Latino Baseball Legends

Latino Baseball Legends

AN ENCYCLOPEDIA

Lew H. Freedman

GREENWOOD

AN IMPRINT OF ABC-CLIO, LLC
Santa Barbara, California • Denver, Colorado • Oxford, England

Library of Congress Cataloging-in-Publication Data

Freedman, Lew.
    Latino baseball legends : an encyclopedia / Lew H. Freedman.
        p. cm.
    Includes bibliographical references and index.
    ISBN 978–0–313–37867–6 (hard copy : alk. paper) — ISBN 978–0–313–37868–3 (ebook)
1. Baseball players—Latin America—Biography.   I. Title.
GV865.A1F7   2010
796.357092′2—dc22 [B]   2010019876

ISBN: 978–0–313–37867–6
EISBN: 978–0–313–37868–3

14 13 12 11 10   1 2 3 4 5

This book is also available on the World Wide Web as an eBook.
Visit www.abc-clio.com for details.

Greenwood
An Imprint of ABC-CLIO, LLC

ABC-CLIO, LLC
130 Cremona Drive, P.O. Box 1911
Santa Barbara, California 93116-1911

This book is printed on acid-free paper ∞

Manufactured in the United States of America

Contents

Preface, ix

Introduction, xiii

PART I

Essays on Latino Baseball, 1

    Countries of the Game, 3

    Cuban Baseball Takes a Dark Turn, 4

    Dreams in the Dominican Republic, 15

    Mexico and Big Thinkers in Monterrey, 24

    Venezuelans Love Their Baseball Heroes, 30

    Beisbol—The Latin Game, 36

    Flavor of the Game, 41

    Latinos and Blacks Common Fates, 44

    Underage Issues, 51

PART II

Icons of Latin American Baseball, 57

    Twenty-five Icons of Latin American Baseball, 59

        Sandy, Sandy Jr. and Roberto Alomar, 59

        The Alou Family Felipe, Matty, Jesus and Moises, 66

        Luis Aparicio, 73

        Rod Carew, 80

        Orlando Cepeda, 87

        Roberto Clemente, 94

        Martin Dihigo, 102

        Ozzie Guillen, 109

        Adolfo Luque, 117

        Juan Marichal, 123

Dennis Martinez, 130

Edgar Martinez, 137

Pedro and Ramon Martinez, 145

Minnie Minoso, 152

Tony Perez, 159

Vic Power, 166

Albert Pujols, 173

Manny Ramirez, 180

Mariano Rivera, 187

Alex Rodriguez, 194

Ivan "Pudge" Rodriguez, 202

Sammy Sosa, 209

Luis Tiant, 216

Fernando Valenzuela, 222

Omar Vizquel, 229

PART III
Seventy-five More Significant Latin American Baseball Figures, 237

Bobby Abreu, 239

Ruben Amaro Sr. and Ruben Amaro Jr., 239

Sandy Amoros, 240

Joaquin Andujar, 242

Luis Arroyo, 242

Bobby Avila, 243

Carlos Baerga, 244

Jorge (George) Bell, 245

Carlos Beltran, 245

Hiram Bithorn, 247

Bobby Bonilla, 247

Pedro Borbon Sr. and Pedro Borbon Jr., 248

Miguel Cabrera, 249

Bert Campaneris, 250

Buck Canel, 251

Jose Canseco and Ozzie Canseco, 252

Rene Cardenas, 253

Rico Carty, 254

Vinny Castilla, 255

Cesar Cedeno, 256

Davey Concepcion, 256

Jose Contreras, 257

Jose Cruz Sr. and Jose Cruz, Jr., Tommy and Hector Cruz, 259

Mike Cuellar, 259

Carlos Delgado, 260

Bobby Estalella (grandfather) and Bobby Estalella (grandson), 261

Tony Fernandez, 262

Ed Figueroa, 263

Julio Franco, 264

Andres Galarraga, 265

Nomar Garciaparra, 265

Juan Gonzalez, 266

Vladimir Guerrero and Wilton Guerrero, 267

Guillermo (Willie) Hernandez, 268

Orlando Hernandez and Livan Hernandez, 269

Teddy Higuera, 270

Jaime Jarrin, 271

Julian and Stan Javier, 272

Andruw Jones, 273

Roberto Kelly, 274

Hector Lopez, 275

Javy Lopez, 276

Felix Mantilla, 277

Jose Mendez, 278

Omar Minaya, 279

Bengie, Jose and Yadier Molina, 279

Willie (Guillermo) Montanez, 280

Manny Mota, 282

Tony Oliva, 282

Luis Olmo, 283

Magglio Ordonez, 284

David Ortiz, 285

Jose Pagan, 286

Rafael Palmeiro, 287

Camilo Pascual and Carlos Pascual, 288

Tony Pena and Tony Francisco Pena, 289

Juan Pizarro, 289

Alex Pompez, 290

Aramis Ramirez, 291

Pedro Ramos, 292

Edgar Renteria, 292

Jose Rijo, 294

Francisco Rodriguez, 294

Cookie Rojas, 295

Manny Sanguillen, 297

Johan Santana, 297

Benito Santiago Jr., 298

Tony Taylor, 299

Miguel Tejada, 300

Cristobal Torriente, 301

Cesar Tovar, 302

Manny Trillo, 303

Zoilo Versalles, 304

Ozzie Virgil Sr. and Ozzie Virgil Jr., 305

Bernie Williams, 306

Appendix A: Hispanic Heritage Baseball Museum Hall of Fame, 309

Appendix B: Twelve Young Hispanic Players to Watch, 315

Appendix C: Latin Americans in the National Baseball Hall of Fame, 319

Appendix D: Roberto Clemente Award, 321

Bibliography, 325

Index, 341

Preface

The most dramatic change in Major League Baseball in the last three decades has been the rise and influence of Latin American players. Where once a player from Puerto Rico, the Dominican Republic, Mexico, or Cuba was a Spanish-speaking rarity on a given team, such players in the 2000s are heavily represented on Major League rosters.

In fact, the number of Latin American players on opening day of the 2009 season approached one-third of all Major League players.

How did this happen? Where did they all come from? Who are the best players? And who were the pioneers that laid the foundation for the hundreds of Latino players making their way through the minor leagues into the top echelon of the game?

Written for students and general readers, this encyclopedia explains the history of the Latino player in the majors dating to the early part of the twentieth century, the expansion of opportunities for Latin players in the middle part of the century, and the explosion of Latin players in the majors near the end of the twentieth century and into the early twenty-first century.

This work is divided into three sections featuring different aspects of the Latin American baseball experience. It encompasses what baseball is like in the nations that are the greatest hotbeds of the game outside of the United States and how what has been perceived as a home-grown American game has really been long embraced by many of the United States' neighbors. Part I of the book includes essays on baseball in several Latin American countries, along with essays discussing a variety of particular topics central to the game. Part II, follows with extended, alphabetically arranged entries on 25 Latino baseball players who have left a lasting mark on the sport. Part III provides concise alphabetically arranged entries on an additional 75 Latino players. Entries cite print and electronic resources for further reading. The encyclopedia closes with four appendices on the Hispanic Heritage Baseball Museum Hall of Fame, the winners of the prestigious Roberto Clemente Award, the presence of Latinos in the National Baseball

Hall of Fame, and short sketches of a dozen Latino ballplayers to watch in the future. The encyclopedia concludes with an extensive bibliography of print and nonprint resources, along with a detailed index. Sidebars of interesting information appear throughout the work, along with a wide range of photos.

Careful study went into the selection of the 25 most significant and influential Latin players of all time. In most cases on-field performance spoke for itself. But much more went into reviewing careers, including the important roles played by pioneers so that others might follow. These are not unknown names to the serious baseball fan. These are the best of the best, Hall of Famers in fact, and Hall of Famers in the making. In many cases they were among the first from their homelands to experience the satisfaction of having a dream come true by making it to the Major League level.

In some cases accomplishment was enhanced by a combination of having more than one member of the same family beat the odds and reach the majors.

Many of the earliest Latin American stars of the game also faced a rockier path to the top than their home-country descendents do today. They came from poverty and spoke little English when parent clubs signed them and assigned them to small towns in the American South or Midwest. Alone, away from home for the first time, they were frightened and lonely, and felt discriminated against because of skin color and the language barrier.

In several instances among these 25 stalwarts, they became heroes and role models to the next generation of ballplayers in their countries and, in some instances, especially in the case of Puerto Rican Roberto Clemente, are esteemed legends today, decades after their careers played out. No pretense is made to rank these players. Their stories are presented alphabetically.

The present-day baseball fan is well aware of Albert Pujols and Alex Rodriguez, the two players vying for the title of best active Major League player—and both of them of Hispanic heritage. Lesser known is the first true Latin American star in the majors, pitcher Adolfo Luque of Cuba. The start of his career dates back nearly a century and although there were a few other notable Latino players before the 1950s, Luque did pave the way.

Clemente, a star of the first magnitude and beloved by many fans of all races, is considered the Jackie Robinson of Latinos. Lesser appreciated by non-Latino fans outside of Chicago, Minnie Minoso is put on a pedestal by many Hispanics.

There is a second tier of 75 additional influential Hispanic baseball figures, making up a list of the 100 most important Hispanic baseball figures. Their careers were significant, as well, though judged to be of slightly less import than the top 25. Many are names not nearly as famous, but through their efforts as players, coaches, and broadcasters drew attention to their home areas and helped along young people. Again, this is not a ranking but an alphabetical listing.

There will be some surprises on the list and some listings that reflect more of the standing of an individual in his home country than his batting average. For example, Ozzie Virgil Sr. is not a name well-remembered by many younger baseball fans. His greatest fame for fans who followed the majors in the 1950s was as the first black player for the Detroit Tigers. But in the Dominican Republic Virgil maintains much greater status and even has an airport named for him. The Virgil example illustrates that there is a parallel world of fandom unknown to the U.S.-based, non-Hispanic baseball follower.

A common theme, in both collections of names, regardless of where individuals came from, are stories of poverty and how the passion of players overrode the limitations on their opportunities to help shape their careers. When a youngster is willing to fold cardboard into the form of a baseball glove, as if he is working in clay, it is apparent how hungry he is to succeed and how much love he has for the sport.

In researching the Latin American baseball experience, it is obvious that politics has sometimes played a role in shaping a country's history with the sport, whether it is Communist dictator Fidel Castro in Cuba, or former dictator Rafael Trujillo in the Dominican Republic.

Every present-day baseball fan recognizes the influx of more and more Latin American baseball players filling up the roster of his or her favorite team. But there has long been a separate universe of winter baseball played in the warm-weather lands that also supply the majors with its talent. At a time when Major League baseball was hostile to American blacks, it was equally inhospitable to dark-skinned baseball players from Latin American countries. Thus, the fates of the two minority groups were inextricably linked. If Major League baseball had not opened up the sport to African-Americans, it would not have opened up the sport to dark-skinned Latin Americans. This world is also explored. To reach their present-day status as exalted stars dominating the game in many instances, Latin Americans were forced to undergo a rough transition to the mainstream, just as American blacks were.

This volume highlights not only the love of baseball in many Latin countries and the careers of the most influential Latin American players and baseball figures, but their struggle for acceptance.

As noted in other sections, there is now a Hispanic Heritage Baseball Museum Hall of Fame, supplementing the list of Latinos who have been voted into the National Baseball Hall of Fame in Cooperstown, New York. And one of the most coveted individual honors in Major League Baseball, recognizing community involvement in conjunction with excellence on the field, is named after a Latino, Roberto Clemente.

Introduction

The chatter between players sitting at their lockers in the clubhouse in the 2000s is as likely to be conducted in Spanish as English. The music from a boom box is as likely to be salsa as hard rock. The official language of Major League Baseball remains English, but it doesn't take a United Nations translator to realize that the sport has become bilingual.

Such a transformation was unimaginable six decades ago, but the reality is undeniable. Baseball's claim as the United States' national pastime was staked out during the first half of the twentieth century. But baseball's hold on the peoples of Latin America is equally deep-rooted. In Cuba, the Dominican Republic, Mexico, Venezuela (and to a lesser extent Panama), baseball is the national passion.

Social scientists long ago declared that it is impossible to know the hearts and minds of Americans without understanding baseball. They were talking about the United States. If anything, baseball has a firmer grip on the national psyche of many Latin American lands.

Baseball is as much a way of life—even more so—in the dustiest neighborhood in the Dominican Republic, in the most remote corner of Venezuela, under Castro's form of Communism, as it is in Boston, St. Louis, or Chicago, those giant hotbeds of Major League ball sprinkled around the United States.

It is no longer a news flash that the best Latin American players are worthy of Major League attention. If the 2000s are measured against the 1940s and the relative welcome of Latin players is compared, then even the densest of fans must recognize that a revolution occurred. This is not a revolution that is underway, but one that has been accomplished. It is over. The revolution was won. At one time, Latin American players of dark skin were banned, just as American blacks were prohibited, from participating at the top level of the sport. At one time, baseball administrators might have thought there was such a thing as too many Latin American players on a roster at one time.

Those days are gone, appropriately buried. Talent is signed, cultivated, developed, and showcased regardless of heritage. At the beginning of the 2009 season, 29 percent of the players on Major League opening-day rosters were of Latin American descent. If a man can hit or pitch he can find a job, regardless of his first language or place of birth. Both the United States and Major League Baseball are more egalitarian societies than they once were. If there were once arguments about whether or not Latin players were good enough, they were long ago put to rest. If there were once concerns about Spanish-speaking players fitting in on a team, they were long ago disregarded.

American attitudes have matured. Change was gradual in coming and long overdue from the standpoint of social justice, but the here and now represents a fairer world than the crueler one of the past. Just as Major League Baseball was slow to accept American blacks, it was just as cold and harsh toward Latin players with dark skin, lumping them under the same umbrella.

It took the arrival of Minnie Minoso, Juan Marichal, Chico Carrasquel, Luis Aparicio, Roberto Clemente, Rico Carty, Bobby Avila, Orlando Cepeda, and so many more stars from Latin America to clarify the point that baseball is all about human similarities, not differences. In the 1950s, if there was one Latin player on a team's roster that was notable. In the 2000s, the numbers are so much larger that no one counts. Rather the discussion focuses on a different plane—whether Albert Pujols or Alex Rodriguez is the best player in the world, or if Johan Santana is the best pitcher in the world.

In the United States it is about the game and the achievements, but it should be noted that the pride in national origin is huge back home. If fans of the Yankees, Dodgers, or Diamondbacks mostly care about the ways the Latin player can aid their team's quest for victory, in the Dominican or Venezuela there is a very distinct puffing out of the chest in claiming hometown ownership of the achiever. The attitude of local boy makes good is prevalent.

The sheer numbers of terrific players from Latin America dotting American League and National League rosters are overwhelming to Latino old-timers. They had to scratch their way to the pros and endure hardships because they did not speak English well or because they were discriminated against for being black. The early comers were pioneers in much the same way that Jackie Robinson, Larry Doby, Roy Campanella, Monte Irvin, and Hank Thompson were among black players erasing the color line.

"The racial problem was so bad," said San Francisco Giants Hall of Fame pitcher Juan Marichal from the Dominican Republic. "We couldn't go through the front door." (Quoted in *Beisbol*.)

Those front doors in hotels and restaurants were blockaded against black-skinned Latinos like Marichal, who broke into the majors in 1960. Many Latino players were assigned to minor-league clubs in the Deep South and had to stay on the team bus when teammates ate at restaurants. Just as their American black counterparts, they also were often assigned to sleep in private, black-owned homes rather than team hotels.

Compounding the difficulties for the young Latino player away from home for the first time, trying to cope with the pressures of launching a successful career, were language challenges. Big league ball clubs did not offer Berlitz courses to their signees. They just turned them loose to fend the best they could.

Rico Carty, a future National League batting champion from the Dominican, played his first ball in the United States in Davenport, Iowa in 1960. He barely spoke English and could not read a menu. "I eat chicken for three months and then after that I eat hamburger for three months 'cuz I didn't understand anything in English," he said. "I feel frustrated, but my teammates start teaching me how to speak the words." (Quoted in Ruck, 157.)

Rod Carew, the seven-time American League batting champion who was born in Panama, was first assigned to Leesburg in the Florida State League and said his black skin was a lightning rod for the narrow-minded. When the bus stopped for lunch on a road trip, he sat on board. When he played the field, racial slurs were shouted at him. It was a sobering and demoralizing experience for a young man and Carew said that he and many other Latin players probably went through "something similar to what Jackie Robinson" did when he broke baseball's color barrier with the Brooklyn Dodgers in 1947. "You had to be twice as good as the white player to have the job," Carew said of his rise to the Minnesota Twins in 1967. In Carew's case, he was. (Quoted in "Viva Baseball!")

One of the biggest helpmates Latino players had in making their case for their talent in the majors in the 1950s, and for decades beyond, was Howie Haak. He was a scout on the payroll of the Pittsburgh Pirates and he was the man with the discerning eye, the always-packed suitcase, and stop watch who was the Santa Claus of Latin America. He had the power to make dreams come true.

Haak was a key figure in spotting Roberto Clemente's talent and in aiding the Pirates in grabbing him from the Brooklyn Dodgers. He specialized in identifying young Latino ballplayers. Haak had frequent flyer miles piled higher than the Empire State Building before there were frequent flyer miles. The arrival of Haak in your community was a bigger deal than New Year's day.

Haak was a hefty man, a former minor league catcher, who became known across Latin America as "Big Daddy." He could rescue a player from a life of poverty. Among Haak's signees for the Pirates were Manny Sanguillen, Omar Moreno, Tony Pena, Jose DeLeon, Joe Christopher (the first player from the Virgin Islands), and Rennie Stennett. Haak's coming to Panama, said Sanguillen, "opened the door for us." (Quoted in Goldstein.)

He went where no man went before from 1950 to 1988. In the United States, Haak was called "The King of the Caribbean." Haak was 87 when he died in 1999 and his wife Crystal said he wanted only to be cremated. "Just throw me in the trash can," Haak's wife said he told her. "He was a tough, old bird." (Quoted in "Ex-Pirates.")

Some Latino players were naïve when they came to the United States. They did not know they might be discriminated against because of their skin color. Others were quite well informed. Future San Francisco Giants Hall of Famer Orlando Cepeda was the son of Pedro "Perucho" Cepeda, considered one of Puerto Rico's greatest players. The older Cepeda understood the racial situation in the United States and advised his son not to seek Major League Baseball as a career. But Orlando Cepeda, then 17, wanted to test himself against the best and disregarded the suggestion.

"He said, 'Are you sure you want to go there, being black?' " Cepeda said. "It was a huge change. You had to sit in the back of the bus." Cepeda also faced a language barrier. He said he lived on apple pie and chili con carne in the United States for three months. "That's all I knew how to get." (Quoted in "Viva Baseball!")

Pitcher Luis Tiant, a future star with the Cleveland Indians and Boston Red Sox, faced a similar dilemma. His father, Luis Sr., was a superstar at home in Cuba who was never allowed to try out for the majors because of his dark skin color. He, too, was cynical and worried about what his son might face in the United States The younger Tiant was also determined to carve out his own path. And he did so very successfully.

Few U.S. baseball fans realize, especially when Latino ballplayers began infiltrating Major League rosters in a trickle in the 1950s, and even now when Latino ballplayers have flooded big-league teams' payrolls, that the countries where those players grew up revere the game and that baseball has been part of their national landscape for nearly as long as it has been in the United States.

Since 1907, the sport has subscribed to the myth that baseball was invented by one-time Civil War General Abner Doubleday when he was stationed in upstate New York. The investigating committee trying to pinpoint the game's origins did a shoddy job and nowadays anyone who believes that Doubleday wrote the rules is considered someone who might also still believe in the Easter Bunny. Doubleday may have seen a baseball game, but the holes in the theory of him inventing the game are large enough to fly a 757 through.

In contrast, labeling the Cincinnati Red Stockings of 1869 as the first professional franchise is considered gospel truth and, regardless of Doubleday's association or not, baseball has always been viewed as the quintessential American created, founded, and played game. The possessiveness of baseball being "our" game is dominant in the United States.

However, credit for introducing baseball to Cuba in 1864 is officially given to a native of the island, not any passerby U.S. soldiers or naval crews. Nemesio Guillot had spent six years studying in Alabama, and when he returned home at age 17 he was carrying a bat and ball in his belongings. The equipment was the first of its type seen in Cuba.

The Civil War had barely ended in the United States when baseball saw its first Latino involvement. Esteban Bellan, a native Cuban who had been sent to school in New York by his parents, played three years of baseball at Rose Hill College, ending in 1868, before turning pro with the Troy Haymakers. That made Bellan the first Latino in the majors. In 1872 Bellan returned to Cuba and helped organize the first club team in his home country.

In the years that followed, baseball took root in the Dominican Republic, Mexico, Puerto Rico, Panama, Nicaragua, Venezuela, Colombia, and Aruba. It was not necessarily recognized as a U.S. export, though. In almost every case, the introduction of the sport to those countries and locales stemmed from contact with Cuba. Although American military outfits displayed their skills in recreational games during shore leave or following invasions to guide the results of regional revolts, they were mainly adding to the storehouse of knowledge already present. The Cubans planted the seeds of baseball growth throughout Latin America.

In 1882, the Providence Grays, then a Major League team, signed a part-Mexican catcher named Vincent Nava from California and assured the world he passed the litmus test of color because he was Spanish. Except at times some referred to him as being Italian. Those who couldn't keep track said he might be from Cuba. Nava was the second Latino major leaguer. Nava, who played through 1886, would be taken for brown skinned if he was merely walking down the street, but he was viewed as "OK" by baseball because he said he was Spanish.

Baseball was more advanced, whether it was new equipment or new stadiums, than anywhere else in the world and there was no dispute the princes of the game were better paid to play in the U.S. than anywhere else. The sport was better organized in the U.S. and by the 1920s could command audiences of more than 50,000 people at a time, unheard of elsewhere.

Soccer was king throughout most of the world, the sport of Western Europe, Africa, and South America alike. And no one would dismiss the importance of soccer in Mexico or Colombia, but even if the cultures of Spanish-speaking, tropical climate nations to the south of the United States had little else in common with the behemoth of the hemisphere, baseball was a bond. For many years, however, it was a one-way love affair. If the best Latino ballplayers aspired to play in the majors, the majors were indifferent at best to their desires and hostile at worst to their hopes.

Once black Americans were exiled from baseball in the 1880s, black Latinos were not welcome in the majors, either. Owners, league presidents, and Commissioner Kenesaw Mountain Landis always protested that there was no policy banning blacks from the game, but while it may not have been written down it was etched in stone. To the best black American ballplayers, from Satchel Paige to Josh Gibson, Cool Papa Bell, and so many others, the denials were poppycock.

Less visible to the sports fan was the same draconian outlook applied to Latinos. While the best black players competed in the separate, but not equal Negro Leagues, most Latin players with dark skin did not even get close enough to embarrass the owners with their presence. They were hundreds or thousands of miles away. The disgrace of Major League Baseball banning blacks is well-known, but lesser known is the strange, almost schizophrenic manner in how baseball dealt with Latin American players who might have graced the sport's rosters. While teams meekly agreed to the ban on American blacks, they sometimes sought to put one over on baseball by signing Latin players with darker skins.

A Latino player with white skin was acceptable in the majors. A Latino player with somewhat darker skin could pass for white possibly by declaring that he was Spanish. If a player could convince a team that he was really of Western European descent, not African descent, he might get a job. Then it was the team's role to sell this approach. No, he's not black, he's Castilian. The process was surreal.

On occasion, such as when the Cincinnati Reds played two Cuban players in 1911, Rafael Almeida and Armando Marsans, they had to sign affidavits that they were not black and were really of European heritage. Before the players were approved for Major League play they were deemed to be "the purest bars of Castilian soap." (Quoted in Burgos, 94.)

During the same time period when baseball teams refused to sign American blacks or black Latinos, they sometimes went to extreme lengths to provide cover stories for whiter Latinos who could say they had no black blood in them. And they also signed a bevy of dark-skinned American Indians. It was permissible for Charles "Chief" Bender, Jim Thorpe, and Louis Sockalexis to play Major League ball. The national pastime needed some time on a psychiatrist's couch to explain itself, though that type of self-examination did not take place until after World War II.

While so many spent so much energy trying to determine black from white and brown from tan, it was possible for a lighter skinned Latino to make good in the game. In 1914, Adolfo Luque, a Cuban right-handed pitcher known as "The Pride of Havana," broke into the majors with a cameo appearance for the Boston Braves. That was the start of a 20-year Major League career for Luque, who won 194 big-league ballgames. The high point of Luque's career came in 1923 when he finished 27-8 with a 1.93 earned run average for Cincinnati, a performance that led the National League in wins and ERA. Luque was viewed as an exception rather than a forerunner of a new source of baseball talent. Luque did gain enduring fame, however, despite his throwing inconsistency, as the first Latino regular to touch upon stardom.

One of Luque's countrymen, Mike Gonzalez, who enjoyed a brief Major League career, but a lengthy coaching career, is all but forgotten despite being the claimant to an important milestone. The Cuban-born Gonzalez became the first Major League Latino manager in September of 1938 when St. Louis Cardinals skipper Frankie Frisch was fired. Gonzalez took over for the season's final 16 games. Again in 1940, Gonzalez served the Cardinals as an interim replacement manager. His lifetime managerial record was 9–13.

During the 1920s, 1930s, and 1940s, as the Negro Leagues flourished and black players continued to be exiled from the majors, some of the most talented baseball players with black skin spent their winters competing in Latin American climes. Satchel Paige and other leading American black players of the day spent the winter months in Cuba, Mexico, or the Dominican Republic, and signed for good paydays. In all of those nations black players were better treated than they were at home. They were feted for their skills and not discriminated against because of their skin color.

Negro Leagues star infielder and future Hall of Famer Willie Wells played winter ball in Mexico and loved the experience. "I am not faced with the racial problem in Mexico," he said. "When I travel with Vera Cruz we live in the best hotels, we eat in the best restaurants, and we go anywhere we care to. I've found freedom and democracy here, something I never found in the United States." (Quoted in Burgos, 164.)

At the same time the top black Americans were traveling to foreign lands to play ball, Martin Dihigo, a Cuban, followed the same path, lighting up Latin American pitching in several countries. A virtual unknown in the United States, some believe he was among the top handful of players of all time. Dihigo, like Babe Ruth, was a success as a pitcher and hitter. A phenomenon who could play virtually any position, Dihigo has been selected for the baseball halls of fame of five countries. He was renowned his for play in the Negro Leagues; Cuba, Mexico, Venezuela, and the Dominican Republic all put him in their halls. Dihigo's two-decades-long playing career began in the 1920s and ended just before integration.

Dihigo was revered by Latinos and admired by his opponents. Buck Leonard, one of the overlooked American Negro Leagues stars later voted into the National Baseball Hall of Fame, said Dihigo could do everything on the diamond, including "run, hit, throw, pitch and manage. You can take your Ruths, Cobbs and DiMaggios. Give me Dihigo. I bet I would beat you almost every time." (Quoted in Wendel and Villegas, 31–32.)

While American blacks were finding freedom in Latin America, they were also fighting for American freedom in Europe and the Pacific during World War II. When the war ended in 1945, there was an even louder outcry for Major League Baseball to integrate. That move finally happened in 1947 and it also paved the way for darker-skinned Latinos to break into the majors.

Players like Orestes "Minnie" Minoso were in the first wave. Minoso was born in Cuba and initially came to the United States to play for the New York Cubans in the Negro Leagues. In 1949 Minoso played for the Cleveland Indians. In 1951, he was the first black man to play for the Chicago White Sox. A seven-time All-Star, Minoso was a daring runner and excellent hitter. He was also flamboyant. At various times Minoso has said he took pride in being the first black player for the White Sox and at other times he said the role did not bother him. "I never felt any really great pressure at being one of the first black players in the major leagues," he said. "I concentrated on playing ball, and during the game, put aside personal problems." (Quoted in Regalado, 47.)

Minoso was the first black player for the White Sox, but he was not a solo Latino player for the team. In 1950 the White Sox had signed Alfonso Colon Carrasquel, better known as "Chico," to play shortstop. A Venezuelan, Carrasquel was the first in a long line of his country's star shortstops—he was a four-time All-Star—and he was venerated throughout his life. One reason was that throughout his 10-year Major League career, Carrasquel always returned home to play in the off-season. Carrasquel never forgot his home fans and they always appreciated him playing for them during the prime of his career. That pattern became an established policy for most Latino Major League stars.

When Carrasquel died in May 2005, Venezuelan President Hugo Chavez declared two days of national mourning. Carrasquel was a national hero. "It is difficult to people outside Venezuela (to realize) how important Carrasquel was to his country," said sports writer Milton H. Jamail. "He was immensely popular because of his accomplishments on the field and his accessibility off it both in Caracas and Chicago. . . . He was the living symbol, more than any other player, of Venezuelan baseball." (Quoted in Jamail, 203.)

The 1950s marked a new day for Latino ballplayers. Once shunned, or merely tolerated, for the first time they were coveted.

The Washington Senators, a perennial last-place finisher in the American League, laid the predicate in the 1930s and 1940s when they turned their attention to Latin America. Team owner Clark Griffith did not have cash to spend wildly. He anointed scout Joe Cambria his agent in Latin America and told him to round up as many promising ballplayers as he could, on the cheap. Catcher Mike Guerra and infielder Bobby Estalella were signed from Cuba. Griffith spent half of his time trying to convince his fellow owners that Cambria's signees were not black.

Between 1935 and 1945 Cambria, who became known in Latin America as "Papa Joe," signed 13 Latinos for Washington. In his long scouting career, from 1932 into the early 1960s, Cambria is estimated to have signed 400 Latinos for pro ball.

Washington's focus on signing Latinos lasted for decades and such skilled players as Camilo Pascual and Pedro Ramos ended up in Senators' uniforms. It was a fruitful connection, but the arrival of Spanish-speaking ballplayers who didn't know what manager Bucky Harris was talking about when he called for a squeeze play or a hit-and-run at times drove him daffy. A frustrated Harris was venomous, saying, "They're trash (of Latin players). They're doing no good and they aren't in place here. They don't fit. If I have to put up with incompetents, they must at least speak English." (Quoted in Regalado, 19.)

The trend toward using more and more Latino ballplayers, who proved quite competent at their jobs, long outlasted Bucky Harris and his archaic views. Before the end of the 1950s, Latin American superstars were among the highest profile and most accomplished players in the game. Luis Aparicio, another Venezuelan, succeeded Carrasquel as the White Sox shortstop. Roberto Clemente of Puerto Rico began a storied career worthy of Hall of Fame induction. Before Clemente's baseball career and his life were cut short in 1972, he would prove himself worthy of induction into the Humanitarian Hall of Fame as well.

Clemente, so skilled, flamboyant, outspoken, and prideful, became the Godfather of all Latin American players. Regardless of their country of nationality, they bowed to the statue erected in his memory on the island possession of the United States.

No one knew it at the time, but Clemente's career marked a turning point between Major League Baseball, the American public, and Latino players. By the time Clemente's career ended, fewer people cared if one of their players spoke Spanish, English, or signed autographs in hieroglyphics. And since the 1970s, the explosion of Latino participation in Major League ball has reverberated throughout the sport.

Joe Cambria was the point man for scouting in Latin America. The Pirates' Haak became a household name in Latin America. The Houston Astros were the first team to construct and staff a baseball academy in Venezuela. Roberto Clemente, Orlando Cepeda, and Juan Marichal, it turned out, were not isolated phenoms. They represented entire populations who could play the game. Major League Baseball was once the province of white-skinned citizens of the United States. In 1947, black players were allowed into the fraternity. Now the latest source of untapped talent was in lands where baseball was beloved and where raw ability was legion.

In the United States, the sport of boxing was always most densely populated by the poorest of ethnic groups. The Jewish, Italian, and Irish immigrants entering the country in the first half of the twentieth century took up the sport because all they had was their fists as means to fight their way out of ghettos. Then blacks replaced the ethnics at the bottom of the socioeconomic scale and took over the sport in the United States. Latin Americans growing up in the United States followed. Basketball became a city game because equipment—all you needed was a ball—was inexpensive.

Paralleling the United States, in Latin America's poorest neighborhoods with the dustiest streets, the barefoot boys with cardboard gloves and bats made from tree branches, bred the hungriest players in the world. Juan Marichal, who grew up in the Dominican, said he was among those who used cardboard wrapped with wire for a baseball glove in the absence of being able to afford real leather. He and his friends dried out a branch from a guasume tree to use for a bat and swiped mothers' and sisters' old socks to wrap around a golf ball before taping it down. Voila, a baseball. Rod Carew said he used a broom stick for a bat. "We played baseball year-round," he said. (Quoted in "Viva Baseball!")

Even after integration the Spanish-speaking player faced difficulties and challenges. Teams were careless in their placement of players in their minor-league system. Black Latinos were sent to small towns in the South that were inhospitable, and they struggled mightily because they did not speak English. Sports writers in Pittsburgh tried to Americanize Roberto Clemente's first name into "Bob." There were several Latino players on the San Francisco Giants in the early 1960s, and apparently it burned manager Al Dark much as it had annoyed Bucky Harris. Dark banned the speaking of Spanish on the bench. Orlando Cepeda, among others, thought the ruling was ridiculous and he did not foresee himself holding chit-chats with Juan Marichal in English. It took time, but the world changed, the sport changed, and Major League Baseball changed.

It became more and more important for teams to scout Latin America. Any team that was closed-minded about employing Latino ballplayers was mapping out its own doom. In Latin America, the male youth of the nation became the crop, the latest annual harvest. The more the scouts looked the more gems they uncovered.

Even more significantly, once a generation of players retired, the chance to stay in the game opened up. Latino coaches became common. The Chicago White Sox named their former shortstop Ozzie Guillen manager, making him the first Venezuelan skipper and the first Latino manager to win a World Series. Dominican Omar Minaya became the first Latino general manager when he took over operations of the Montreal Expos in 2002. And Mexican-American Arturo Moreno became the first Latino owner of a Major League franchise when he bought the Los Angeles Angels in 2003.

In the Dominican Republic, Venezuela, and other Latin baseball hotbeds, the boys loved the game and they lived the game. They dreamed how the game could rescue them from poverty, could uplift their families from poverty. Baseball in the United States could be their savior.

"Oh, baseball for me and my family was like a religion," said Detroit Tigers outfielder Magglio Ordonez, who is from Venezuela. (Quoted in "Viva Baseball!")

The doors closed on Cuba as a baseball talent mecca in 1961 under the regime of Fidel Castro. As much as Castro, a one-time player, reputedly with a good pitching arm, loved baseball, he was more concerned with a Communist revolution. He decreed there would be no more professional baseball, only the amateur game, played in Cuba. Many major leaguers could not travel home for years and friends and family were lost to them. Cuba did become the pre-eminent amateur baseball power in the world.

Cuba had introduced baseball to its Latin neighbors, and when Cuban professional talent dried up, many of those countries welcomed the fame and money offered by U.S. scouts when the need to find more players to stock expansion teams grew acute from the early 1960s on. Baseball was a sport of 16 Major League teams essentially for the first six decades of the twentieth century. But by the twenty-first century the number of teams had nearly doubled to 30. With an increasing number of young American boys choosing basketball and football over baseball, the Latino player filled the labor need.

The opportunity is a gift. The top Latino athletes still favor baseball. There is no real interest in football and basketball is a minor sport, at best. The foremost dream of a Dominican Republic infielder is to be prized by a big league scout. The biggest thing that can happen to a Venezuelan pitcher is to be sought and signed by a Major League scout. Discarding poverty in favor of a lifetime of riches is an easy choice. It is not easy to make the journey to the end of the rainbow, but it is a possibility for the young man with the right talent and connections.

Author Samuel O. Regalado writes of a "special hunger" that resides in the breasts of young Latino baseball players. In the past they might not have had a chance to make money doing anything but working on sugar plantations. The odds remain against any single Latino ballplayer emerging from the worn playground on his small-town corner, but there are many role models who have made good. To dream the dream is not so far-fetched because a teenager can look around and see proof that others just like him have risen from poverty and staked out a new life through baseball.

"Many of us came from families that didn't have the money to send us to college or anything like that," said long-time Major League infielder Octavio "Cookie" Rojas from Cuba. "So the only way of bettering ourselves and our families was to make it in baseball." (Quoted in Regalado.)

The hunger is very real. So is the payoff.

Further Reading

Beisbol: The Latin Game (video) Major League Baseball, Narrator Esai Morales, Lead Producer Alfonso Pozzo, 2007.

Burgos, Jr., Adrian, *Playing America's Game* (Berkeley, Calif., University of California Press, 2007).

"Ex-Pirates Scout Howie Haak Dies," Associated Press, February 28, 1999.

Goldstein, Richard, "Howie Haak, Baseball Pioneer In Latin America, Dies at 87," *New York Times*, March 1, 1999.

Jamail, Milton H., *Venezuelan Bust, Baseball Boom: Andres Reiner and Scouting on the New Frontier* (Lincoln, University of Nebraska Press, 2008), p. 203.

Regalado, Samuel O., *Viva Baseball: Latin Major Leaguers and Their Special Hunger* (Champaign, Illinois, University of Illinois Press, 1998).

Ruck, Rob, *The Tropic of Baseball: Baseball in the Dominican Republic* (Lincoln, Nebraska, University of Nebraska Press, 1999).

Viva Baseball! Baseball Hall of Fame Exhibit on Latin American Baseball, in taped interview, 2009.

Wendel, Tim, and Luis Villegas, *Jose Far From Home: Latino Baseball Players in America* (Washington, D.C., National Geographic Society Books, 2008).

Part I

Essays on Latino Baseball

Countries of the Game

The Latin American nation with the longest and richest involvement in baseball is Cuba. The island country, located just 90 miles from the United States, picked up the sport ahead of other Latino countries and exported it as a popular pastime to many of the other nations in the hemisphere.

Cuba, long a winter home for Major League players, at one time possessed an AAA minor-league club in Havana, and produced several superstar players. Cuba's more recent history of the game has taken on overtones of tragedy. Following the Communist Revolution led by Fidel Castro, all ties to the United States were cut, including those to baseball. Major League stars no longer practiced their craft in Cuba during the warm winters; Cuban-born Major League players were no longer permitted to travel back and forth to play for U.S. professional teams. Castro shut down the pro game and emphasized amateur play.

Sequentially to the elimination of Cuba as a source of big-league talent, baseball-playing countries such as the Dominican Republic and Venezuela came of age. In addition, players emerged from Puerto Rico, Mexico, Panama, and, to a lesser extent, Nicaragua and Colombia.

As each year passed, Latin American players assumed greater importance in Major League Baseball. The number of Hispanic-origin players continues to expand, and the influence of Spanish-speaking ballplayers continues to grow.

Cuban Baseball Takes a Dark Turn

The devotion to baseball runs just as deeply in Cuba as it does in the United States, and that love and passion date back nearly as far as they do in the United States. But Cuba is the Latin American anomaly, the nation that sticks out as different. Unlike the Dominican Republic, Mexico, Puerto Rico, and Venezuela, the state of the game in Cuba is not measured by the success of young players being paid millions of dollars for their efforts in the United States.

Cuba is the outcast, the outsider, the nation with its nose pressed to the glass looking in, though not with a feeling of desperation, but with a feeling of curiosity. For nearly 50 years now Cuban ballplayers have been exiles from the highest level of the sport, have been shut out of the major leagues because they are shut in on their own island.

Once the missionaries of the game—spreading love of baseball throughout Latin America—Cubans have been locked in a prison of their leaders' own making since the early 1960s. Once the leading baseball proselytizers in the region, Cubans now must make do with amateur play. Instead of allowing their finest players to make good livings as professionals, Cuban players have lived within the Communist system first imposed by dictator Fidel Castro and now by his brother Raul. The highlights of competition for Cuban players are their own league play in the National Series and challenges against the best of the rest in the world on special occasions on foreign diamonds in the Pan American Games, the Olympic Games, and the World Baseball Classic.

Contrary to popular belief, baseball, regarded as the quintessential American game, was not introduced to Cuba by U.S. military troops.

Esteban Enrique Bellan, who was studying in the United States at Fordham University in New York, became the first Cuban and first Latin American professional baseball player when he signed with the Troy Haymakers of the National Association of Professional Base Ball Players in 1871. But he was not the person who introduced the game to his home country. In 1864, a young man named

Nemesio Guillot, returned from study in the United States carrying a bat, a ball, and diamond wisdom, according to accounts. (Quoted in Regalado, 10.)

In 1866, sailors from a U.S. ship landed on the island and in their spare time played the locals in an exhibition. This event likely led to the legend of American military introduction of the game. The first recorded all-Cuban game took place in 1868 with teams from Havana and Matanzas. When Bellan enrolled at Fordham, he already knew about baseball due to the game against the U.S. sailors. After his schooling in the United States, Bellan returned to Cuba and was one of the early pioneers of the sport at home. He stayed in baseball as a player and manager until 1886. By then, a Cuban writer named Wenceslao y Delmonte observed, "Baseball . . . had rooted itself so strongly in this land as proven by the hundreds of clubs in almost all parts of the island." (Quoted in Regalado, 10–11.) By 1900, baseball was clearly part of the fabric of Cuban life and such American stars as Ty Cobb and Christy Mathewson began making visits, enjoying the mild off-season climate.

Cuba, located just across a strip of the Atlantic Ocean from Florida, has about 11.5 million people. The island is 42,803 square miles in size and the climate is tropical. Per capita income is $4,819 a year and there is little doubt that the best baseball players would benefit mightily and increase their income massively if allowed to play professionally in the United States.

The earliest Latin players in the majors came from Cuba, notably pitcher Adolfo Luque, who spent most of his 20-year career with the Cincinnati Reds and won 194 games after breaking into big-league play in 1914. Like their dark-skinned U.S. counterparts, dark-skinned Cubans could find no place in the majors until Jackie Robinson cracked the color barrier with the Brooklyn Dodgers in 1947. The first black Cuban star in the United States was Orestes "Minnie" Minoso. Minoso, who initially came to the United States to play for the New York Cubans in the Negro Leagues, became a major leaguer in 1949 and was a seven-time All-Star.

For the next dozen years, Cubans who previously had not been sought by American teams gained the opportunity to join minor and major league teams. Typically, the players spent summers in the United States and off-seasons in Cuba, and still enjoyed the applause of their countrymen in winter ball. Cuba was regarded as a fun place to play: the night life was lively; the food was tasty; ballplayers were welcome. And the travel distance from the United States was insignificant. The Havana Sugar Kings, an AAA minor-league outfit, were members of the International League from 1954 to 1960. Many U.S. players were playing winter ball in Cuba when the government of Fulgencio Batista fell to Fidel Castro's hordes coming down from the hills.

An increasing number of Cubans had become major leaguers in the 1950s and many more had signed contracts and were working their way through minor-league chains. One of the first signs that baseball in Cuba would change in a major way was the decision by Commissioner Ford Frick to move the Sugar Kings to Jersey City, New Jersey. The U.S. government, responding to Castro's pledge to re-make Cuba's image into a socialist state, pressured Frick to make the call. Soon after, Castro decreed that there would be no more professional baseball in Cuba and henceforth Cuba would concentrate on training amateur teams for international competition playing for medals and the glory of the motherland.

In January 1961, Cuban natives Pedro Ramos, Camilo Pascual, and Minnie Minoso were detained in Cuba as they attempted to leave for spring training. This sent out an alert that made major leaguers wonder if their careers were in jeopardy. This was also the year of the botched Bay of Pigs invasion, the first U.S. attempt to overthrow Castro. Relations between the two countries had escalated from talking to shooting. When Minnesota Twins shortstop Zoilo Versalles realized he could not get his wife out of Cuba he was so distraught he left the team for a month. "I'm worried," he said. His wife did get out, but Versalles no longer returned to Cuba. "There is nothing worse to a man than to lose his home," Versalles said. (Quoted in Regalado, 141.)

Many Cubans decided they could not risk returning to their home in the Major League off-season. They felt they would be detained and have their careers destroyed. This decision resulted in Cuban baseball figures not seeing family members for years, for decades, or, in some cases, forever. Among the Cuban ballplayers affected by Castro's policies were Luis Tiant, Preston Gomez, Leo Cardenas, Tony Gonzalez, Mike Cuellar, Bert Campaneris, Jose Cardenal, Sandy Consuegra, Tito Fuentes, Jackie Hernandez, Marcelino Lopez, Pancho Herrera, Luis Arroyo, Tony Oliva, Sandy Amoros, Joe Azcue, Diego Segui, Tony Taylor, Roman Mejias, Zoilo Versalles, and Cookie Rojas.

Just as he became the paramount figure on the island in all walks of life, Fidel Castro also dominated the baseball landscape.

There is a persistent myth in baseball that if one of the Major League teams most intensely scouting the Caribbean in the early 1950s had convinced Fidel Castro that his right arm would carry him to the majors, perhaps the history of the region would have been dramatically different.

The young Fidel (much like the older Fidel) was a huge baseball fan. When Castro was a young man he was a pitcher and supposedly had the makings of a Major League curveball, but he did not have the strength to throw a Major League fastball.

There are varying reports about the assessments of scouts from the Pittsburgh Pirates, the Washington Senators, and the then-New York Giants. Some suggested that Castro was not worth signing; others suggested that he was worth a small bonus and should be given a chance to play in the minors.

Unlike the young men periodically spotted lighting up pickup games on Spartan sandlots, Castro had a track record: pitching well enough for Belen University and the University of Havana to earn a look-see. The key to Castro's repertoire was his curve. It was a first-rate breaking ball. But he was a sketchy prospect at best. One report had the Giants offering Castro a $5,000 bonus to sign. Another report said it was the Senators. The Pirates projected Castro as unlikely to advance beyond the AA minors.

Because Castro became a famous world figure, it is not easy to sort out fact from fiction about this part of his life. Peter C. Bjarkman, perhaps the foremost U.S. authority on Latin American baseball, gives little credence to comments that Castro was close to being signed. The idea that famed Senators scout Joe Cambria offered Castro $5,000 to sign is wrong in his mind. "The truth is that popular legend about Castro's prodigious hurling talent has little basis in fact," Bjarkman wrote. "Scattered references in the literature repeatedly mention Cambria's scouting of Castro, yet no documented or believable account suggests that any scout assessed the future dictator as a legitimate prospect." Bjarkman cites other sources. Senators owner Calvin Griffith was quoted as saying, "Uncle Joe scouted Castro and told him he didn't have a Major League arm." (Quoted in Bjarkman, 17.)

Pirates scout Howie Haak was one of few contemporaries and equals of Cambria at ferreting out Latin American talent for his Pittsburgh club. He, too, was aware of Castro, but he authored a report to general manager Branch Rickey indicating the future leader of his nation was not worth the trouble to develop. Castro might wage civil war from the hills, but he was not necessarily someone to stand poised and irresolutely on the rubber. Castro, apparently, was much more likely to get shelled on the mound than in the war. So the Pirates offered no contract.

In the late 1950s, as Castro fomented unrest in the hinterlands against the regime of Fulgencio Batista, he rallied students for a change in government. Periodically, he appeared at local ballparks with groups of agitating young people. Don Hoak, who played winter ball in Cuba and was the third baseman on the Pirates' 1960 World Series championship team, recounted a tale where he was in the batter's box when the game was interrupted by student demonstrations. Castro walked to the mound, asked for the ball, and motioned to Hoak to step up to the plate. Hoak did so.

Castro threw a couple of curveballs, Hoak remembered, and some came in high and tight. After four pitches, with a 2–2 unofficial count, Hoak said he motioned for the game to continue. Play resumed. "Looking back on it, I think with a little bit of work on his control, Fidel Castro would have made a better pitcher than a prime minister," Hoak said. (Quoted in Hoak and Cope.)

While Castro never laced up spikes for a United States professional team, he remained an avid fan and dictatorially ruled the sport. Castro banned professional play and was often a spectator at major baseball events in the country.

In an amusing photograph, Castro is shown taking a swing at a pitch before a tournament in 1977. He is full-bearded, as is his trademark, wearing his usual khaki revolutionary military attire. In 2009, Castro wrote a 300-word baseball column in advance of the World Baseball Classic. An American sportswriter took note of the writing and called it a departure in description and competence from most "socialist sportswriting," which he called "quite crummy. *Granma*, the Cuban Communist party newspaper runs baseball stories all the time and most of them sound like they were written by a third apprentice undersecretary in charge of boredom, and then edited by a committee of 37 people who had never seen a baseball game." The author of the Classic piece signed it "Comrade Fidel." (Quoted in Siegel.)

Comrade Fidel never came close to playing U.S. pro ball. Just maybe, Bjarkman wrote, picking up on a theory advanced by Jorge Figueredo, a former Cuban sportswriter, Castro or his followers exaggerated the entire baseball scenario to make him look good. "(They) likely fostered the popular legend simply to add luster to the dictator's popular image," Bjarkman wrote. (Quoted in Bjarkman, pp. 16–17.)

Starting in 1962, Cuba became an international power in amateur baseball. The national team won the gold medal 15 times in the Pan American Games and 35 times in the World Cup. In five Summer Olympics, the Cubans won gold three times and silver twice. The team was regarded as virtually unbeatable in international competition.

Various players wanted more than that. Realizing that their skills were marketable, top Cuban players began defecting. Often slipping away from their teams while housed in hotels overseas, or resorting to the same type of desperate measures as their lower profile countrymen by buying their way onto small boats trying to cross the water to Florida, many Cuban stars seeking their fortune made their way to the United States. Such defectors included well-known pitchers Jose Contreras, Livan Hernandez, Orlando Hernandez, and Danny Baez. Many others joined them.

When Castro took control of the country, Pedro "Preston" Gomez, was 37 years old and still trying to make his way onto a Major League roster after years of trying. After hitting a fine .286 in eight games with the Washington Senators in 1944, the second baseman could never again crack the big league club's lineup. His minor-league apprenticeship became an odyssey.

After 1959, although his parents and all of his close relatives still lived in Cuba, Gomez did not return to his homeland until 1970. One of his greatest triumphs was managing the 1959 Havana Sugar Kings to the championship of the International League and the title in the Junior World Series, emblematic of minor-league supremacy.

In 1969, Gomez became the first manager of the expansion San Diego Padres. Three years of 100-plus-season losses doomed Gomez in the position, but he bounced back as a coach with the Houston Astros and in 1974 took over as manager of that team. Gomez also managed the 1980 Cubs, but from 1981 to 2008 Gomez was in the game as a coach, scout, and ultimately served as assistant to the general manager of the Angels.

Gomez was managing the Padres when he gained the rare opportunity to visit Cuba and see his aging father Pedro, who was sick with cancer, and his immediate family. At the end of the trip, Gomez was able to bring his mother Elia out of the country with him. In Cuba, Gomez watched top players and lobbied Garcia Bando, director of sports, to let him take home a player. "I would like to take that fellow," Gomez said. Bando simply laughed. No amateurs were going pro on his watch. (Quoted in Dozer.)

Gomez also had a face-to-face meeting with Castro. The dictator popped in on Gomez when he was eating dinner at a restaurant. Castro asked Gomez to evaluate Cuban talent and asked about Cuban exiles and other Latinos in the majors. "I tell you, that man has a memory," Gomez said. "He knew all the names." (Quoted in Murphy.)

Gomez gave three previously unscheduled baseball clinics and said going to his homeland again was a memorable experience. He also predicted that Cuban baseball stars, facing a ceiling on the highest level they could play, would one day go to the United States to play in the majors. "I think many of the Cuban ballplayers would like to come to the U.S. to earn a good living," he said. "Some day they will. Perhaps not now." (Quoted in Murphy.)

The words foreshadowed future defections.

Gomez was still active in baseball when he was in an automobile accident in 2008. Seriously injured, he died as a result of the crash 10 months later at age 85.

In the mid-1970s, Bill Veeck, owner of the Chicago White Sox, endorsed scouting Cuban talent even though Major League Baseball had a hands-off policy. In 1976, a travel agent who said Veeck asked him to check into a way to get him into Cuba went public about the owner's interest. "I've investigated it," Veeck said. The travel agent, Vince Bytner, from Albany, New York, said, "Ping-pong opened up China. Baseball will open up Cuba." It hasn't happened yet. (Quoted in Murphy.)

Long before Cubans began dotting Major League rosters, big-league teams and players visited the island, many for organized winter ball. Others were on off-season tours. In an era when there was no television and salaries were low and many players needed winter jobs to make ends meet, the biggest American baseball stars undertook popular barnstorming tours to make money and to bring the game to communities far from big-league cities. Babe Ruth led one such tour to Cuba in 1921 and watched power hitter Cristobal Torriente mash big-league pitching for three home runs while he could only flail at Jose Mendez' fastball. "Tell Torriente and Mendez that if they could play with me in the major leagues we would win the pennant by July and go fishing for the rest of the season," the Yankee slugger said. (Quoted in Rubin.)

A visiting sportswriter compared Mendez favorably with "The Big Train," Walter Johnson, and his flaming fastball, saying the Cuban "is every bit as classy as Walter Johnson." (Quoted in Regalado, p. 33.)

Of course, Torriente and Mendez were not able to play with Ruth, or any other major leaguers, because they were dark-skinned. Decades later, their excellence was recognized (and Ruth's talent judgment justified) when they were both selected for the Hall of Fame in Cooperstown.

In 1999, with the permission of the U.S. State Department, the Baltimore Orioles made a goodwill trip to Cuba and played exhibition games against a team of Cuban all-stars. "People were crazy about baseball when I was growing up," said Tony Perez, the retired Cincinnati Reds slugger who would later be inducted into the Hall of Fame. Perez was born in Ciego de Avila, Cuba in 1942 and at the time of the exhibitions was working in the Florida Marlins front office. "We followed the majors closely by reading the newspapers and watching the Game of the Week." (Quoted in Rubin.)

There were demonstrations among Cuban exiles in the United States against what was perceived as appeasement or a thaw by the government toward Castro. One prominent American baseball figure, Tommy Lasorda, was vehemently opposed to the exchange involving the Orioles. Lasorda, the long-time Los Angeles Dodgers' manager, had been active in Cuban winter ball as a player and was in Havana the night Batista fled. "I have many, many Cuban friends in Miami, people who were persecuted and stripped of their property and wealth by Castro," Lasorda said. "I don't want to play baseball over there against the wishes of these people." (Quoted in Rubin.)

Americans who love baseball have sought entry into a country that has no diplomatic relations with the United States. They can take advantage of opportunities offered by entrepreneurs. A baseball aficionado searching the Internet can find options.

One company, called "CubaTours," books fans on trips to Cuba to watch regular-season National Series action for a week by departures through Canada. Another company urges fans to sign up to play baseball in Cuba. "Spend a week in the forbidden isle doing what you love, playing baseball," an ad reads. The trick for the traveler is to be part of a U.S. amateur team, not a professional.

In a world some may view as upside down, this circumstance may be seen as ironic. Instead of Cuba importing its best players to compete in the United States, the United States is exporting mediocre players to compete in Cuba.

Over the decades various stars on the Cuban national team chose to defect from their home country rather than continue to play as amateurs, but one stalwart stayed on message his entire career and was regarded as a local hero.

Omar Linares was a special third baseman for the Cuban National Team, and he was the big fish that got away from the majors.

Over a 20-year career playing for the Pinar del Rio club in the National Series league, Linares recorded a .368 batting average with 404 home runs and 1,547 runs. He could run, too, stealing 264 bases despite being 6-foot-1 and 225 pounds. When he was past his prime, Linares played three seasons in Japan's Central League with the Chunichi Dragons, but not as a regular starter.

Linares was Castro's exemplar on the national amateur team. The Cubans repeatedly won world championships (six with Linares in the lineup) and won gold medals in the 1992 and 1996 Olympics and a silver medal in 2000 once baseball was added to the Olympic program. Linares was a fixture on all of those medal-winning Olympic teams.

For two decades, Linares was the biggest star in Cuba. Linares was recognized everywhere he walked in Cuba and his swing was imitated by sandlot players. He said he was never going to take the Major League money and run. "None of it means anything to me," Linares said. Defecting, he added, "would be an act of treason. It will never happen." (Quoted in Fainaru.)

The best players in Cuba were rewarded with higher subsistence pay and owned fancier houses than the average Cuban, but the money was spare change compared to the money to be made in the majors.

As far as Linares could tell, life could not get any better. Baseball, he said, "is the nourishment of the people. Money doesn't interest me." (Quoted in Fainaru.)

At the same time, defections of first-class Cuban talent continue. Experts in the sport hint that one day Aroldis Chapman may be among the most famous players to ever play the game.

Regarded as a prodigy because of his powerful left arm, Chapman was the up-and-coming star of the Cuban National Team when he defected in Rotterdam, The Netherlands before setting up temporary housekeeping in Barcelona, Spain, and then Andorra, awaiting a fate being mapped out by agents and scouts of Major League clubs. Ultimately, Chapman signed with the Cincinnati Reds and began making a splash in spring training in 2010. Chapman's fastball has been clocked at 102 mph on a radar gun.

As many previous defectors on Cuba's pre-eminent amateur national team had done, Chapman made a run for it while the team was on the road.

Chapman's departure from Cuban territory and Cuban handlers was not so dramatic as other tales, however. The Cuban team was in Rotterdam to compete in an event called the World Port Tournament. On July 1, 2009, with his sights set firmly on the future, he stealthily watched for a chance to skip out on his club. Chapman made an aborted dash for freedom in 2008 and when caught had been chastised in a face-to-face meeting with Raul Castro, the new leader.

Chapman was suspended for the rest of the Cuban baseball season but was reinstated for the World Baseball Classic in March 2009. Undeterred by his warning, Chapman headed for the hills as soon as he could in The Netherlands. The implications were huge if he was caught, but his getaway went smoothly. "I walked out easily," he said, "right through the hotel door and I hopped into a car and left. It was easy. Now the plan is to sign with a Major League team." (Quoted in Arangure, "Top Cuban.") Soon enough, he did.

Chapman, who said he was 21, stands 6-foot-4, but his weight was given as 179 pounds, meaning he needed to add meat and muscle to his bones. Chapman has a shaved head and the look of a very young man.

Chapman is regarded as a pitcher who despite his raw tools and solid collection of pitches needs some seasoning and maturity. He does not have a large body of work behind him. Once reinstated for Cuban play in 2008, Chapman threw 118 1/3 innings with an 11–4 record, but his earned run average was a pedestrian 4.03. He was barely on display in the World Baseball Classic, and he pitched one inning for Cuba's gold-medal team in the Pan American Games in 2007.

The last very high profile pitching defector from the Cuban baseball team before Chapman was Jose Contreras. Contreras, a success with the New York Yankees and Chicago White Sox before moving on to the Colorado Rockies in the summer of 2009, was in his 30s when he defected and there was always a question about his true age. However, he still signed long-term, multi-million-dollar contracts. There was little doubt that Chapman was in line for a large payoff once it was determined which team was the best fit.

When Chapman defected, he left behind his mother and father, two sisters, and a newborn baby that he did not see. Although Chapman had survived Raul Castro's "conditional reprieve," he never wavered in his desire to reach the U.S. mainland and play in the big leagues.

On the night Chapman chose to dash for freedom, he decided almost spontaneously after assessing the circumstances. He was hanging out with a teammate and told him he was going out to smoke a cigarette. So when Chapman left the hotel he was carrying only two personal items on his person—a pack of cigarettes and his passport. He was picked up and whisked out of the area.

As Chapman adjusted to Western technology—he fell in love with iPhones, text messaging, and fancy cars immediately—he followed a workout regimen designed to show him at his best for Major League clubs seeking to rent his pitching services.

"I'm very happy," Chapman said after he was safely away from the Cuban team. "This is the plan that I had and this was a decision I took. I wanted to test myself in the highest levels of baseball." (Quoted in Arangure, "Top Cuban.")

"I want to be the best pitcher in the world," he said. "I'm not yet. But with work I can be." (Quoted in Arangure, "New World.")

Surprise, He's Latino

A Gold Glove-winning third baseman for the Florida Marlins and the Boston Red Sox, and winner of the 2007 World Series Most Valuable Player Award, Mike Lowell's off-field story is even more compelling.

His mixed background, drawing heavily on Latin American history, is an example of the United States' long tradition of being a melting pot. And Lowell's challenge in overcoming testicular cancer in 1999 on his way to the top of his profession is an example of the long history of athletes battling great obstacles to succeed.

Born February 24, 1974, in San Juan, Puerto Rico, but of Cuban heritage, Lowell made his Major League debut for the New York Yankees in September 1998. The 6-foot-3, 210-pounder was named to the All-Star team for the first of four selections in 2002.

Lowell's grandfather was born in Chicago and was an American citizen but was raised in Cuba. After World War II, Lowell's grandfather worked in California and his father Carl was born there. When Lowell's dad was two years old, the family returned to Cuba and lived there until his father was 11. By then Lowell's father was an accomplished baseball player. However, Lowell's grandfather did not like the initial signals from Fidel Castro's revolution and with foresight he moved the family to Puerto Rico in the early 1960s.

Mike Lowell's bride Bertica—also Cuban—had a father who had been imprisoned as a political prisoner for 15 years under Castro's regime. Lowell's wife was actually conceived on a conjugal visit while her father was held in jail. She was born in 1974 and her father was released from prison three years later.

When it was reported that Castro was seriously ill (the illness that led to him temporarily relinquishing power to his brother Raul), a Boston reporter asked Lowell what he thought about the matter. Lowell said, "I hope he dies." (Quoted in Lowell and Bradford, 37.) That phrase was printed in gigantic type on the front of the newspaper.

With the last name of Lowell, the player has not always been immediately recognized as being of Hispanic origins, but he is fluent in Spanish and English.

Further Reading
Lowell, Mike and Bradford, Rob, *Deep Drive*, New York, Celebra Books, 2008.

It was way too soon to tell if Chapman's saga would have a happy ending and if he would fulfill his dreams and make some U.S.-based baseball team very happy, or if his multi-million-dollar arm would let him down. The adventure was just beginning, but no one was more interested in how it would all turn out than the baseball fans of Cincinnati.

Further Reading

Arangure Jr., Jorge, "New world of hope awaits Chapman," *ESPN The Magazine*, August 12, 2009.

———, "Top Cuban prospect defects," *ESPN The Magazine*, July 3, 2009.

Bjarkman, Peter C., "Baseball with a Latin Beat" (Jefferson, North Carolina, McFarland & Company, Inc. Publishing, 1994).

Dozer, Richard, "Veeck Eyes Cuba for White Sox Talent," *The Sporting News*, October 23, 1976.

Fainaru, Steve, "Revolutionary: playing for the love of the game," *Boston Globe*, December 3, 1995.

Hoak, Don and Cope, Myron, "The Day I Batted Against Castro," *Sport Magazine*, June, 1964.

Murphy, Jack, "Gomez' Visit to Cuba Includes Chat With Castro," *The Sporting News*, February 21, 1970.

Regaldo, Samuel O., *Viva Baseball!* (Champaign, Illinois, University of Illinois Press, 1998).

Rubin, Bob, "Cuban relives big-league baseball ties," *Miami Herald*, March 28, 1999.

Siegel, Jeff, "Fidel Castro, Baseball Writer," iVoryTowerz, http://www.ivorytowerz.com, March 16, 2009.

Dreams in the Dominican Republic

The richest men on the island play a little boys game and the poor little boys dream of growing up and playing, too.

Baseball is the game of the rich and the poor—and almost everyone in-between—among the 10 million people of the Dominican Republic. Everyone has his part in the stage play. The men who go away to the United States earn top dollar being among the elite players in the world. The little boys do their best to emulate them—playing baseball with rudimentary, home-made equipment, on poorly maintained fields, on unpaved streets, on grass faded brown from the sun. The others, the men who harvest sugar cane, the sisters and mothers who raised them, are spectators at the ballparks.

There is no other profession in the Dominican that promises such riches to the talented, a way out of poverty to the genuinely skilled, as playing baseball. Everyone on the island that once belonged to Spain knows the names of those who have succeeded and upgraded their station in life. Everyone understands the system of how even the poorest of the poor can be noticed by a Major League scout. The heroes of the past and those playing now paved the way and created a climate of opportunity and inflamed an atmosphere of hope.

Although it has been only in the last 50-or-so years that Dominican players have populated Major League rosters, baseball has been the most popular sport on the island for more than a century. Cuban exiles brought the game to the Dominican and helped organize the sport in 1894 or 1895. U.S. military interventionists played games in the Dominican while stationed there in 1916. Just like Cuban and Afro-Americans, however, black Dominicans were outcasts from the U.S. major leagues until after Jackie Robinson's barrier-breaking arrival with the Brooklyn Dodgers.

Long before Dominicans routinely became prominent figures in the majors, high-level baseball was played on the island, much of it featuring American Negro Leagues stars. Perhaps the most famous series in Latin American history that did not involve pursuit of an amateur gold medal took place in the Dominican Republic in 1937.

Guns and gamesmanship were involved. Satchel Paige was on the mound for one side, soldiers lined the edges of the grandstands, and dictator Rafael Trujillo watched from a place of honor as a very interested spectator.

Truth, exaggeration, drama, and fiction are all rolled into reports of this intramural showdown, almost entirely due to the imaginative mind of Paige, who liked his stories to feature maximum adventure with no constraints imposed by accuracy. Paige's version of this baseball tale may be more fanciful than realistic.

Born October 24, 1891, Trujillo had a reputation as a brutal dictator. He rose to power in 1930 and immediately set about enriching himself by nationalizing the sugar and rum industries and maintaining his stranglehold on the country by siccing secret police on dissidents. He loved baseball, and in 1937 when facing one of his most dangerous political challenges he tried to use the game to enhance his popularity. Trujillo recruited the best available baseball players for his Los Dragones team.

Paige, the biggest star in the American Negro Leagues, was a pitcher with a suitcase always packed, ready to move on where the grass and the cash seemed greenest. If a man with a plan had a stash of cash, Paige was ready to roll. Trujillo sent an emissary to Paige at a New Orleans hotel with $30,000 as an inducement to jump the Pittsburgh Crawfords and spend the summer in the Dominican. Paige signed on the dotted line faster than the time it took his fastball to reach the plate.

Paige then rounded up other Crawfords and Negro Leagues players whom he knew could use good paydays. Not only did Paige offer more money, but Crawfords owner Gus Greenlee, a noted numbers runner, was having troubles with the law. The Dominican seemed like a good alternative. The $30,000 payout was for Paige to divvy up how he saw fit for an eight-week season. He kept $6,000. The great Josh Gibson, Cool Papa Bell, Bill Perkins, Leroy Matlock, and Sam Bankhead were among those who joined Paige in the Caribbean. "Ol Satch was making good money," Paige said, "but $30,000 was more than $3,000 apiece, even if I didn't skim some off for managing the whole thing." (Quoted in Ribowsky, 149.)

One player imported from Puerto Rico for Los Dragones was Pedro Cepeda, the father of future Hall of Famer Orlando Cepeda. The team was loaded, but it was not unbeatable. Surprising Trujillo, the club's main rival, the Aguilas Cibaenas, stockpiled its own recruited talent. Also raiding the Negro Leagues and scouring Latin America, the Cibaenas featured pitchers Chet Brewer and Luis Tiant Sr. under the managerial leadership of Martin Dihigo. The Estrellas Orientales, the team Trujillo most feared, was also tough. This team included the best of the homegrown players. Trujillo believed he had cobbled together a super power, but he underestimated the opposition.

The Negro Leagues stars lived like kings, drinking and dancing in nightclubs until late hours, dining on steak and turkey, bodysurfing, and fishing. Games were played on weekends, leaving considerable time for revelry.

Paige won eight games and Gibson batted .453 and Trujillo's team won the regular-season crown. In a case of foreshadowing, the Orientales represented San Pedro de Macoris, the Dominican town that decades later would be the most productive in rearing Major League players. The local guys were pretty good in 1937, too. To clinch the championship the Negro Leagues transplants had to win a best four out of seven series against the Orientales.

All season long—and this is where Paige's story-telling creativity comes into play—the U.S. players were somewhat on edge. They were hired to play ball, but, as the summer passed, they convinced one another that if they didn't win the title Trujillo would have them killed. No pressure. "I had it fixed with Mr. Trujillo's polices," Paige said. "If we win, their whole army is gonna run out and escort us from the place. If we lose, there is nothing to do but consider myself and my boys as passed over Jordan." (Quoted in Ribowsky, 140.)

Neither Paige nor his American teammates spoke much Spanish, so they suffered from a communication gap with the locals. Trujillo, always one to embrace a show of force, had his soldiers line the field at the ballpark each night and periodically raise their rifles, fire at the sky, and yell, "El Presidente doesn't lose!" (Quoted in Ribowsky, 153.)

In Paige's telling, the players took this display to mean that their own lives would be forfeited if they didn't win the championship and please the big man. Whether the actions were for show, or Trujillo was trying to get a message across to his hired hands (or perhaps both) is an open question. For the rest of his life, Paige told everyone that the players competed with great fear and the belief that if they did not win for Trujillo they would not leave the island alive.

Cool Papa Bell, who was not regarded as a wild story teller, buttressed Paige's stories. When Bell realized that things might get serious he was quoted as saying, "They kill people over baseball?" The answer was: "Down here they do." (Quoted in Holway, p. 90.)

Jimmie Crutchfield, another Negro Leagues player friendly with Bell in later years, said that Bell was a nervous wreck, to the point of trembling when he recounted the Trujillo adventure. The imports had lost a big series to the group in San Pedro de Macoris and when they returned to their hotel they were met by a general. "Look, you play for the presidente," the general said. "We don't lose." Bell said the officer then pulled out a .45 and began blasting the walls. (Quoted in Ribowsky, 155.)

Sometime during the stay in the Dominican, Paige said that he acquired a lucky charm from a voodoo priest that had been illegally smuggled in from Haiti. Paige didn't really know if the charm was for real or designed to actually bring him bad luck. "Or was it perhaps an evil charm designed by Trujillo's enemies to ensure a Paige defeat?" historian Peter J. Bjarkman wondered. "Whatever the facts, in a land filled with black magic such stories seem highly plausible, if not probable." (Quoted in Bjarkman, 170.)

At season's end, emotion and hysteria were racheted up considerably among fans and players. The Los Dragones fell behind in games 3–0 in the final series and Paige didn't like their chances of a comeback. The night before the fourth game, the man who recruited Paige for the team met with him and Paige said it was a testy, nerve-wracking encounter. Paige wondered how he and his players would get back to the United States if they lost and all the other man "could do was wring his hands." Not exactly a vote of confidence. The Paige-led Trujillo team rallied to tie the series at 3–3. (Quoted in Ribowsky, 156.)

The U.S. players on Trujillo's team were rounded up the night before the deciding game and placed in jail. Some interpreted that as a message about their futures. But it was later said Trujillo's troops put the Americans in jail for their own protection. Oh, for a fluent Spanish speaker to straighten out the mess. Chet Brewer, the Negro Leagues pitcher on the Orientales team, went to see his American friends at their hotel the night before the big game. When he asked where everyone was, he was told, "In the carcel," and the respondent aimed his thumb in the direction of the jail. Later, Paige said, "You'd have thought we had the secret combination to Fort Knox." (Quoted in Holway, 90.)

The next day, with Paige on the mound and his team trailing 5–4, he said, "You could see Trujillo lining up his army. They began to look like a firing squad." (Quoted in Ribowsky, 156.) However, the Los Dragones rallied and won. Paige reported that he and his compatriots made a hectic dash for the hotel, zoomed down to the docks, and hopped on the next ship headed for home. But other reports indicate that while the other players split promptly, Paige hung around the beaches for a while. Such a leisurely departure pace would have undermined the drama of Paige's tale.

Several details were murky or contradictory when Paige related the affair. "The American consul heard what a worrisome situation we was in" (Quoted in Ruck, 41), Paige wrote in a 1948 book, "and they flew us out in a bird that same night." In a 1962 version of his life story, Paige wrote, "I hustled back to our hotel and the next morning we blowed out of there in a hurry. We never did see Trujillo again. I ain't sorry." But Larry Tye, a 2009 Paige biographer, uncovered other Paige comments indicating he did hang around the Dominican for a little while (Quoted in Tye, 115–116.)

Paige never let the facts get in the way of a good story.

For all of Trujillo's supposed devotion to Dominican baseball, his reckless spending and the other clubs' attempts to match him in 1937 bankrupted the sport for years. "We spent too much money to bring these players here and because they were the best in the world it cost too much," said Cuiqui Cordova, a Dominican sports reporter, years later. "That killed baseball here" (Quoted in Baseball Almanac.com.)

Seriously wounded it, but only temporarily. Professional baseball resumed in the Dominican Republic in 1951. The repressive regime of Trujillo continued and his methods of governing became harsher. In 1961, Trujillo met his death by assassination.

By then Dominicans were making inroads in the top level of the sport. The first Dominican in the majors was Ozzie Virgil, Sr., when he played for the New York Giants in 1956. Two years later Virgil was the first black player on the Detroit Tigers. In the decades since, Dominicans have become featured players on all teams. At no time since 2000 has the chance to play Major League baseball been better for Dominicans. Once it became clear to U.S. teams that the pool of talent was deep and that infielders, pitchers, and outfielders might well be the most valuable export on the island, teams sent scouts galore to drive into distant towns, forests, or anywhere there might be a field. And when there proved to be even more players than scouts could handle or manage, teams set up their own training academies in the Dominican to evaluate the teenagers with promise and sign the best of them.

One after another superstars emerged from the tropics, estimable followers to the pioneer players of the 1950s like Virgil and the Alou brothers, bettering their achievements and staking out jobs on rosters in stunning numbers. One after another they struck it rich and uplifted the game with their whippet arms, fast legs, and powerful bats. Once regarded as rare jewels, now hundreds of Dominicans have reached Major League rosters, and if anything the pace is increasing. As of 2009, approximately 500 players born in the Dominican have become big-league ballplayers. (Quoted in *Beisbol*.)

Among the best of the best born in the Dominican Republic: Albert Pujols, Felipe, Matty and Jesus Alou, Cesar Cedeno, Vladimir Guerrero, Juan Marichal, Pedro Martinez, David Ortiz, Manny Ramirez, Sammy Sosa, Miguel Tejada, Juaquin Andujar, George Bell, Adrian Beltre, Robinson Cano, Tony Fernandez, Julio Franco, Rafael Furcal, Freddy Garcia, Cesar Geronimo, Alfredo Griffin, Pedro Guerrero, Julian Javier, Ramon Martinez, Jose Mesa, Manny Mota, Jose Offerman, Carlos Pena, Tony Pena, Aramis Ramirez, Hanley Ramirez, Jose Reyes, Jose Rijo, Juan Samuel, and Alfonso Soriano.

These players are household names in the United States, but they are household gods in the Dominican Republic. Many do good works in the communities where they are anchored in the United States. Many more do good works in the communities they came from. Those communities are more in need of every type of good work. Ortiz, known as "Big Papi," is famous in the United States and Dominican as much for his booming bat as his easy-going smile. A big man at 6-foot-4 and about 240 pounds, Ortiz seems to cultivate good will among children, who sense the friendliness behind his size.

"In my opinion, he's the Babe Ruth of our era," said Boston Red Sox teammate Jonathan Papelbon of Ortiz, given his long distance swats and Pied Piper image among children. (Quoted in *Beisbol*.)

Rico Carty, a star outfielder with the Braves in the 1960s, won a National League batting title, but as long as he was healthy he always also played winter ball. "I feel a real obligation to play here because I owe my country a lot," he said, "because they pushed me so much here (to be good)." (Quoted in Ruck, 117.)

There is a sense of responsibility, a feeling of wanting to give back to the less fortunate, among Dominican baseball stars. When they go home to visit parents and siblings, they cannot duck out on the scenes of poverty in their old neighborhoods. The per capita income in the Dominican is about $8,700 a year. Players may drive past ramshackle adobe homes with corrugated tin roofs. They may pass fading chicken farms used to sustain families with a dozen or more people. They know they are needed. They know they are inspirations. "If we could do it, why can't they?" said Pedro Martinez, a pitcher bound for the Hall of Fame. "I want them (the kids) to know that I was born there, that I grew up there." (Quoted in *Beisbol*.)

Baseball is played all over the Dominican Republic. Professional teams have constructed good, solid fields at their academies, but boys too young to sign contracts, who are still growing and improving, carve out their own fields wherever they live. They may live in sugar cane country or in the mountains, but they find a way to design their own fields and even if their families have no money to give them spikes, they play barefoot. They make gloves out of cardboard, shaping orange juice containers and the like into makeshift mitts to field.

Baseball is a complex industry in the Dominican, not just handing cash to young players as a gift. Intermediaries, sometimes acting as agents between players and their families and big-league teams, collect payoffs. Other baseball figures on the island are in the employ of Major League teams, teaching the young people fundamentals at the academies, showing them how to act and respect the game if they are sent to the United States. Much is at stake. A player may get one chance and be sent home, his dreams crushed. It is imperative, at all times, to be ready for opportunity if it knocks. "It's the sport that gives you money," said Victor Mata, who ran a New York Yankees academy in the Dominican. "The sport that gives you the ability to support a family." (Quoted in Forreo.)

One of the most amazing success stories in sports is the miracle of San Pedro de Macoris. Both a province and the name of a capital city with a population of

300,000, the community may not possess the fountain of eternal youth sought by Ponce de Leon, but baseball experts bemusedly agree there must be something magical in the water. The port city on the Caribbean Sea southern side of the Dominican manufactures baseball players the way Detroit manufactures cars, the way Cuba produces cigars, and the way Battle Creek, Michigan manufactures cereal.

At one point, San Pedro de Macoris was known as "the city of infielders," but that description is 20 years out of date. The community does not discriminate against players by position. It may just be that fathers place baseballs in the cribs of their new-born sons now, just to make sure they get an early start in the game that brought stardom to local luminaries like Rico Carty, Sammy Sosa, Tony Fernandez, Robinson Cano, Jose Offerman, Joaquin Andujar, George Bell, Alfonso Soriano, Juan Samuel, and so many other players, from Mariano Duncan to Luis Castillo, from Manny Alexander to Johnny Cueto.

"San Pedro right now is the top city in the world to develop ballplayers," said Vic Power, the one-time Puerto Rican star in the American League who used to work with young prospects back home. "I've been asking everybody what they do over there, what do they eat? So I can bring the secret to Puerto Rico." (Quoted in Krich, 89.)

If there is a secret, it has never been exported, except in the form of the players themselves. They are highly motivated. There is not much of a fallback position if they don't make it in baseball. It's not as if it is easy to carve out middle-class careers in San Pedro. It is more of an all-or-nothing approach. How it all came to pass is open to conjecture and speculation and not really founded in any type of fact. One thing everyone agrees on is that those who have made it big are role models for those who want to make it. Also, because of the lack of discretionary income, as one way to put it, teenagers do not have the chance to become distracted playing computer games. They spend their waking hours practicing, practicing, practicing in hospitable weather. It is always baseball season in the Dominican Republic and time invested helps develop skills.

"These boys are hungry," said a one-time Dominican player named Pedro Gonzalez who worked with the young people of San Pedro, teaching them the game. "There's not a lot of work in San Pedro these days. And what job could pay what they can make in the majors?" (Quoted in Ruck, 170.)

There has never been enough work in the Dominican, and indeed, no job would ever pay as much as a star player could earn in the majors. That may provide a focus for the athlete, but something more is at work. The love of the game throughout the country nurtures the environment to succeed.

When author John Krich first visited the Dominican in the late 1980s he was overwhelmed by the country's devotion to and appreciation of baseball, wherever

Howie Haak's Great Dominican Signing

Howie Haak was a single-handed Pittsburgh Pirates Latin American bureau when he toured the rain forests and the bushes for baseball players.

If the episode helping the Pirates steal Roberto Clemente from the Dodgers was Haak's signature moment in the scouting business, a later incident became legendary, too. On one of his journeys to the Dominican, Haak experienced the type of nirvana moment all talent spotters dream about. Watching winter league ball, he saw a left-handed pitcher named Diomedes Olivo dominate Pirates first baseman Dick Stuart. The self-promoting Stuart, who had hit 66 home runs in one minor-league season, never let anyone forget his feat and considered himself one of the top sluggers in the world. Haak watched Olivo strike out Stuart nine straight times. There was only one problem. Olivo was already an old man by baseball standards. Haak telephoned the home office and spoke to general manager Joe L. Brown. "This guy can pitch in the big leagues," he told Brown. "Stuart didn't even get a foul ball off him. Do you have the guts enough to let me sign him?" Brown did not shrink from the challenge. "If you've got the guts enough to do it, go ahead." (Quoted in Newhan.)

Haak collected Olivo's John Hancock on a contract and that's how the unknown Dominican became a rookie at age 41 in 1960. The glory didn't last long—three Major League seasons—but Olivo appeared in 62 games, all but one in relief in 1962 and compiled a 5-1 record, with seven saves, and with a 2.77 earned run average.

For aspiring Latino players—apparently regardless of age—Haak was a rainmaker.

Further Reading

Newhan, Ross, *Los Angeles Times*, "The King of the Caribbean," date missing, 1990, Baseball Hall of Fame Library archived.

he traveled and to whomever he talked. "Welcome to the country disguised as a tryout camp," Krich said, "where play-by-plays are broadcast on buses, where children take their cuts in every cane field with sugar stalks for bats, where short-stops outnumber scholars or honest politicians." (Quoted in Krich, 103.)

Baseball, it became obvious to him very quickly, was far more valued than as a recreational outlet. It was a way of life in the Dominican Republic.

For all of the effort put into making raw, young ballplayers into skilled pro prospects, one historian studying the Dominican Republic felt fans still brought a different approach to the ballpark to watch their favorite local teams. They wore shirts identifying more with the local clubs than Major League clubs and ditto with baseball caps. In the stands they were louder, more uninhibited than their American counterparts. Pride in being Dominican showed through and when asked about their display of allegiance to the hometown teams rather than a Major League team, the interviewer heard that feeling come through even more pointedly. "Dominicans have been so successful at the game that they sense they are in charge of it," author Alan M. Klein said, "that they are at least the equals of the North Americans. The Dominicans have shown how a form of foreign popular culture can be used to resist hegemonic influences, and at least symbolically, they have contradicted the notion that economic domination automatically results in cultural domination and cultural inferiority." (Quoted in Klein, 117.)

It is doubtful that the 16-year-olds summoned to sit down with a scout to discuss their baseball future think very much about economic policy that transcends their own family circumstances. They just want to play ball and they keep on proving that they can do it as well as anyone in the world.

Further Reading

Baseball Almanac, http://baseball.almanac/com.

Beisbol—The Latin Game (movie), lead producer Alfonso Pozzo.

Bjarkman, Peter C., *Baseball with a Latin Beat* (Jefferson, North Carolina, McFarland & Company, Inc., 1994).

Forreo, Juan, "Cultivating a Field of Dreams," *Newark Star-Ledger*, July 5, 1998.

Holway, John B., *Josh and Satch* (Westport, Connecticut, Meckler Books, 1991).

Klein, Alan M., *Sugarball: The American Game, the Dominican Dream*, (New Haven, Connecticut, Yale University Press, 1991).

Krich, John, *El Beisbol* (Chicago, Ivan R. Dee, 2002).

Ribowsky, Mark, *Don't Look Back: Satchel Paige in the Shadows of Baseball*, (New York, Simon & Schuster, 1994).

Ruck, Rob, *The Tropic of Baseball* (Lincoln, University of Nebraska Press, 1991).

Tye, Larry, *Satchel: The Life and Times of an American Legend* (New York, Random House, 2009).

Mexico and Big Thinkers in Monterrey

Baseball dates to the 1880s in Mexico. The true start date is difficult to pinpoint, as is the starting place for the sport in the country. Several communities claim links to the game, but it is easier to agree on when baseball was played by in Vera Cruz (1886) or Nuevo Leon (1889), than it is to agree on when it was first played in those towns.

It is understood that baseball was an export from the United States, but it is not readily apparent who precisely imported it into the country. There are even some suggestions that U.S. troops, still remembering the Alamo and trying to take over their southern neighbor, introduced baseball in 1847. The cavalrymen played the game for recreation.

By 1925, Mexican ballplayers could play the game for money. That is when the Mexican League was founded in its first incarnation. Almost all games were played in Mexico City, and the rosters of the teams were stocked with Cubans because few of the homegrown Mexicans were first-rate players.

Ultimately, the passion for the game helped develop top-caliber local players who could compete on a higher level. Mexican players were no longer content to remain spectators and honed their skills sufficiently to be taken seriously. Baldomero Almada was the first Mexican to make the jump to the majors in 1933.

He joined the Red Sox as an outfielder and spent seven years in the majors with four teams. His lifetime batting average was a respectable .284.

Few fans of Major League play in the United States paid any attention to the Mexican League until the 1940s. The Pasquel family, headed by rich brother Jorge, made a unilateral decision to upgrade play in his home country. To provide the Mexican League with more credibility he set out to steal players from the United States.

In an era well before free agency, when U.S. players had to seek winter jobs when their season ended, he found a receptive audience when he waved around contracts for $10,000 or more. Pasquel thought big and even tried to seduce Ted Williams and Joe DiMaggio into abandoning their American League franchises to play in Mexico. They ignored his entreaties. Others did not. Although only about a dozen U.S. players jumped to the Mexican League in the 1940s, their departure caused great concern among Major League owners.

Commissioner A.B. "Happy" Chandler decreed that any U.S. player who abrogated his contract with a Major League club would be banished from the majors for life. Still, several took the chance, perhaps most prominent among them pitcher Sal Maglie.

But the Pasquels' dream was short-lived. Paying higher salaries without a commensurate increase in attendance virtually bankrupted Mexican teams and ran the Mexican League into the ground. Depressed at their failure, the Pasquels decided to lure no more players and one by one the U.S. men wooed to play in Mexico tried to go home. Chandler rescinded the lifetime bans, reduced most banishments to five years, and some sentences even more, and eventually, anyone who wanted to return to the majors could do so.

The Pasquels nearly wrecked top-caliber baseball in Mexico and it took until 1955 to regenerate the league. By that time a despondent Jorge Pasquel had died in a plane crash. Facing ruination, Anuar Canavati, president of the Monterrey Sultanes, negotiated working agreements with Major League teams. With time and effort the Mexican League gained strength. There are now 16 teams in the summer league and eight in winter ball and more than 100 Mexicans who played in Mexico have gone on to Major League careers.

That took time, but a bright future for Mexican baseball was heralded in the Little League World Series in Williamsport, Pennsylvania in 1957, when the Monterrey representative stunned American audiences by becoming the first foreign team to win the crown.

Angel Macias, 12 years old, was on the mound in the championship game for Monterrey against La Mesa, California. In a performance that caught U.S. spectators off-guard, Macias pitched a perfect game to give his underdog country the title.

"A majority of us came from economically disadvantaged areas," he said decades later, "but a lot of doors opened for us immediately. We received high school and college scholarships." (Quoted in Sanchez, "History of baseball . . .") Macias, who said he never realized he was pitching a perfect game until it was over, played professionally for 11 years.

From that year forward, many of the important milestones or developments in Mexican baseball have been linked to Monterrey. Monterrey is the location of the Mexican Baseball Hall of Fame, or Salon de la Fama. It was established in 1939 with an inaugural class but lay fallow until 1964. It has been a going concern since then with about 200 inducted members.

One player who competed for a Monterrey team, as well as two others, in a long career is the late Hector Espino, whose nickname was the "Mexican Babe Ruth." In his 22-season career between 1962 and 1984, Espino smacked 453 home runs. Although he had several offers to play for Major League teams, he ignored them in favor of staying with his family in Mexico and because he feared discrimination in the United States.

Espino was content to be a big fish in his native land and is revered because of it. "There have been many great players in Mexico," said Hall of Fame director Magdalena Rosales Ortiz, "but Hector Espino was very unique. He was an outstanding athlete, but an even better person. He will be remembered as the kind and dignified gentleman who would treat the batboy with the same respect he treated the owner of a team." (Quoted in Sanchez, "Hall honors . . .")

The popular slugger died at only 58 in 1997.

Many baseball fans in the United States may not recall that when the Montreal Expos franchise was failing and it became clear the team needed a new home far from its Canadian roots that one of the locales demonstrating the keenest interest in taking in the club was Monterrey.

Through mismanagement and an appalling lack of fan interest in the fortunes of the National League team, in 2003 the Expos were on their way . . . to where, exactly? Out of Montreal, for sure, but already under a receivership being run by Major League Baseball, the team was in search of a new home. While Commissioner Bud Selig and owners of the other 29 teams flipped through travel brochures and debated the best landing location for the Expos, cities such as Washington, D.C., Portland, Oregon, Las Vegas, San Juan, Puerto Rico, and Monterrey embraced a lobbying and bidding process that fell short of what the International Olympic Committee supervises every several years but was seen as the communities' best chance to gain a big-league team.

This was not come-lately interest expressed by Monterrey. On April 4, 1999, in its efforts go to global, the majors kicked off the regular season with a game between the San Diego Padres and the Colorado Rockies in Monterrey's 26,000-seat stadium (with standing room it could hold 30,000). It was a one-night-only performance and marked the first time the majors had played a season opener anywhere but in the United States or Canada. Tickets for the game were sold out within three hours of the announcement that it would be played. Even then there were murmurings that Monterrey could be the site of a future expansion club. Major League baseball officials did not say such a thing explicitly but did speak in grand terms. "It's part of our plan to grow the game worldwide," said MLB Vice President Timothy J. Brosnan. "Mexico is our neighbor, and there's a great Latin baseball tradition. We want to bring the game to our fans." (Quoted in Dillon.)

Prior to that milestone game, the Los Angeles Dodgers had played exhibition games in Mexico and the New York Mets and the Padres played a regular-season series in Monterrey in 1996.

Monterrey city fathers decided to go after the Expos when they became available. A well-off community that hoped to legitimize itself in the eyes of North Americans as big-time, Monterrey was very serious about going pro. The prosperous business community rallied to back the idea. "It's no secret why we have the best universities in Latin America here, and that this is Mexico's wealthiest community," said bid spokesman Jose Maiz. "The great businesses are steering the future here. That future includes a Major League baseball team." (Quoted in Sandoval.)

Monterrey's ballpark was the largest in the country, the city had a vast network of Little League teams, and the Mexican Baseball Hall of Fame is situated there. "Having the major leagues open their season in Monterrey is a point of pride for us," said Governor Fernando Canales Clariond. "We have great fans and we feel very close to baseball." (Quoted in Dillon.)

Mexico City, the capital, made a short-lived, more half-hearted attempt to inject itself into the process, but despite having a large population base the move to acquire the Expos was not considered a very serious one. If Mexico was going to go big-league it would be in Monterrey. Although the 30,000-seat stadium was smaller than what would be needed, it was a jumping off point and there was a belief the building could be readily expanded. It was also predicted that residents of the southern portions of Texas would become Monterrey Expos (or whatever the name the team ended up being called) fans. At the time there were 1,500 Dallas Cowboys season ticket holders in the Monterrey area. Monterrey is located about 120 miles from Texas, so there was some back-and-forth documented.

It certainly would have been a change for Expos players to move from a predominantly French-speaking city to a predominantly Spanish-speaking city, but Monterrey's effort failed. The Expos found a temporary home in San Juan, playing numerous home games there for a season, but eventually relocated to Washington, D.C. and became the Washington Nationals.

Baseball has been popular in Mexico for well over a century, but the caliber of play in the Mexican League has fluctuated wildly. Before Jackie Robinson's ascension to the Brooklyn Dodgers in 1947, the Mexican League was often a haven for top Negro Leagues players. The rift provoked by the Pasquel family kept U.S. players away for some time in the 1950s, and the league's attendance dropped dramatically.

In 1971, expansion gave the Mexican League 12 teams for the first time since 1936. The time was ripe. Playing in much smaller ballparks than the U.S. majors, the teams across the land began to draw well. Opening day of 1971 attracted 25,000 fans to a game hosted by the Mexico City Reds. Other teams in smaller

Arturo Moreno

In 2003, Mexican-American billionaire Arturo Moreno became the first Latino owner of a major North American sports franchise when he bought the Anaheim Angels from The Walt Disney Company for $180 million.

Moreno, 56 at the time of the purchase, is the oldest of 11 children who grew up in Tucson, Arizona. Ranked as one of the richest men in the world, Moreno made his personal fortune by constructing billboards and then selling his company for $8.3 billion. A long-time baseball fan, Moreno previously owned a small share of the Arizona Diamondbacks. Prior to that, he was a part-owner of the Salt Lake City Trappers minor-league club.

Moreno made headline news quickly, stating he wanted to compete for fans with the Los Angeles Dodgers, by cutting the price of tickets and beer at the Angels' ballpark, and by signing free agent superstar outfielder Vladimir Guerrero before the 2004 season. Guerrero, whose first language is Spanish, speaks little English and when he struggled a bit at his introductory press conference, Moreno stepped in as translator, creating laughs. "It's one thing to have the means to buy a baseball team," Moreno said, "but more important, do you really respect the opportunity?" (Quoted in Gregory.) Moreno was making the point that he wants to win. Under Moreno's stewardship, the Angels emerged as a perennial playoff team and the kingpin of the American League Western Division.

When chatting with his Latino players, Moreno often slips into Spanish, many times clearly putting them at ease. Having an Hispanic owner was a milestone for baseball. But it also marked the first time many of the Latino players talked their own language with a major authority figure on a team they played on since leaving home.

Further Reading
Gregory, Sean, "Arturo Moreno," *Time* magazine, August 13, 2005.

cities drew 12,000 or 15,000. Later, the league developed into a 16-team circuit with affiliations to U.S. clubs. When *The Sporting News* covered all minor leagues, the Mexican League saw regular round-up coverage in the U.S. publication.

In 1977, prominent San Francisco-area sports columnist Art Spander took a trip to Mexico to explore the baseball situation. He jokingly noted that one of the first ways a U.S. tourist realized he was not in his home country anymore was that O.J. Simpson wasn't in the Hertz ads. Also common, he observed, were fans avidly reading what he took to be a daily version of *The Sporting News*. Spander also found that the daily newspapers gave ample space to the majors, as well as the Mexican League.

Fernando Valenzuela, Enrique Romo, Aurelio Rodriguez, and Jorge Orta are only a small number of Mexican players known for their stays in the majors.

The popularity of baseball has only increased in Mexico since and although the fleeting opportunity to make Monterrey a player on the big-league scene evaporated, expansion proponent Maiz said he believed it would work out well if the majors chose his city. "We'd treat them real well here," he said. "We all speak English and the quality of life is better than anywhere else in Latin America." (Quoted in Sandoval.)

Further Reading

Dillon, Sam, "Beisbol Si! But Can U.S. Players Drink the Water?" *New York Times*, March 31, 1999.

Sanchez, Jesse, "History of baseball in Mexico," MLB.com, January 7, 2004.

———, "Hall honors Mexican greats," MLB.com, January 7, 2004.

Sandoval, Ricardo, "Monterrey making pitch for baseball," *Dallas Morning News*, November 8, 2003.

Spander, Art, "Baseball Is Big In Mexico," *The Sporting News*, August 13, 1977.

Venezuelans Love Their Baseball Heroes

The images of joy on the fans' faces as Ozzie Guillen returned to his native country bearing the Major League trophy signifying that his Chicago White Sox were World Series champions were as telling as the images of joy on the fans' faces in Chicago.

Throwing confetti, fans paraded in the streets of Chicago in celebration of the White Sox' first title in 88 years. Fans paraded in the streets of Caracas, throwing confetti, to celebrate the first World Series championship won by a Hispanic manager.

For Venezuelans, it was personal. One of their own had become a rare Hispanic manager. Then he had done his predecessors one better by winning a title. All the while, Guillen, who had been a prominent player for the White Sox when he was younger, talked of his Venezuelan heritage, his background, and learning the game. One of their own had reached the pinnacle of the sport and the Venezuelan fans were proud.

Venezuela is one of the hotbeds of baseball in Latin America, with a long history of sending its best players to the majors. There is a special connection between Venezuela's top-flight shortstops and the majors, starting with Chico Carrasquel. Carrasquel was the pioneer and became the standard bearer when he moved into the White Sox' starting lineup in 1950. He was followed by Luis Aparicio and a tradition began. Guillen was part of that tradition. So was Cincinnati's Davey Concepcion. The older players helped the younger players and as the years passed Venezuela became identified in the United States with superior shortstops. Gradually, that singular distinction expanded and quality players at all positions gravitated to the United States.

Now Venezuela is regarded as one of the most reliable and prominent suppliers of fresh talent to the majors each year. Among the best players from Venezuela in recent years are pitcher Carlos Zambrano of the Cubs, Freddy Garcia, who helped pitch the White Sox to that 2005 title, outfielder Magglio Ordonez of the Tigers, pitcher Johan Santana of the Mets, outfielder Bobby Abreu of the Angels, relief pitcher Frankie Rodriguez of the Mets, and first baseman Miguel Cabrera of the Tigers.

Venezuela Loves the White Sox

Venezuela's connection to the Chicago White Sox dates back to Chico Carrasquel becoming the team's shortstop in 1950. The connection remained strong even after the revered Carrasquel was traded to the Cleveland Indians in 1956 to make room for the next great Venezuelan shortstop Luis Aparicio.

Ozzie Guillen continued the trend and kept the link alive during his tenure holding down the same position for the Sox between 1985 and 1997. But Guillen's stature rose significantly in 2004 when he was named the first Venezuelan manager of a big-league team. Guillen was hired to supervise his old team, the White Sox.

The excitement grew in 2005 when Guillen piloted the White Sox to an American League Central Division crown and on to the World Series. Throughout Venezuela fans were glued to their television sets watching the White Sox-Houston Astros World Series but, above all, rooting for Guillen to win it all.

"There's always been Sox fans down here, but now, because of Ozzie, every Venezuelan is a White Sox fan," said Antonio Jose Herrera, who was the owner of the La Guaira Sharks. That was the winter ball club Guillen played for during his years with the White Sox. More White Sox ties: the 2005 manager of the Sharks was scheduled to be Joey Cora, but because he was the White Sox bench coach, he was late to start his winter season.

The Sharks honored Guillen, their predecessor, in a unique way after the White Sox captured the American League pennant. The Sharks players all wore No. 13 patches, Guillen's number, and black socks that matched that part of the Chicago uniforms.

Even before Guillen led the White Sox to their first World Series title in 88 years, Hugo Chavez, president of Venezuela, proclaimed himself a fan. Guillen was a guest on Chavez's weekly radio show. "All of us here in Venezuela are so proud of you," Chavez said. (Quoted in Dellios.)

Many times Guillen spoke of his pride in his Venezuelan heritage. He called Carrasquel his hero and shed tears when Carrasquel died early in the 2005 season and he was unable to attend the funeral because his death occurred during the White Sox season.

Further Reading
Dellios, Hugh, "Venezuela Wild About Sox," *Chicago Tribune*, October 22, 2005.

The South American country on the northern coast of the continent has about 27 million people. It is a tropical land, where winter is unheard of, and the possession of key oil reserves makes the nation an international player economically. Like most of the other countries in the region Venezuela was colonized by the

Spanish before declaring independence in 1811, though it was not until 1821 that the new nation's government was stable. At about $11,400, the per capita income is much higher than several other Caribbean area countries.

In 1992, Hugo Chavez staged a coup and took over the reins of power. In the years since he has solidified his hold on the country, moving the politics to the left and frequently demonizing the United States. Unlike Fidel Castro, who had a personal involvement in baseball and changed the administration of the game in Cuba, which altered the lives of thousands of players, Chavez has been hands off in regard to the sport. Rather, he has used his pulpit to praise and honor any heroes of the game that have achieved milestones in the United States. Either through congratulatory events in the case of Guillen, or commiseration when Carrasquel died early in 2005, Chavez has shrewdly used the moments to ally himself with popular sentiment.

The mix of politics and sport has sometimes been volatile. In December 2002, when opposition politicians organized a general strike in the nation because of Chavez' policies, the Venezuelan winter league called off play for a period of time. Americans trying to improve their game during the off-season from the minors or majors cut short their stays in the country.

As Chavez moved more to the left and aligned more closely with Castro and Communist Cuba, there was speculation in 2007 that he might even ban Venezuelan professionals from returning to the United States. The discussion arose because that is what Castro did in the early 1960s when tightening his grip on Cuba. Venezuelan players, however, doubted it would come to that in their country. "I don't think he (Chavez) would do that," said Venezuelan pitcher Carlos Carrasco, who was affiliated with the Philadelphia Phillies. "He's real proud of what we do here." (Quoted in Zolecki.) Although Chavez nationalized telecommunications and electric industries in a move toward socialism, at one point Chavez said he would not follow Castro's lead and prohibit Venezuelan players from playing in the majors.

However, Venezuelans do have the Cubans to thank for their interest in baseball. The sport was introduced to Venezuela by Cuban workers who set up a cigarette factory in Caracas in the early 1890s. The progenitor of the factory and the game was Emilio Cramer and his workers. The El Caracas Base Ball Club was formed and the first game was played on May 23, 1895.

"It is a common misconception that the Marines introduced baseball to the Caribbean during frequent interventions," according to Milton H. Jamail, a journalist and author. (Quoted in Jamail, 16.)

That first game was an exhibition to raise money for Cuba's war effort against the United States. The team of 22 players was split in half and played against each other in front of 2,000 fans. A photograph was taken of the team, helping future generations note the date of the sport's founding in Venezuela. The sport grew from there, spreading to other communities. It also eclipsed soccer in popularity, quite rare among South American countries.

One of the most important games in the nation's history was the 1941 victory over Cuba that gave Venezuela the World Amateur Baseball Championship. The celebration was long and loud. Government offices and schools closed, fans danced in the streets, roses were dropped from airplanes. No business was conducted when the conquering team returned home from Havana.

Although Chico Carrasquel was the idol for an entire generation of Venezuelans when he became a major leaguer, Carrasquel himself had a different role model. The first Venezuelan to reach the majors was Alex Carrasquel, a pitcher who broke in with the Washington Senators in 1939 and compiled a 50–39 record with a 3.73 ERA. That Carrasquel, born in 1912, was Chico's uncle. In an eight-year career interrupted by World War II, Alex Carrasquel was mostly a relief pitcher. He also jumped to the Mexican League. Alex Carrasquel had been traded to the White Sox and didn't want to go to Chicago. Instead, he signed a three-year deal with the Pasquel brothers when they were throwing money around raiding the majors for talent as part of their grand scheme to upgrade the Mexican League.

Omar Vizquel, another in the long line of all-star Venezuelan shortstops nearing the end of his career, is a likely future Hall of Famer. He considers baseball far more popular in his homeland than soccer and said it has gained in popularity during his 20-year career. "The sport has never been more popular," Vizquel said. "Like basketball in America, baseball is seen by poor Venezuelan teens as a way to trade poverty for Porsches. My country is overrun with scouts from America looking for a scrawny kid with the potential to become the next superstar." (Quoted in Vizquel and Dyer, 36.)

For years, it has been tradition for Latino players to return to the neighborhoods of their upbringing in the off-season to compete as full-time regulars with local teams in winter ball. This was tiring, but it was a way to show the locals that the player had not become a big-timer and forgotten his roots. Vizquel said he played winter ball for 10 years in Venezuela before he ran out of gas. The key rivalry in the eight-team winter league was between a team from Caracas that he played on, and one from Valencia. Emotions ran high when the teams met. "Those games make Yankees-Red Sox games seem tame," Vizquel said. (Quoted in Vizquel and Dyer, 55.)

Venezuela has become one of the major producers of big-league talent, but the numbers are still not in the ballpark of the Dominican Republic's. Compared to the Dominican, Venezuela is a late bloomer, with Major League teams slower to commit full-time scouts to the country and to build baseball academies as has been done in the Dominican (partially because of the uncertainty of the political situation).

The Minnesota Twins, who featured the versatile Venezuelan, Cesar Tovar in the 1960s, were ahead of the much of the competition. That's how they signed

Johan Santana (although they couldn't afford to pay him the multi-millions the New York Mets could when he became a free agent). "We're proud of Venezuela and Venezuelan baseball," Santana said. "People in America don't realize it, but we've got 25, 30 million people here, and so many of us love baseball. This is a great place to look for talent." (Quoted in Souhan.)

The Twins did open a scouting academy in Venezuela and that presence helped the club find young prospects. Santana was the outstanding example, but they signed infielder Luis Rivas and pitchers Carlos Pulido and Juan Rincon, too.

One aspect of life in Venezuela holding back Major League teams from committing more scouting resources to the country is the growth industry in kidnapping. Venezuela can be a violent place and the upsurge in kidnapping is a deterrent to displaying wealth and status and to roaming around solo and unprotected. Not even baseball players can be sure of their safety.

Born in Caracas in 1974, Ugueth Urbina was a top-tier relief pitcher when his mother was kidnapped in 2004. Urbina, a two-time All-Star, led the National League in saves with 41 in 1999, and he helped the Marlins win the 2003 World Series. Urbina was with the Detroit Tigers when his mother was kidnapped from his ranch and held in the jungle 300 miles away for ransom before $6 million was paid to rescue her. In 2005, Urbina, who has 237 lifetime saves, was charged along with friends with attempted murder for pouring gasoline on and waving a machete at five farm workers whom he accused of stealing a gun. In 2007, he was sent to prison for 14 years and is still incarcerated.

Outfielder Richard Hidalgo, who frequently showed impressive power during his career with the Houston Astros and other teams, was the victim of violence in his home country in 2002. In November of that year he was shot in the arm in a car jacking while visiting Venezuela.

Those high profile incidents make current Venezuelans think carefully about personal security and the security of loved ones. Francisco Rodriguez, called K-Rod, set the Major League record for saves in a season in 2008 with 62. Rodriguez played with the Angels and then moved on to the Mets in New York, but has maintained a home in Venezuela. His residence was as fortified as an old Western fort on the Plains. The Rodriguez home was surrounded by eight-foot walls with electrified fencing and the grounds were patrolled around-the-clock by armed security. Security cameras also scanned his property.

"You can't even walk outside without protection," Rodriguez said of the climate of violence targeting citizens of wealth. "Anybody with money is a target. They know baseball players make pretty good money and they're going to find a way to take it. If they have to kidnap a member of your family, they're going to do it." (Quoted in Eisenberg.)

If Rodriguez's security measures seemed extreme, he only took action follow-ing the Angels' 2002 World Series triumph when his brother and mother (on dif-ferent occasions) were robbed in the street. Rodriguez tried to convince 13 members of his extended family to move to the United States, but they refused. Instead, he built them a stronghold for protection. This was not the way the Venezuelan dream was supposed to play out.

Such worries are the domain of only the wealthy few and the vast majority of Venezuelan ballplayers will never make the millions that K-Rod has banked. But as more Venezuelan stars rise to the top of the game, more and more players will try to make it to the majors.

Further Reading

Eisenberg, Jeff, "Venezuelan major leaguers take protective measures," *Riverside Press-Enterprise*, May 20, 2007.

Jamail, Milton H., *Venezuelan Bust, Baseball Boom* (Lincoln, University of Nebraska Press, 2008).

Souhan, Jim, "Baseball's Frontier: Venezuela fertile ground for Twins," *Minneapolis Star-Tribune*, January 14, 2003.

Vizquel, Omar and Dyer, Bob, *Omar!* (Cleveland, Gray & Company Publishers, 2002).

Zolecki, Todd, "Long arms of Chavez could hold Phils back," *Philadelphia Inquirer*, March 4, 2007.

Beisbol—The Latin Game

In 2007, under the auspices of Major League Baseball, a movie was released telling the story of baseball in Latin American countries. Cognizant of the growing number of Hispanics populating rosters—approaching 30 percent of all players—organized baseball leaders saw the need to explain the history, the background, and the personalities of the sport in the Dominican Republic, Venezuela, Puerto Rico, Mexico, and other locales. One impetus was the implementation of the new World Baseball Classic, an event that brings together the best players in the universe for the first time because it includes not only amateurs, but major leaguers.

The movie explores the roots of the game in Latin American countries by taking viewers into neighborhoods filled with cinder-block houses lining dirt streets, zooming in on youngsters who play the game during every daylight hour on their dirt playgrounds, on the beach, and in the street, with shabby homemade equipment. Cardboard juice boxes are shaped into gloves, tree branches are wielded as bats, and balls are created by wrapping thick tape around pairs of socks.

The difficulties faced by Latin American pioneers who came to the United States without knowledge of English and walking into a society prejudiced against dark-skinned people are shown. Players of the 1950s laid a foundation and became role models for future generations of players from their own country and other nearby countries with their ability and dignity in the face of discrimination. Throughout the film, wherever the camera roams, the importance of baseball to fans, players, and the people in general is documented.

"We have passion for this game," said Hall of Fame pitcher Juan Marichal, who is from the Dominican Republic.

Of his home country of Venezuela, Chicago White Sox manager and former shortstop Ozzie Guillen said, "They breathe, they eat, they talk baseball."

Quotations from the movie *Beisbol—The Latin Game*, lead producer Alfonso Pozzo, narrated by Esai Morales, 2007.

In 2004, Guillen became the first Venezuelan manager in the majors. In 2005, he became the first Latin American manager to guide a team to a World Series championship. For all of his and his players' joy, and the glee shown by the people of Chicago as the White Sox won their first title in 88 years, Guillen said no one was happier than the people of Venezuela. Soon after the Chicago victory sweeping the Series from the Houston Astros, Guillen brought the championship trophy back to Venezuela and paraded it around the baseball-mad nation.

The ascent of the Latin American player does represent a revolution. Before World War II there were only small numbers of Hispanic players in the major leagues. Any player with dark skin was classified as black and was locked out of the big leagues, just as African Americans in the United States were. When Jackie Robinson broke the color line in baseball he also broke it for Latinos. A steady arrival of Latino players followed during the 1950s, with such teams as the Washington Senators, Pittsburgh Pirates, and San Francisco Giants opening the gates to their stadiums a little bit wider.

Once skin color receded as an impediment to obtaining a job on a Major League roster, the language barrier reared up. There were no Spanish-speaking managers or coaches with big-league teams. There was no infrastructure in place to help transplanted Dominicans or Mexicans adjust to New York, Chicago, or Cleveland and especially not on the lonely journeys through the small towns in the heartland of the United States that were home to minor-league clubs. There were cases where players felt they were misunderstood as well as discriminated against, were homesick, and in places where they felt they had to be stars, not merely the best man at the end of the bench, to stick on final cuts.

Gradually, all of those issues dissipated. Baseball teams wised up and hired Latino or Spanish-speaking managers and coaches. They smoothed the way for young prospects away from home for the first time. Eventually, Major League baseball teams established dozens of academies to screen prospects in their home areas and to teach them the fundamentals of English in addition to the hit-and-run.

The change has been dramatic. From a situation where a few teams featured Latin American players to all teams having Latin American starters and stars, the big leagues have changed demographically. "It's a matter of if you are not down there you are not going to be a winning organization," said New York Mets general manager Omar Minaya, who became the majors' first Latino general manager with the Montreal Expos. "What you are seeing is an explosion."

USA Today baseball writer Jorge Ortiz agreed. "Teams don't excel without Latin players anymore," he said.

Puerto Rican Bernie Williams, the long-time centerfielder for the New York Yankees who retired in 2006, is also a musician. He said during his playing days the type of music played on boom boxes by teammates changed with the makeup of the players. "We hear a little bit less country music in the clubhouse and more salsa and meringue, that's for sure," Williams said. Nor does Williams think there is any more prejudice in recruiting of Latino players. The poorest of the poor can get a chance as long as they can play the game at a high level and it has been proven many times. "That's just part of the American dream"—or the Latin American dream.

Tribute was paid to the fulfillment of that Latin American dream in 2005 when Major League Baseball oversaw the selection of a Latino Legends lineup of baseball stars with votes from fans across the country. Wearing suits, but accented with the baseball caps of their teams, the stars were introduced to tumultuous applause in Houston before the fourth game of the 2005 World Series. "It's about time we as Latin Americans are given our due in the game," said Hall of Famer Rod Carew. "For so long we weren't."

The Latino Legends' very exclusive lineup included: Starting pitchers Juan Marichal, Fernando Valenzuela, and Pedro Martinez and relief pitcher Mariano Rivera; catcher Ivan Rodriguez; first baseman Albert Pujols; second baseman Rod Carew; shortstop Alex Rodriguez; third baseman Edgar Martinez; and outfielders Roberto Clemente, Vladimir Guerrero, and Manny Ramirez. Clemente was represented by his grown sons, Roberto Jr., and Luis.

Although they were not singled out, the runners-up, or second team, according to ballots cast were: Starting pitchers: Luis Tiant, Johan Santana, and Bartolo Colon and relief pitcher Jose Mesa; catcher Tony Pena; first baseman Orlando Cepeda; second baseman Robby Alomar; shortstop Luis Aparicio; third baseman Bobby Bonilla; and outfielders Sammy Sosa, Bernie Williams, and Tony Oliva.

"To be named to such an elite group of names, to me it's a moment of joy and pride," said Pedro Martinez.

Catcher "Pudge" Rodriguez echoed the sentiment, saying, "To be where I am tonight, it's an honor for me."

Major League Baseball found the son of Martin Dihigo, whom old-timers consider the greatest all-around player of the first half of the century. Dihigo was a five-tool player who could also pitch, but as a dark-skinned Cuban he was never accepted into the majors. He was a star in the Negro Leagues and throughout Latin America. On camera, Dihigo's son Gilbert held up a picture of his deceased dad and although it was clear his main language is Spanish he said in English, "Some people say he was the greatest player ever."

Integration of Major League Baseball came far too late to help Dihigo. Marichal, emerging as an All-Star in the late 1950s, was right on time. But he mused about the acceptance of Hispanic players now and a half century ago. "Latino players have come so far," he said.

Paramount credit for changing the way some fans looked at Latino players and for leading the revolution of Hispanic players on Major League fields is given to Clemente. During his 18 years in the majors, all with the Pirates, the Puerto Rican native was a twelve-time All-Star and redefined coverage of right field. He concluded his career with 3,000 hits and a lifetime batting average of .317. Clemente won four National League batting titles.

"He was unapologetically Hispanic," said baseball historian John Thorn. "He was proud and he conveyed it with every step he took on the field." When he was a young star on the rise from Panama, Rod Carew said Clemente took him aside and urged him "to always take care of the young Latin players." Carew took the advice to heart and tried to mentor young Hispanic players.

Former Cardinals catcher Tim McCarver, now a national television broadcaster, was a contemporary of Clemente's and noted there was a lot of pressure on the Puerto Rican. "He responded to being looked up to," McCarver said.

Clemente thrust himself into the forefront of issues. He was not meek, and he spoke out if disturbed by any matter. "I am from a minority group," Clemente said almost defiantly. "I am from the poor people."

Just as it did when the first Latino players were called to the majors, baseball is a symbol of opportunity in poverty-stricken areas of countries where all of the conveniences are not available. No small nation has made a bigger impact on Major League baseball than the Dominican Republic. Star after star has emerged, following in the footsteps of Marichal. Boston Red Sox designated hitter David Ortiz, known for his community good works in the United States and the Dominican, summarized the life facing young people in his land. "We don't have choices," Ortiz said. "We have to work our way out."

Ortiz, like so many of his countrymen, returns to the Dominican in the off-season, mingles with the fans, gives money to good causes, and works with young people, holding clinics. Homegrown Dominican baseball stars are the most popular people in the country. They are the rock stars and movie stars of the land, but even bigger because they are accessible. They followed a path from the same place and the same circumstances to prove anyone with skills can make it. "These fellows are viewed as the idols, the heroes, role models," said Dominican President Leonel Fernando Reyna. "Just having some kind of personal communications is so important for youngsters and for the people in these communities."

When Felipe Alou joined the Giants organization in 1956, an alumnus of hard-knocks fields in the Dominican, he spoke little English and what he did speak was with a thick accent. Naturally, people he encountered in the United States asked where he was from. When he replied that he was from the Dominican Republic hardly anyone knew a thing about the island, he said. "Nine out of 10 people didn't know where the Dominican Republic was," Alou said.

My, how times have changed. Even the most casual of baseball fans knows about the Dominican now. It is fair to say that the baseball stars of the island have put their country on the map in a way that far exceeds its tiny size. When the Red Sox won the 2004 and 2007 World Series titles, their key sluggers were Ortiz and Manny Ramirez, both from the Dominican Republic. Team president Larry Lucchino said the hard-hitting duo had created a new fan base for the Bostonians. "Make no mistake about that," Lucchino said. "Red Sox Nation extends into the Dominican Republic."

Stars like Ortiz and Ramirez live double lives. They are the heroes of their American teams for what they do on the field, but they are the heroes of their Dominican fans because of where they come from. Their success is linked to their heritage, but their demeanor when they come back to share their success is critical to how they are viewed. It is important for the Latino stars to show respect to their forebears and to remember how difficult life is for many of their countrymen. Generosity, with money, attitude, and time do count. Clemente set that bar and he set it high.

If Clemente sought to pass on wisdom to up-and-coming Latin players and worked to make sure the lineage was passed through players like Carew, Carew is glad to see the tradition passed on. "All these young players in the game today will take the torch and carry it on from there," he said.

Each group of youngsters that comes along is looking for role models. Clemente is the patron saint of all Latino players. Marichal and Cepeda, Carew and the Alous are no longer in the daily limelight making fresh headlines on ESPN's Sports Center, so there is a demand for new faces, new heroes to identify with whether the youngsters are in the Dominican, Venezuela, or Puerto Rico. Given the large numbers of players following the pipeline to the majors, they should never run out of new idols.

Not unless the stars of today forget where they came from. And with players like Carlos Delgado and others around that will not happen. Delgado returns to Puerto Rico each off-season. Going back to the fields he played on as a youth is a reminder of the distance he has traveled, not so much in miles, but in changing worlds. "It's pretty humbling," Delgado said. "This is where it all started. These are my roots. I can never go away from this."

As time goes on and more and more Latino players reach the big leagues, the All-Star game, and become famous, it will always be easy for a young player in the Dominican, Venezuela and Puerto Rico to obtain a reminder about the Latino players of the past. All he has do is turn to the movie, *Beisbol—The Latin Game*, to learn his own heritage.

Flavor of the Game

Party at the park. Fan festival every day. The Hispanic game is a swirl of color and pageantry, a cacophony of music and song. The passion and devotion to baseball is on display every day in the Dominican, Venezuela, Mexico, Puerto Rico, and elsewhere in the Caribbean. The game is a daily circus, a sporting event that combines all the flavor of Latin American life. Far more than being caught up in watching the hit-and-run, baseball fans in Latin America enjoy the spectacle of the evening.

Women wear dresses of yellow, green, and red. Men wear colorful hats. Allegiances are worn on the sleeve. Cheers come from the soul and jeers come from the gut. And sometimes the two get confused, mixed up in the emotion and desire to see excellence and frustration when errors or failure intrudes.

"The fans in Venezuela are outrageous," said homegrown shortstop star Omar Vizquel. "When they get on a guy, they don't stop. One fan always stood behind home plate and screamed the entire game. He hated our second baseman and rode him constantly. The abuse wasn't just verbal. The ballpark sold lots of oranges. They were sold in halves, and the fans would peel them, eat the inside, and save the peels for when somebody made an error. They threw beer at you, too. The outfielders had to wear batting helmets to protect themselves from the junk that would fly out of the stands." (Quoted in Vizquel and Dryer, 56.)

Jokingly, Vizquel, then starring for the Cleveland Indians, said such intense fan reaction prepared him for playing against the Boston Red Sox in Fenway Park and against the New York Yankees in Yankee Stadium.

Even though Puerto Rican great Orlando Cepeda was nicknamed "Cha-Cha," the sounds of music at Latin American ballparks are usually salsa and meringue. Bare-midriff-clad young women sometimes stand up and gyrate at their seats in the stands to the tunes. There is a less inhibited crowd at ballgames throughout Latin America than are found in Major League stadiums. The entertainment for the whole family extends beyond the game itself. Nonetheless, the results, the caliber of play, are taken very seriously. It is common to see street corner debates about players and teams in Venezuela and Cuba.

Citing the discussions he saw among fans in Venezuela, Dodgers' Spanish-language broadcaster Jaime Jarrin said, "Latinos have a passion for baseball that is infectious." (Quoted in Viva Baseball.)

American writer John Krich was quite taken by meringue music he heard played in the Dominican and felt it fit the place. "By dint of its utter sincerity, madcap turns, and infectious hilarity, the music has overpowered more sophisticated island rhythms. It's an awfully urgent beat for such a sleepy place, but the perfect sound for a country both so blessed and looted. In no other music on earth does the happiness sound so sad, or the sadness so happy." (Quoted in Krich, 113.)

Also part of the show: rum on ice in paper cups, papitos (a kind of potato chip), and pork rinds. Bookies on the premises take bets on games, something that would give Major League Baseball officials heart attacks.

During his heyday with the Chicago Cubs, Sammy Sosa ruled the clubhouse. It was as if his ability to hit more than 60 home runs in a season three times (more than anyone in history), empowered the native of the Dominican Republic to play his favorite Latino tunes loudly on a boom box. Sosa was the big man in the lineup and that made him the sergeant of arms of the locker room, the chief judge of what was desirable to hear in pre-game and post-game music. It was like being assigned to ride shotgun next to the driver on a long-distance drive. Sosa hit his own long-distance drives and as a result in essence controlled the radio.

Before things soured between Sosa and the Cubs in the early 2000s, he was the happiest guy in baseball. His trademarks included a wide smile, a little hop when he thought a ball he had powdered was traveling out of the stadium for a homer, blowing kisses to his mother, and a tap on his chest with his fingers to express love. He was exuberant and charming and the fans loved his gushing personality. Fans loved Sosa because not only did he produce, he acted the way they felt they would act if they were being paid a fortune to play Major League baseball. He was having fun and he let everyone in on it.

Sosa outgrew Chicago and became a phenomenon across the United States during the 1998 season when he and Mark McGwire were chasing Roger Maris's single-season record of 61 home runs. Sosa was the outgoing, jocular one.

Sosa had more showmanship in his game than most players. This is true of several Latino players. The basic, conservative, simple, just-fundamentals style demanded by some American managers did not always play well at home. The comparison could be made that Latino baseball had elements of American playground basketball in it, where it was OK to complicate a simple play with flash as long as the basic mission was accomplished. That sometimes meant that those athletic shortstops could handle the ball the way a basketball playmaker did, flipping it behind the back to a second baseman to complete a double play, spearing a grounder out of mid-air bare-handed to ensure that the throw made it to first base before the runner. Some people might call it showboating, but if the job got done, it added spice to the play. And sometimes, just like a behind-the-back basketball pass, that was the best way to get the job done.

"They come with that style," said U.S. slugger Gary Sheffield of Latino players in the majors. "It adds fun to the game." (Quoted in *Beisbol—The Latin Game*.)

Venezuelan Victor Martinez, late of the Cleveland Indians, who was traded to the Boston Red Sox in 2009, was known for his innovative handshakes in Cleveland. The shimmying and shaking went way beyond "slap-me-five" territory. Martinez developed individual routines for different teammates. It was a wonder he could remember which act went with which player. Shortstop Orlando Cabrera, from Colombia, and most recently of the Minnesota Twins, is also renowned for his complex handshakes.

Nowhere was the pageantry of Latin American baseball style on display more vividly than in the 2006 and 2009 World Baseball Classics. The best teams in the world gathered, major leaguers included, to chase the tournament title. Latino countries led the way in flag waving, blaring music, and patriotism on display. "Nothing quite matches the passion that the Latin Americans have for the game," said former big leaguer and national baseball broadcaster Tim McCarver. (Quoted in *Beisbol—The Latin Game*.)

Passion. The word comes up again and again when baseball people describe the underlying emotion in Latino baseball.

Moises Alou, son of Felipe and nephew of Matty and Jesus, all of Giants outfield fame, had his own long career in the sport. Dominican by heritage although he was born in Atlanta, Georgia, Moises appreciated the dancing and music that accompanied baseball in Latin America and that was a prominent feature of the World Baseball Classics. Alou, who retired in 2009, had played for seven Major League teams, but nowhere he had been matched the color that fan supporters brought to the sport in Latin America. "You hear the drums and the sirens," Moises Alou said, "things you never see in the States." (Quoted in *Beisbol—The Latin Game*.)

Further Reading

Beisbol—The Latin Game (movie), lead producer Alfonso Pozzo.
Krich, John, *El Beisbol* (Chicago, Ivan R. Dee, 2002).
Viva Baseball! Exhibit at National Baseball Hall of Fame.
Vizquel, Omar and Dryer, Rob, *Omar!* (Cleveland, Gray & Company, Publishers, 2002).

Latinos and Blacks Common Fates

It is no accident that Jackie Robinson is a member of the Hispanic Heritage Baseball Museum and Hall of Fame. The African American who broke the Major League color line when he was promoted to the Brooklyn Dodgers in 1947 opened doors not only for the United States' ballplayers of dark skin, but also for Latinos who had been barred for the same reason.

Essentially, for the first half of the twentieth century, the only baseball players of Latin American extraction who were welcome in the majors were light-skinned. Adolfo Luque was a prime example of a Cuban with lighter-toned skin who carved out a 20-year pitching career between 1914 and 1935.

Although Luque was able to show off his talents with the Cincinnati Reds and other teams, such phenomenal players as Jose Mendez and Martin Dihigo were banned from the majors because of their darker skin. Although both men were eventually voted into the National Baseball Hall of Fame, it was not because of their records in the majors.

Besides excelling in winter leagues throughout the Caribbean, from Cuba to Venezuela, a multitude of Latin stars also performed in the U.S. Negro Leagues. Minnie Minoso was an All-Star with the Chicago White Sox and the Cleveland Indians, but he came to the United States from Cuba to play for the New York Cubans. Dihigo, who was selected for five different baseball halls of fame, played for the Cuban Stars in the United States and spent 12 seasons in the U.S. Negro Leagues. Mendez pitched for the Cuban Stars and the Brooklyn Royal Giants, as well as being a Cuban star back home.

Many of the greatest Negro Leagues stars also competed overseas, supplementing their income with appearances in Cuba, Mexico, the Dominican, Puerto Rico, and Venezuela in winter play. The black Americans felt they were treated better in Latin America than they were in their home country where they faced discrimination at many hotels and restaurants. For them, playing ball was liberating. For the fans in the Latino countries, it was good fortune to watch some of the best players in the world in person, regardless of skin color.

The magnificent power-hitting African American catcher Josh Gibson made his mark in Puerto Rico, once hitting a 500-foot home-run that left teammates and opponents gaga. But it was also said that Gibson, not a natural catcher, benefited greatly from the extra time spent on the field during the cold-weather months. "Josh didn't really learn how to catch until he played winter ball," said Buck Leonard, the Hall of Fame first baseman whose dark skin also kept him out of the majors. (Quoted in Holway, 74.)

During Gibson's prime, when he was smashing home runs with ferocity and for great distances, he was called "The Black Babe Ruth." However, while equally admired in Puerto Rico, he had a different nickname on the island. He was called "Trucutu." This was a comic strip character that had the powers of a Superman. (Quoted in Ribowsky, *The Power and the Darkness*, 216.)

Gibson and the marvelous Satchel Paige were more often a pitching battery, competing on the same team, but as they traveled the hemisphere, playing exhibitions, Gibson and the lanky pitcher had their hitter-thrower confrontations. They always teased one another about who would come out best when they faced one another, but Paige seemed to triumph more often. He had a better gift for psychology than the straight forward, serious Gibson, and he employed it as a weapon when they met on the field. Paige got the better of Gibson in Puerto Rico most of the time. Gibson was the strong, silent type. Paige was an endearing blabbermouth who talked more than a campaigning politician and he worked on Gibson's mind from the mound. Once when Paige zipped a fastball past Gibson, he yelled, "S'matter Josh, too hot for ya?" (Quoted in Ribowsky, *The Power and the Darkness*, 216.) It was nothing for Paige to address hitters in the middle of an at-bat.

Paige was the king of the barnstormers and the star of the exhibition circuit. If a promoter waved dollar bills in his face, he was ready to go. That meant playing for teams from North Dakota to Mexico. During Paige's remarkable career that lasted nearly 40 years, the limber thrower came up with a lame arm only once. He was pitching in Mexico and had to give up a season and return to the United States when his arm went dead. The aches that cost Paige his fastball and trickiness stayed with him for more than a year and many owners and players thought he was washed up. The loss of his best tool in making a living frightened Paige like no other experience in his life.

Paige jumped his contract with Gus Greenlee and the Pittsburgh Crawfords and headed to Mexico in 1938. Highly paid and highly publicized, Paige joined a team in Vera Cruz. But he was dismayed when he couldn't fire with his usual velocity and his arm betrayed him. "It kinda burns in there, feels like somebody pinched off the blood," Paige said. "My arm. I couldn't lift it." (Quoted in Ribowsky, *Don't Look Back*, 169.)

That was almost the end of Satchel Paige as we knew him. His legend was almost truncated. But he recovered and returned to Latin America many times. The U.S. black ballplayers and the Latino black ballplayers were like a brotherhood. They understood where they ranked in the United States. They had no gripes with one another. They were the colorblind baseball people of the era.

"Winter ball must have been near to heaven for blacks of that generation," wrote one author who studied Latin American baseball. "In their Caribbean brethren these men must have recognized themselves and discovered that Africans are everywhere in the Americas." (Quoted in Krich, 134.)

Buck O'Neil, the Kansas City Monarchs star first baseman and later manager, became an eloquent spokesman for Negro Leagues teammates and friends as he out lasted them in life into his 90s. He, too, had his share of Latin American baseball experiences. His first Latin American trip, he said, came when he was a young man and affiliated with a U.S. team named the Black Spiders. O'Neil tells the story in his autobiography of playing exhibitions in Mexico and of being so well-received that the Mexican League was going to take his group into the league as an entity. All the Spiders had to do was beat one more team, O'Neil said. It was all or nothing. Win and the Spiders were in the league, or lose and go home. "We would be spending the winter in Mexico City with the senoritas and the tequila, and that sounded like a good deal," he wrote. "Only trouble was, we lost. You know it's a tough league when they deport you for losing." (Quoted in O'Neill, Wulf, and Conrads, 65–66.)

Buck Leonard, the slugging first baseman for the Homestead Grays, enjoyed playing in Mexico. There was a relaxed pace to the season. "We only played Tuesday, Thursday, Saturday and Sunday," said Leonard, a perennial .300 hitter in Mexico. "We had about half the time off. They only allowed three (U.S. players) on each team—black players and white players. The best ball was played over here. I played 17 years in the United States and five years in Mexico." (Quoted in Kelley, 33.)

Those five seasons spent in Mexico were between 1951 and 1955, after the Grays were defunct and the Negro Leagues were headed in that direction. Leonard was at the tail-end of his long career, but could still bash the ball, and he played winter and summer in Mexico, splitting his time between the Torreon Peas (or Black-Eyed Peas as the players called themselves) and Durango in the summer and Obregon and the Xalapa Hot Peppers in the winter. Although Leonard liked the competition, being able to extend his career, and the people, his stomach had trouble adjusting upon re-entry each year. "Every year when we would go down there that water would give you dysentery," Leonard said. "It would last a couple of weeks and then get all right." (Quoted in Leonard and Riley, 214.)

One teammate was Charolito Orta who had a little boy named Jorge, later a player for the Chicago White Sox. Leonard used to bounce the toddler on his lap and carry him around the ballpark. Leonard also encountered the fathers of future Hall of Famers Luis Aparicio and Orlando Cepeda. Leonard's manager with more than one team was Martin Dihigo and Leonard raved about Dihigo's baseball knowledge. "He was a good teacher of baseball and he could tell you all about playing," Leonard said of the Cuban great. (Quoted in Leonard and Riley, 215.)

With half the week off, Leonard had plenty of time for relaxation and socializing. "In Mexico, everybody went out and sat in the plaza and watched people walking around," Leonard said. "And that's how people passed the days and nights. I spent a lot of leisure time watching bullfights and cockfights." (Quoted in Leonard and Riley, 217.)

In addition to his long-time play in Mexico, Leonard also played winter ball in Puerto Rico, Venezuela, and Cuba when he was younger. Leonard's personal tour of the Caribbean was almost as extensive as Dihigo's. And he was welcome wherever he traveled and played.

Latinos who came in the opposite direction during the first half of the twentieth century were not so warmly received as black Americans who went to the tropics. Dihigo, who could both hit and pitch, joined the Cuban Stars in 1923 when he was just 17. The pay seemed fine to him, but the life in the United States for a dark-skinned man angered him. "My first contract with the Cuban Stars was $100 a month," Dihigo said, "but more than all that, I began to experience firsthand the hatred of 'gringos,' going through lots of hardships and vexations, and having to struggle daily for subsistence." (Quoted in Burgos, 120.)

Dihigo's all-around skills as a baseball player made him a god in Cuba, where he grew up, and wherever he played throughout Latin America. Yet no matter how well he hit and no matter how fast he pitched in the United States, he was looked upon with disdain by a large segment of society. Major League baseball fans of the time missed out on seeing one of the great talents of all time, but they either didn't know or didn't care.

Willie Wells, the skillful Negro Leagues infielder (like Dihigo) later elected to the National Baseball Hall of Fame in Cooperstown, New York, was born in Austin, Texas in 1905 and played from 1924 to 1948 in the Negro Leagues. But he breathed most freely when in Hispanic foreign lands, where he was welcomed on and off the field. He was particularly fond of Mexico. "When I travel with Vera Cruz," Wells said, "we live in the best hotels, we eat in the best restaurants, and can go anyplace we care to. I've found freedom and democracy here, something I never found in the United States. I was branded a Negro in the States, and had to act accordingly. Everything I did, including baseball, was regulated by my color. They wouldn't give me a chance in the big leagues because of my color, yet they accepted every other nationality under the sun." (Quoted in Burgos, 164.) It was a stinging indictment of his home country.

Once Jackie Robinson made his debut, the color barrier came down. However, the 16 Major League teams of the time did not rush with equal enthusiasm to embrace the opportunity to add men of color to their rosters. The Cleveland Indians, under Bill Veeck's stewardship, did so immediately. The New York Giants were quick to integrate, as were the St. Louis Browns. The Washington Nationals had been pro-active in Latin America, but did not sign a black Latin American immediately. While the Dodgers added several black players to their team in the years following Robinson's ascension, some teams were quite slow to integrate. It took until 1959, when the Boston Red Sox added infielder Pumpsie Green to the club, for all teams to be integrated.

On the landmark list of individual barrier breakers by team, four of the 16 players credited with being the first black players on a team are also Hispanic. Cuban Minnie Minoso, who became a regular with the White Sox in 1951, is the first and also the most notable player, a seven-time All-Star whom many feel should be in the National Baseball Hall of Fame.

The Cincinnati Reds' first black player in 1954 was Nino Escalera. Escalara, from Puerto Rico, played 73 games in the outfield for the Reds and batted .159 that year. That was his only season in the majors. Cuban outfielder Carlos Paula joined the Washington Senators in 1954 and spent three years with the club, compiling a lifetime .271 average. Ozzie Virgil, Sr., from the Dominican Republic, broke in with the Giants in 1956, but was the first black with the Detroit Tigers in 1958. He played nine seasons as a third baseman and a catcher while hitting .231.

Minoso made the greatest impact. After a slow start with the Indians he was popular from the get-go in Chicago. Minoso smacked a home run in his first game at old Comiskey Park and as a base-stealing fiend with an active bat and daredevil running in the field and on the bases, the local fans cheered him wildly. That did not mean his existence in the United States, with the New York Cubans, the Indians, and White Sox, while visiting various cities was stress free.

"The Negro Leagues was an experience all its own, and not one I would trade for the world," Minoso wrote in his autobiography. "We slept a lot and usually ate our meals on the bus. Racial segregation was rampant in the South, so there were only certain places we were allowed to get off the bus and buy things." (Quoted in Minoso and Fagen, 29.) A naturally upbeat man, Minoso was gregarious regardless of the situation, but he spoke Spanish first and English with an accent, so he sometimes fretted about making himself understood. He maintained his inner strength by being himself. "I never let the world hurt me," Minoso said. "The world didn't break me. They used to call me terrible things. I let it go in one ear and out the other. None of it stayed with me. I never wanted them to know my feelings on the inside. On the outside, I just gave them my smile. My smile all the time." (Quoted in Wendel and Villegas, 39.)

Minoso became an icon for many younger Latino players, especially Cubans. They watched him succeed in the majors and felt because he had done so, they could do so. The superb Cuban pitcher Luis Tiant, who also became a great success in the majors with the Cleveland Indians and Boston Red Sox, called Minoso "my idol growing up. He was the first one to stand up for black Cubans. Guys like me. You see somebody like that make it and you have some hope. You start to believe that maybe one day you can reach the big leagues, too." (Quoted in Wendel and Villegas, 35.)

The welcome mat was out—supposedly—for dark-skinned Latinos after 1947. But if a qualified player of Hispanic heritage could now get a job, it still took extra effort to get noticed and make the final roster. That welcome was conditional at first, borderline players learned. And even the best players, like Minoso, were not free from discrimination. Handling the demands, the tough times, was going to be the difference maker at least throughout the 1950s and 1960s. From then on, the talent level of vast numbers of Latinos was undeniable. It became more of a sellers market and teams really did not care what the color of your skin was.

Minoso had more challenges than the Latino players of today, but he persevered and became one of the most revered players in White Sox history. "I get a great thrill when I hear how I paved the way for future Latin ballplayers," Minoso said. "Those like myself who were black had to deal with both racial discrimination and a language barrier. Sure it made things more difficult, but never impossible. I always felt that I was defending my uniform every time I put it on. To me, it was like defending the American flag. I respected my uniform, and I wore it as if I was defending the American flag." (Quoted in Minoso and Fagen, 131.)

The hatred for some Latinos entering the U.S. baseball world was palpable. Many were taken aback and quite surprised by their treatment. Vic Power, the flashy Puerto Rican first baseman who could not make it out of the minors to become the first black New York Yankee, but later starred with the Athletics, Indians, and Twins, endured some rough treatment in the minors while traveling in Florida. He was the only black player on his team and often stayed on the bus when teammates went into restaurants or stores. Once, while stopped at a gas station, Power climbed out to buy a cold drink from a soft-drink machine. The proprietor jumped onto the bus and angrily demanded that Power return the bottle. Power said he had purchased it for a quarter. The man shouted, "I don't want your quarter. I want the bottle back." Then the man called the police and had Power arrested for using obscene language. Teammates had to post $500 bail. Horrified by the entire nightmare experience Power said, "What kind of country is this?" (Quoted in Relagaldo, 65–66.)

It was a country that had been founded on principles of liberty and justice for all but took at least two centuries to grow into its idealistic notions, and even then it seemed very much a work in progress.

"Orlando Cepeda and Felipe Alou told me what to expect," said Manny Mota, the long-time Dodgers' star pinch-hitter from the Dominican Republic about the advice he received from other Hispanic players. "Another coach prepared me mentally to face it (racism) and that's what I did. I never realized it was going to be that bad." (Quoted in Relagaldo, 65.)

Times changed. Tolerance in American society improved. Barriers between races on and off the baseball field crumbled. The influx of Latin Americans into the United States made Hispanics the fastest-growing ethnic group in the country. In 1997, statistics showed that for the first time since the color barrier fell in 1947, the number of Latino players in the majors surpassed black U.S.-born players. "And the gap has continued to widen." Baseball, some concluded, was the advance vanguard of "the browning of America." (Quoted in Relagaldo, 243–244.)

Whatever impediments to Latino players reaching the majors that previously existed, whether it was because of the prejudice against skin color, or the lack of development in their skills from lack of coaching and proper equipment, have long ago evaporated. Ironically, it was Fidel Castro who talked revolution for the way of life in Cuba, but baseball, one of the aspects of life he attempted to control the most strictly, has become a symbol of cooperation between the United States and Latin America.

Further Reading

Burgos Jr., Adrian, *Playing America's Game* (Berkeley, California, University of California Press, 2007).

Holway, John B., *Josh and Satch* (Westport, Connecticut, Meckler Books, 1991).

Kelley, Brent, *Voices from the Negro Leagues* (Jefferson, North Carolina, McFarland & Company, Inc. Publishers, 1998).

Krich, John, *El Beisbol* (Chicago, Ivan R. Dee, 1989).

Leonard, Buck and Riley, James A., *Buck Leonard: The Black Lou Gehrig* (New York, Carrol & Graf Publishers, Inc., 1995).

Minoso, Minnie and Fagen, Herb, *Just Call Me Minnie* (Champaign, Illinois, Sports Publishing LLC, 1994).

O'Neil, "Buck" John, Wulf, Steve, and Conrads, David, *I Was Right On Time* (New York, Simon & Schuster, 1996).

Regalado, Samuel O., *Viva Baseball!* (Champaign, Illinois, University of Illinois Press, 1998).

Ribowsky, Mark, *Don't Look Back: Satchel Paige in the Shadows of Baseball*, (New York, Simon & Schuster, 1994.)

————, *The Power and the Darkness* (New York, Simon & Schuster, 1996).

Wendel, Tim and Luis Villegas, Jose, *Far From Home: Latino Players in America* (Washington, D.C., National Geographic Society Books, 2008).

Underage Issues

Compared to other big-time sports in the United States like professional football and basketball, Major League baseball has traditionally paid minimal attention to players who spend several years playing in college before turning pro. Not so many years ago those players were overlooked altogether. That attitude has changed somewhat and players with college backgrounds reach the majors regularly now.

However, the mindset of getting a player into a team's organization as early as possible is still a staple of talent development. Nowhere is this more evident than in signing players from Latin American countries who were never going to attend U.S. colleges and be eligible for the regular domestic talent draft. For decades, Major League teams have scoured the playgrounds and sandlots in poverty-stricken communities searching for prospects with potential that could be signed cheaply.

The idea was to sign the players as young as possible, preferably at age 16, and provide them with several years to develop their skills in the minors. Residents of the Dominican Republic, Puerto Rico, Venezuela, and other Latin American lands dreamed of being anointed, of being awarded the chance to escape dismal living conditions and become rich. The young players were eager to sign, viewing the opportunity as a once-in-a-lifetime chance. A player could sign with the Pirates, the Blue Jays, the Giants, the Astros, or one of the other teams that put so many resources into Latin America and harbor hope of a better life, and no less gain it by doing something he loved—playing baseball.

Over time, players became savvy enough to surreptitiously challenge the system. There were always prominent players in the majors whose age was questioned. This was notably true of Cuban defectors who might have been 33, but who claimed to be 30. Knowing what U.S. teams wanted, some players who when signed claimed to be 16, but in reality were 19 years old. This bought them extra time to succeed. This deception could be life-altering. A Major League team signing a 19-year-old who aged into a 22-year-old in AA ball might well decide to cut its losses and cut the player. The same player, who was signed under the guise of being 16, would only show up as 19 in the bookkeeping and might well be given additional time to mature and earn another summer look or two.

The sketchiness of records availability hindered teams' ability to discover the truth. However, much of this changed in 2001. When terrorist attacks leveled the World Trade Center and hit the Pentagon, the United States Congress passed several measures tightening security. Among those changes was firmer proof of age for foreign nationals seeking to work in the United States. Many ballplayers that had provided false ages to their teams now had to show proof of age, and it was demonstrated that they had engaged in lying for their own benefit. Major League Baseball even opened an office in the Dominican to cope with the growing issue.

In 2008, a reporter for the *Houston Chronicle* traveled to the Dominican Republic to unearth information that showed that one of the Astros' up-and-coming pitchers, Wandy Rodriguez, had once been an outfielder playing under another name and was older than he claimed. He was deemed to have potential when he became a pitcher (and indeed has done well for the Astros), but he was already 19, an age when big-league clubs were unlikely to touch him. A contact in Dominican baseball told Rodriguez, who had dropped out of school at age 15 to devote his life to baseball, what had to be done for him to have a chance at a pro contract. "Consult with your uncles and parents," the man said. "They consulted and found their decision. I didn't have a part in that because I didn't want to have that responsibility. When the boy has a younger age, he has a better chance and you'll figure out what to do from there. Then his uncle told me they found him a name." (Quoted in Ortiz.) In these types of situations, often a cousin's credentials are substituted.

One of the most prominent players in the game who admitted that he had pulled the age scam when he was starting out is Miguel Tejada. When Tejada, a six-time All-Star, signed with the Oakland Athletics in 1993 he told the team he was 17. In 2008, Tejada confessed that he had been 19 at the time and was 33, not 31, as he was then listed on the Houston Astros roster. A Dominican whose talent was spotted by Hall of Famer Juan Marichal, the pitcher said he had nothing to do with the age switch. Tejada said he did what he had to do. "I was a poor kid," Tejada said. "I wanted to sign a professional contract and that was the only way to do it. I didn't want or mean to do anything wrong. At the time, I was two years older than they thought." (Quoted in "Tejada . . . ") There has been almost no general discussion about the premium teams put on the extreme youth of the Latin American signees, failing to allow for natural growth and maturity seen in an 18- or 19-year-old compared to a 16-year-old.

After being exposed in age fraud in a completely different set of circumstances, shortstop Rafael Furcal, then with the Atlanta Braves, came clean about his true age in 2000 after being stopped for DWI—and underage alcohol consumption. That charge was dropped because Furcal proved that he was really 22 and not 19 as he had claimed. When he spoke to reporters about the incident, Furcal said he was urged in the Dominican to tell Major League teams he was 16 in order to better enhance his chances of signing a pro deal.

The publication *Baseball America* reported in 2009 that 300 professional players in the majors and minors were found to have provided false information about their ages. Although discrepancies began showing up in the early 2000s, the pace of disclosure stepped up over the last few years when Major League baseball began administering DNA tests to players. The testing program was not aimed simply at determining true ages, but true identities. It was learned that many Latin American prospects were displaying fake or borrowed birth certificates as "proof" of age. A news story of a scandalous nature emerged in 2004. A pitching prospect from the Dominican Republic was paid a $400,000 bonus to sign with the Arizona Diamondbacks. It was later shown that neither his age nor his name was genuine. Investigation showed that the player was really three years older than he claimed.

In 2009, the U.S. Consulate in Santo Domingo, Dominican Republic requested that Major League baseball investigate more than 40 recent signings of young players. If it was shown that those players lied, their visas for the United States could be revoked. In July of that year, the New York Yankees voided a contract with a young Dominican player on the grounds that he lied about his age and name.

Over the last few decades several Major League teams set up baseball academies in the Dominican Republic as a way to try out young talent without committing much money to the process. By outfitting the players, giving them opportunities to show their stuff on higher-quality fields in front of scouts, the teams weeded out the true prospects without bringing them to the United States as young teenagers.

Later, realizing what a difference a comparatively small amount of cash could make in the life of the player and his family, teams signed up groups of young players wholesale. For several years teams signed as many as 15 Dominican players who were young and raw, but offered the promise of development. The deals were typically for $10,000, meaning a club could invest $150,000 (true pocket change to a Major League franchise) and hope that one player would make it all of the way to the big time.

The teams signed up this large coterie of players in the hopes that talent would shine and rise to the top, taking a chance on volume producing quality, "the same way somebody might buy 15 lottery tickets," as one sportswriter put it. (Quoted in Torre and Verducci, 446.) The market for top high school draft picks and top college picks with longer track records had soared. The price of signing those draft picks had escalated into the millions of dollars. Signing a young Dominican player could produce a diamond in the rough. Eventually, even the price for better known young Dominican players jumped, too. Savvier players and their families, with smarter representation, could command $50,000, whereas once $10,000 was the ceiling. Now the $10,000 price tag has gone the way of the nickel cigar.

One of the players the Cleveland Indians signed for $10,000 out of the Dominican was pitcher Fausto Carmona. Carmona matured into a 19-game winner for the team. Or, as the same sportswriter observed, "The Indians had won the lottery." (Quoted in Torre and Verducci, 449.)

There was another way that young Latin American baseball prospects worked to get around Major League baseball rules. No team was supposed to sign a player who was under 16. So teenagers and their representatives worked both sides of the fence. Players who were 15 came up with proof to show that they were already 16. Players who were 19 came up with proof to show that they were only 16.

For a time, the combination of scouting in remote areas, in foreign countries, where there was desperation by players and their families to be noticed and signed, even if they had to lie about their ages, resulted in unchecked wheeling and dealing. Signings were made by teams only too willing to believe that a teenager was whatever age he was supposed to be. Tiring of the ruses, Major League Baseball officials stepped in to try to halt the practice. In 2000, the Los Angeles Dodgers were punished by the game's administrators for changing documents relating to the signing of hot prospect Adrian Beltre. According to *USA Today*, "The murky politics of local boosters handing off players to scouts for a little kickback has been a sordid, but accepted part of the Latin American baseball scene for years. Falsified birth documents—about $200 for a convincing one—have been part of it." (Quoted in Beaton.)

The sheer number of Latin American players coming into the big leagues made it mandatory for Major League Baseball to work at ensuring that rules were followed. In the past, there had been periodic questioning of Latin American players' true ages. But the number of Latin American players was small and the number of Latin American players who were stars whose ages were in question was even smaller. There was probably more speculation about Cuban defector Orlando "El Duque" Hernandez' real age than any other Latino notable. Getting hold of El Duque's birth certificate was not going to be an easy assignment when relations between the United States and Cuba were so contentious. Another *USA Today* observation: "One of the oldest guessing games in sports is knowing the real ages of players from Spanish-speaking nations." (Quoted in Weir.)

Occasionally, a player might simply smile enigmatically when asked about his age. It was to dodge the question and the question was not often pushed very hard. If the player was truly exceptional, few cared how old he was anyway. Luis Tiant, the star pitcher for the Indians and the Boston Red Sox in the 1960s and 1970s into the 1980s was pretty much the poster player for this example.

By 2008, Major League concern over falsified birth certificates and fake names had taken an even uglier turn. Scouts for several teams were accused of taking kickbacks from Dominican agents for signing their players, or for diluting signing bonuses from Major League teams to the young players and keeping a chunk of the payouts for themselves. It was revealed that sometimes "buscons," or intermediaries supposedly helping less sophisticated young players and their families obtain the best deals, also required payoffs.

What began as an in-house investigation by Major League Baseball expanded into a criminal investigation by officials of federal law enforcement agencies. Scouts and representatives for several teams were fired from their positions because of hints of shady behavior or outright accusations. Among those teams dismissing officials were the Washington Nationals, the New York Yankees, the Chicago White Sox, and the Boston Red Sox. In some cases the teams fired long-standing employees and simply summarized their departure under the heading of "violations of team policy." What was apparent was that the pursuit of young Dominican baseball players had degenerated into the wild, wild West, with rules being ignored.

The biggest name to fall was Washington general manager Jim Bowden, a long-time administrator in the big leagues. Upon his dismissal at the end of February 2009, Bowden said he was the victim of "false allegations" and "there has been no indication that parties have found any wrongdoing on my part." (Quoted in Robinson and Schmidt.) Former Cincinnati Reds star Jose Rijo was also fired by the Nationals at the time. The Chicago White Sox fired a long-time front office executive, as well as two Dominican scouts. White Sox senior director of player personnel David Wilder was let go after he allegedly brought $40,000 of undeclared money with him through customs in Miami when returning to the U.S. from the Dominican.

It was clear that Major League Baseball was angry about apparent shenanigans brought to its attention in the pursuit of Dominican talent. Bob DuPuy, president and chief operating of Major League Baseball, said the sport's governing body had become concerned about allegations and poured more resources into discovering the truth. "We have spent the last year trying to clean it up," DuPuy said. (Quoted in Robinson and Schmidt.)

The Dominican Republic—and Latin America in general—remains a must-stop on the itinerary of U.S. Major League scouts. And that country and the other standbys remain fertile territory for teams seeking future professionals and stars. No system is perfect, but Major League Baseball is seeking to ensure that all transactions are on the up-and-up. Dreams can still come true for Latino players, but the challenge in the process is to make certain that everyone is telling the truth.

Policing of the process to make sure that a 16-year-old is really a 16-year-old requires vigilance. So does making sure that the cash money promised to the genuine prospect gets into his hands.

Further Reading

Beaton, Rod, "Baseball cracks down on underage signings," *USA Today*, February 8, 2000.

Ortiz, Jose De Jesus, "Lying about age not uncommon for Dominican baseball players," *Houston Chronicle*, May 4, 2008.

Robinson, Joshua and Schmidt, Michael S., "Nationals' G.M. Resigns as Scandal Deepens," *New York Times*, March 1, 2009.

"Tejada admits to being two years older than he had said," ESPN.com, April 18, 2008.

Torre, Joe and Verducci, Tom, *The Yankee Years* (Doubleday, New York, 2009).

Weir, Tom, "For some players, fudging age might be the key to success," *USA Today*, February 8, 2000.

Part II

Icons of Latin American Baseball

Twenty-five Icons of
Latin American Baseball

The following 25 selections encompass a group of outstanding Latin American baseball stars based on their lifetime achievements on the field, in some cases their accomplishments beyond the field, and in some cases because of their unique circumstances and roles in the sport.

The names will be familiar to baseball fans of all persuasions and represent the game's heroes from Cuba, Venezuela, the Dominican Republic, Puerto Rico, Mexico, Panama, Colombia, and Nicaragua.

In some instances those chosen represent hallowed families of the game. In others, the timing of their careers was considered essential, including the difficulties and challenges faced in simply reaching the major leagues.

All of these players were deserving of being singled out for special recognition for their performances and contributions to baseball.

Sandy, Sandy Jr. and Roberto Alomar

Santos Alomar was never very big, but he had a big heart and he had a big glove. Born in Salinas, Puerto Rico in 1943, the shortstop with quick hands forged a 17-year Major League career with the Milwaukee Braves, Chicago White Sox, California Angels, and four other teams. He also spent his free time raising a family dynasty.

The 5-foot-9, 155-pound Alomar came from a baseball-playing family. Three brothers played the game at a fairly advanced level in the Mexican League and the U.S. minors. Alomar made it bigger than they did and then produced two offspring who exceeded his own accomplishments during long Major League careers.

Sandy's strength was his fielding, and he won numerous accolades for his range and throwing arm as he worked his way through the minors in the Milwaukee system. Before he even reached the big leagues there was newspaper

Sandy Alomar (left) and Sandy Alomar Jr., two of the three members of the famous Alomar playing family when their careers intersected with the New York Mets. Sandy, the father, was a coach and Sandy Jr. was near the end of his career as a catcher. Not pictured is Sandy Jr.'s brother, second baseman Roberto, a sure-fire future Hall of Famer. (AP Photo/Richard Drew)

speculation that he was destined to be the team's top man at short. One newspaper story in 1963 referred to Alomar as "a sleeper" for the next season's club and suggested he was one of the best "young prospects in baseball." (Quoted in Wolf, "Puerto Rican . . .")

At the time Bobby Bragan was managing the Braves and his research on Alomar seemed quite up to date. "He's the Luis Aparicio type," Bragan said in comparison to the American League's premier shortstop, "small, fast, and a great fielder." (Quoted in Wolf, "Puerto Rican . . .")

No one was raving about Alomar's hitting, however. He grew up as a switch-hitter, believing it would better enhance his chances of making the majors. But when he reached the high minors, his hitting capability from the left side of the plate did not keep up. There was such a disparity between Alomar's batting on the left and the right that minor-league coaches ordered him to bag his left-side swinging in favor of exclusive right-side hitting. Once he did so, Alomar's average shot up. The improvement, coupled with his always reliable fielding, put Alomar in the majors while he was still 20 years old.

"I was down around .190 in June," Alomar said of his slump, "and then they told me to quit switching. I like that much better." (Quoted in Wolf, "Alomar...") Alomar never changed back, remaining a right-handed batter for the rest of his career.

Sandy Alomar played just 19 games for the Braves in 1964 and batted .245. Although he tripled his playing time the next year and went with the Braves to their new home city of Atlanta, he never became a full-time player until he was a member of the White Sox in 1968. For three years in the early 1970s with the Angels, Alomar led the majors in games played and was selected to his only All-Star team with California in 1970 after shifting to second base. Once he found a home at second, it was hard to move Alomar back to the bench. In 1971 he recorded an 18-game hitting streak and he had 689 official at-bats that season, a pace that kept Alomar very busy. At one point, stretching into 1973, he had a consecutive games played streak of 648. The streak ended not because of injury, but because of a hitting slump that dropped Alomar's average to .188. With no end in sight, Alomar was benched.

Alomar's term in California was truncated when he broke his left leg. That facilitated a move to the Yankees, and he was a good fit on a team looking for a second baseman. The new arrival helped spark a revival in New York. The Yankees were last in their division, but picked up speed with Alomar in the lineup. "They have gone from the bottom of the pile to the top," a sportswriter noted. "The improvement is too striking, the statistics too overwhelming for it to be mere coincidence." (Quoted in Pepe, "Yanks...")

Although he was a prominent player from Puerto Rico, Alomar had only a personal acquaintanceship, not a close personal friendship, with Roberto Clemente. He said his ball-playing brothers knew Clemente better than he did. However, after Clemente died trying to bring food and medical supplies to earthquake-torn Nicaragua, many efforts were made to raise money and help Clemente's dream of a sports city for youngsters become reality. Alomar played a major role in the fundraising for two Yankee benefit exhibition baseball games in San Juan in March 1975. "One friend of mine bought 50 tickets," he said. "It has been 16 years since I haven't been home at this time of year. I was always playing baseball at this time." (Quoted in Pepe, "Alomar...")

Alomar was a great believer in Clemente's mission to provide sports opportunities and coaching for kids. At that time his son Sandy Jr. was 9 and Roberto was 7. "The kids now play in vacant lots," Alomar said. "There are not enough baseball fields. The kids clean out the lots just to play baseball." (Quoted in Pepe, "Alomar . . .")

What Alomar, who retired in 1978, could not have imagined was that his two boys spending all of their free time on those dusty sandlots were destined to also make the major leagues and eclipse his own accomplishments.

Sandy Alomar Jr. was born in 1966 and he did not fit the family mold of small-ish infielders. Sandy Jr. was 6-foot-5 and weighed 215 pounds. His position was catcher and anyone trying to get to the plate had a brick wall to skirt. As much as he loved baseball and was influenced by his father, Sandy Jr. was not single-minded. He liked competing at other games and playing with toy trucks and riding his bicycle. Early in his teens he took a break from baseball and concentrated on dirt-bike racing and karate. Still, that familial influence was powerful. Sandy Alomar was so popular in his hometown of Salinas that his face was painted on the outside of the local Estadio Manuel Gonzalez. He loomed over the action like the protective father he was.

Catching was very much choosing his own path, but perhaps counting on his genes, the San Diego Padres signed Sandy Jr. when he was 17. After piling up impressive credentials in the minors (two minor league player of the year awards), the Padres used him in just a single game in 1988 and just eight more in 1989. Alomar hit well and gunned down runners trying to steal second with a strong arm. But the Padres really didn't know what to do with him because they already had an All-Star receiver in Benito Santiago.

San Diego put all of the training into Sandy Jr.'s catching future but reaped none of the benefits. In 1990 he was traded to the Cleveland Indians and became an instant All-Star, as well as the American League rookie of the year. "I feel very happy to win," Sandy Jr. said. "You only get one chance." (Quoted in Moton.) After six years in the minors Sandy Jr. was wondering if that chance would ever come. He hit .290 with 9 homers and 66 RBIs in his 132 games behind the plate for the Indians.

Sandy Jr. embarked on a 17-year career and was chosen for six All-Star teams. Sandy Jr. considered himself more of a self-made ballplayer than his brother Robby, who had more pure talent. "Robby is 'The Natural,'" Sandy Jr. said. "He has a God-given gift. Hey, there were at least three players on my Little League team better than me." (Quoted in Bloom, "Favorite . . .")

Sandy Jr. was a better hitter than his father. He hit 111 home runs and batted .273 for his career and never forgot his roots. Each winter he returned to Salinas and played ball in his hometown. It is difficult to say how much effect this might have had on Sandy Jr.'s prime years' performance, but playing year-round he never got the chance to fully rest and recover after playing the most demanding position in the majors. Although he lasted 17 years on Major League teams,

Sandy Jr. did not play more than 100 games in a season between 1998 and his retirement after the 2004 season. Still, he wanted to play in front of Puerto Ricans, even if he knew the year-round task would be challenging. The obligation was a mixed blessing if he had an off day or showed fatigue and couldn't hit. "We're from here," Sandy Jr. said of his family in Salinas, "so if you don't do well, the fans hammer you. They're tough. They're very demanding." (Quoted in Bloom, "Favorite . . .")

As a multi-year All-Star, Sandy Jr. had some great moments. In 1997, he hit the game-winning home run in the exhibition classic. To make the blow sweeter, the contest was played before the local fans at Jacobs Field in Cleveland. Sandy Jr. also played key roles in Indian pennants that carried the team to the World Series in 1995 and 1997.

Father Sandy stayed in the game after retirement and was a coach with the Padres while Sandy Jr. excelled. Robby, two years younger, also broke into the majors with San Diego. As Sandy Jr. noted, young Roberto was the most talented of the three, a dazzling fielder with more natural quickness than his dad or brother.

Papa never expected to have two sons follow him into the majors, but he was thrilled that it occurred. "It would have to be in the blood," he said. "The whole family has been baseball players. I feel like any father who sees his kids succeed. We're proud of all three of them, and I'm including a daughter (Sandia), who is a college graduate. The thing I like is that people always speak well of them. That makes you feel like you've done a good job." (Quoted in Johnson.)

Alomar, who was constantly traveling during the kids' youth, said his wife Maria deserved more credit than he did for bringing them up well. "That's why they are the kind of people they are," he said. (Quoted in Johnson.)

Yet Sandy Jr. said his father was a good role model and also deserves credit for their tight relationship and sound advice handed down even after the son was playing big-league ball. He knew where he could go for help whenever he was discouraged. "My dad kept me going many times when I was down," Sandy Jr. said. "He's a real strong part of my life. He's really taught me everything I need in baseball and life." (Quoted in Johnson.)

Roberto Alomar was not as big as his big brother, but was bigger than his father. He stood 6 feet tall and weighed 185 pounds. He was not a featherweight, but a sturdy second baseman. When Robby was brought to San Diego for the 1988 season he became an infield starter right away, playing 143 games and hitting .266.

While Sandy Jr. was frustrated either in the minors or on the bench, his younger brother earned raves hitting the majors as a 20-year-old. By his third season, Robby was an All-Star for the Padres. After his two seasons of almost no Major League action, Sandy Jr. shifted to the Indians and during that 1990 season both second-generation Alomars were All-Stars. It was the first of 12 All-Star selections for Roberto, who, in 17 years, playing primarily with San Diego, Toronto, Baltimore, and Cleveland, earned 10 Gold Glove awards. He is considered one of the greatest fielding second baseman in history, and, in a rarity for his position, Alomar also compiled a .300 lifetime average.

Sandy Sr. was also part of the game as a coach for the National League and he was one beaming father having two sons on the field for the same All-Star game. "An indescribable moment," Sandy Sr. said. (Quoted in Bloom, "Alomar . . .")

Roberto did not hesitate naming his hero growing up. Standing right with his father, he pointed. "This man right here," the youngest Alomar said. "He took good care of me when I was a kid. I'm real proud of him. I'm real proud of my brother, too. I love my brother very much. If it wasn't for him I might not be playing baseball now." (Quoted in Johnson.)

Roberto tried catching as a youngster, but Sandy Jr. stepped to the plate and when he stepped into a pitch his bat hit his brother in the head. Roberto promptly moved to shortstop. "I did him a favor," jokes Sandy Jr. (Quoted in Antonen.)

Not only did the Alomar brothers meet in the same All-Star game, when they were both in the American League their clubs met in the playoffs. They competed to knock one another out of the post-season. Roberto gained the most satisfaction out of the playoffs, being part of Toronto Blue Jay teams that won the World Series in 1992 and 1993. The bigger the stage, the better Roberto played. By 1992 he was a full-fledged star whose acrobatic fielding won him comparisons to the greats of the past. That season he was voted the American League's Most Valuable Player. At 24, he was the youngest player to win it.

After two years with the Blue Jays, the young man who grew up in Puerto Rico and traveled to the major cities in the United States with Major League baseball was a hero in Canada. Yet in some ways he showed he was still a boy at heart. He was making millions of dollars and was probably the most popular athlete in Ontario who didn't ice skate, but Roberto was still living in a hotel room. Not just any hotel, though. The Toronto Sky Dome had a hotel built into the side of the ballpark. Alomar likely had the shortest commute in the majors. All he had to do was take an elevator to the ground floor and he was at the office.

Alomar just didn't want to hassle with home buying and all of the accessories necessary to make a comfortable residence out of the real estate. "You have to go through all kinds of stuff to get furniture and cable," he said. "All I need is a bed and that's about it. I have cable in the room. I have a fridge. If I need laundry done, I call the laundry, and if I need food, I call room service." (Quoted in Newman.) Any more questions?

As a single guy in the public eye, Alomar's biggest worry, if one could call it that, was being hounded by women who wanted to make his acquaintance.

Hotel security arranged a routine that enabled Alomar to reach his room after games without being followed. A system with the switchboard also intercepted Alomar's calls for screening purposes. The adults running the show at the hotel seemingly adopted Alomar and did everything possible to make sure their famous guest was not bugged by insistent fans at all hours.

In the era of free agency, where players whose contracts are up can depart for bigger money, there was a sense of paranoia evident in jokes tied to his residence that Alomar would forego the Blue Jays for brighter lights. It was suggested that one day he would just check out and disappear, only to surface with the Yankees or some other big spender. But Alomar didn't complain about his four-year, $18 million deal when others signed for more.

"When (Cub Ryne) Sandberg signed (for $28.4 million), people said, 'Roberto, what about now?' " Alomar said. "But I don't let money determine my happiness. Ryne Sandberg earned his money. I think I can live with $18 million. How many 24-year-old guys are earning the kind of money I make?" (Quoted in Newman.) Roberto spent five years in Toronto and eventually made many million dollars more with other teams.

While highly paid baseball players often shift allegiances for even larger contracts, the biggest controversy of Robby Alomar's career did not revolve around cash but a more heinous offense that surprised and appalled the baseball establishment and fans. On September 27, 1996, Alomar spit in the face of umpire John Hirschbeck during an argument at home plate. Roberto, then playing with the Orioles, took a called third strike and disputed Hirschbeck's judgment. It is a no-no to argue balls and strikes at all and umpires have great discretion to toss out a player who does.

This debate escalated into more than a passing comment and the two men were toe-to-toe when Alomar unleashed his saliva. Alomar said Hirschbeck called him "a fag" and used a racial slur and was grumpy because his son had died of a rare disease. Infuriated, Hirschbeck attempted to physically confront Alomar. No one condoned the player's actions. Condemnation of Alomar was swift and loud from many quarters. He was suspended for five games and contributed $50,000 to charity. The incident tarred Alomar's good-guy image and has been long-remembered even though he apologized to Hirschbeck and the men publicly shook hands five months later before a game.

"We became good friends after that incident," Alomar said. "Unfortunately it happened, and unfortunately, people still talk about it. But me and John, we moved on. It was in the heat of the moment. I wish it wouldn't have happened. We both understand that." (Quoted in Lott.)

Roberto Alomar's last season in the majors was 2004 and his lifetime performance will almost certainly land him in the Hall of Fame in Cooperstown soon. When that occasion arrives there will certainly be an Alomar family reunion.

Further Reading

Antonen, Mel, "Roberto Alomar gives credit to sibling for baseball career," *USA Today*, October 10, 1997.

Bloom, Barry M., "Alomar, As In All-Star," *Sport Magazine*, March 1991.

———, "Favorite Son," *Sport Magazine*, May, 1998.

Johnson, Chuck, "Alomar sons deepen roots in baseball," *USA Today*, July 13, 1990.

Lott, John, "Another level; As Roberto is honoured by Blue Jays, the star hopes fans forgiven an old mistake," *The National Post*, April 4, 2008.

Moton, Tom, "Unanimous vote names Alomar best rookie," *The National*, November, 1990. Date missing, National Baseball Hall of Fame Library archives.

Newman, Bruce, "Home Suite Home," *Sports Illustrated*, June 8, 1992.

Pepe, Phil, "Alomar Glad to Do His Bit For Friend He Seldom Saw," *New York Daily News*, March 19, 1975.

———, "Yanks Built Their High Rise Upon a 'Sandy' Foundation," *New York Daily News*, September 21, 1974.

Wolf, Bob, "Alomar to Take Over at Shortstop for Braves," *Milwaukee Journal*, September 15, 1964.

———, "Puerto Rican Whiz on Way," *Milwaukee Journal*, November 8, 1963.

The Alou Family Felipe, Matty, Jesus and Moises

The three baseball-playing brothers named Alou from Haina in the Dominican Republic were among the first from their island nation to make an impact in Major League ball and their names and fame were enhanced by the uniqueness of their situation.

The odds against one individual becoming a Major League player are astronomical. The odds against a trio of brothers reaching the highest level of the game and succeeding are probably in the one-in-50-million range. Few families have been as accomplished as the Alous. Felipe, the oldest brother, was born in 1935, Matty in 1938, and Jesus in 1942. Moises is Felipe's son and a generation later established his own top-notch career.

All scouted and signed by the San Francisco Giants, Felipe, Matty, and Jesus gained the distinction of being the first threesome of siblings to play in a Major League outfield in the same game.

When Felipe broke in with the Giants in 1958 he was the first native-coached Dominican to reach the big leagues. He was followed by Matty in 1960 and Jesus in 1963. Imagine the glee of scouts when Felipe was asked if there were any more like him at home. Yes, indeed, he replied.

The Brothers Alou. Left to right: Jesus, Matty, and Felipe became the first trio of brothers to share a Major League outfield when they appeared in a game for the San Francisco Giants against the New York Mets on September 10, 1963. The Dominican natives were among the first Major League stars from their country. (AP Photo)

Felipe enjoyed a 17-year playing career. He hit 206 homers with a lifetime average of .286 and was selected to three All-Star teams. Matty posted a lifetime average of .307 and won the National League batting title in 1966 for the Pittsburgh Pirates when he hit .342. Matty was a two-time All-Star during his 15-year career and recorded 231 hits in a single season. Jesus played 15 seasons and hit .280.

Along with pitcher Juan Marichal, a contemporary with the Giants, the Alous were among the first Dominicans to make a lasting impression in American baseball. The novelty of three brothers fortunate to play together helped gain them extra attention beyond the worth of their solid abilities.

Felipe Alou was the family pathfinder, the one first chosen to live the Dominican dream of transcending the sandlots in the big time. But his road was not any easier to follow than it was for Roberto Clemente or other Latino players in the 1950s. He moved from the comfort of a tropical island existence surrounded by family to a lonelier lifestyle where he struggled to make his thoughts understood in a place that oftentimes seemed unfeeling.

"We are not American," Alou said. "We are different. Maybe that is why we are able to survive. When I came over here I didn't know English. I was supposed to be a 'darkie.' I had no baseball teaching. I didn't know about the racial encounters that I was going to endure. I didn't know about winter or snow. I survived that. Hundreds of Latins will tell you the same thing. The only reason we survived is because we are different. We are survivors. We never give up. We never quit. We quit when we die. This is the spirit of the Latin. We are a hard people to put away." (Quoted in Marantz.)

Life in Haina, a small Dominican community, was not easy for the Alous, either. They were raised solo by Jose Rojas, a blacksmith and carpenter after their mother, Virginia, died young. Another future Major League player, pitcher Mel Rojas, is a cousin. Felipe Alou's father bought him his first pair of baseball spikes when he was 14, but as an illustration of the family's poverty, later reclaimed them, removed the cleats and used them as his own shoes at work. Before his excellence in baseball resulted in a career change, Felipe was dedicated to studying to become a surgeon. His family could not afford the cost of the education, however.

By the time the Alou threesome finished with baseball they could afford just about anything they wanted. Big brother led the way—and he continued to do so later in life by becoming a Major League manager for the Montreal Expos and the Giants. He was manager of the year in 1994. Alou always had a dignified demeanor and he carried a Bible with him close at hand on road trips. He took big swings but was difficult to strike out.

"I think Felipe Alou is the most underrated ballplayer I've ever seen," said Atlanta Braves third baseman Clete Boyer when he shifted from the American League to the National League. "He can do everything and do it well above average. He's really outstanding. He surprised me. I don't think he's been given near enough credit." (Quoted in Rumill.)

As a youth, Felipe Alou said he was inspired by a 1948 visit to the Dominican Republic by the Brooklyn Dodgers to play an exhibition game. Jackie Robinson was in uniform in his second season and just seeing a dark-skinned man wearing the colors of a big-league club was moving for the 13-year-old.

Calling it a "proud moment," Alou said "To see Robinson in the Brooklyn lineup gave us hope. We didn't have much besides baseball. No college scouts came looking there for football or basketball players. But there was a black man out there with a Major League uniform on." (Quoted in Donnelly.)

Felipe really was the big brother. He stood 6 feet tall. Matty Alou, the middle brother, was 5-foot-9, although Jesus grew to be 6–2. As a result, Matty was called "Little Matty" in the majors. Before reaching the Giants at an overlapping time period, the brothers got the chance to play together on a team in Santo Domingo, taking over the entire outfield. Matty joked that fans referred to the trio as "The Telephone Outfield" because "when you pick up a telephone in our country you say, 'Alou.' That means hello." (Quoted in Grieve.)

"Just like any kid in the Dominican Republic—then and now—this bug, or whatever it is about the game, runs in the veins of every Dominican boy."

—Felipe Alou, comparing the 1950s to the present day. (Quoted in Latinos and Barriers in Baseball, http://umich.edu.)

Unlike his older brother, who had to put up with more prejudice, Matty seemed to have escaped very much discrimination. He also had praise from the hometown fans and San Francisco's relationship with the players, some of whom were homegrown and some of whom moved West from New York when the team relocated. "Best fans are here," Matty said. "They love baseball. They never go to the park to holler at the players. Nobody yells, 'You bum.' They like me. They like everybody. We like them." (Quoted in Grieve.)

Although once Jesus arrived after a tour of the minors the Alous had the prospect of sharing the outfield long-term it did not work out that way. The brothers were not playing at an equally high level. Felipe was always a step ahead—entrenched, experienced, more valuable. Matty brought a lively attitude to the team, but not a big bat. He struggled for most of the parts of six seasons he spent in San Francisco.

His best chance to shine was 1965 when he played in 117 games. But Matty could hit just .231 that season. Not even rooming with his brother and absorbing biblical advice helped his at-bats. One thing that might have hurt all of the Alous was the revolutionary disruption back home that resulted in the U.S. Marines moving in to occupy the Dominican and quell unrest. It was a very disconcerting time.

As soon as Matty was traded to the Pirates, he blossomed. His career high .342 average was recorded in 1966 and that was the first of four straight years when the middle Alou batted at least .331. The tremendous performance marked the first time a Dominican won the National League batting title. In the off-season, among other accolades Matty gathered, was a gold medal presented by Dominican Republic President Joaquin Balaguer. As most of the top Latin stars did, Alou also played winter ball at home during his time off from the Pirates and the first time he came to the plate the fans roared and gave him a standing ovation. "It made me feel good inside," Alou said. (Quoted in Biederman.)

By the late 1960s Matty Alou was among the best hitters in baseball. Although he was a small man, he wielded the lumber of a slugger. Alou used a

40-inch-long, 37-ounce bat, a tree-like weapon that would have been more commonly employed in the early 1920s. In Pittsburgh, it may have been that Matty Alou was just in the right place at the right time with the right mentor.

Pirates manager Harry Walker urged Alou to pick up the heavy bat and to forego pull hitting. For a week in spring training he forced Alou to hit every pitched ball he saw to left field. With these manipulations, Walker promised Alou that if he listened and practiced them his regular-season average would go up 50 points. "I did what he told me and gained 111 points," Alou said. "I owe him my thanks. I look over the defense to see how they're playing me. I basically use the shortstop as my guide. If he's playing me toward second base, I try to hit to his right. If he's over in the hole, I try to go up the middle." (Quoted in Broeg.)

Alou also picked up a new nickname in Pittsburgh. Catcher Jim Pagliaroni took to calling him "Topo Gigio" after the mouse that talked through a ventriloquist's voice that was all the rage on "The Ed Sullivan Show" at the time. If anything, the comparison would have been better made with *The Mouse That Roared*, the name of a popular book and movie.

The funny thing about Matty Alou's hitting success was that the better he got the uglier his swing was. He would not be posing for instructional videos. What was suggested by Walker and worked for him was not for everybody. Ted Williams, the great Red Sox slugger who retired with a .344 lifetime batting average and is regarded by many as the greatest hitter of all time, made a science out of his at-bats. He studied pitchers and understood what balls in what places near the plate gave him the best chance of connecting and hitting a pitch solidly. When he looked at Alou's mish-mash of an approach Williams practically cringed. "He violates every hitting principle I've ever taught," he said. Future Hall of Fame pitcher Steve Carlton once said, "Alou is the worst-looking .300 hitter I've ever seen." (Quoted in Christine.)

Alou recorded more than 180 hits in a season five times with his high of 231 in 1969. He was on fire all season and provoked his general manager Joe Brown into suggesting, "You'll be the first man to get 500 hits in one season." (Quoted in McHugh.) A slight exaggeration, but when Alou was on he made that type of impression. He looped singles into the outfield and hit high choppers that never made it out of the infield that he could beat out to first. It wasn't pretty, but it was effective.

Always keeping Walker's advice fresh in his mind, Alou said he hit so poorly with the Giants he was looking for assistance when he came to the Pirates. "When you hit only .231, you had better listen to someone." (Quoted in Feeney.)

While Felipe was the family pioneer and Matty had to overcome the image that he was too small and couldn't hit, third brother Jesus had to match the expectations of those who felt he would be a star because his brothers were. When Jesus came up to the Giants in 1965, observers felt he might be better than both of them. When Felipe was complimented as a young player, he said, "I'm not so good. Wait until you see my brother." When Matty came up someone asked, "Are you that brother?" Matty said, "Oh, no, Felipe was talking about our younger brother, Jesus. He's the greatest." (Quoted in Stevens.)

It was a nice thought, but things didn't work out that way. Jesus Alou made his debut in 1965 and seemed to hit his stride that year when he hit .298. Sporadically, Alou put up some low .300s seasons, but he never hit for power and his RBI totals were always low. He was good enough to stick around the majors with four teams for 15 years, but he never made an All-Star team. Alou was a good fielder, but he had to be merely to survive in Candlestick Park's right field where the wind blew almost constantly and at certain times of the afternoon the sun glared brightly in the right-fielder's eyes.

Felipe said Jesus possessed "the base-hit stroke," and Jesus hit over .336 four times in the minors. Felipe predicted his younger brother would win a batting title in the majors. But Jesus never connected quite as consistently as he did in the minors. Jesus, who overcame a 75-stitch cut from a base-running collision against the Mets early in his career, had one bad habit: He couldn't control his urges to swing at pitches thrown outside the strike zone. "He could hit .320 every year if he'd just quit swinging at bad pitches," said Hank Sauer, the Giants' hitting coach. (Quoted in McDonald.)

Alou was too aggressive at the plate. He didn't wear pitchers down and he walked all too rarely, taking bases on balls only 13 times during the 1965 season. That was an average of one walk every two weeks during the campaign. Some batters could just stand still with the bat on their shoulder and obtain more walks. "He's got to narrow the number of bad pitches down himself," Sauer said. (Quoted in McDonald.)

Jesus listened, but although he agreed he was swinging too freely, he found it tough to change his patterns. He admitted making up his mind to swing in certain situations before the pitcher threw, even when he had a favorable hitter's count. After peaking with poor pitch selection in 1965, Alou vowed to change. "I try to cut it down this year," he said in 1966. "Sometimes, maybe, I forget, but I gonna cut it way down, I think." (Quoted in McDonald.)

For most his career, though, Alou's on-base percentage hovered closer to the .300 line than the .400 line. Yet he usually got his share of hits, batting as high as .324 in 77 games for the Houston Astros in 1978.

One of the three Alous was in the majors between 1958 and 1979 and, combined, Felipe, Matty, and Jesus played in 5,129 games. Then, after an absence of 11 years with no Alou in the majors, Felipe's son Moises made his debut in

1990. A six-time All-Star, by the time he retired in 2009 Moises had displayed more power than his older relatives, frequently clouting 30-plus homers in a season. Also an outfielder, Moises placed in the top five of the National League's batting average list four times. His lifetime average was .303 after 17 seasons.

Moises got the rare chance to play for his father between 1992 and 1996 when Felipe was managing the Montreal Expos. In 2005 Moises signed a contract with the San Francisco Giants that permitted him a second chance to play under Felipe. "This is one of the years I've been looking forward to the most," said Moises, then 38 and nearing the end of his playing days, "coming back to play for my dad and to play for a great team." (Quoted in "For the . . .")

Unlike his father and uncles, Moises was born in the United States, in Atlanta, when his father was playing for the Braves. But he maintained the family ties to the Dominican Republic and frequently was reminded by long-time baseball fans of the family's distinguished past in the game.

"I'm very proud," Moises Alou said. "Everywhere I go in the Dominican Republic, people ask about my dad and my uncles and tell me how they carried themselves off the field. It made me a better person and player." (Quoted in "For the . . .")

Pride was always a prominent characteristic among the Alous. Felipe was soft-spoken, but became gradually more outspoken about Latino concerns as a player. Then as he worked his way into position to become the first Dominican manager by managing in winter ball, by putting in 12 years in the minors, and coaching three years in the majors, he tried to shed light on what he felt was the issue of whites being favored for such leadership jobs.

"This game looks for certain conditions before they hire a manager," Alou said after obtaining his first Major League managing job for the Expos at age 57. "Ideally, (teams look) for a white manager. I believe that's the No. 1 condition." (Quoted in Hill.)

Alou's remark was not terribly controversial at the time. Major League Baseball under Commissioner Bud Selig had already declared that teams had to interview more minority candidates when filling managerial openings. Even if the words seemed jarring, Alou's viewpoint was timely.

Alou managed the Expos from 1992 to 2001. The team was coming unglued and on the verge of extinction when his tenure ended before it relocated to Washington, D.C. as the Nationals. Alou coached for the Detroit Tigers, but was startled and pleased to get a fresh chance to manage with his first-love team, the Giants, for the 2003 season.

"I'm going back home to where I started," said Alou, then 67. (Quoted in "Alou signs . . .") And, he said, he hoped the full-circle job running the Giants would be the sweetest and last job for him in the majors. At the least, it seemed appropriate to have an Alou in a San Francisco uniform one more time.

Further Reading

"Alou signs three-year deal to manage Giants," ESPN.com, November 13, 2002.

Biederman, Les, "Bat King Matty—The Man Everybody Knows," *Pittsburgh Press*, March 25, 1967.

Broeg, Bob, "Matty Alou: The Talking Mouse Who Soared At the Plate," *St. Louis Post-Dispatch*, August 29, 1968.

Christine, Bill, "Matty Magic," *Pittsburgh Press*, June 18, 1969.

Donnelly, Joe, "Alou Bridged the Gap For Latin Americans," *Newsday*, September 8, 1971.

Feeney, Charles, "They've Stopped Calling Matty 'Lucky Alou,' " *The Sporting News*, August 2, 1969.

"For the Alous, a Father-Son Reunion Comes in Giants Uniform," Associated Press, March 6, 2005.

Grieve, Curley, "Matty Ready To Go; Leg Gets Doc's OK," *San Francisco Examiner*, May 12, 1962.

Hill, Thomas, "Alou: Teams want white managers," *New York Daily News*, May 22, 1999.

Marantz, Steve, Current Biography, http:/vnweb.hwwilsonweb.com. The H.W. Wilson Company, adapted from *The Sporting News*, June 21, 1993.

McDonald, Jack, (headline missing), National Baseball Hall of Fame Library archives, *The Sporting News*, April 2, 1966.

McHugh, Roy, "Matty Alou Goes By His Own Book," *Pittsburgh Press*, April 10, 1969.

Rumill, Ed, "Boyer calls Alou 'most underrated,' " *Christian Science Monitor*, August 21, 1967.

Stevens, Bob, "Jesus Alou Could Be the Best in Family," *The Sporting News*, July 3, 1965.

Luis Aparicio

Luis Aparicio was the second coming in the great Venezuelan shortstop lineage, succeeding Chico Carrasquel not only as the starter for the Chicago White Sox but as the new national hero in his home country.

As a young player in Maracaibo, Aparicio idolized Carrasquel. Not from such a distance, either. Aparicio had the good fortune to grow up in a baseball family where his father and uncle coached and taught. The home instruction was as professional as any available in Venezuela and gave Aparicio a head start in making his mark in the majors.

Chicago White Sox shortstop Luis Aparicio, shown here getting the New York Yankees' Tony Kubek out, was a genius at turning the double play during his Hall of Fame career. Aparicio continued the tradition of great Venezuelan shortstops and for 2010 allowed another in that line, Omar Vizquel, to use his previously retired White Sox No. 13. (AP Photo/Matty Zimmerman)

"I came from a baseball-playing family," Aparicio recalled. "My father used to be a ballplayer. My uncle also used to be a ballplayer. They took me to the ball park and each helped me a lot." (Quoted in Forman.)

Aparicio, who was born in 1934, was advanced in the game as a teenager and was playing for Maracaibo's main team when big-league scouts discovered him in 1953. Red Kress, who briefly played in the majors, was managing in Venezuela and was impressed by young Aparicio. He tipped off the Cleveland Indians that there was a diamond in the rough manning short and suggested the club sign him. The Indians listened to Kress, sent scouts south, looked over Aparicio, and decided he was too small to ever become a big leaguer.

Aparicio never grew to be more than 5-foot-9 and 160 pounds, so he was small in stature, but the misjudgment was quite costly to the Indians, especially when Aparicio was signed by their American League rival the Chicago White Sox. By 1956, Aparicio, whose skills were much larger than his physique, was starting for the Sox and his one-time hero Carrasquel was playing for Cleveland.

The nickname "Little Looie" stuck with Aparico throughout his career, but he definitely played big. Aparicio made his Major League debut on April 17, 1956— opening day at Comiskey Park. Oh yes, the opponent was the Cleveland Indians. The Sox won the game, 2–1, behind the pitching of southpaw Billy Pierce. Aparicio went one-for-three at the plate in his debut and in what would become a regular sight, participated in a double play that included second baseman Nellie Fox. The two eventual Hall of Famers became the premier double-play combination of the 1950s.

Various teammates over the years said they were awestruck by the ground balls that Aparicio reached with sprawling dives, great flexibility, and tremendous instinct. The ball shot off the bat, a fielder shrugged at the realization that the opponents had a hit, and then all of a sudden Aparicio would glove the ball and throw the man out at first. Aparicio led American League shortstops in fielding for eight straight seasons between 1959 and 1965 while playing for the White Sox and the Baltimore Orioles. He was just as much of a weapon on the bases, leading the AL in stolen bases nine straight seasons between 1956 and 1964 during an era when the long ball was prevalent.

"That shortstop of yours," Yankee manager Casey Stengel said to a Chicago-based inquisitor, "really hurts me. He steals base hits from us. He's a pest on the bases." (Quoted in Roberts.)

In 1959, the White Sox ended a 40-year drought by capturing the American League pennant. Aparicio and Fox gave the team extraordinary fielding strength up the middle and manager Al Lopez, himself a Hall of Famer-to-be, raved about the duo. Lopez touted the Aparicio-Fox entry as the greatest keystone combo of all time. "I have been around a few spectacular second-shortstop machines," Lopez said, "but never have I seen any better than Fox and Aparicio. They are so great because both are in their prime and they can do a lot of things apart from defense." (Quoted in Daniel.)

As a rookie, Aparicio stole 21 bases. His second year he stole 28. In 1958 he stole 29. Then he made a quantum leap, stealing 56 during the pennant year and 51 in 1960. Aparicio recorded league-leading 50-plus steal seasons three more times, including a career high of 57 in 1964. He totaled 506 stolen bases during his career. Aparicio drove opposing pitchers, catchers, and managers nuts with his derring-do. He worked the hurler for a decent lead, got a good jump, and out-ran catchers' arms.

"Sometimes we give him the steal sign," Lopez said. "But usually he's going on his own. After all, he knows better than anyone else when he's got a good chance to make it. He uses exceptional judgment. He doesn't take an exceptionally long lead like most good stealers. But he gets the fastest start of anyone I've seen in a long time." (Quoted in Roberts.)

The 1950s, when all-time sluggers like Mickey Mantle, Hank Aaron, and Willie Mays were breaking into baseball and Ted Williams and Stan Musial were still ripping the cover off the ball, highlighted homers more than steals, so Aparicio's less obvious running and fielding skills may have been comparatively underappreciated. One admirer was Paul Richards, the former White Sox skipper who managed Aparicio with the Orioles. The White Sox not only won the pennant in 1959, they were contenders for a few years surrounding that magical season. They would not have been riding so high without Aparicio,

Richards contended. "I'll tell you how good he is," Richards said of Aparicio when he was still with the Sox. "If the Sox didn't have him, they'd be in seventh place." (Quoted in Roberts.)

Aparicio always credited his upbringing in Venezuela and Chico Carrasquel as a role model for his own success. "Chico was my idol," Aparico said of the four-time All-Star who was the first player from his country to be selected for All-Star game play. "He's a tremendous guy and he helped me a lot. If he hadn't played in the big leagues, I don't know if other (Venezuelans) would have had the opportunity. He's so likeable and back home everyone idolizes him." (Quoted in Forman.)

Representing a nation of shortstops, from Carrasquel to Davey Concepion, Ozzie Guillen and himself, Aparicio gave considerable thought to what it takes to make a player successful in the role. Lucky for all of those players, size was not a prerequisite. Shortstop can be a smaller man's position and none of those men were ever faced with the career choice of becoming either NBA power forwards or shortstops.

"I think you need three things to be a good shortstop," Aparicio said. "Good hands, quick reflexes and smarts, and I think I had them all, so I guess I turned out to be a good shortstop." (Quoted in Forman.)

Sometimes athletes who excel with a specific talent cannot explain to observers what they do. They cannot connect in words the smooth action of their muscles playing out their natural role. When asked what made him a superior base stealer Aparicio seemed to have no clear-cut answer, only attributing his success to the same basic abilities he brought to playing the field.

"Like I said earlier," Aparicio noted, "you need good, quick reflexes to play shortstop. I think I had that and it helped me steal bases." (Quoted in Forman.)

When Aparicio first joined the White Sox he was quiet in the clubhouse. Part of the reason was his partial discomfort with English. Spanish was his first language, but Aparicio spoke more English than many Latino players breaking into the big leagues and his vocabulary grew steadily. Aparicio established his game and style with his performance and seemed more at ease after that, too. After four years in the majors, his father, also named Luis, said his son "has gotten more playful now that he's older." (Quoted in Rogin.)

As might be expected of someone who was on the small side as an adult, Aparicio was diminutive as a youth. Although his official listed Baseball Encyclopedia weight is 160 pounds at various times he played at 150 or 155. Aparicio was slow to grow and for a brief period of time as a youngster he voiced a desire to become a jockey. His father put the kibosh on that aspiration and steered him back to baseball. For a while, Aparicio and Yankee Hall of Fame catcher Yogi Berra used to tease one another on the field, calling each other "Shorty." Berra started it, but Aparicio checked out some statistics and discovered that his listed height was one inch taller than Berra's. He gave him additional grief for that.

Once Aparicio loosened up in the clubhouse and on the field he was a more vocal leader. At the start of White Sox games he was the first to run out to his position. He yelled as he went and made sure (a superstition) to always step on the first base bag as he scooted past to shortstop.

When asked during his prime years how he spent his free time Aparicio said his life was very simple. He concentrated on baseball most of the time and spent his free hours with his wife Sonia and his four children. Baseball dominated his thoughts, awake or sleeping. "I think I dream about baseball almost every night," Aparicio said. "You can't get that baseball out of your mind. I try to, but I can't. I dream I make a real bad job. You always wake up in the best part, the worst part. You know, in dreams, you make an error, you wake up." (Quoted in Rogin.)

Aparicio probably made more errors in his sleep than he did in the field.

In 18 years with the White Sox, Orioles, and Boston Red Sox, Aparicio was a .262 lifetime hitter. He scratched out singles and worked to get himself on base every which way, but his memorable performances were built around slick fielding and hot-footing it to second base in a cloud of dust. Aparicio is most closely identified with the White Sox as part of the 1959 ensemble labeled the "Go-Go White Sox" and he admits that season was very special to him. Not only was he sharing the infield glory with his good friend Nellie Fox, the players around them rose to the occasion.

The White Sox had been decimated by the Black Sox Scandal of 1919 when Commissioner Kenesaw Mountain Landis banned eight players for life. The Sox floundered for decades before becoming a contender in the 1950s and the 1959 season was the culmination of the journey.

"Nineteen-fifty-nine was an unbelievable year," Aparicio said. "To win a pennant, you've got to have at least 10 or 15 guys have good years. And that's what happened with us. We had real good pitchers, guys like Early Wynn, Bob Shaw, Billy Pierce and Dick Donovan. Plus, we had Gerry Staley and Turk Lown as the stoppers in the bullpen. We also had a good defense and Sherman Lollar was a great catcher." (Quoted in Forman.)

Aparicio batted .277 that season and led the American League in stolen bases and league shortstops in fielding. The White Sox lost the World Series to the Los Angeles Dodgers in six games, but that team and its stars, Aparicio included, are still revered in Chicago. Aparicio's No. 11 uniform was retired. A 10-time All-Star, Aparicio has also been honored by the team in another way. An etching of the former star is displayed on the left-center field wall at U.S. Cellular Field, the White Sox' current home park.

It was a bit of a shock to Aparicio and to White Sox fans when "Little Looie" was traded to the Baltimore Orioles before the 1963 season. Aparicio was sent to Baltimore with outfielder Al Smith and the White Sox obtained shortstop Ron Hansen, third baseman Pete Ward, outfielder Dave Nicholson, and future Hall of Fame reliever Hoyt Wilhelm. Aparicio had shown no sign of slippage in the field or on the bases, and, in fact, led the American League in his usual two categories, top fielding percentage and stolen bases, again in 1963.

Aparicio was still in the prime of his career and his accomplishments in Baltimore matched his accomplishments in Chicago. So did the thrills. Although it was fun and memorable to reach the World Series with the White Sox, Aparicio experienced the one thing the White Sox did not do. With the Orioles, Aparicio was part of a World Series winner.

"Nineteen-fifty-nine was nice, but '66 was my favorite year," Aparicio said, "because we not only were in, but won, the World Series (over the Dodgers). Everyone seemed to have a great year in '66. Our pitching was super, our hitting was strong, and we also had a good defense." (Quoted in Forman.)

Although Aparicio's Orioles number is not retired, in 2004, to observe the club's half-century in Baltimore, the team that began as the St. Louis Browns conducted a poll selecting the 50 most popular Orioles of all-time. Aparicio was one of the individuals chosen.

Despite his success in Baltimore, Aparicio was dealt back to the White Sox in 1968. He was not leading the AL in his two favorite statistics each year, but he was still good enough to represent the Sox in the 1970 All-Star game. A year earlier Aparicio notched a stat proving he had not just been hanging around all those years. He passed the 2,000-hit mark with a sharp single to right field against the Detroit Tigers on May 16. Aparicio was 14 years into his Major League career but, unlike the sportswriters quizzing him, felt it was extremely unlikely his body would hold up long enough for him to reach 3,000.

"I don't think I can make 3,000," Aparicio said. "That would take another seven years. But I do believe that I can play as a regular for at least four more years. I'm 35 now, but my legs are still good. I don't steal as many bases as I used to and maybe I'm not quite as fast. However, my legs are as strong as ever because I've always kept them in good shape." (Quoted in Munzel.)

Aparicio was only half kidding when he said he wanted to stay in the majors until his son, Luis III, then 12, was brought up and replaced him. Luis III never did make the majors, however.

Aparicio also predicted that he was probably good for 700 more hits in his career. Whether he used Taro cards or a crystal ball, Aparicio's feelings were very close to reality. He concluded his career with 2,677 hits and he was a regular for exactly four more years, one with the White Sox and three more seasons with the Boston Red Sox. Aparicio made two All-Star appearances for Boston, too.

Although there was never a specific indication one way or another that the installation of artificial turf in 1969 as part of a refurbishment of Comiskey Park helped or hurt Aparicio's longevity, he said he liked it. Given that he was a fielder whose savvy made him a wiz at positioning and who got to every ball that bounced his way, Aparicio seemed to adopt the turf as a bonus aid.

"I liked it right from the start because there are no bad hops on our AstroTurf," Aparicio said. "Not only is every bounce true, but I believe you get more big hops than you do on regular turf. I've had no trouble adjusting to the AstroTurf because I've always fielded about 50 grounders before a game to see how the ball reacts. Even grass infields are all different." (Quoted in "Aparicio likes . . .")

Aparicio once had to pick up grounders on rocky playground fields near his Maracaibo, Venezuela home. A decade-and-a-half into a Major League career he was still plucking ground balls on the most modern field available in the world.

Aparicio played in 132 games for the Red Sox in 1973 and batted .271. He fielded .966, not much under most of his top seasonal figures. But he called it a career after that year and returned to Venezuela, where he has resided since.

In 1984, Aparicio was elected to the Baseball Hall of Fame, eclipsing the accomplishments of his childhood idol Chico Carrasquel. Aparicio was elected along with slugger Harmon Killebrew and pitcher Don Drysdale.

As the years passed and firmly entrenched in Venezuela, Aparicio only periodically returned to Chicago for public appearances. Sometimes he traveled north to sign autographs at sports memorabilia shows. Sometimes he appeared at U.S. Cellular Field for a White Sox function. When the White Sox reached the World Series in 2005—the first time since 1959—Aparicio attended some games. When the survivors of the 1959 team were recognized in June 2009 for a 50th anniversary celebration, Aparicio also appeared.

But the most meaningful visit to a White Sox event for Aparicio occurred in 2006. The White Sox unveiled a dual statue of Aparicio and Nellie Fox completing a double play. The life-sized bronze stands on the 100 level behind center field at U.S. Cellular Field. Fox, who died young of cancer, was not present for the unveiling. Aparicio expressed sorrow that Fox could not be present and when speaking about his old friend the great shortstop teared up.

The keystone partners made special memories for White Sox fans, and the statue freezes a moment in time when the Hall of Fame twosome was hard at work doing what they did best. The sculpture immortalizes Aparicio and Fox in bronze, capturing nostalgia one step beyond the haze of memory.

Further Reading

"Aparicio Likes AstroTurf on White Sox Park Infield," *The Sporting News*, September 20, 1969.

Daniel, Dan, "Fox, Aparicio Rated Greatest by Al Lopez," *New York World Telegram & Sun*, August 24, 1959.

Forman, Ross, "Little Looie," *Sports Collector's Digest*, June 28, 1991.

Munzel, Edgar, "2,000 Hits for Looey, Still a Chisox Pillar," *The Sporting News*, May 31, 1969.

Roberts, Howard, "Tiny Tormentor," *Chicago Daily News*, (date missing, National Baseball Hall of Fame Library and Archives).

Rogin, Gil, "Happy Little Luis," *Sports Illustrated*, May 9, 1960.

Rod Carew

Rod Carew wielded a baseball bat as if it was the baton of a symphony orchestra conductor. The bat was an extension of his arms, not an inanimate wooden object. And like such conductors, the maestro made beautiful music.

Few among baseball's all-time greats could hit with the precision, the authority, and the focus of the 18-time All-Star for the Minnesota Twins and the California Angels. Although he was not a slugger, Carew was one of the greatest hitters who ever lived, with his bat control a throwback to Ty Cobb and Major League Baseball's dead-ball era pre-1920.

Fifteen times Carew hit over .300 and he won seven American League batting championships. In 1977, when the 6-foot, 182-pound native of Panama batted .388 (the highest average of his career), many thought Carew would become the first player since Ted Williams in 1941 to hit .400.

Carew was born in 1945 in Gatun in the Canal Zone of Panama, the greatest player ever produced by his nation. Never a chatterbox who touted his own feats, Carew was nonetheless so dominant as a second baseman and then first baseman that he never lacked for recognition. He broke into the majors with the Twins in 1967 and was an immediate All-Star. The only time Carew was not an All-Star in his 19-year career was 1985, his final season.

To say that Carew was born in his parents' hometown of Gatun is a slight exaggeration. His mother, Olga, and father, Eric, were on their way to a hospital 40 miles away to ensure her the best care. However, mom went into labor in the "colored" section on a train packed with boxing fans headed to a major bout. A nurse on her way to work at the same hospital assisted, and then a doctor was called from the white section of the train to aid in the final moments of the delivery. Carew was named for the doctor: Rodney Cline Carew. The nurse,

During his days as an infielder with the Minnesota Twins and Los Angeles Angels, Hall of Famer Rod Carew proved to be the best position player ever from Panama. Over the course of his 19-season career, Carew stroked 3,053 hits. (AP Photo/Rod Boren)

Margaret Allen, a stranger to the family, was named godmother. Word spread that a baby had been born and Carew received the first round of applause of his life. It was not easy to picture that two decades later crowds of 40,000 or more would be cheering for him.

Carew lived in Gatun, a community of 2,000 within walking distance of the Panama Canal, until he was 8 and then the family moved to Gamboa, with a population of 4,000. When Carew was 15 his family moved to New York City. But his earliest memories were formed in Panama. To those he met in New York, Panama was a mystery, an alien place. If those he came into contact at first knew anything about the Central American country it was as its famous role as the transfer point for huge cargo ships from the Atlantic to the Pacific Ocean.

"I've been asked, 'What's it like to grow up in a grass hut in the jungle?'" Carew said in his autobiography. "Well, I didn't grow up in a grass hut. I didn't grow up in the jungle." (Quoted in Carew and Berkow, 12.)

Carew said he lived in an everyday apartment in both small towns, but was so close to the Canal he could hear the foghorns of the huge ships as they chugged past. Sometimes he walked over to the locks to watch the ships from various countries sail through on their long journeys. He waved to foreign sailors and they waved back. It was big industry at work in one of the world's busiest shipping zones. "It's a thrilling sight," Carew said. (Quoted in Carew and Berkow, 13.)

The apartments Carew lived in with his mother, father, brother, two sisters, and grandparents were all new housing, constructed for workers in the Canal Zone. He remembers the streets being spacious and clean—more so in both instances than New York City. "People spent a lot of time in the street, sitting in front of their houses," he said. "Kids played. Adults talked and played dominoes. I remember at World Series time everybody would plug in their radios and come down and sit on boxes and play dominoes and listen to the game." (Quoted in Carew and Berkow, 14.)

Yet Carew's entire existence in Panama was segregated, from schools to homes. Carew said his grandparents were recruited as workers at the Canal from the West Indies. The local swimming pool had a no trespassing sign on it, Carew said. "We knew that meant us," he said since only white kids were allowed to use it. (Quoted in Carew and Berkow, 16.)

Baseball became a passion early in Carew's life, though he and his friends had very little in the way of needed equipment. Many years later, in an interview for a National Baseball Hall of Fame Latin American display, Carew thought back about how the youngsters made do because they were so hungry to play. He and his friends used broomsticks for bats and tennis balls instead of real baseballs and made their own gloves out of cardboard or paper bags. Play baseball is what boys did. It was the main free-time activity. "It's bigger than any other sport (in Panama)," Carew said. "We played baseball year-round." (Quoted in Viva Baseball!)

Although the games broadcast to Panama via Armed Forces Radio were played far away, the young players dreamed of making it to the big-time, of transplanting their games to the United States and playing for the New York Yankees or another Major League club. For most such thoughts were far-fetched fantasies. Carew realized that his hopes of becoming a major leaguer were unlikely to come true. It is impossible to know if he would have been discovered if he had not moved to New York, though the outlook toward Latin America was broadening at the time.

The move to New York broke up Carew's parents. It was his mother's wish, and he and his brother were satisfied with the decision because they had come to see their father as unnecessarily cruel and distant from them. Carew's uncle Clyde became an influence in his life as the boy enjoyed Coney Island and became addicted to movies—his next favorite pursuit besides baseball—as he learned English. During his adaptation to New York, Carew actually gave up baseball for a couple of years. He resumed playing baseball as a high school senior—when he weighed just 150 pounds at his full height of six feet.

For all of his inexperience, Carew showed a natural flair on the diamond and several teams began scouting him. However, the Twins signed him after his high school graduation in June 1964. Always a clutch player, Carew went seven-for-eight at the plate when he was being closely observed. Scouts ran for their pens and contract forms.

Carew played shortstop in school and on the sandlots, but the Twins made him a second baseman because they felt he lacked arm strength. Carew was 18 in his first season in the minors at Cocoa Beach in the Florida State League. There he discovered his fielding needed more nursing than he had as a baby on that Panama train.

"What relaxed me was my hitting," he said. "I always thought I could learn to field." (Quoted in Carew and Berkow, 56.)

Carew was right. His hitting set him apart, and he did learn how to field sufficiently well to fit in as a big leaguer. He was only 21 when he broke in with the Twins as the club's second baseman in 1967 and batted .292. Carew was named the American League Rookie of the Year.

In spring training of 1967 it was not yet clear if Carew would make the cut and stick with the Twins, but the team was already touting him as a player to watch. "Carew can do it all," said team president Calvin Griffith. "He can run, throw and hit. He has had some growing up to do, but it looks like he has made some great strides. He could be the American League All-Star second baseman if he sets his mind to it." (Quoted in Nichols, "Rookie Rod . . .")

No pressure. This would not have been a crazy prediction if Carew had slowly worked his way up through the minors and starred at AAA. However, he was trying to make the move directly to the majors from the Class A Carolina League. But Griffith actually looked like a genius for making such a dead-on prediction when Carew had not yet secured a starting job. While the vote of confidence was nice from a higher up, Carew had not yet won the approval of more discerning judges of talent known to be hard to please—infield coach Billy Martin and manager Sam Mele.

"I say Carew has a chance," Martin said. Mele was more reticent than Martin. "I'm considering him," the field boss said. "I want to see more of him before I say more." (Quoted in Nichols, "Rookie Rod . . .")

Even coming out of spring training, Twins officials weren't sure if Carew would benefit more from another year in the minors or if he could make it with the big club. When they were mulling his future he went eight-for-nine at the plate to cinch his new job. It was a performance reminiscent of his timely hitting in high school that won over scouts. Carew showed enough to those Twins older students of the game to play in 137 games in 1967.

Minnesotans loved Carew from the start. A Midwest enclave where actions are prized more than words, the communities of Minneapolis and St. Paul embraced Carew and his work ethic. Although Carew was careless on the bases at first, frequently getting thrown out while trying to stretch hits, he had conquered his earlier fielding woes and was hitting around .300. By mid-season it was apparent that Carew had matured quickly on the field.

"Last spring I expected him to have more problems fielding than hitting," Mele said. "But he has played terrific baseball at second base. It's amazing how much advice and instruction he has been able to absorb." (Quoted in Nichols, "Lightning Rod . . .")

As Carew gained experience, he became a better and better ballplayer. He sometimes clashed with reporters or seemed moody to them, but he often made quiet, off-the-record visits to hospitals to cheer up ill children. Carew was never a home-run hitter, but one of his supplemental skills was base stealing. He recorded a high of 49 steals in 1976 and showed he was one of the true swipe artists who had the daring in his soul to steal home plate. Except for Jackie Robinson, stealing home had become a lost art among major leaguers roughly by 1930. Carew, who stole home 17 times in his career, stood out in his generation—and since—as the only player who could accomplish the feat with any type of regularity. Carew also tied a Major League record by stealing home seven times in a single season in 1969.

Stealing home is remarkably difficult to pull off. The pitcher, who is throwing home anyway, has to be caught off-guard. The runner must beat a 90 mph throw to the plate over the distance of 90 feet from third. There is considerable pressure to make the bold move pay off, as well, because if the attempted thief is out, he has just sacrificed a runner in scoring position for his team. The odds are against success, but certain players have had a knack for the dazzling play. Ty Cobb, who stole home 50 times in his career, was by far the most successful. When the play works it can demoralize the opposition and excite the crowd. Even the attempt leaves baseball people buzzing.

"I was never the fastest guy around," Carew said, "so if I can do it, others can, too. What it takes mostly is a willingness to study pitchers and a manager who'll let you go when you see the chance. The first thing you check for is whether the pitcher is using a windup or a stretch when you're on third. Of course, it's easiest when he's using a windup because you get a better head start. Then you check to see if he holds the ball in his hand or his glove when he's on the mound. A pitcher that holds the ball in his glove is easiest to steal against because he has to make an extra move before he can throw." Carew never underestimated the importance of surprise in making the entire enterprise work, either. (Quoted in Klein.)

By 1969, the lanky Carew, who had filled out somewhat, was already a two-time All-Star. But that season represented a coming out party for him, and Carew catapulted into a higher echelon of stars. His always-sharp batting eye grew even sharper with experience. That year Carew hit .332 and won his first AL batting crown.

Carew put together top-notch statistics year after year, but he out-did himself in 1977. It was a milestone season, one that raised his profile in the sport even higher. That year Carew hit 14 homers, equaling his career high and uncharacteristic for him. He also knocked in 100 runs, the most of his career. He led the American League in hits with 239 and triples with 16. And that was the season he made a bid to hit .400 before settling for a career-best .388 average. It was the type of season that had baseball people gushing about his talents anew.

"He doesn't have one weakness that's evident," said future Hall of Fame pitcher Nolan Ryan. "I don't try to out-fox him anymore. I just throw hard stuff, as close to the outside corner as possible." (Quoted in Durslag.)

While the Red Sox slugger Ted Williams finished the 1941 season with a .406 average, the last time any hitter broke the magic barrier, Carew said he didn't think he would be able to duplicate the achievement. "Pitching today is more varied and scientific," Carew said. "Defensive players are faster and more agile. They wear better gloves. And today's hitters are handicapped by longer schedules, longer travel and less rest." (Quoted in Durslag.)

Actually Williams had long before reflected on Carew's chances to join him as a .400 hitter. In 1969, Williams, who was then managing the Washington Senators, had seen enough of Carew by mid-season to respect his chances. "I keep saying it is possible with luck and hitting in the right ballpark," Williams said. "Who knows about Carew? I know how he looked against us. In fact, Mr. Carew looks terrific to me." (Quoted in Lamey.) Carew was at .408 in mid-May of that year before tailing off.

One thing Carew could do that Williams never indulged in was bunt for a base-hit. Once again that made him more like the throwback players of the 1910s and 1920s. As patient as Carew seemed to most players, he said he did regularly go after bad pitches and that would probably cost him as the season went on. Attention built as Carew carried his high average deep into the summer. He appeared on the cover of *Time* magazine, sitting on a floor, legs crossed, baseball bat held in front of him under the headline, "Baseball's Best Hitter."

In 1977, Carew was 31 and more polished. He batted .486 in June alone and was still hitting .411 in July. Carew revealed that he did not keep his 34 ½-inch, 32-ounce bats made from ash with the rest of the Twins' hitting lumber, but cared for them separately on his own. He also said he would never slam a bat on the ground after making a frustrating out. "That bruises them, makes them weaker," Carew said. "I couldn't do that. I baby my bats, treat them like my kids, because using a bat is how I make my living." (Quoted in "Baseball's Best . . .")

During his ultimately unfruitful quest, Carew was featured in *Sports Illustrated*, *People*, *Newsweek*, *Black Sports*, *Sport*, and on various television shows. He received stacks of fan mail, and despite changing his home phone number more than once, he kept getting calls from fans. In the end Carew had to "settle" for a .388 average.

"Someone said I was only eight hits short of hitting .400," he said. "It would be so easy for me to pick out eight balls that I'd like to have over again, hard-hit balls that someone made a terrific play on. But I wasn't terribly disappointed at falling short." (Quoted in Carew and Berkow, 209).

Although Carew never wrote history for hitting .400, his seven batting titles made him one of the most accomplished hitters of all time. His production was not quite as impressive with the Angels after he moved West in 1979, but he punched out his 3,000th hit with California and concluded his career with 3,053.

Although Carew frequently had to face great expectations and pressures on the field, there was only one dark cloud during his career that stemmed from off-field activity. Carew married a white, Jewish woman named Marilynn Levy in 1970, at a time when Americans were not especially open to intermarriage. Racists seized on their high profile union and the Carews received hate mail and even death threats.

The Carews encountered bigots in restaurants in Florida disparaging them for being together, received hate mail, and a late-night threatening telephone call to their home. Carew infuriated the diners by bluntly asking, "Is it any of your business if my wife is yellow or green or pink?" And eventually, the FBI was brought in to investigate the death threat. It was an uncomfortable time, but the marriage persevered and those days of facing up to narrow-minded racists were left behind. (Quoted in Gross.)

Carew was not happy to leave baseball behind when he retired in 1985. His contract was up with the Angels, but he felt he could still hit—as always. Only no Major League team offered him a job. He left the sport with little fanfare.

As expected, Carew's election to the Hall of Fame followed his retirement by a suitable length of time. He was inducted in 1991. It was the appropriate capstone to a brilliant career.

Only later did Carew return to the majors. He became the Angels hitting coach (and later for the Milwaukee Brewers, too)—a perfect match. But that tenure was marred by sorrow in its fifth year when his teenage daughter Michelle contracted leukemia and fought a public battle for her life. Carew and his wife were crushed when Michelle died at age 18 in 1996. A nationwide campaign for a bone marrow donor brought out 70,000 people willing to try, but no match could be found. Instead, the offers were used to help save other lives.

When his little girl died peacefully, never relinquishing her smile or hope, Carew was overcome with tears, sadness, and love.

The journey of thousands of miles Carew embarked on when he was born on a train in Panama made him the pride of that country, but it was beyond his power to keep everyone in his family safe.

Further Reading

"Baseball's Best Hitter Tries for Glory," *Time* July 18, 1977.

Carew, Rod, and Berkow, Ira, *Carew* (New York, Simon & Schuster, 1979).

Durslag, Melvin, "A stroke of genius," *TV Guide*, September 3, 1977.

Gross, Milton, "Death Threat to A Batting Champion," *Sports Today*, August, 1971.

Klein, Frederick, "Carew: Master thief of home," *Wall Street Journal*, May 14, 1980.

Lamey, Mike, "Carew Wins Support as Possible .400 Swatter," *The Sporting News*, July 12, 1969.

Nichols, Max, "Lightning Rod—Twins' Go-Go Rookie," *The Sporting News*, June 10, 1967.

———, "Rookie Rod Carew Stakes Out Claim to Twin Keystone," *The Sporting News*, March 25, 1967.

Viva Baseball! National Baseball Hall of Fame exhibit interview, 2009.

Orlando Cepeda

Orlando Cepeda's nickname was "The Baby Bull," and the San Francisco Giants All-Star from Puerto Rico was indeed strong like one. He was also the hard-hitting son of a local legend, Pedro, or "Perucho," who many felt was his equal on the diamond. Perucho was an admired hitter whose dark skin denied him even a glance from Major League Baseball during his prime.

As part of a terrorizing batting order for the San Francisco Giants alongside Willie Mays and Willie McCovey, Orlando Cepeda, known as "The Baby Bull" was one of the best early power hitters from Puerto Rico. A seven-time All-Star in 17 seasons, Cepeda overcame difficulties in his personal life to become a Hall of Famer. (AP Photo)

Born in 1937, Cepeda was raised in poverty, but baseball was always a priority in his Ponce household, and his father was a great influence. Orlando learned by watching his dad play and from hearing his words of advice. As a teenager, Cepeda served as a batboy for the Santurce team, one of the island's most storied clubs.

When Orlando exhibited great power and fielding skills and said he wanted to try his luck in the United States, his father was against it. He foresaw only heart-break for his son because of discrimination against blacks. But Cepeda's association with Santurce paid dividends. The owner, Pedro Zorilla, saw Cepeda's potential and urged Perucho to allow his son to attend a New York Giants' tryout camp. Perucho did not live to see him succeed, however; he died at age 48, only days before Orlando played his first game in the minors. Cepeda used his $500 signing bonus to pay for his father's funeral.

Still, the father recognized what type of ability his son possessed long before Orlando saw it within himself. His father used to tell other baseball people that as good as he was, Orlando "is going to be a better player than I was." (Quoted in Orr.)

To the gain of Orlando, the Giants, and U.S. baseball fans, the son was determined to play in the best league available and he became a popular star regardless of skin color and his reliance on Spanish. It did not take long for the 6-foot-2, 210-pound smooth swinger to join Willie Mays in the Giants' lineup. In 1958, Cepeda's rookie year, he played in 148 games, hit 25 home runs, drove in 96, and averaged .312. There were no debates about whether or not he belonged. Cepeda practically took over, and was named National League Rookie of the Year. That was the beginning of a 17-year Major League career as a first baseman and outfielder that featured seven All-Star selections.

Cepeda had to be special his first year because the Giants were loaded with rookie talent. In the same year they were blessed with the arrival of outfielders Felipe Alou, Willie Kirkland, and Leon Wagner, plus third baseman Jim Davenport. The scouts should have found huge Christmas bonuses in their paychecks that year. Manager Bill Rigney, who recognized the significance of what he saw, called the rookie group, "the greatest collection I've ever seen." (Quoted in Orr.)

Sharing the middle of a batting order with Willie Mays did wonders for both Cepeda and Mays, forcing pitchers to gingerly approach them. "He is annoying every pitcher in the league," Mays said. "He is strong, he hits to all fields, and he makes all the plays. He's the most relaxed first-year man I ever saw." (Quoted in Orr.)

Being relaxed, fun-loving, and laid-back was just part of Cepeda's personality and it helped him make friends. It also earned him a second nickname, "Cha-Cha." Cepeda idolized Mays, whom he first met when the veteran played winter ball in

Puerto Rico, and it did not take long for him to make friends with the icon and the other up-and-coming Giants. In the early 1960s San Francisco fielded one of the most feared lineups of all time. A pitcher had to face Mays, Cepeda, and Willie McCovey, all future Hall of Famers, and all able to bash the ball from the confines of Candlestick Park to Los Angeles it seemed.

Cepeda was an All-Star by his second season and in 1961 he was the most dominant hitter in the National League, leading the circuit in home runs with 46 and RBIs with 142. His average was a fine .311. Cepeda was in a zone all season long. When pitchers saw him coming to the plate they started complaining of shoulder pain to their managers. The biggest problem Giants management had was how to take full advantage of having Cepeda and McCovey on the roster. They both were natural first baseman and there was little doubt that first was their best position. Neither could cover much ground in the outfield, but Cepeda was a little bit quicker and mobile, so he sometimes got the call to roam the grassy plains. It was not his favorite duty.

"I'm a first baseman," Cepeda said when quizzed about his preference. "I am more comfortable at first base, but the manager says it is better for the team to have McCovey at first base sometimes, so I play where I am told." (Quoted in Gross.)

There is no statistical evidence to suggest that being shuttled around in the field disrupted Cepeda's hitting. Twelve times he hit 20 or more home runs. One of the testimonies to Cepeda's power and strength was his willingness to swing a 36-ounce, 41-inch bat at times. That approximated the dimensions of Fred Flintstone's club. Actually, Cepeda even dabbled with a 39-ounce bat. The man had muscles to spare, and his enthusiastic flair swinging—and making contact—made him a fan favorite in San Francisco and especially when he returned to Puerto Rico in the off-season. Cepeda seemed to be one of the all-around hitters who could connect without much batting practice or warm-up and still be a threat to hit the ball deep. It was a fun time to be a member of the Giants. Gleeful about obtaining Major League Baseball, the city was welcoming and granted a honeymoon period to a team that seemed as if it could do no wrong. If there was a "boo" to be heard in the late 1950s it was definitely either misunderstood or directed at the opposition.

"When I talk to Latino players today, a lot of them don't even realize how hard it was for us then."
—Orlando Cepeda on coming from Puerto Rico to the Continental U.S. in the 1950s. (Quoted in Quote Sea/Latin Quotes, http://www.quotesea.com.)

"The city went bonkers for us immediately," Cepeda said in his autobiography. "Bay Area fans had been expecting Major League Baseball since the end of World War II, so we were the talk of the town. Win or lose, we were big-time conversation. The five Bay Area newspapers made us front-page news." (Quoted in Cepeda and Fagen, 46.)

Cepeda was only 17 when he signed with the Giants and he was 20 when he made his Major League debut. Although the scouts touted him, fans didn't know what to expect from a comparative unknown. Cepeda thinks he helped cement his image with the spectators and even in his own mind as someone who belonged during a stretch in early May 1958. In the first game of a series against the Pittsburgh Pirates he hit two straight home runs. Then he hit another homer the next day and added a fourth in three days.

"The fans went wild," Cepeda said. (Quoted in Cepeda and Fagen, 49.)

Cepeda's rookie year was greeted with great fanfare when he returned to Puerto Rico in the off-season. Teams that had lagged in scouting the Latin American baseball market took the short flight from the mainland of the United States to the island. Cepeda, pleased to be following in the footsteps of Minnie Minoso, Chico Carrasquel, and Mexican Bobby Avila, who won the American League batting title in 1954 for the Cleveland Indians, also heard from an older generation of Puerto Ricans. They told him his father would have been proud of his play.

"Even my staunchest critics considered me a worthy successor to my father," Cepeda said. (Quoted in Cepeda and Fagen, 59.)

As blissful as Cepeda's early years with the Giants were, schisms began to form on the team in the early 1960s. Cepeda and Mays grew apart a bit, though there were no overt problems between them. But another problem for the team's cohesiveness was that manager Al Dark and the Hispanic players never seemed to be on the same page. Although the Giants won the 1962 pennant (losing the World Series to the New York Yankees), they could not repeat. There was tension in the dugout and clubhouse. At one point, in what has been categorized by baseball historians as an act of racism, Dark banned the speaking of Spanish at the ballpark, even in casual chats between players whose first language was Spanish. This edict was resented and it created festering disgruntlement. It symbolized Dark being culturally tone deaf about the diversity of the men on his team. Cepeda rebelled at the language rule and said he told Dark, "Alvin, I won't do that. I'm Puerto Rican, others are Dominican, and I am proud of what I am. This is a disgrace to my race." (Quoted in Cepeda and Fagen, 75.)

Cepeda said Dark avoided the Latin players except to yell at them, and he prohibited the playing of Latin music in the locker room. Cepeda said he felt singled out for criticism and that discipline was not equally meted out to players—white, black, or Latino. "To be blunt, on many occasions Alvin made my life a living hell," Cepeda recounted in his autobiography. "Things got so bad at times that there were days I didn't want to go to the ballpark. I believe that Alvin's racial attitudes were harmful to the best interests of the ball club in general, and to the Latin players in particular." (Quoted in Cepeda and Fagen, 73–74.)

Cepeda said that while appearing at an old-timers game in the 1990s, Dark "offered me an apology of sorts." (Quoted in Cepeda and Fagen, 73.)

Like any hitter, Cepeda had the occasional slump (though not many of them in his first seven seasons), but in 1962 he flunked his driver's test because of poor vision. This was counterintuitive for anyone who could usually pick out the seams on a 90 mph fastball rotating toward the plate. As a result, the Giants ordered an in-depth vision test. Instead of showing any deficiency, Cepeda came through with 20–20 vision in his right eye and an even sharper capability of 20–15 in his left eye. That helped explain why he could see the ball so well right before he smacked it. Cepeda had gone into a homer slump for a while and felt something might be wrong with his vision, but once he was screened he had no explanation for a possible problem. Whatever bothered Cepeda was cured.

"You and I should have eyes as good as his," the eye doctor reported to Giants owner Horace Stoneham. (Quoted in McDonald.)

Cepeda experienced bigger health worries after the 1964 season when he underwent ligament surgery on his knee. Despite rehabbing all winter, he was not ready to play when spring training began and the injury never came around. For the first time, Cepeda had the frustration of not being an everyday player. He appeared in just 33 games with only 34 at-bats. It was a lost season. He also resented hints from Giants officials that he was malingering. He wanted to prove to Dark and then Herman Franks, the successor as manager, that he could still play. Franks suggested he was faking and that the pain was all in his head.

"And I tried, believe me," Cepeda wrote. "But I was in pain, real pain. I was sitting in the clubhouse one day very depressed. I was almost crying. I had taken enough—too many accusations." Cepeda said that to ease his anguish when a friend offered him a marijuana cigarette, he smoked it. (Quoted in Cepeda and Fagen, 95.)

Although it took months for the arrangements to play out, Cepeda was nearing the end of his term with the Giants. In 1966 he played in only 19 games for the team before he was shipped to the St. Louis Cardinals in a trade for pitcher Ray Sadecki. Fan reaction in San Francisco was hostile to the deal. They wanted Cepeda to stay. Cepeda never thought he would play for another team. "Initially I was crushed," he said. "The day I was traded I sat by my locker and cried." (Quoted in Cepeda and Fagen, 100.)

Cepeda was uneasy about moving to another team, and he said he did not know many players on the Cardinals. One player who made him feel welcome immediately, he said, was Tim McCarver. McCarver, an All-Star catcher who spent 21 years in the big leagues before embarking on a lengthy broadcasting career that has kept him in the limelight, approached a gloomy-looking Cepeda when he showed up in the clubhouse of his new club.

"He broke the ice immediately," Cepeda said. "He told me, 'Orlando, you're here now. Screw the Giants. Screw Herman Franks. We really want you here.' " (Quoted in Cepeda and Fagen, 102.)

The fresh start was invigorating for Cepeda. He no longer had to worry about competing for playing space on the field with McCovey. His knee was healthy again. And he had no more spats with Franks or doubting Giants officials. Cepeda played 120 games for the Cardinals during the remainder of the 1966 season and all of them were at first base. With the Cardinals alone he cracked 17 home runs and drove in 58 runs while batting .303. McCarver was right—the Cardinals really did want him.

The key for Cepeda was regaining strength in his knee. The key for St. Louis was that Cepeda had regained his equilibrium and was the old Orlando. He filled a critical need for the Cardinals and when they made a run at the 1967 pennant, Cepeda was one of the leaders on the field. His hitting stroke back in prime form, Cepeda smashed 25 homers, drove in a National League-leading 111 runs, and batted .325. The performance earned Cepeda the NL Most Valuable Player award, and he helped lead the Cardinals to the World Series championship. His victory represented the first unanimous vote in the history of the league.

St. Louis also let Cepeda be Cepeda. He was allowed to play Latin music in the locker room and he even danced on a chair and sung to his teammates. This type of revelry followed many wins. As the song ran its course, Cepeda yelled, "Who wins the game?" His teammates, English speakers as well, responded, "El Birdos!" Conducting the crowd as if it was an orchestra he then shouted, "What's the magic word?" "Nuts to Herman Franks," the Cardinals retorted.

It was telling and symbolic that when Cepeda won the MVP trophy he praised St. Louis trainer Clarence "Doc" Bauman. The message was inescapable: In San Francisco he was ridiculed, in St. Louis he was helped. Cepeda thanked Bauman "for the hard work that helped me to recover from my injured knee. This is so very big, especially when I was so close to quitting baseball because of my knee injury." (Quoted in Vecsey.)

The MVP culminated a glorious comeback and year of triumph for Cepeda. After that, however, Cepeda had only sporadic success. He slumped in St. Louis; but in 1969, he turned in a brilliant year for the Atlanta Braves with 34 homers, 111 RBIs, and a .305 average. Cepeda declined in earnest after that, although in 1973 he had a solid 20-homer, 86 RBI year as a designated hitter for the Boston Red Sox. It was the first year the designated hitter rule was in use in the American League. His single season in Boston won him a new group of fans.

Cepeda finished his career in 1974 with the Kansas City Athletics, unaware that the greatest challenge of his life was soon to follow.

In December 1975, Cepeda was arrested and charged with illegal possession of 165 pounds of marijuana at the San Juan International Airport. Eleven months later, Cepeda was convicted and sentenced to five years in prison. Once a hero in Puerto Rico, Cepeda was placed behind bars in disgrace, the ever-present smile wiped off his face by his troubles. Cepeda served 10 months in a federal prison camp in Florida before being paroled.

It took time for Cepeda to deal with his mistake. He refused to admit guilt until 1978, although it was obvious that such a volume of marijuana was not simply for personal use, and he was depressed and seemingly lost for some time after his release from prison.

"When I got out of jail, I wasn't really ready to deal with a lot of things," Cepeda said. "I was going through the motions in many ways. My mind was like an empty apartment. If you came knocking at the door, more often than not you would find nobody home. I had a tough time coping." In 1988, nearly 13 years after his arrest, Cepeda did not feel terribly guilty about his crime. "I have nothing to be ashamed of," he said. "Look, it was only grass. I didn't kill anybody or hurt anybody." But he could not explain why he got involved with a major marijuana deal in the first place. "I've asked myself that so many times. Obviously, if I had been thinking clearly, I wouldn't have." (Quoted in Chapin.)

Cepeda was slow to put his life back together, but he eventually did so with the help of family. He admitted letting his fans down, but as time passed they rallied around him. Cepeda regained his stature in Puerto Rico and among Giants fans, who re-embraced him. He became an eloquent spokesman for Latin American baseball pioneers of the 1950s and participated in documentary film projects on the topic.

In 1999, Cepeda was rewarded with the ultimate restoration of his reputation when the National Baseball Hall of Fame Veterans Committee made him the second Puerto Rican (after Roberto Clemente) to be selected to the Hall—warts and all. "I cried this morning, along with my wife," said Cepeda, who was 61 at the time. "When they told me I was selected, I lost my mind." (Quoted in Roderick.)

With his ascension to the Hall of Fame, it might be said that Cepeda was paroled again. For a second time he was walking out of prison a free man.

Further Reading

Cepeda, Orlando and Fagen, Herb, *Baby Bull: From Hard Ball to Hard Time and Back* (Dallas, Texas, Taylor Publishing Company, 1998).

Chapin, Dwight, "Cepeda can't get to first in post-baseball life," *San Francisco Examiner*, May 22, 1988.

Gross, Milton, "Cepeda Grows Up; He's Starting to Act Like A Team Man," *Pittsburgh Press*, July 2, 1961.

McDonald, Jack, " 'Nothing Wrong With Cepeda's Eyes,' Says Medic After Exam," *San Francisco Examiner*, November 10, 1962.

Orr, Jack, "Cepeda's For Real," *Sport Magazine*, October, 1958.

Roderick, Joe, "End of a Giant Journey," *Contra Costra Times*, March 3, 1999.

Vecsey, George, "Now Cepeda Has His," *New York Times*, November 8, 1967.

Roberto Clemente

With his death in a plane crash while on a mission of mercy in 1972, the already esteemed Roberto Clemente gained the ultimate role of patron saint of all Latin American baseball players.

Clemente, who grew up in Puerto Rico, was already a hero on his home island and looked to as a guiding light for Spanish-speaking ballplayers in the major leagues and for those who aspired to make the grade. Even now, four decades after his death in a fiery crash into the sea, Clemente is viewed by many as the greatest all-around Latino player of all-time. He was a superstar on the diamond and for the way he handled himself off the field.

The legendary Roberto Clemente of the Pittsburgh Pirates was a role model for not only fellow Puerto Ricans, but all Hispanic ballplayers. Clemente was regarded as one of the best fielding outfielders of all time and won four batting titles. He died in a plane crash on a mission of mercy to bring supplies to earthquake-stricken Nicaragua on December 31, 1972. In his honor, Major League Baseball annually presents a Roberto Clemente Award for Humanitarian Service. (AP Photo/J. Spencer Jones)

Always proud, always insistent on recognizing his Latin American heritage, Clemente displayed a sense of behavior in an alien land like the United States that encouraged young Latino players. That was in day-to-day matters. His other actions, aimed at helping the less fortunate, ultimately at the sacrifice of his own life, transformed him into an icon. A statue of Clemente stands in Puerto Rico. Major League Baseball honors recipients each year with a humanitarian award in his name. This is not solely because the man could hit a fastball or throw out foolish runners testing his arm.

Roberto Clemente was born in Carolina, Puerto Rico on August 18, 1934. Although the first-name diminutive "Bob" can be seen on his earliest baseball cards, Clemente never used the Anglicized version of his name. Clemente was first signed by the Dodgers, but he was picked off in a supplemental draft due to savvy scouting by Latino expert Howie Haak, resulting in the everlasting joy of the Pittsburgh Pirates. Clemente broke in with Pittsburgh—the only team he played for during his 18-year Major League career—in 1955.

This was a culturally less-sensitive time in American history. People with dark skin faced resolute discrimination in most walks of life. A person who spoke a foreign language in an overwhelmingly English-speaking field confronted additional difficulties. Clemente could speak English, but he did so with a thick accent, and he often groped for the right words to match his thoughts. The sportswriters covering the Pirates, however, were impatient and frequently displayed insensitivity. It irked Clemente when he saw his words twisted by misinterpretation and in ways that he felt made him sound illiterate.

During Clemente's first trip to Florida for spring training he experienced first-hand discrimination. He swiftly learned that the black players did not stay in the same hotels as white players or share the same restaurants.

"When I started playing in 1955 . . . every time I used to read something about the players, about the black players (the writers) have to say something sarcastic about it," Clemente said. "When I got to Fort Myers (Florida), there was a newspaper down there and the newspaper said, 'PUERTO RICAN HOT DOG' arrives in town. Now, these people never knew anything about me, but they knew I was Puerto Rican, and as soon as I get to camp they call me a Puerto Rican hot dog." (Quoted in Maraniss, 69.)

The phrase "hot dog" did not refer to the popular ballpark cuisine, but rather was a synonym for a player who was a showboat on the field. To conservatives who saw themselves as guardians of the game, this might mean criticizing someone who had a different type of batting stance or someone who caught the ball with one hand instead of two.

In Latin American baseball, whether it was played in Cuba, the Dominican Republic, Puerto Rico, Venezuela, or other locales, this merely represented expressing individualism. Fans placed more of a premium on style and were disinclined to applaud stuffiness. As long as the player got the job done and caught the darned ball, no one cared how he did it. This was just part of the entertainment package. "No other aspect of Dominican life, except perhaps for meringue, has provided as much joie de vivre for this Third World country, as baseball, its highest art form," one historian noted. This was Clemente in a nutshell, the personification of the point. (Quoted in Ruck, xx.)

Whether it was Roberto Clemente, or any other Latino, a ballplayer in the majors had to beware of stereotyping. If a coach ordered the player to catch the ball with two hands and he resisted, he might be labeled a bad actor. Alfredo Griffin, a one-time shortstop for the Dodgers and Blue Jays over an 18-year career starting in 1976, said he was given advice on this score from Hall of Famer Rod Carew. "He tells us that you got to show that you can play every day," Griffin said. "He said if we wanted to make it, we could give them no excuse to get rid of us." (Quoted in Klein, 94.)

Clemente ran afoul of the media periodically because he suffered from several nagging injuries. He was branded a hypochondriac, something else that infuriated him. Over the long term, however, Clemente grew into a bigger and bigger star with his all-around hitting, running, fielding, and throwing skills and his true personality emerged from behind the wall of Spanish. Pittsburgh embraced him. Then the world of baseball embraced and appreciated him.

Clemente was selected to 12 All-Star teams. He accumulated 240 home runs and 1,305 runs batted in while batting .317. He earned four batting titles, played on two World Series champions and was Most Valuable Player in the 1971 Series. It seemed he could do anything on the field and morphed into a clubhouse leader off of it, particularly in tutoring young Latino players. But Clemente's magnificence transcended race and heritage.

"During my career, Roberto Clemente of the Pirates has been consistently the toughest of all the great players against the Cubs," wrote Chicago Hall of Famer Ernie Banks in a newspaper column when both men were still active. "When you play the Pirates in Pittsburgh and a ball is either hit to right field or if you're on first when there's a base hit out there, it calls for extreme caution. Roberto, who plays a shallow right field, has been known to throw out batters at first base on drives hit on the ground." (Quoted in Banks.)

Clemente never wanted to be anything other than a baseball player when he was growing up, and he was good right away. By the time he was 12, he was holding his own with much older players. "Roberto was born to play baseball," said his mother, Luisa Walker de Clemente. "I can remember when he was five years old. He used to buy rubber balls every time he had a chance. He played in his room, throwing the ball against the wall and trying to catch it. There were times he was so much in love with baseball that he didn't even care for food."

In the scrapbook his mother kept, there was a passage in an article where Clemente reminisced about his youth. He described a game that lasted 7½ hours, and he said he hit 10 home runs during that game. (Quoted in Carmona.)

Although misunderstandings and misperceptions clouded Clemente's relations with sportswriters—and often through them, with fans—at various times Clemente expressed his gratitude to Pirates fans. "People there (Pittsburgh) are my friends," Clemente said. "They cheer me and this peps me up. Funny thing, I play better before large crowds. It does something to me. I seem to let down with small crowds. Applause stirs me up, helps me." (Quoted in Biederman, "Hitting . . .")

Clemente batted just .255 as a rookie. He posted his first .300 season the next year, but it took until 1960, when the Pirates won the world championship, for Clemente to become a regular .300 hitter. As he matured, he improved at the plate and in all facets of the game. He worked hard and at a time when he was still struggling for national recognition maintained no false modesty about where he felt he belonged in the mix of best players. If no one else was going to pump him up, Clemente, whenever asked, said what he thought about his ranking.

The only thing he couldn't measure up to against the Willie Mays', Hank Aarons, and Mickey Mantles was in hitting home runs. He never would, either, as long as he played in cavernous Forbes Field, which did not offer such inviting outfield targets as were available in those others' home parks.

"I believe I can hit with anybody in baseball," Clemente said. "Maybe I can't hit with the power of a Mays or a Frank Robinson or a Hank Aaron, but I can hit. As long as I play in Forbes Field I can't go for home runs. Line drives, yes, but not home runs. I'm a better fielder than anybody you can name. I have great respect for Mays, but I can go get a ball like Willie and I have a better arm." (Quoted in Biederman, "Clouter . . .")

Clemente tried to be a big brother to other Latin players when they arrived in the majors. Sometimes he was even protective of them during interviews. On one occasion, when New York Mets outfielder Joe Christopher (who broke in with Pittsburgh) was being interviewed pre-game on the field on the topic of why it seemed to take a long time for some Latino players to reach their potential, Clemente jumped in and answered the question.

"We need time to get adjusted here like you would need time to get adjusted in our countries," Clemente said in 1964. "In the early days, segregation baffled us, but this has eased very much in recent years. You have no idea how this held some of us back, however. The people who never run into these problems have no idea at all what kind of an ordeal this can be." (Quoted in Biederman, "Latin . . .")

Clemente rose above all challenges to imprint his name, face, personality, and accomplishments into the fabric of Pittsburgh. On July 24, 1970, 15 years after Clemente joined the team, the Pirates held a "Roberto Clemente Night," complete with gifts and honors. In part, the message in the program read, "Tonight we honor you, Roberto Clemente. You have had many special 'nights' on the playing field, but this is something different. Tonight we pay tribute to you as the complete ballplayer, the legitimate superstar, and a polished performer with the glove and the bat.

"We thank you for the thrills you have given us—the clutch line drive, the sliding catch, the spectacular throw and the extra base you dared to take. Pittsburgh is proud you are a Pirate." (Quoted in "Roberto Clemente . . .")

Less than a month later, Clemente revealed details of a frightening criminal incident that took place a year earlier in San Diego. Clemente told a story of being kidnapped in May 1969 by four armed men, who forced him at gunpoint into a car near the Pirates' team hotel. He had just come back from a restaurant and was carrying leftover chicken in a bag.

Clemente said that once in the car the men ordered him to strip to his undershorts and threatened him by putting a pistol in his mouth. He realized some of the men were Spanish-speaking and he conversed with them in their own tongue. He told them he was a baseball player but didn't tell them his name. He thought he might be killed, but he kept talking and said it was fine to take his $250, but no death was worth any amount of money.

Somehow, Clemente proved more persuasive than expected. The robbers returned his clothes and money and let him go. They began driving off but then circled around, and he got worried they were coming back after him. Instead, he said, the men reached out the window and handed him his bag of chicken before driving off.

Clemente said he never reported the confrontation to the police and told only a few members of the Pirates about it. He went public in the interests of accuracy, he said, when the story began to make the rounds.

"Why should I report it?" he said. "I am alive, no? I got everything back that they took, all my money, my All-Star ring, everything. They didn't hurt me and nobody knew about it." Clemente said part of him thought the men would shoot him and dump his body in the woods, but at the same time he was never truly afraid. "I knew nothing was going to happen to me," he said. "I knew for sure. I don't know why. I can't explain it. I just knew." (Quoted in Christine.)

Given what loomed on the not-so-distant horizon for Clemente's fate, the superstitious might say the emotions were connected to an awareness that he was destined to do bigger things with his life considering how he exited this earth.

Some of those bigger things were on the diamond. The 1971 Pirates were champions of the National League, but not favored to beat the Baltimore Orioles in the World Series. Clemente put his team on his broad shoulders and guided the group to an unexpected championship. Clemente hit in all seven games of the Series and made spectacular plays in the field. Clemente became the first Latin

American player to win the Series MVP award. But beyond that, the fun-loving Pirates were a team that incorporated the largest racial mix of players on one club to date. The team was a showcase for racial harmony. Besides Clemente, such Latino players as Manny Sanguillen and Jose Pagan shared the roster with blacks like Willie Stargell, Al Oliver, and Doc Ellis, and whites like Richie Hebner. At one point during the regular season manager Danny Murtaugh started nine players with dark skin. It was the first time in Major League history. Clemente played his usual right field that day.

Not only were the Pirates feted in Pittsburgh after defeating the 101-win Orioles team, but when Clemente returned to Puerto Rico after the triumph he was mobbed. His jet plane was surrounded on the runway at San Juan International Airport as thousands of fans greeted him. "It makes me feel good to know that the people have always been with me and I feel that the people of Puerto Rico (realize) that I try my best while representing them in the States," Clemente said. "If not, it would be an empty victory." (Quoted in Stevens and Beltzer.)

By October 1971 Clemente had given considerable thought to what he could do beyond entertaining fans with baseball to help the lives of the less fortunate. He took advantage of the forum he was given as the Series MVP to announce that he had grander aspirations than simply winning baseball championships. He said "the biggest ambition of my life" was to build a sports city to benefit the children of Puerto Rico. Clemente, 37 at the time, said he would quit baseball right away if the funding for such a project materialized. Clemente chose this avenue to make a difference after years of working with deprived children, many of them from one-parent households. "One of the biggest problems we have today," he said, "is the father doesn't have time for the kids and they lose control over the children." (Quoted in Chass.)

In Clemente's vision children would have constructive activities to keep them off the streets, and they might also develop into top-flight athletes with good coaching to follow their dreams to professional sports.

Clemente did not retire after his glorious 1971 season. He had at least one milestone to go in capping his career. He entered the 1972 baseball season 118 hits shy of 3,000. The 3,000 hits level for a hitter is a special mark. It states that a batter has been a first-class hitter for a long time. Hitters who attain that figure are automatic Hall of Famers.

A total of 118 hits in a season was not ordinarily a great feat for Clemente. He exceeded that number in 16 different seasons. However, the 1972 season was not an easy one for Puerto Rican star. He dealt with injuries and played in only 102 of the Pirates' 162 games. As it so happened, Clemente was still just shy of the needed 118 entering the last game of the season on September 30. Pittsburgh was at Philadelphia, and it was a game won, 4–3, by the Pirates. Attendance

Quotations from and about Roberto Clemente

Among Latino baseball fans and players, Roberto Clemente is the king, the ultimate royalty of Hispanic heritage. He is the symbol of greatness for players who hail not only from his native Puerto Rico but for all Spanish-speaking players from Latin America. In the nearly four decades since his premature death in a 1972 plane crash, Clemente has been elevated to near-sainthood in the Hispanic world.

With neither the man nor a body to pay homage to, Clemente's deeds, words, and actions live on through those inspired by him.

Roberto Clemente Said

"Nobody does anything better than me in baseball." (Before the 1971 World Series in which he batted .414 and was the MVP of the Series.) (Quoted in *Baseball Almanac*.)

"When I put on my uniform, I feel I am the proudest man on earth." (Quoted in *Baseball Almanac*.)

"The sportswriters make it 'Me Tarzan, you Jane.'" (Clemente's objections to how his speech was portrayed in the media.) (Quoted in Maraniss, 174.)

"Nobody can say Roberto is mean. I might look mean, but I really respect people." (Upon being told his frown scares some people.) (Quoted in Maraniss, 172.)

"I don't want to get 3,000 hits to pound my chest and holler, 'Hey, I got it!' What it means is I didn't fail with the ability I had." (Quoted in Maraniss, 279.)

What Others Said about Roberto Clemente

"He was a baseball machine." (Pirates teammate Steve Blass.) (Quoted in *Beisbol*.)

"He was a better person than he was a player—and that says a lot." (Pirates teammate Al Oliver.) (Quoted in Beisbol.)

"He gave the term 'complete' a new meaning. He made the word 'superstar' seem inadequate. He had about him the touch of royalty." (Baseball Commissioner Bowie Kuhn in a eulogy.) (Quoted in *Baseball Almanac*.)

Further Reading
Besibol—The Latin Game, movie, 2007.
Maraniss, David, *Clemente: The Passion and Grace of Baseball's Last Hero*, New York, Simon & Schuster, 2006.
www.baseball-almanac.com

was just 14,157. Clemente made outs in his first three plate appearances but singled off of Phillies' hurler Bill Wilson in his fourth at-bat. The season ended with Clemente precisely at a career total of 3,000 hits. He would be able to add to it the next season and pass a number of star players on the all-time list.

Only next season never arrived.

Just after Christmas in 1972 a massive earthquake struck Managua, Nicaragua. Clemente lent his name to the relief effort in Puerto Rico, and he also was hands-on in gathering medical and food supplies to deliver to the injured and homeless in the Central American country. On New Year's Eve, December 31, when a rickety, overstocked airplane took off from Puerto Rico to deliver the relief supplies, Clemente was aboard.

The plane crashed into the Atlantic Ocean on take-off, killing Clemente and others on the mercy mission. Clemente's body was never found. His wife Vera, his three elementary school-aged sons that grew up without a father, and all of baseball, mourned him then and mourn him still.

"He had about him the touch of royalty," said then-Baseball Commissioner Bowie Kuhn. (Quoted in "He Had . . .")

Testimonials to Clemente flooded newspaper columns and the air waves. "His work with the relief effort was typical," said Pirates teammate Willie Stargell. "Roberto was always trying to help someone." Pirates General Manager Joe L. Brown said, "We have lost not only a great baseball player, but a very wonderful human being." (Quoted in "He Had . . .")

In the years that have passed since Clemente's death, his legacy has only grown stronger. His face has appeared on a United States postage stamp. His sports city was built in Puerto Rico. And on each milestone anniversary of his death, old teammates, players, and younger generations of Latin ballplayers take a moment to pay respects and recall the player many refer to simply as "The Great One."

Further Reading

Banks, Ernie, "Ernie Banks Rates Clemente Toughest Star He Ever Faced," *Chicago Tribune*, July 6, 1968.

Biederman, Les, "Clouter Clemente Popular Buc," *The Sporting News*, September 5, 1964.

———, "Hitting In Daylight (.411 Versus .302) Best For Clemente," *Pittsburgh Press*, March 11, 1962.

———, "Latin Player Faces Many Tough Barriers in U.S., Roberto says," *The Sporting News*, September 5, 1964.

Carmona, Emilio, "Clemente Once Hit 10 Homers in One Game," *San Juan Star*, June 26, 1960.

Chass, Murray, "Clemente's Dream: A Utopian Sports City," *New York Times*, October 21, 1971.

Christine, Bill, "Clemente Reveals Close Call With Kidnappers," *Pittsburgh Press*, August 22, 1970.

"He Had The Touch of Royalty," *Newsday*, January 2, 1973.

Klein, Alan M., *Sugarball: The American Game, The Dominican Dream* (New Haven, Connecticut, Yale University, 1991).

Maraniss, David, *Clemente: The Passion and Grace of Baseball's Last Hero* (New York, Simon & Schuster, 2006).

Roberto Clemente Night Program, Pittsburgh Pirates, July 24, 1970.

Ruck, Rob, *The Tropic of Baseball* (Westport, Connecticut, Meckler Books, 1991).

Stevens, Tito and Beltzer, Yvonne, "Clemente Gets Hero's Welcome," *San Juan Star*, October 22, 1971.

Martin Dihigo

The shame of Martin Dihigo's brilliant baseball career is how little remembered he is today among average baseball fans in the United States. Asked to identify him, a ballpark devotee might only shake his head, face blank in response to the mystery of the name. The modern spectator does not know the name, the statistics, or any of the calling cards that led to Dihigo's election to the National Baseball Hall of Fame.

Cuban great Martin Dihigo never played in the majors because of his skin color and the discrimination governing baseball before 1947, but he is revered throughout Latin America as one of the most versatile pitcher-hitters of all time, and he was chosen for the Hall of Fame in 1977. (Transcendental Graphics/Getty Images)

But if any man can muster credentials to challenge Babe Ruth as the greatest all-around hitter-pitcher in the history of baseball, it is the Cuban superstar. Dihigo was born too soon, too far away, and with the wrong color skin pigmentation to be appreciated in the United States.

Yet he is catalogued as the most versatile and accomplished multitalented player to ever wear spikes in Latin countries and to star in the U.S. Negro Leagues. Dihigo was both a contemporary of and an equal to Satchel Paige, Josh Gibson, Buck Leonard, and Cool Papa Bell among luminaries whose abilities made them famous to Latin American and African-American audiences despite being shunned by Major League baseball.

Was Dihigo a better pitcher than Paige? Probably not. Was Dihigo a more powerful batsman than Gibson? Probably not. Was Dihigo a faster runner than Bell? Not likely. But Dihigo was worthy of a slot in the comparative discussion with each of the other superstars in their specialties. Dihigo hit over .300 and as a right-handed pitcher mowed down hitters. He could play the infield or outfield, run with speed, and throw with accuracy. When scouts eye young talent they talk of the ideal player being a five-tool talent. Dihigo was a five-tool talent as a position player, plus one—he could also pitch. And when his legs lost their spring he used still another talent, his brain power, to manage teams.

"He was the only guy I ever saw who could play all nine positions, manage, run and switch hit," said Hall of Fame first baseman Johnny Mize. (Quoted in Anderson.)

Dihigo was born in Matanzas, Cuba on May 25, 1906. He died in Ciefguegos, Cuba, May 20, 1971. The distance between the two island communities was not so great and Dihigo would certainly have been a greater traveler if Major League Baseball's policy of banning black-skinned players from its rosters did not coincide with Dihigo's playing years between 1922 (when he was still 16) and 1947. Cities with the brightest lights and biggest ballparks like New York, Chicago, Philadelphia, and St. Louis would have been his playgrounds if societal mores had been more liberal and civilized at the time. Instead, Dihigo was more of an in-the-shadows phenomenon in the United States with the Homestead Grays and the Cuban Stars, making his mark outside the view of mainstream media.

Dihigo glowed most brilliantly in Cuba and throughout Latin America, where he was a virtual deity for his prowess. Dihigo was blessed with the seemingly perfect athletic physique of 6-foot-3 and somewhere between 185 and 200 pounds, which did not hurt him during an era before weightlifting and when players were generally of smaller stature.

During winter league play in Cuba for the 1926–27 season, Dihigo batted .413. During the 1927–28 season, he hit .415.

In 1932 and 1934, while pitching in Venezuela, Dihigo tossed no-hitters. In 1935, Dihigo played in the first East-West Classic, the Negro Leagues All-Star game. In 1937, while playing for Vera Cruz, he pitched a no-hitter in Mexico. The next year Dihigo recorded a six-for-six day at the plate and led the Mexican League in hitting. All the while he posted double-figure seasons in home runs. In 1938, Dihigo won the Mexican League batting title with a .387 average, but also notched a 0.90 earned run average with an 18–2 pitching mark. In 1939, Dihigo posted an 18-strikeout game.

Some statistics in Dihigo's career are sketchy, but he is generally credited with batting over .300 for his entire winter and summer leagues combined career in various countries. Various sources suggest Dihigo won between 205 and 260 games on the mound, but the research of esteemed Latin American baseball historian Peter C. Bjarkman's produced a claimed record of 288–142. The popular nickname attached to Dihigo by his Latin American teammates and fans was "El Maestro," The Master, and the numbers alone suggest the reason why.

Handsome, with a long face and penetrating eyes, Dihigo was a matinee idol of sorts, as well. There is little evidence that he was voluble, but he was not above demonstrative displays of glee when he did something well on the field. Out-smarting the opposition, whether by using the hidden ball trick to pick a man off second base or yelling at a pitcher, was just part of Dihigo's vast repertoire. He was such a good all-around baseball player that he sounds like the dashing figure who stars in a series of ads for a certain Mexico beer claiming to be "The Most Interesting Man in the World." For many, Dihigo was definitely the most interesting man in baseball.

Long-time Philadelphia sports promoter and professional team owner Eddie Gottlieb raved about Dihigo. "Martin Dihigo was one of the greatest black players who ever lived," Gottlieb said. "He could play any position. In fact, I saw him over a period of two or three games—I saw him do everything. I saw him one day (at the Phillies' Shibe Park) stand up against the fence and rifle a ball in on a line right to the catcher, as accurate as it could be. Great all-around player." (Quoted in Petition . . .)

When the great Boston Red Sox slugger Ted Williams was inducted into the Baseball Hall of Fame in 1966, his acceptance speech urged selectors to open the Hall to the many black stars of the past who had been denied the opportunity to play in the majors because of racism. The Hall soon began the process of accepting nominations and inducting several such stars. In 1974, municipal officials and newspapermen in Dihigo's home town in Cuba mounted a campaign to gain him recognition. Their petition quoted many notables from the sport endorsing his worthiness.

"Any baseball fans of the black leagues will admit, as will any player, that the greatest all-around player, ever, was the Latin giant, Martin Dihigo," said Hall of

Famer Monte Irvin, a Dihigo contemporary in the Negro Leagues and in Latin American play. (Quoted in Petition . . .)

Voters did soon acknowledge Dihigo's greatness by installing him in the National Baseball Hall of Fame in Cooperstown, New York in 1977. Meanwhile, almost any country where Dihigo took a swing during his career recognized his brilliant play, and Dihigo is also a member of halls of fame in Venezuela, Cuba, Mexico, and the Dominican Republic.

Like many of the Cuban baseball stars who followed him, Dihigo came from no great wealth and as a teenager was more interested in playing baseball than doing anything else. He was not yet 17 when he began playing with a Cuban club in 1922, and his ability was noted by such black baseball stars of the period as Oscar Charleston and John Henry "Pop" Lloyd. They supported him; and if Dihigo was rough around the edges at the plate because of his inexperience, within a year he was making himself known on the island.

It did not take long for Dihigo to emerge as the best player in Cuba and his services were in demand everywhere but in Major League baseball. Dihigo played ball year-round, following the bouncing ball through the winter leagues and summer leagues with teams in various countries that offered the best pay-checks. When fans, sports writers, and the like were not referring to Dihigo as "El Maestro," he was described as "El Immortal," The Immortal.

Youngsters who desired to make it big in baseball revered Dihigo as a role model. One of them was Orestes "Minnie" Minoso, who did gain stardom in the majors in the United States after growing up poor in Cuba. Minoso, who moved to Havana to be raised by relatives after the death of his parents, was a small boy with big aspirations when he was young. He attached himself to Dihigo with enthusiasm. "Dihigo once let me carry his shoes and glove and that's how I got into the ballpark down there when I was kid," Minoso said. "He was a big man, all muscle, with not an ounce of fat on him. He helped me by teaching me to play properly. It is difficult to explain what a great hero he was in Cuba." (Quoted in Bjarkman, "Martin . . .")

Dihigo followed the sun as a ballplayer. Eventually, opportunity led him to the United States. There is nothing to suggest that Dihigo felt going to the Negro Leagues was much of a change from his usual country-hopping. He signed with the Cuban Stars, but found out there was one major difference in the United States. He encountered racism of a kind he never experienced in Latino nations.

"My first contract with the Cuban Stars was $100 a month," Dihigo said of his 1920s U.S. debut. To him that was good money. However, he had to wonder if the payday was worth the aggravation that came with it. "But more than all that, I began to experience first-hand the hatred of gringos, going through lots of hardships and vexations and having to struggle daily for subsistence." (Quoted in Burgos, 120.)

The treatment may have surprised Dihigo, but it was no surprise to American black players, whether they had grown up in the South or in other regions of the country. Players traveled to away games by bus and frequently had to stop for roadside luncheons. In most places during the first half of the twentieth century, black players were not welcome inside those restaurants. And when they arrived at their destination, there was a very good chance the black players would be housed in black-owned hotels or in private homes owned by black baseball fans. No distinction was made between blacks from the United States and blacks from Latin America. The problem was compounded because the Latinos in many cases did not speak English. But they were viewed more as foreign invaders than foreign guests.

Dihigo was born too soon to be accepted by the majors, retiring from active play just two years before Jackie Robinson broke the American game's color barrier. "Of all the dark-skinned Cubans who faced bitter rejection from baseball's hypocritical barons of the pre-World War II epoch, none had more reason to grieve than mountainous Martin Dihigo—the Babe Ruth, Christy Mathewson and Ty Cobb of Cuba rolled into one massive, black-skinned frame," wrote historian and Latin American baseball expert Bjarkman. "The . . . Cuban giant was perhaps the most versatile player ever in any country, in any epoch, in any league!" (Quoted in Bjarkman, "Baseball . . ." 16–17.)

In addition, Bjarkman, a great admirer of Dihigo, wrote, "Of the legendary dark-skinned Latino stars none has greater mythic stature than Cuba's Martin Dihigo." (Quoted in Bjarkman, "Baseball . . ." 172.)

Bjarkman contends that baseball's racial policies robbed Dihigo not only of the wealth and fame he was due but also deprived him of the positive statistical proof of his greatness because he was often stuck playing in leagues that did not keep accurate records. The assertion is valid. Baseball, above all other sports, is a strict caretaker of its records, a stickler for accuracy and more than any other sport has fans who have bought into the notion of being able to compare different eras of competition based on numbers. There is much hue and cry now as baseball seeks to come to terms with the recent steroid era and the validity of home runs and other power numbers posted by players later found to be using performance-enhancing drugs.

In the case of U.S. black players and Latinos who were banned from the sport, it is impossible to know what types of records they would have recorded. The absence of play cannot be measured numerically; as a result, players like Dihigo are forever doomed to being discussed in conjecture. No doubt even more infuriating for a talent such as Dihigo was the knowledge that he would have been accepted in the majors if he was a Cuban of lighter skin hue. The evidence, in the person of Adolfo Luque, and his two decades long Major League career, stared Dihigo right in his black face. Luque was accepted in the 1920s and beyond because he was lighter skinned, not because he was a better ballplayer. They were two men, contemporaries from Cuba, from towns located approximately 50 miles apart, but, logically or not, destined to live out different fates in baseball.

Cristobal Torriente was another tremendous Cuban ballplayer of the pre–World War II era whose skin was too dark to earn him a place on a Major League roster. Torriente and Dihigo were friends and teammates at different times, both knowing, like so many other black U.S. stars, that they belonged in the big time. Clear victims of injustice, it was not easy for a man to cope with the discrimination that prevented him from making a better living and gaining more widespread recognition of his skills. Although it is not clear if this contributed to Torriente's demise, he became addicted to alcohol; in the late 1930s, Dihigo and another player found him on a street in Chicago. Dihigo brought Torriente to New York and tried to help him, but Torriente would not stop drinking and died in 1938. Even fewer baseball fans outside of Cuba and Latin America recognize Torriente's name today than Dihigo's. (Quoted in Bjarkman, "Baseball . . ." 179.)

It is Dihigo's name that still resonates among the oldest Cuban baseball fans, those who have researched his career, and those who had the chance to talk baseball with his contemporaries before they died off in recent decades. "He was the greatest all-around player I know," said Buck Leonard, the Hall of Fame first baseman who was called "The Black Lou Gehrig" and who died in 1997. Leonard believes Dihigo might have been greater than anyone who played before or since. "I'd say he was the best ballplayer of all time, black or white," he said. (Quoted in Bjarkman, "Baseball . . ." 219.)

Max Manning, a pitcher who played for the Newark Eagles in the Negro Leagues, but also played under Dihigo when the older man was a manager in Mexico, said he was very impressed by the Cuban and wishes he had seen him play during his younger years rather than as a fill-in player-manager in middle age. "He was a marvelous physical specimen—height, weight, broad shoulders," Manning said. "You could see the power that this man had. One regret I have is that I never saw Martin Dihigo play in his prime." (Quoted in Holway, 127.)

Interest in the Negro Leagues and how Latino players performed in their home countries during winter ball was almost non-existent when Dihigo was at the top of his game. Starting in the 1970s, baseball historians began to delve more deeply into the lives and skills of unknown terrific players whose exploits were spread by word of mouth among surviving older guys. By that time Dihigo had passed away and his voice was never truly heard. Unsolicited testimonials about his abilities piled up in interviews with elderly former players such as Burnis "Wild Bill" Wright, a former Nashville Elite Giant who also played in Mexico, who said that Dihigo was the best player he saw.

Wright is one of several who mentioned Dihigo. "I think Martin Dihigo was the best player because he could hit, he could pitch, he could play first base, he could play outfield, he could play second base," Wright said. "Big guy, too—about 6–5 (actually closer to 6–3). He could throw. He could bring it about 92 (mph)." (Quoted in Kelley, 30.)

Dihigo's style and grace left impressions on his teammates and foes that even years and years later could recall the way he could beat an opponent with his bat, glove, or arm. Some remembered his mound work better than other attributes. Some favored his hitting. But many raved about his qualities. "Dihigo . . . he could do almost anything," said one-time Homestead Grays catcher Josh Johnson. (Quoted in Kelley, 39.)

It was Dihigo's misfortune to come along too early to gain the widespread recognition that would have come by playing in the majors. After Dihigo's death, his prime years as an athlete often could not be remembered by surviving contemporaneous players when historians interviewed them. Dihigo pre-dated many of their careers, or overlapped them only partially, when he was an aging ballplayer and they were young and on the way up. Dihigo's reputation preceded him, but it was like catching up to Willie Mays in his final days with the New York Mets as opposed to watching him run free in centerfield during his glory days in the Polo Grounds for the New York Giants.

Mahlon Duckett was only 17 when he joined the Philadelphia Stars in 1940. Dihigo was nearing the end of his career. Duckett said he could tell Dihigo still had it even if he was slowing down. "Martin Dihigo, he could do everything," Duckett said. "I played against him, but I played against him when he was a little older and he was still great then." (Quoted in Kelley, 94.)

The main evidence that Dihigo possessed a certain degree of showmanship or vanity are the reports that many times he played nine different positions in a game. This has been done very rarely at the Major League level—Bert Campaneris and Cesar Tovar come to mind. Dihigo's weakest position was catcher, but he didn't mind dropping onto his haunches for an inning or so.

Dihigo last took a swing in earnest in 1947, but he was very much a man of his country. He supported Fidel Castro's revolution—and knew him personally. To protest the regime of Fulgencio Batista, Dihigo did not return to Cuba from 1952 until after Castro took over the government in 1959. Dihigo managed teams in several Latin American countries for years after his playing days, and he became a baseball instructor in Cuba after Castro eliminated professional baseball.

Dihigo was living with his son Martin Jr. in Cienfuegos when his health began failing. He was in and out of the hospital many times before he died in May 1971. (Quoted in Bjarkman, "Martin . . .")

Dihigo remains a baseball legend in Cuba, Mexico, and other Latin American lands. Regrettably, despite his achievements, he has never become a widely known name in the United States.

Further Reading

Anderson, Dave, "In Old Cuba With Dihigo And Lasorda," *New York Times*, March 23, 1999.

Bjarkman, Peter C., "Martin Dihigo: Baseball's Least-Known Hall of Famer," *Elysian Fields Quarterly*, Spring, 2001.

————, *Baseball With A Latin Beat* (Jefferson, North Carolina, McFarland & Company, Inc., Publishers, 1994).

Burgos Jr., Adrian, *Playing America's Game* (Berkeley, California, University of California Press, 2007).

Holway, John B., *Black Diamonds* (Westport, Connecticut, Meckler Publishing, 1989).

Kelley, Brent, *Voices From the Negro Leagues* (Jefferson, North Carolina, McFarland & Company, Publishers, 1998).

Petition for inclusion of Martin Dihigo in the Baseball Hall of Fame, July 20, 1974.

Ozzie Guillen

When he was a young player with the Chicago White Sox, Ozzie Guillen fielded ground balls with All-Star skill. As the first Major League Venezuelan manager, also with the White Sox, he fields questions from the media with the same type of All-Star aplomb.

To listen to Guillen expound on his team, opponents, the sport, and his own life during his daily chats with beat writers prior to White Sox games is to be treated to a stand-up comedian during open-microphone appearances. Guillen wears his emotions on his sleeve and he says whatever comes into his head. He can make listeners laugh and make them think. In early 2010, Guillen added Twitter messages to his repertoire and gained thousands of followers. If ever a sports figure was worthy of his own television show, it is Guillen. "I will tell the truth, whether you like it or not," Guillen said. (Quoted in Price.)

Occasionally, it may be the truth just for a moment, such as when a frustrated Guillen announces he doesn't need managing and might quit at the end of the season. Or an exasperated Guillen who doesn't think his boss, general manager Kenny Williams, is providing enough talent to win the American League Central Division. On such occasions, Guillen might be better off with adhesive tape over his mouth until his emotions cool. But Ozzie wouldn't be Ozzie if he was not blunt about everything that swirls around in his life. And the stress of keeping silent

One of the most colorful figures in the game, Chicago White Sox manager Ozzie Guillen of Venezuela became the first Latino field leader to win a World Series in 2005. Guillen, an American League Rookie of the Year as a player, and a sharp fielder, is shown here high-fiving former Sox player Orlando Cabrera in celebration during the 2008 season. Guillen brought the World Series trophy home to Venezuela to show it off. (AP Photo/Brian Kersey)

would likely give the energetic, shoot-first-and-ask-questions-later Guillen a heart attack.

Sometimes Guillen can be inflammatory in his remarks. He said Alex Rodriguez had no right to play for the Dominican team in the World Baseball Classic because he grew up in Miami. But Rodriguez was eligible because of his heritage. He slammed former White Sox outfielder Magglio Ordonez over a perceived slight. But Guillen has a unique, humorous manner of getting his point across when mentioning every-day occurrences with his team. One day Chicago relief pitcher Scott Linebrink essentially called in sick. He said he couldn't pitch that day because of a headache. Guillen said he believed Linebrink's excuse. "I believe him because he's a real religious guy," Guillen said. "Someone else tells me they have a migraine, I know they are hung over." (Quoted in "They Said It.")

Oswaldo Jose Barrios Guillen was born in Oculaire Del Tuy, Venezuela in 1964. As many of his countrymen did, he aspired to play Major League baseball and like so many youngsters at home he dreamed of becoming a shortstop. Following in the footsteps of Chico Carrasquel, whom Guillen called his hero, and Luis Aparicio, whom he knew well after playing for Aparicio's father's team, and Davey Concepcion, the shortstop for the Cincinnati Reds' Big Red Machine teams of the 1970s, Guillen did make it in pro ball playing the position Venezuelans most venerate.

Guillen was regarded in baseball circles as a hot, young talent, but White Sox fans did not know anything about his game or his bubbly personality when he was acquired at the end of his minor league days in late 1984 as part of a six-player trade that sent Cy Young Award-winning pitcher LaMarr Hoyt to the San Diego Padres. While fans were skeptical, Guillen made the deal pay off—and continues to do so because of his long, successful association with the Sox.

Guillen stepped in as the White Sox's starting shortstop in 1985. Playing in 150 games, Guillen batted .273 and fielded a league-leading .990. He was chosen the American League Rookie of the Year. The Guillen award provided redemption to White Sox general manager Roland Hemond, who engineered the controversial trade. "I took some flak for that deal," Hemond said, "but it worked out just great for us. Wherever I went to speak during the season and since the end, people have told me he reminds me of Luis Aparicio. You can't say anything finer than that." Aparicio was elected to the National Baseball Hall of Fame just the year before. "You will seldom see anyone play the game with more enthusiasm than Ozzie. He's going to be a big favorite in Chicago for a long time." (Quoted in Lang.)

Hemond was dead-on with his prediction about Guillen's longevity and popularity in Chicago. Probably just because he came from Venezuela and was not very tall or heavy at 5-foot-11, 150 pounds, Guillen was compared to Aparicio in Chicago even before he began playing for the White Sox. But Guillen never made the comparison. He recognized Aparicio was a superior player with a gaudier record and this was one time he was careful not to say anything that might unintentionally antagonize a man he held in high esteem.

When Guillen was sent to Chicago in the trade, he did contact Aparicio and ask for information and advice about his new city. He did not encourage the idea that he was "the next Aparicio," which sportswriters seized upon. "I've never seen him play," said Guillen, who was 21 at the time, 12 years after Aparicio's retirement. "But he told me a lot about Chicago. I'm not going to try to play like him. I just want to keep my job and help the team win. If people say I'm a super shortstop and we lose, it doesn't mean anything. If we win, they don't care how good I am. It's too early to say I'm better than Luis Aparicio, or that I'll play 18 years like him. I'm just trying to stay in the big leagues." (Quoted in van Dyck, "Guillen Shrugs . . .")

Ironically, Guillen was the type of hitter that as a manager he hates to send to the plate—a free-swinger who doesn't have the patience to wait for walks. During his final year in AAA ball at Las Vegas, Guillen had 463 at-bats and walked only 13 times. Guillen never had a very good on-base percentage in the majors, but in 16 seasons, 13 of them with the White Sox, he collected 1,764 hits and batted .264.

Guillen's first All-Star selection came in 1988. In a sense that put him on the map. In 1990 and 1991, both years during which Guillen hit in the .270s, he was also chosen for the All-Star game. His excellent range and flashy pick-ups won him the spots more than anything. It became clear that he had grown into the heart and soul of the White Sox and his energy was contagious. "Ozzie's the MVP," said Detroit Tiger manager Sparky Anderson in 1990. (Quoted in Sherman.)

"Ozzie" was not a common name, but it just so happened that the best short-stop in the National League was Ozzie Smith, the St. Louis Cardinals' fielder who was on his way to the Hall of Fame. Ozzie Guillen played in the American League and was searching for his own recognition. At the end of several seasons, Guillen felt he was deserving of a Gold Glove for his fielding, but by 1990 he had not yet won one. "If I don't win this year, the hell with it," Guillen said. "There's too much political stuff. I've been overlooked before. I don't know why. Maybe they don't want to pick someone from a last-place team." (Quoted in Sherman.)

The White Sox were playing better and Guillen did win his only Gold Glove in 1990. "He's got great instincts," then-White Sox coach Ron Clark said of Guillen's glove work. "He knows where the ball is going to be hit. There's not a better shortstop in the league." (Quoted in Sherman.)

Guillen's bread and butter was his fielding. His capabilities with the glove made his reputation. He hit well enough not to be a liability at bat but went through periodic slumps that made White Sox coaches gulp. Scooping up grounders came naturally to Guillen but keeping the rhythm of his stance and swing did not. Unexpectedly at one point during the 1990 season, Guillen, never a serious home-run threat, had compiled three intentional walks. Typically, he joked about the situation. "Would you want to pitch to me?" he asked. However, only a season earlier pitchers were lining up to pitch to Guillen. He was out of sorts at the plate and highly regarded hitting coach Walt Hriniak cringed when Guillen stepped in to hit for the White Sox. "He was swinging at pitches the Good Lord couldn't hit," Hriniak said. Working with the knowledgeable hitting coach soothed Guillen and got him back on track. (Quoted in Sherman.)

By 1992, as a three-time All-Star, Guillen was established in the sport. He was also established in other players' minds as a chatterbox, a gabby Ozzie who never stopped talking. When *Sports Illustrated* wrote a feature on Guillen, it talked as much about his motor mouth as his motor skills in the field. Guillen and the writer even speculated about the possibility of him hosting a talk show in Venezuela.

He had clearly given thought to the idea, including such details as what time of day he wanted to be on the air. "Not 6:30 in the morning when everyone is going to work," Guillen said. "And not 12 o'clock at night when everyone is sleeping. You gotta give me a good hour. And I will talk about politics, what is going around Venezuela, problems. Not just about catching a ground ball. Yes, I am available for that. And when I open the show, what will I say? I will say, 'Let's talk about something!' " (Quoted in Hoffer.)

Guillen was blessed with quick hands and the gift of gab. Both came naturally to him. But Guillen practiced his conversational give-and-take, if not consciously for a talk show rehearsal then just because he felt like talking. He spoke to opposing runners who got to second base and he talked to White Sox infielders when their pitcher was in his windup. "He's non-stop, never shuts up," said White Sox third baseman Robin Ventura. Not one unspoken thought. He's talking about something he saw on TV, about the batter, about how some event here might translate in Venezuela. He's talking to me, he's talking to the umps, he's talking to fans, he's talking to base runners." (Quoted in Hoffer.)

He also talked to reporters in the clubhouse. Guillen became in the sportswriting trade what is known as a "go-to quote man." That meant simply that sportswriters hard up for someone to speak to after a hard loss would turn to Guillen because they always knew he was willing to talk despite disappointment. Guillen was visited often in good times, too, because he was entertaining. For all of the attention, Guillen never wavered in his comparison between himself and the other Venezuelan shortstop icons. He might tease by saying, "Already I am beyond compare," but then list Carrasquel, Aparicio, and Concepcion. Carrasquel he called "Pops." But Guillen slipped in a joke: "Ozzie, he is the richest." (Quoted in Hoffer.) Given the eras in which the men played and collected their big-league salaries that was indisputably true.

In 1998, Guillen played briefly for the Baltimore Orioles and then moved to the Atlanta Braves. He spent the 1999 season with the Braves and finished his playing career with the Tampa Bay Devil Rays in 2000. Early that year, shortly before Guillen changed teams, his homeland was devastated by tragedy. A torrent of rain pounding an 8,900-foot mountain outside of Caracas turned into a disaster area for nearby villages. The record rainfall created avalanche conditions and a swirling, angry combination of water, mud, and boulders crushed homes and slides swept them away.

Galvanized by the people's plight, Guillen raised $120,000 through his own foundation and worked to obtain another $50,000 in donations from other Latino baseball players, not all of whom sounded as if they were his friends beforehand. "Yeah, he has a big mouth," said Eddie Perez, a Guillen contemporary and catcher with the Braves. "He talks too much. But when you need something, he's right there for you. If you're ever in trouble, he's right there with you." (Quoted in "Guillen gives . . .")

Guillen, who was distraught and touched, inspected the affected area by helicopter and saw a father burying three children. His first-hand look at the destruction prompted him to commence the fundraising. "I wanted to give something back to these people," he said. "I wanted to make their lives a little better. What they need more than anything is love for their soul." (Quoted in "Guillen gives . . .")

The spunky shortstop showed his heart was in the right place, but his active career ended a few months later with 63 games played for Tampa Bay. The end of Guillen's playing days marked the end of one chapter in his career, but he became a coach with the Montreal Expos in 2002. A year later, Guillen was the third-base coach for the Florida Marlins when they won the World Series. Within weeks after the Series concluded, Guillen was back with the White Sox after being named their new manager for the 2004 season.

It was a grand and popular homecoming for an up-and-coming leader still shy of his 40th birthday. This was a dream come true for Guillen, who throughout his playing days told teammates he would one day become a Major League manager. One of those teammates was Kenny Williams, whose playing career was much briefer and less spectacular than Guillen's, but whose administrative career was on the rise. The general manager of the White Sox said he wasn't sure Guillen was the right guy for the job. "We knew he had the knowledge and gamesmanship," Williams said of Guillen's playing tenure, "but there was the goofball side of him and we thought that maybe no one would take him seriously." (Quoted in Greenstein, "White Sox . . .") Williams saw beyond Guillen's fun-loving side to determine he could very well take him seriously. Owner Jerry Reinsdorf, who always had a soft spot for Guillen, played a role in getting the message across that the young shortstop was now a wiser old head.

Guillen was thrilled to be re-joining the team he represented for so long and so well. "It's an honor for me to be back," he said. "I hope this is the last uniform I ever wear." He was explicit in what he expected from players. "When you come to this ballpark, you'll see that every player who wears this uniform is going to play the game right. If they don't, they won't play for me. I don't want selfish players. Give me players who want to win, not good players who don't care." (Quoted in Greenstein.)

Guillen always cared and he repeated this philosophy regularly in his early years as Sox manager. With his black, curly hair and thick mustache, Guillen looked distinguished but also retained a youthful appearance. From the start, in talking about players, the games, the situations, he was candid. Some thought he was a bit too candid when he sprinkled his commentaries with four-letter words. Guillen did not keep any secrets, however. He came right out and let it be known if a player was underperforming or disappointing him. If the player was coming through he earned praise for that.

There was some question about whether or not Guillen could co-exist with star slugger Frank Thomas, who was nearing the end of his long tenure with the White Sox, but in spring training of 2004, Guillen's first year, Thomas was a defender of Guillen as a savvy guy. "He has pulled every trick in the book and played forever," Thomas said. "Ozzie was up in the big leagues (when he was) around 18 years old. He knows what to expect and he knows when guys are (testing him)." (Quoted in Mullin.)

When Guillen was hired he announced that he was not going to change his stripes, and that he was going to be the same Ozzie Guillen that people had always known. He has remained true to his word. In some ways, just by gaining experience, Guillen did change—he worked to pick up the knowledge that a manager needs to succeed. He was learning on the job as a rookie manager. "Obviously, every day you learn something," Guillen said. "You learn something about the game. But I love it. I am always going to have fun in this game." (Quoted in van Dyck, "Guillen grades . . . ")

If people listened to Guillen every single day of the season, they would not believe that statement. Sometimes he suggested that his players would drive him nuts or give him an ulcer by not performing. When exasperated, he threatened to quit. Most of that talk was chalked up to Guillen's emotions. In 2005, his second season on the job, Guillen led the White Sox to the World Series title. It was the franchise's first title since 1917. Guillen was the toast of Chicago. He raised the championship trophy during a parade through the city's streets. Guillen received a congratulatory phone call from Venezuelan President Hugo Chavez, who told him, "I dare to say that you are like the king of Venezuela. Your triumph is the triumph of all Venezuela." (Quoted in "Guillen 'like . . . ' ") Then Guillen brought the trophy to Venezuela.

On January 20, 2006, however, Guillen was sworn in as an American citizen, along with his wife Ibis and oldest son Oney, who was born in Venezuela. Guillen's two other children were born in the United States.

The magic of 2005 was not immediately replicated, but Guillen also led the White Sox to playoff spots in 2007 and 2008. He was the same old Ozzie, sparking controversy with strong statements, making light of game happenings, commenting that sometimes his team was out to get him with its mistakes. Major League Baseball required Guillen to undergo sensitivity treatment after he insulted a former Chicago sports columnist with unwarranted language, but he never backed down from media repartee. In a 2006 interview with the HBO show "Real Sports with Bryant Gumbel," Guillen said, "I like trouble. Why not? A lot of people have their way to say stuff. I got my way. You know, all those little things about the game. People don't face it. Attack. Attack. I never take the first punch, never. Believe me, you throw me rocks, I'm gonna F-16 and just try to kill you. That's my style." (Quoted in Greenstein, "Guillen shoots . . .")

It is not Guillen's style to nursemaid his players, either. He has said that he loves his guys, but he apparently believes in tough love. As the White Sox began the second half of the 2009 season just a couple of games behind the American League Central Division-leading Tigers, Guillen provided a very direct assessment of a young starting pitcher who had been slumping. "This is not the Instructional League," he said. "I don't (want to) see another outing like the last few because we need to win." (Quoted in van Dyck, "Richard revival . . .") And of the centerfield spot that was giving him stomach pains, he said, "No matter who I put there, the same results (occur). Hopefully those guys out there make my life a little bit better." (Quoted in van Dyck, "Obama . . .")

Not so much sensitivity to the feelings of the pitcher or the outfielders, but Ozzie Guillen is never going to sugarcoat his thoughts. As he said, he needs to win.

Further Reading

Greenstein, Teddy, "Guillen shoots from hip in HBO interview," *Chicago Tribune*, February 5, 2006.

———, "White Sox name Ozzie Guillen their latest manager," *Chicago Tribune*, Nov. 3, 2003.

"Guillen 'like the king of Venezuela,' " Associated Press/United Press International, October 31, 2005.

"Guillen gives back to ravaged homeland," Associated Press, February 25, 2000.

Hoffer, Richard, "Heeeere's Ozzie!" *Sports Illustrated*, April 6, 1992.

Lang, Jack, "Guillen named AL's top rookie," *New York Daily News*, November 27, 1985.

Mullin, John, "Guillen playing to rave reviews; Humor, wisdom boost manager's stock as a leader," *Chicago Tribune*, March 22, 2004.

Price, S.L., "War of the Words," *Sports Illustrated*, February 20, 2006.

Sherman, Ed, "The world discovers the other Ozzie," *Chicago Tribune*, July 8, 1990.

"They Said It," *Sports Illustrated*, March 24, 2008.

van Dyck, "Obama makes nice pitch for marketing department," *Chicago Tribune*, July 19, 2009.

———, "Richard revival is vital," *Chicago Tribune*, July 19, 2009.

van Dyck, Dave, "Guillen grades himself an 'A,' " *Chicago Tribune*, May 31, 2004.

———, "Guillen Shrugs Off Aparicio Label," *The Sporting News*, April 29, 1985.

Adolfo Luque

If teammates with the Cincinnati Reds, Boston Braves, or other National League clubs Dolf Luque pitched for during a 20-year Major League career suggested that the Havana, Cuba-born righty danced to his own tune, they were correct. Not only did Luque carry a phonograph and a personal stash of Latin beat records with him in his luggage on road trips, he also taught dancing back home in the off-season.

Luque, whose nickname was "The Pride of Havana," was born in 1890 and broke into the majors in 1914 with a cameo appearance for the Braves. Luque's luck was that he was a light-skinned Latino, so he passed the color litmus test for U.S. professional ball during a time period when black-skinned players were forbidden to be signed.

Luque took up baseball as a young lad and also was immersed in the popular cockfighting culture of his home island at an early age, a hobby he kept up in adulthood. It might be said that Luque adopted the same take-no-prisoners attitude of his fighting roosters. In 1912 Luque began playing baseball professionally in Cuba. He was spotted by a Cuban businessman who also had interests in New Jersey, including a Long Branch baseball team in the New Jersey-New York State League. He brought Luque to the United States. An immediate success, Luque's pitching prowess was noted by Braves manager George Stallings during an exhibition game and Luque signed a contract.

Shown throwing for the New York Giants in 1933, right-hander Adolfo Luque of Cuba was the first Latin American star in the majors. In a 20-year career, primarily with Cincinnati, he won 194 games, including a league-leading 27 in 1923. Luque made his Major League debut with the Boston Braves in 1914. (AP Photo)

Although Luque spent most of the next couple of years in the minors, he became the first of what would be an unending stream of Latino stars to make an impression in the majors. Luque was not overly large, standing 5-foot-7 and weighing 160 pounds, and the fastball was not his main weapon. He possessed a superb curveball that was tricky enough to leave most batters flailing at the air. Luque kept his pitches low, except when he was aiming for a batter's head, and took pride in his thread-the-needle control.

Introduced by a college-aged student who had matriculated in the United States, baseball had been entrenched in Cuba for three decades. Leading up to the Spanish-American War in the late 1890s, Cubans, seeking to break away from Spain's yoke and hoping to establish a fresh identity, embraced baseball as something that had no connection to the imperial power. When American troops occupied the island some of the first diplomatic relations between Cuba and soldiers took place on the diamond.

Luque was said to have a fiery temperament and while that was a stereotype of the times, he was quick to anger. He spoke English as a second language, which is to say, at times broken but understood English, and he could make himself understood to impatient teammates with effort. Players marveled at the crispness of his curve and some asked where he learned to throw it so effectively. Luque replied with a word taken to be "Marty." The questioner said, "Who?" Luque took him for a dummy, saying, "What's the matter? You don't know Marty?" Marty was actually Matty, as in Hall of Fame pitcher Christy Mathewson.

Luque's first sip of Major League clubhouse coffee came with the Braves in 1914, when he appeared in two games and finished 0–1. He didn't get much more of a chance to pitch in 1915, either, and was shipped to the Reds, where he blossomed, slowly. In 1917, Luque went 6–3. In 1918 his record was 10–3. After that Luque was a regular in the Reds' rotation. The Reds were not very good, so he took many lumps and his record of 13–23 in 1922 certainly did not herald Luque's overpowering magical All-Star season of 1923 when everything went right.

That season, Luque's best, the slick thrower finished 27–8 with a 1.93 earned run average. Luque led the National League in wins, ERA, winning percentage (.771), and shutouts (six). Although Luque never again came close to matching those numbers (he didn't even win 20 games again), he did lead the NL in earned run average (2.63) again two years later.

It was Luque's misfortune to play on a multitude of bad ball clubs when he had his best stuff, but he had staying power and won 194 Major League games in his career. He might well have won many more games if he had been surrounded in the order by batters who hit for higher averages.

Luque battled batters on every pitch and battled on and around the diamond in every way possible if he felt slighted. The notion of Latins always owning hair-trigger tempers is an ages-old image. It may be that Luque actually helped establish the stereotype with his actions. Luque became embroiled in several incidents that were looked at with bemusement during his playing days, yet during the 2000s would have led to lengthy suspensions and massive fines by Major League Baseball.

Unhappy with the way the balls and strikes had been called, Luque once marched in from the mound to the plate, confronted Hall of Fame umpire Bill Klem, yanked up the arbiter's protective mask, and knocked him down with one punch. Such action today would lead at least to a year-long banishment, if not a lifetime suspension. From a logic standpoint alone, such abuse of an ump was never going to win Luque the close calls on the inside corner.

This confrontation was ironic because early in his career Luque formed the idea that he could not pitch with maximum efficiency unless Klem was the umpire assigned to call balls and strikes. Umpires traveling in four-man crews take turns at bases around the diamond. One day when Luque realized Klem was umpiring, but at first base, the pitcher offered him $10 to trade positions with the home-plate ump. The transaction was not concluded. Not long after, Luque was again the scheduled pitcher on a day when Klem's crew was working the game. Klem was again assigned to first base. This time Luque offered Klem $25 to trade spots with the home-plate ump. Klem laughed about the incidents, apparently merely chalking the actions up to Luque's foreign upbringing. "So Bill explained to the Cuban star that baseball wasn't played that way in the United States," a sportswriter penned. (Quoted in Condon.)

Baseball in the 2000s is a genteel game compared to baseball in the 1920s. Heckling, not only by fans, but from opposing players, was a more accepted part of the sport. Riding an opposing player to make him lose concentration was a common strategy and often the tenor of the shouts was insulting and personal. In Luque's case, players in the opposition dugout might make fun of his accent. The wisest and most placid of players ignored the taunts, but Luque was not one of them.

One day the New York Giants were all over Luque's case, ripping him from the bench inning after inning. One player in particular let loose with a constant stream of invective. The crowd of players in the sheltered dugout, however, provided anonymity and Luque could not tell who his abuser was. Eventually, though, he blew his top. Luque placed the ball in his glove, laid his glove on the mound, and charged into the Giants dugout and attacked outfielder Casey Stengel. Luque's punch flattened Stengel. But he got the wrong guy. Stengel hadn't yelled a thing at Luque all day and the then-unidentified guilty perpetrator escaped Duque's wrath. (Later the big mouth was said to be Bill Cunningham.) Luque was so infuriated that it took a quartet of police officers and some of his teammates to haul him out of the dugout and eject him from Crosley Field. By the time he was wrestled out of the Giants dugout, Luque had picked up a bat to use as a weapon.

While with the Brooklyn Dodgers, either in 1930 or 1931, one fan got under Luque's skin. He was pitching well and the fan kept screaming, "Lucky Luque!" The hurler resented the aspersions on his talent and informed manager Wilbert Robinson, "I'm gonna club this loudmouth with a bat." (Quoted in Condon.) The boss talked him out of it.

However, no one was around to intervene the time Luque chased after Babe Pinelli with an ice pick because the fielder made a game-costing error. Luque chased Pinelli in the clubhouse, but never got close enough to skewer him. "We finally broke it up, but from Luque's remarks, he meant business," said Luque's catcher at the time Clyde Sukeforth. (Quoted in Biederman.)

Sympathetic historians attribute many of Luque's blowups to the tense racial atmosphere of the times. Even if Luque was light-skinned enough to acceptably pass for white in a whites-only environment, he still was not completely accepted as an equal and his Hispanic background led to on-field haranguing. Typically, Luque used the pitcher's best weapon for intimidation—the brushback pitch, high and inside, to drive a batter into the dirt, as his retaliation. Sometimes he exploded.

One author noted: "lighter skin color and ethnic background offered only momentary relief in an institution that closely scrutinized ancestry for any tell-tale signs of a false racial claim. Although they may not have been discernibly black, few of their contemporaries viewed them as white. They lived between racial poles along the color line." (Quoted in Burgos, 145.)

Near the end of his Major League pitching career, Luque was picked up by the New York Giants, nearing the end of their own run mostly under legendary manager John McGraw. Luque was in his 18th Major League season but lucked into an opportunity he took advantage of. When called upon in relief in the 1933 World Series, he quelled a Washington Senators threat. When Mel Ott hit a home run in the 10th inning, Luque got the victory.

"The two things I remember about Luque were his curveball and his temper," said Sukeforth, later a long-time Major League coach who scouted Jackie Robinson for the Dodgers. "He has one of the finest curves I ever saw and an explosive temper to match. Luque was always angry when a batter got a hit. In his mind there were no base hits. He figured everything should have been caught by his fielders. He was a great pitcher all right." (Quoted in Biederman.)

During his long Major League career, Luque also pitched winters in Cuba and in other Latin countries. His Cuban pitching record was 103–68. This enhanced his reputation and both during his playing years and after his retirement as an active player he managed for years in Latino hotbeds of baseball. Luque won at least eight pennants as a field boss. Long after his prime years, Luque occasionally returned to the mound for a pitching appearance. Paralleling the ageless Satchel Paige, Luque made some relief showings when he was 55 years old.

Luque must have suffered insults during this period that were no doubt of the same variety that all managers endure about their pitching changes, lineups, and hit-and-run calls. Luque, as usual, continued to fight for what he believed in. This meant if Luque felt a player was not hustling for him, not giving his all on the field, he would be threatened by an irate manger waving a pistol. Luque was definitely not a turn-the-other-cheek type of fellow.

Luque was a no-fear and no-nonsense pitcher. He was very territorial, making sure that batters knew what parts of the plate he claimed for his own. He threw inside and tried to make that strategy work for him. Sometimes he hit batters that he felt deserved it. That did not always make him friends. "Luque was probably one of the nastiest guys . . . I ever met," said former Negro Leagues player Max Manning, who also played in Latin America. "One thing Luque couldn't stand: pitchers walking batters. He would turn red and come out there, snatch the ball out of your hand and spit on your shoes, all around the mound, and cuss you out in Spanish." (Quoted in Holway.)

Manning said he witnessed Luque and Boojum Wilson, the other player whom he considered about on par with Luque for nastiness, in a bizarre clubhouse confrontation. Luque marched over to Wilson's locker carrying a pistol. Luque pulled the trigger and shot a bullet into the ceiling. "That was supposed to scare Boojum," Manning said. Rather than quake in his spikes, Wilson reached into his locker, pulled out his own pistol, fired it at the ceiling and said, "What about that?" Manning said the situation was a standoff. (Quoted in Holway.)

At his best as a pitcher, Luque was very good. Besides his one stupendous season, Luque won 10 or more games in the majors 11 times. When he aged he morphed into an effective late-inning reliever. *The Sporting News*, then the Bible of the sport, called Luque "Cuba's greatest gift to our national game." (Quoted in Regalado, 22.)

Among Luque's attributes as a player was his ability to field his position. They didn't give out Gold Gloves in Luque's day, but he was a vacuum cleaner when it came to scooping up dribblers and bunts and throwing out runners who thought they had it made getting to first. In the early 1930s a young player for the Boston Braves named Randy Moore came to the plate against Luque in an obvious bunting situation. Thinking about the veteran's reputation, Moore felt he would be buzzed by a high, hard one for sure. Instead, Luque tossed a slow curve up to the plate. Moore happily took advantage, laid down his bunt, and ran safely to first. However, his teammate Wally Berger was thrown out trying to go from second to third. Luque had planned the scenario all of the way. He jocularly yelled to Moore, "Hey, kid, sometime you learn, eh?" (Quoted in Daley.)

Any twirler who lasts two decades in the majors adds a certain amount of craftiness to his repertoire regardless of how much natural talent carried him to the world's best baseball league. Luque used his smarts in critical situations over and over as he got older. The most visible situation, carrying the highest stakes, was in the deciding game of the 1933 World Series. Luque was on the mound, with two runners on, as lefty-swinging Senator Joe Kuhel came to the plate. Just one out stood between New York and the Series title.

The Giants' manager, Bill Terry, debated the right move. He didn't know if he wanted to summon another pitcher to face Kuhel. "I pitch," Luque responded. It was the right idea. Later, Luque explained what happened in the pitcher-hitter confrontation. "I look at this Kuhel," Luque said. "He stands way back. I pitch a curve on the outside corner. Umpire says strike. I look again. This time his feet are close to the plate. I pitch inside curve. Umpire say strike. I look again. He has moved back. I pitch outside curve. He swing." (Quoted in Daley.) Strike three. Game over. The Giants became world champs.

Rather humorously, Luque became one of those athletes who announced his retirement but always kept coming back. He long pre-dated boxers Muhammad Ali and Sugar Ray Leonard and basketball star Michael Jordan in this pattern. In March 1940, the Cincinnati Reds were taking spring training in Cuba. Luque took the mound for three innings of work on behalf of the Selections de Cubans team in Havana. When the game ended he announced that he would never pitch again.

"I'm going to be 50 in August," Luque said. "I cannot pitch anymore, so I'll never pitch again. Tomorrow, I will stay in bed all day. I must have rest. I'm not as young as I used to be." (Quoted in National Baseball . . .)

He sounded sincere, and Luque may even have believed his own words. It's unlikely that he would have imagined himself pitching again soon, or especially not pitching in five years when he was 55. Although Luque was inducted into the Cincinnati Reds team Hall of Fame in 1967, his more enduring legacy is in Cuba. He was very much appreciated during his lifetime, and his baseball accomplishments provided inspiration for youngsters. In 1937, a sportswriter talked to a friend of his who worked with the United States amateur boxing team on a visit to the island. The official, Paul Gardner, reported that he polled Cuban youngsters as he met them, asking them about their baseball heroes. "All of them named Luque," Gardner said, "and many of them put him at the top of their lists." (Quoted in Mercer.)

With the flood of Latin American talent pouring into the big leagues, Luque's achievements can be overlooked. But whatever his personality, as a Cuban-born player he was a pathfinder for later arrivals in the majors. He established a litany of firsts, including being the first Latino player to appear in a World Series (twice throwing in relief in 1919 for Cincinnati) and to lead a league in any major statistical category as he did during his phenomenal 1923 season. "Dolf Luque was indisputably the first genuine Latino hero," observed baseball historian Peter C. Bjarkman. (Quoted in Bjarkman, 8.)

Luque died of a heart attack in Havana at 67 in July 1957. New York sports columnist Frank Graham wrote that it was hard to believe because Luque seemed indestructible. "He was a tough man, this one, stocky, gnarled, hard-visaged, hard-thinking, unyielding in combat," Graham wrote. "Few hitters ever liked to go up to the plate against him." (Quoted in Graham.)

No, Adolfo Luque did not take the mound to make friends. He pitched to make outs.

Further Reading

Biederman, Les, "Dolph Luque Had Temper To Match Fine Curve," *Pittsburgh Press*, July 7, 1957.

Bjarkman, Peter C., *Baseball With A Latin Beat* (Jefferson, North Carolina, McFarland & Company, Inc., Publishers, 1994).

Burgos Jr., Adrian, *Playing America's Game* (Berkeley, California, University of California Press, 2007).

Condon, David, In the Wake of the News column, *Chicago Tribune*, July 6, 1957.

Daley, Arthur, "The Cuban Curver," *New York Times*, July 14, 1957.

Graham, Frank, "Adolfo Luque Is Dead?," *New York Journal-American*, July 17, 1957.

Holway, John B., *Black Diamonds* (Westport, Connecticut, Meckler Books, 1989).

Mercer, Sid, National Baseball Hall of Fame Library archives, unattributed newspaper, January 5, 1937.

National Baseball Hall of Fame Library archives, unattributed newspaper, March 28, 1940.

Regalado, Samuel O., *Viva Baseball!" Latin Major Leaguers and Their Special Hunger* (Champaign, Illinois, University of Illinois Press, 1998).

Juan Marichal

The left leg kicking so high that fans wondered if Juan Marichal would boot himself in the forehead or at least knock down a villain with a karate-like kick remains a memorable trademark of the greatest pitcher to come from the Dominican Republic.

Few pitchers in history have completed their Major League careers more than 100 games above .500 as Marichal did when he retired after 16 big-league seasons with 243 wins and 142 losses. The mark was testimony to the remarkable

Dominican Republic star Juan Marichal of the San Francisco Giants is still considered the greatest Latin American pitcher 35 years after his retirement. Right-hander Marichal won 243 games and was inducted into the Hall of Fame in 1983. His lifetime earned run average of 2.89 is one of the best ever for a modern-era pitcher. (Focus on Sport/Getty Images)

domination Marichal demonstrated after breaking in with the San Francisco Giants in 1960. A master of control, Marichal was not an overpowering strikeout artist, but he did fan more than three times the number of batters he walked.

Among the notable trademarks of the long-limbed, 6-foot, 185-pound Marichal's career were his high number of innings pitched each season and his high number of complete games. When Marichal went to the mound the manager didn't have to worry very much about his bullpen. The righty hurler had staying power.

Marichal was born in Laguna Verde in the Dominican Republic near the border with Haiti in 1938, and he was in the first wave of star baseball players to emerge from his country. His father died when he was three, leaving he, his older brother, and his mother broke and living in a palm-bark shack. Even the first teams that Marichal played baseball for in the mid-1950s were poor organizations, and they sometimes rode horses to away games. Marichal almost missed out on a chance to play any baseball. He nearly drowned while swimming after eating too much and suffering cramps. He slipped under the water and was in a coma for six days. One doctor even pronounced him dead, but he fooled the medical experts with his resiliency.

Word of Marichal's pitching prowess spread locally. Before he was noticed by big-league scouts, Marichal was drafted in a different manner. Ramis Trujillo, the son of the nation's dictator, sent a letter informing Marichal that the Air Force wanted him. Not to fly planes, it turned out, but to represent the country in amateur baseball. Marichal pitched for the Dominican Republic in the Pan American

Games. While in Mexico City for the tournament, Marichal said he was surrounded by a group of threatening men who pulled knives and were armed with pistols pointed at him, and who ordered him to lose his game. "Today you lose quick, little one," the thugs said. Marichal was 16 and weighed just 150 pounds at the time. He fled from the bullpen. "I was a child," he said. "I wet my pants, but I don't quit." (Quoted in Stump.)

As a baseball player, Marichal was earnest, a hard worker, driven to succeed, and proud of his ability to baffle hitters. One of Marichal's signatures on the field was running back and forth to the dugout. He said it was the vestige of a lesson learned in the minors in 1959. A coach named Andy Gilbert in the Eastern League stressed to all of his players that they should always hustle. To Gilbert, that meant running out ground balls and bunts and running out to the field and back to the bench. If a player didn't follow those instructions he was fined $1. Although in modern terms a penalty of $1 seems like a joke because players earn millions of dollars, the terms of punishment had an impact a half century ago.

"Andy made it a habit for you to run," Marichal recalled years later. "I've never forgot it. Or the $1 fines I lost, either. I don't like to see anybody hit the ball at somebody and then turn back from the plate to go back to the dugout. It is not big league." (Quoted in Stevens.)

Marichal was a nine-time All-Star and twice led the National League in wins. In 1963 he was 25–8. In 1966, he was 25–6. In 1968 he was 26–9. Eight times Marichal won at least 18 games in a year. Marichal competed during an era when many of the other top National League clubs had an ace to match against him. The Braves featured Warren Spahn, the winningest left-handed pitcher of all time. The Dodgers featured Sandy Koufax, who had as dominant a stretch over five years in the 1960s as any pitcher who ever lived. And the Cardinals featured Bob Gibson. All three, as well as Marichal, were voted into the Hall of Fame.

A Marichal showdown against Spahn is one of the epic games in baseball history. The 16-inning Giants-Braves contest in 1963 resulted in a 1–0 victory for Marichal with both twirlers throwing complete games. Marichal gave up eight hits and no runs. Spahn gave up nine hits in 15 1/3 innings. Such pitching lines are inconceivable today when pitchers might be lifted by their itchy trigger-finger managers before the double shutout went past nine innings.

Giants' manager Al Dark, indeed, wanted to remove Marichal from the game—twice, in fact—but Marichal resisted when the boss visited the mound. "I begged Mr. Dark to let me stay a few more innings, and he did," Marichal said. "In the 12th or 13th he wanted to take me out, and I said, 'Please, please, let me stay.' Then, in the 14th, he said, 'No more for you,' and I said, 'Do you see that man on the mound?' I was pointing at Warren. 'That man is 42 and I'm 25. I'm not ready for you to take me out.' " Marichal said he had a cheerleader on his side, too.

Catcher Ed Bailey kept telling him, "Don't let them take you out. Win or lose, this is great." (Quoted in Sandomir.)

And it was. The longevity and brilliance of the pitchers made the game memorable, even more worthy of mention now because such a drama will likely never play out in such a manner again. While present-day baseball people would have been freaked out by the notion of two such valuable pitchers hurling so many innings on one night, Marichal did not complain of arm aches afterward. His back hurt a little bit, though.

Five times Marichal recorded at least 22 complete games in a season, and in 1968 when he completed 30 games he also led the NL in innings pitched with 326. That's nearly double the work load of what present-day starters consider to be a season's worth of effort.

Brilliant at painting the corners of the plate, Marichal did not dilly-dally on the mound between pitches, nor did he want to throw more pitches than necessary to any hitter. Jack Hiatt, one of Marichal's catchers with the Giants, said he'd love to see Marichal make more batters lunge. "He throws too many strikes," Hiatt said. "Juan pitches his own game and better than anybody who might have ever played this game. Me? I like to tease the guy (the batter) a little. With Marichal's control he could drive the batters wild by flicking at a corner here, a corner there. But no, he rears back and pours the ball through the strike zone as though somebody might take the zone away before he gets the next pitch off." (Quoted in Stevens.)

No one ever doubted that Marichal knew what he was doing, however. His lifetime earned run average of 2.89 is one of the best ever. Marichal just never gave up many runs.

A reflective man, Marichal realizes that he was lucky that he was good enough to be noticed by Giants scouts at a time when few Dominican Republic players were sought. He began playing baseball on the local sandlots near his home, and until he was 12 focused on playing shortstop. Inspired by local hero Bombo Ramos, Marichal became a pitcher and found his ticket to the United States and the majors.

"In my day, any kid who wanted to play Major League Baseball had to work very, very hard," he said. "It was difficult to come to the United States and not speak English. We didn't know how to order anything besides water and chicken." (Quoted in Wendel and Villegas, 7.) If that wasn't challenging enough, Marichal's minor-league environment of Michigan City, Indiana resembled the Dominican Republic about as much as Jupiter did.

When told he was being sent to the Lake Michigan resort town not far from Chicago in 1956, the community did not ring a bell to Marichal. His first question: "Where is Michigan City, Indiana?" (Quoted in Regalado, 94.) It was in Class D, that's where.

Marichal said he initially suffered grievously from homesickness. To cure his mood he often played salsa music and other upbeat music that harkened back to his upbringing. However, he gloomily decided that made things worse. He decided to Americanize. When he got more money, Marichal opted for steak as a main staple in his diet. More telling, when he realized that playing the music did not provide happy memories but only distracted and depressed him, he took drastic action, "that made me so sad that I finally took my records and broke them one by one and stopped listening to Dominican music at all." (Quoted in Regalado, 128.)

Whether that cleared his head or not, Marichal's outward mood certainly made a positive impression during the remainder of his brief stays in the minors in Springfield, Massachusetts and Tacoma, Washington. In Tacoma he was described in glowing terms, called "Laughing Boy" and praised for his "ever-present grin and sunny disposition" and when Marichal got the call-up from the Giants he was missed as "one of the most personable and likeable of the Tacoma players." (Quoted in Regalado, 128.)

Marichal was welcomed to the majors in mid-season of 1960. He pitched a shutout in his first game against Philadelphia. In 11 starts (six completed), Marichal compiled a 6–2 record. The next season he was a regular in the Giants' rotation, going 13–10. In 1962, as the Giants won their first pennant after relocating to San Francisco, Marichal went 18–11. He received his first All-Star invitation that year.

Those who watched Marichal pitch in the majors raved about his performance and his style. One sportswriting observer referred to Marichal as an artist for the ages, saying, "He brought to the mound what Van Gogh and da Vinci brought to the canvas—beauty, individuality and class." (Quoted in Regalado, 130.)

By the mid-1960s, Marichal was at the top of his game and at the top of the game. He was making $100,000 a year. But he was not always content. He, like Felipe Alou and Orlando Cepeda, was resentful when manager Al Dark forbade the speaking of Spanish in the Giants dugout. The happy-go-lucky youth in Tacoma, who was just trying to fit in and find his way in baseball and American society, had still experienced enough prejudice to be disgruntled. He felt there was a double standard applied to Latino players, that they were sometimes taken advantage of because of the language barrier.

"Our skins may be lighter," he said, "but the breaks we get from baseball and on the outside are much less than the Negro player gets." At the time Marichal noted he was being asked to make breakfast, lunch and dinner appearances all over the Bay Area, but was having trouble getting the proper permits to build the house he wanted for his family." (Quoted in Stump.)

Unlike many Latin stars, Marichal was inclined to make his main home in the United States. He briefly played winter ball in Dominican Republic, but when he was in a night club in Santo Domingo one New Year's Eve and a riot broke out, he was attacked by a mob and had to fight his way to his car. Then he was arrested. The publicity about the incident brought telephone death threats to his home.

In the mid-1960s, the Dominican was coping with political unrest, as well, and the United States sent in the Marines supposedly to keep order. However, Marichal had regained enough stature that in 1966 Juaquin Balaguer, running for president, invoked Marichal's name in his campaign. Balaguer, who won the election, used the slogan, "Balaguer is the Marichal of the presidential palace!"

Marichal did not issue a specific endorsement, but spent $1,200 of his own money urging Dominicans to turn out and vote. Rafael Trujillo, the country's dictator from the 1930s until his assassination in 1961, had many brutal crimes attributed to him. His regime was still fresh and some still feared reprisals in mentioning their political opinions. When pollsters asked potential voters who they preferred in the election and they wished to avoid committing, they said, "Let's talk about Marichal." (Quoted in Whitten.) That phrase was a pseudonym for "No comment."

The one great blemish on Marichal's career was a moment of temper loss that has never been forgotten when baseball confrontations are listed. The Giants and Dodgers transplanted their heated rivalry from New York to California when the teams moved West in the late 1950s. The intensity of their regular-season series ranked as high as any in baseball.

In an August 22, 1965 game between the Giants and Dodgers, Marichal was pitching. Emotions were percolating early and Marichal decked Dodger players Ron Fairly and Maury Wills with inside pitches. In the third inning at Candlestick Park, he came to the plate. Johnny Roseboro was catching for Los Angeles. Before the inning ended, the teams were battling on the field and Roseboro had a cut on his head where Marichal had hit him with his bat—and kept on swinging it at him. Roseboro raised his left arm to ward off blows. The frightening display battered Roseboro and led the Dodgers to declare Marichal should be thrown out of baseball.

Marichal said when Roseboro threw the ball back to Sandy Koufax on the mound his toss was so close to his own head that it nicked his ear. He turned to Roseboro and said, "Why did you do that?" (Quoted in Ziff.) There was disagreement on whether Marichal then swung the bat first and connected with Roseboro's head or Roseboro tried to throw a punch. Dodger manager Walter Alston took his catcher's side. Benches and bullpens emptied and skirmishes erupted all around the field. Although there were some minor injuries from punches, the major damage was done to a woozy and furious Roseboro who had a knot on his head that was growing into the size of a baseball. Taken to a hospital, he needed 14 stitches to close his head wound. Marichal was ejected from the game and the park.

Although the Dodgers called for Marichal to be banned from baseball, Major League officials instead slapped him with a $1,750 fine and an eight-game suspension.

Years later, Roseboro said he was angling to mix it up with Marichal given the slightest chance and admitted throwing the ball close to his head to enrage the pitcher. "When Marichal came up to bat, I tried a knockdown from behind the plate, throwing the ball close to his nose when I returned it to the pitcher," Roseboro said. "I expected Marichal to attack me in some way. If he had said anything to me, I had studied karate, and I was ready to annihilate him." (Quoted in Merron.) Only Marichal surprised Roseboro when instead of calling him out and assuming a boxing stance, he clobbered him with his bat.

"I wish it had never happened," Marichal said years later. (Quoted in King.) He always expressed regret and could offer no good explanation for the explosion of his temper in such an uncontrolled way. He often said that he and Roseboro later became good friends.

Fans may be horrified to learn that at times coaches urged Marichal to tamper with his identifiable leg kick and become a more compact thrower. It made no sense to mess with success and Marichal would not. "The Giants tried to change that delivery, but he refused to budge," said teammate Felipe Alou. It's true, Marichal said. "When I got to spring training in 1961, they wanted to change my motion. They didn't want me to kick my leg because they claimed I wasn't watching home plate." (Quoted in Haft.) Whether the ball got to the right place by radar or some other secret Marichal miracle, it found home plate OK.

Marichal had few down years during his first 12 seasons with the Giants and notched his 200th career victory in 1970 when he was only 33. He was coming off a disconcerting spring when he was sick more than healthy and on his way to a pedestrian 12–10 season. Late in the year, though, he seemed to regain his touch and was feeling great again when he beat the Pirates 5–1 in September for the milestone victory.

"It's fun again," said Marichal, who held up a baseball with the number 200 written on it for photographers' benefit. "I can throw the ball now the way I did last season and the season before. On every pitch I feel like I'll get the guy out. Now I know I can go on playing for several years." (Quoted in Frizzell.)

As it turned out, Marichal was wrong. Although he posted one more good year with San Francisco in 1971, his career quickly petered out and he was out of the majors by 1975 after a brief cameo with, of all teams, the Dodgers.

After the disappointing falling out with people in the Dominican, Marichal's status was restored. He eventually became minister of sport and helped bring the Pan American Games to his home island. The bad days are long forgotten. Marichal is now regarded as one of the country's primary sports heroes for his pioneering days in the majors. When he was inducted into the National Baseball Hall of Fame in the United States in 1983, Marichal was the first from his nation.

"This is a very big day for my country," Marichal said in his induction speech, admitting he was very nervous. Not knowing how many Dominicans would follow him into the majors, Marichal said he hoped, "others from my country will make it some day." (Quoted in "Marichal's . . . ")

In the ensuing years, Marichal has expressed pride at the influx of more and more Dominicans arriving in the majors. He makes regular public appearances on behalf of the Giants and at sports memorabilia shows. With gray flecks in his hair, frequently wearing a suit, and remaining trim, Marichal resembles every inch the elder statesman of the game that he is.

Just when Marichal believed he had received every honor possible from baseball, he was surprised to learn that the Giants were dedicating a nine-foot bronze statue of him outside their new San Francisco ballpark in 2005. "I never dreamed I'd have a statue made of me," Marichal said. (Quoted in Bloom.)

It was less of a surprise that the image of the great pitcher had him kicking his left leg high toward the sky, the pose frozen for eternity.

Further Reading

Bloom, Barry M., "Giants to dedicate statue of Marichal," MLB.com, May 16, 2005.

Frizzell, Pat, "No. 200 Restores Marichal's Wide Grin," *The Sporting News*, September 12, 1970.

Haft, Chris, "High-Kicking Excellence," *San Jose Mercury News*, May 18, 2005.

King, David, "Marichal is a man of many hats," *San Antonio Express-News*, April 11, 2004.

"Marichal's induction hailed in 2 countries," Associated Press, August 2, 1983.

Merron, Jeff, "Put Up Your Dukes," ESPN.com, April 24, 2003.

Regalado, Samuel O., *Viva Baseball!* (Champaign, Illinois, University of Illinois Press, 1998.)

Sandomir, Richard, "When Marichal and Spahn Dueled for a Game and a Half," *New York Times*, July 2, 2008.

Stevens, Bob, "Why Does Marichal Run? He Remembers $1 fines," *The Sporting News*, July 21, 1968.

Stump, Al, "Always They Want More, More, More," *Saturday Evening Post*, July 29, 1967

Wendel, Tim, *Far From Home: Latin American Baseball Players in America* (Washington, D.C., National Geographic Society Books, 2008.).

Whitten, Leslie H., "Marichal's Political Magic," Hearst Headline Service, June 3, 1966.

Ziff, Sid, "Dodgers on Marichal: 'Kick Him Out,' " *Los Angeles Times*, August 23, 1965.

Dennis Martinez

With his fine control, crisp fastball, and long career piling up victories, Dennis Martinez, the first Nicaraguan to play Major League baseball, was nicknamed "El Presidente." The moniker was evocative of the idea that the right-handed

Dennis Martinez not only won 245 games, primarily for the Baltimore Orioles and Montreal Expos, during a 23-year career, he threw a rare perfect game for the Expos in 1991. One of the most popular athletes in Nicaraguan history during his playing career, it was suggested that Martinez might end up as president of his home country. (AP Photo/Craig Fujii)

pitcher was so popular in his native country that he might return home and be elected president.

Although that never happened, Martinez, regarded as the greatest athlete produced by his land along with the late world champion boxer Alexis Arguello, does hold the record of 245 wins, the most by a Latino pitcher. His total ranks just ahead of Juan Marichal's 243 on the list. And if anyone doubted the notion of a sports star being so admired that he could obtain high office in Nicaragua, it should be noted that Arguello was mayor of Managua, the capital, when he died in 2009. Instead of running for public office, Martinez had Nicaragua's national stadium named after him. The 30,000-seat stadium, home to Managua's popular soccer club Deportivo Walter Ferretti, is called Dennis Martinez National Stadium.

Martinez was born into poverty in 1955, in Granada, Nicaragua about 25 miles from Managua and emerged as a prospect in the Baltimore Orioles' chain in the 1970s. Martinez had a dark mustache and a winning smile but was not the prototype large, flame-throwing pitcher. He stood 6 feet tall, but played at 185 pounds. Despite various setbacks, Martinez was durable enough to spend 23 seasons in the majors. His 245 victories (against 193 losses) represent the most wins ever for a Major League pitcher who did not win at least 20 games in a season once.

Martinez definitely had his proud moments, however. He is best remembered as one of only 19 hurlers to pitch a regular-season perfect game and one of only seven in National League history. The monumental achievement was recorded against the Los Angeles Dodgers in 1991.

The Nicaraguan star broke into the majors with four appearances in 1976, going 1–2. Within a year, though, Martinez was a full-fledged member of the Orioles' pitching rotation and turned in an excellent 14–7 record. That was the true start to Martinez's lengthy career that included four All-Star game selections. Six times between 1977 and 1985 Martinez won between 13 and 16 games for the Orioles. He was consistent, reliable, and always won his share without being over-powering. Martinez might have posted his best year in 1981, but the season was interrupted by a strike. His 14 victories led the American League that year.

The grassroots playing tradition of high level baseball is not as strong in Nicaragua as it is in Cuba, the Dominican Republic, or Venezuela. Also, the generation of potential players that might have taken advantage of the boom in signings of Latin American players was stunted in the 1980s during the country's civil war between the Sandinistas and Contras. The socialist Sandinista National Liberation Front took power in Nicaragua in 1979 and ruled the country until 1990 following the overthrow of dictator Anastasio Somoza Debayle. The Contras were the U.S.-supported-insurrectionists trying to install leaders more sympathetic to the United States.

Martinez never publicly expressed agreement with one political side or the other. He mainly worried about the health and safety of family members still in the country. He once heard that when Somoza was being run out of office, he ordered a pilot to bomb Granada, Martinez's hometown. It did not occur, he heard, because the pilot came from that community. (Quoted in Newman.)

During this time of upheaval there was more focus on developing a functioning government than on who was throwing the best curveball. Although politics was a touchy subject, Nicaraguans agreed on idolizing Martinez, who continued his exploits in the United States during the fighting. A writer who traveled widely throughout Latin America to study baseball reported that while watching the movie *Under Fire* set in Nicaragua during the war, "I'd noticed that the film-makers established authenticity with a shot of a young boy trying to throw a hand grenade with the motion of his hometown idol, the Orioles' Dennis Martinez." (Quoted in Krich, 180.)

Actually, the movie is very specific in making Martinez a point of reference. Nick Nolte, playing an American news photographer, is confronted by the young male who informs him that Martinez is the greatest pitcher, even better than Sandy Koufax. The fighting Sandinista adds that he has a better curve than Martinez and asks Nolte to deliver a baseball to his hero. Seconds later the character is shot and killed. "I was shocked when I saw it," Martinez said of the scene in the movie.

"See, the Sandinistas thought I was with them and the Contras thought I was with them, but I wasn't with either." (Quoted in Newman.)

Nicaragua was one of the Latin American countries that happily accepted the inclusion of baseball as an Olympic sport for a chance to show what it could do against powers like Cuba and the United States. Nicaraguans were disappointed when their team got knocked out earlier than hoped for in the 1984 Los Angeles Games. "That night even the Contras cried," it was said. (Quoted in Krich, 181.)

Baseball in Nicaragua dates to the late nineteenth century, at least to the 1880s in some form. Students from Nicaragua picked up the sport while visiting Cuba and brought back some form of the game. Many credit the U.S. Marines for popularizing the sport during military actions around the turn of the twentieth century, but passionate fans and those who dislike American foreign policy and its interventionism prefer to favor the story of student origin. A U.S. Navy base was constructed in Nicaragua that included a playing field—for the seamen, not the natives.

Making son Dennis Martinez into a Major League baseball player was not a high priority in the boy's immediate family. It was to him, but not his parents. His mother was determined that he would go to college to study engineering and she saved her coins to help build a college fund for him. She was not thrilled when Martinez embarked for the United States to become a pitcher studying quite different angles. "All mothers care about the future of their sons," Martinez said. "They want to see their sons have good careers. I told her that if I had a few years in the minor leagues I could save enough money to pay for my engineering courses." (Quoted in Vecsey.) As it turned out, she could bank on that promise—and more. Martinez fared much better than he might have imagined, though he never did pick off those school subjects.

Actually, there was more urgency for Martinez to take some other courses. His English was very limited when he was playing in the minors in Miami. A misunderstanding led to Martinez stepping up his learning curve. He was on the mound in the late innings of a game when the manager came out to ask if he was tired. Martinez thought he was being asked if he was OK, so he said yes. The manager assumed Martinez was saying he was fatigued so he got yanked. "I was so mad," Martinez said. When the pitching coach explained what happened, Martinez laughed and said, "I knew I had to learn how to speak English." (Quoted in Vecsey.)

Martinez played for the Orioles from 1976 to 1986, the Montreal Expos from 1986 to 1993, the Cleveland Indians from 1994 to 1996, the Seattle Mariners in 1997, and the Atlanta Braves in 1998. By then he was 43 and had lasted much longer in the game than many thought possible.

Life did not always go smoothly for Martinez. In 1978, he finished 16–11 for the Orioles and in 1979 he was 15–16. The Orioles were renowned for their tough starting pitching during that era and 20-game winners were common. Martinez was expected to be a full-blown star in 1980, but shoulder miseries held him to a 6–4 record. The year represented two giant steps backward. Also, any time a pitcher is sidelined with an arm ailment, teams begin to worry about their future. There were rumors that other teams came sniffing around seeking Martinez in a trade, but Martinez reassured the Orioles he was still part of their future when he had a phenomenal year throwing winter ball in Puerto Rico. Martinez went 6–1 with a 1.39 earned run average. Forget the shoulder problems.

"He was as good as I've ever seen him," said Ray Miller, the Baltimore pitching coach. "He was throwing everything for strikes and he threw the change-up any time he wanted. I didn't see any signs of arm trouble. In fact, he got stronger as he went along." (Quoted in Nigro, "Martinez' . . .")

Concerns spiked. Martinez was back. He came through with that 14–7 strike-disrupted season. Included during the first half of the 1981 season was a 10-inning shutout of the New York Yankees. The Orioles were short on starters at that point and manager Earl Weaver called on Martinez again ahead of his regular turn. "I wasn't too sure with bringing him back with only three days rest," Weaver said. "But the guy was sitting on top of the world after that game and I figured it was better to bring him right back with three days rest than give him five and have him sitting around." (Quoted in Nigro, "Dennis . . .") Martinez threw a nine-inning complete game.

Martinez was happy in Baltimore. Along with his wife and children he made it his home. The season was already underway in 1986 when Martinez was shipped to the Expos for a player to be named later, and it was reported that the Orioles still had to pay a hefty chunk of Martinez's $500,000 salary. The Nicaraguan who had adapted to the United States and learned English was now playing for a team in Canada where French was more commonly spoken.

Believing he would be a career-long Oriole, Martinez took some time to adjust to his abrupt departure and he spent some time sorting out why he was an ex-Oriole. "The Orioles put a lot of pressure on me and no one knows this like me," Martinez said. "They always expected me to be a 20-game winner. They'd say, 'We don't know why Dennis hasn't won 20 games. He has the talent. He should do it.' Well, I believe that, but maybe I've never done it because of the pressure they put on. They never left me alone to pitch the way I want. It was always, 'Dennis, change this. Dennis change that.' There was always something they didn't like. After a while, I began to wonder, 'Why am I still here if I do so much wrong?' The answer was that I was winning. That was the only reason. When I stopped winning, I was gone." (Quoted in Hyman.)

Martinez got into 19 games with the Expos in 1986 and finished 3–6. The team had a young, set staff and his opportunities were few. Martinez was a free agent, but had no record to stand on to snare a major contract. He began the 1987 season in the minors with Miami and showed enough stuff for Montreal to sign him for $225,000 and deposit him with Indianapolis in AAA. He spent seven weeks with Indianapolis. Almost forgotten, Martinez bounced back and when he returned to the majors he posted an 11–4 record, throwing sharply when he was deployed in his 22 starts. "You have to humble yourself once in a while in life," Martinez said of returning to the minors and working his way back to the top. "I didn't care what people thought." (Quoted in "Expos' . . .")

His first-rate 1987 performance showed the Expos that he was not over the hill and at 33 had plenty left in the tank. Martinez's best years were ahead of him in Montreal. During the summer of his return to form, Martinez revealed details of a painful period in his life that likely contributed to his failures in Baltimore. He said that he was an alcoholic and had battled for the previous few years to shed his addiction and keep his drinking problems from interfering with his pitching career.

Arrested for drunken driving while with the Orioles, a depressed Martinez checked himself into a rehabilitation center for eight weeks after the 1983 season, he said. While trying to kick his booze habit, Martinez, who was raised a Catholic in Nicaragua, said he turned to God again for help and guidance. "I got picked up for drunk driving in Baltimore," Martinez said. "I'm happy it happened that way before I killed somebody and I killed myself. God was on my side.

"I was willing to go to any lengths to stay clean. It doesn't mean I'm cured, but the demon is away from me now. I do my praying every night and I do it when I get up. It took from '83–to–'87 to get all the pieces together. I didn't become an alcoholic in one or two years and I knew the recovery would take time. My concentration is getting back and my confidence is back again." (Quoted in Serby.)

A healthy, sober Martinez won 15 games in 1988 and went 16–7 in 1989. Then he was selected to the National League All-Star team three straight times. An older, more reflective pitcher, Martinez demonstrated the same type of speed and control he had as an up-and-comer. He was back to normal. "Dennis Martinez has emerged as the ace of our staff," said Expos manager Buck Rodgers in 1988, words Martinez wondered if he would ever hear. "He's our stopper and our big-game pitcher. Dennis has done a super job of being our main man." (Quoted in MacDonald.)

After kicking his alcohol addiction, Martinez said he became a smarter pitcher, not merely a young hard thrower who could get the best hitters out on natural talent. "Before, when I was drinking," he said, "I used to think I was good. I didn't think about pitching. I used to throw hard and more hard and more harder.

Now I think. I throw a fastball on the corner and then the other corner. I used to just try to throw the ball past the hitter. Now I think. I don't say it makes it easy, but it makes it easier." (Quoted in MacDonald.)

It is generally agreed that there is no such thing in life as perfection. But in baseball, a pitcher can be perfect for one game. They call it perfection when a pitcher sets down 27 batters in a row in nine innings without allowing a base-hit, a walk, a hit batsman, or anyone to reach on an error. Never was Martinez better than on July 28, 1991 at Chavez Ravine, the home of the Los Angeles Dodgers, when he took the mound for the Expos.

There were 45,560 on hand, unaware they were about to witness a master-piece. The opposing pitcher was Mike Morgan. Over the 2 hours and 14 minutes of play, Morgan pitched a notable game. Morgan was perfect for five innings. He surrendered just four hits and two runs to the Expos in his own complete-game effort, though he was not helped by two Dodger errors. The Expos scored both of their runs in the 2–0 game in the seventh inning.

Martinez faced 27 batters and retired them all. He pitched nine innings of perfect baseball while striking out five men. Among the heavy hitters in Los Angeles's lineup that night were future Hall of Famer Eddie Murray and slugger Darryl Strawberry. Nobody touched Martinez's best stuff.

In all there have been 20 Major League perfect games, including Don Larsen's perfecto for the Yankees in the 1956 World Series. The other 19 have been thrown in regular-season play, going back to the origins of the National League in 1876, at a rate of slightly more than once a decade. It took 13 years for another perfect game to be pitched in the NL after Martinez's. It was a breathtaking accomplishment.

"I was really going from the first hitter to the last hitter," Martinez said. "The way I always do. I was concentrating on the game more than the no-hitter." Martinez had a low-key reaction at first. "I was blank," he said. "There was nothing in my mind. I had no words to say. I could only cry. I didn't know how to express myself. I didn't know how to respond to this kind of game. I didn't know if that was me down there. I thought I was dreaming." (Quoted in "Martinez . . .")

There is always a certain amount of good fortune when a pitcher throws a no-hitter or a perfect game. Not only must he be on fire, but the ball has to bounce his way. The last out of the game was made by pinch hitter Chris Gwynn. Gwynn hit a deep fly ball to center field, where Marquis Grissom gathered it in. The ball was hit hard enough to make Martinez nervous, but not deep enough to spoil things. "It was scary," Martinez said. "I thought he hit it very well." (Quoted in "Martinez . . .")

The game was broadcast by Radio Nicaragua and Martinez's accomplishment set off celebrations in his home country after it was reported on the front page of local newspapers. A teacher said only a Nobel Prize by a Nicaraguan would receive such general acclaim. "I dedicate this one to my people," Martinez said in an interview a day after the game. (Quoted in "Nicaraguans . . .") President Violeta Chamorro issued congratulations and said that Martinez's accomplishments were a source of pride for the nation and "should serve as an example" to the country's children.

When it came to serving as an example, Martinez had been much more active than throwing a baseball. He volunteered his time to many good causes, started his own foundation to help others, and aided refugees displaced by the civil war.

Martinez's services were in less demand as he passed 40, but he put in two solid seasons for the Cleveland Indians after signing as a free agent and made the American League All-Star team in 1995. A personally satisfying performance enhanced his short stay with the Braves. On August 10, 1998, Martinez defeated the San Francisco Giants for his 244th career victory, making him the winningest Latino pitcher in Major League history. That surpassed Juan Marichal by one win and it was Martinez's next-to-last triumph before he retired.

"I've been grateful to play as long as I've been playing," Martinez said. "This is another record, most wins, but the perfect game, nobody will ever take that away from me." (Quoted in "Martinez surpasses . . .")

Further Reading

"Expos' Martinez reaping success," Associated Press, August 8, 1987.

Hyman, Mark, "Will Martinez and Montreal mix?" *Baltimore Sun*, June 26, 1986.

Krich, John, *El Beisbol* (Chicago, Ivan R. Dee, 2002).

MacDonald, Ian, "Heeding Expos' Call for Arms," *The Sporting News*, September 12, 1988.

"Martinez Attains Perfection in L.A.," Associated Press, July 29, 1991.

"Martinez surpasses mark in Marichal's home," *USA Today*, August 11, 1998.

Newman, Bruce, "Return of the Native," *Sports Illustrated*, December 30, 1991/January 6, 1992.

"Nicaraguans cheer Martinez," *USA Today*, July 30, 1991.

Nigro, Ken, "Dennis Martinez Is O's Hit," *The Sporting News*, June 27, 1981.

———, "Martinez' Turnaround Is Eye-Popping to O's," *The Sporting News*, February 28, 1981.

Serby, Steve, "Expo Martinez savors escape from alcohol," *New York Post*, August 5, 1987.

Vecsey, George, "Nicaragua's Best Pitcher," *New York Times*, 1981).

Edgar Martinez

Edgar Martinez was 10 years old in 1973 when the American League adopted a new rule to benefit hitters and put more offensive action into the game. Neither Martinez nor the Seattle Mariners could have imagined that a decade-and-a-half in the future the Puerto Rican youngster would become the prototype model of the most efficient designated hitter of the weapon's first 37 years.

Martinez was actually born in New York on January 2, 1963, but grew up in Dorado, Puerto Rico. During his 18 years in the majors, Martinez distinguished himself as the most productive, effective, dangerous, and flat-out best practitioner of the designated hitter role. Depending on how voters view that position in the context of everyday play, Martinez could become the first full-time DH to be selected for the Baseball Hall of Fame.

As a youth, Martinez was like every other baseball player. He wanted to play as often as possible, hit as often as he could, and play a position in the field

Puerto Rican Edgar Martinez was such a reliable hitter for the Seattle Mariners that on his retirement Major League Baseball named the award for the game's best designated hitter each year after him. Martinez could become the first designated hitter to earn Hall of Fame recognition. The city of Seattle named a street after the highly respected player. (Stephen Dunn/Getty Images)

full-time. During Major League Baseball's first century, that's the way it worked for all players except for pitchers. The rules changed in 1973 when some baseball officials sought to put more pop in the lineup. It was felt by many that pitchers batting simply represented a wasted at-bat. In an attempt to rev up offenses the American League adopted the designated hitter rule. The National League declined to do so. Although the rule does not state that American League teams must substitute a designated hitter for a pitcher in the batting lineup, from a practical standpoint that is what has occurred. In the American League, the pitcher throws and plays the field but never hits. The designated hitter bats but never plays the field.

Martinez made his Major League debut in 1987, playing 13 games for the Mariners. He was used in only 14 games the next year and in 65 in 1989. At that stage of his career Martinez was a third baseman. In 1990, Martinez became a full-time regular, starting at third. He did that job for two years and blossomed as a hitter, batting more than .300 both seasons.

A smooth-swinging batter with a good eye, Martinez was merely warming up. In 1992, the 5-foot-11, 175-pound Martinez hit .343 and won his first batting title and made his first All-Star team. He was on his way to recording seven All-Star selections and a lifetime .312 average. Until then Martinez's position was third base and he had merely dabbled in the designated hitter role. It took until 1995 before Martinez assumed the Mariners' DH job full-time, but he rarely spent time in the field again before retiring following the 2004 season.

Throughout his career, Martinez was a man of few words. He did not brag about his deeds, nor did he make brash predictions about his team. He was known as a friendly, warm person, but not one who embraced the limelight in any way beyond swinging a powerful bat. The Seattle Mariners were not one of baseball's best-known and most popular teams. Based on the West Coast, the Mariners' night game results often went unrecorded in the morning newspapers of the nation's largest cities on the East Coast. It also did not help that for years during Martinez's time with the Mariners they were one of the sport's losingest franchises, a team that did not make the playoffs or earn national television attention. For all of those reasons, Martinez remained an anonymous star.

The casual baseball fan might take a glance at the American League batting statistics and see the name "Martinez" nestled in the top five and then pause and say out loud, "Who's Martinez?" There were other players with the common Latino name and the exploits of Seattle's Martinez were often difficult to catch up with outside of the Pacific Northwest.

When Martinez won that first batting title in 1992, he also led the AL in doubles with 46. Since he was not one of the league's extraordinary home-run belters, the double seemed to define Martinez's offense. He got his share of homers

(309 lifetime), but he smashed 514 doubles. (Given his below average foot speed triples were not part of his repertoire.)

While the batting championship put Martinez on radar screens, he immediately suffered through two injury-riddled seasons that buried him in obscurity again. Martinez missed 120 games in 1993 and barely played in half the Mariners' games in 1994. When he returned at full strength in 1995, he returned with all engines firing, hitting a career high .356 to claim a second batting title. "He's the No. 1 hitter in this league," said then-Mariners manager Lou Piniella in 1995. "There are a lot of great hitters in this league, but he's No. 1." (Quoted in Keegan.)

That was a compliment too large for the self-effacing Martinez to digest. He did not claim to be the No. 1 star on his own team, a team that featured outfielder Ken Griffey Jr. and pitcher Randy Johnson, two players definitely bound for the National Baseball Hall of Fame. When Martinez was told what his manager said about him he did all but blush and immediately concede the title to Griffey. Martinez might have the batting titles on his resume, but Griffey was a natural who could do more damage in more ways at the plate. "I think I'd trade with Junior," Martinez said. "I just enjoy to watch him hit. His swing is very easy looking. It looks perfect to me. I'd love to have his swing." (Quoted in Keegan.)

As Griffey's long career wound down he had almost exactly twice as many home runs on his resume as Martinez (more than 600), but nary a batting title. They were two different types of hitters. Although Seattle does not have the same significantly large Hispanic population of a New York, Los Angeles, or Texas, Martinez was a local hero once he established his .300-plus hitting. Some called him "Edgar The Great." Spanish-speaking fans held up signs in the Kingdome reading, "Edgar Esta Caliente." Translated that said, "Edgar is hot." That might have been a reference to Martinez's dark good looks, but was most probably describing his phenomenal all-around 1995 season.

That year Martinez not only hit .356, but recorded a stunning .479 on-base percentage. He knocked in 113 runs while slamming 29 homers, scoring 121 runs, and collecting 52 doubles. He also walked 116 times. In a season shortened slightly by one of baseball's many labor battles, Martinez appeared in all 145 games, leading the American League in that category too. After that season any baseball fan, whether living in Seattle, Florida, or Alaska, would have to be statistically blind not to recognize Martinez's value.

Mariner teammates were sometimes in awe of the Quiet Man's contributions. Jay Buhner, the bald-headed slugger stationed near Martinez in the lineup, raved about Martinez' all-around abilities. "Look at all he does," Buhner said. "Look at his average. Look at his on-base percentage. Look at his slugging percentage (.628). It's the total package." (Quoted in Keegan.)

Baseball purists have argued that being a designated hitter means a player is only a half a player. The flip side of the role is being stuck in the role of permanent pinch-hitter. Pinch-hitting once a game or once in a while is no easy task. A DH is a full member of the lineup, and must stay sharp and ready to hit when his turn comes around. That is usually four times a game, the same as the starting first baseman or catcher. Readiness is critical. Concentration and focus are imperative. "It takes a different type of animal to be able to do that," Buhner said of a designated hitter. "I can't do it. He is magical with a bat in his hands." (Quoted in Keegan.)

The designated hitter must be patient, must stay in the flow of the game, and be ready when his turn at bat arrives. He has the freedom to sit in the dugout and schmooze with teammates and he has the freedom to retreat to the clubhouse to do anything that makes sense to him to maintain his sharpness. Before and during games Martinez was focused on his hitting. He took lots of batting practice and he took lots of practice swings with a two-pound, weighted batting doughnut attached to his personal bats. Martinez swung the bat repeatedly with the added weight in order to develop quickness in his swing. "Hitting a baseball isn't easy, so you do everything you can to stay sharp," Martinez said. "That's why I use the doughnut. It adds weight to the bat and it makes swinging (in batting practice) more of a challenge." (Quoted in Pearlman.)

A designated hitter makes his living with excellent eyesight, good judgment on approaching fastballs, and quick reflexes. He is not asked to take infield field-ing practice, but being merely an average hitter won't cut it in the big leagues if the DH can't make noise at the plate. That is, after all, why he is on the roster. Once considered an oddity, the designated hitter position is entrenched in the American League even if the true oddity now is that the National League doesn't play by the same rules. Accepting the logic that fans would rather watch another professional hitter swing away than a pitcher strike out or hit feeble ground balls, the DH is in use in most minor league baseball, college, and amateur play.

After 37 seasons, it is Edgar Martinez who emerged as the premier DH. His high average, steady power, and RBI numbers (six seasons of more than 100) stand out. Martinez's work ethic was nearly as renowned as his batting average.

"Edgar out-works everybody I've ever played baseball with," said Mariner teammate Mike Blowers. "A lot of it started when he moved from third base to DH. Edgar at the time felt a lot of pressure: 'I really have to hit now.' That's when you saw him hit the weight room a lot harder. He wanted to drive the baseball a little bit more. He hits from the time he shows up at the ballpark, usually about 2 (for a night game), until the time the game starts, and sometimes even after. Every-body talks about the work, but he is also extremely talented." (Quoted in Edgar Martinez . . .)

Martinez was one of the successful baseball players who let his bat do most of his talking. He was friendly to one and all in the Mariners' clubhouse, respectful to management, and open to fans. But he was not a chatterbox. He was not the type of guy to sound off to a player, but was a dignified presence. As he aged, Martinez became the key veteran in the clubhouse as Griffey, Johnson, and then Alex Rodriguez, the other top stars, went on to other teams. He was looked up to both for his demeanor and the results he produced.

"You talk about how hard these guys work, and the great ones work very, very hard," said Mariners Chairman Howard Lincoln, "but Edgar, his work ethic is in another orbit. Nobody works harder than he does. I'm not sure anybody ever has in baseball. In the dead of winter, he's down there in the cage by himself. His self-discipline is just incredible. His eyes actually sparkle. You meet a few people like that who just light up a room and he's that way. He's a very special person. Foremost, he is a true gentleman. He is an absolute gentleman in every sense of the word. He's a wonderful human being. I've never met a nicer man in my life. He's just that kind and decent a guy." (Quoted in Edgar Martinez . . .)

Throughout the late 1990s and into the early 2000s, Martinez was a hitting machine. He could always be counted on to produce one of the top batting averages in the American League, but he mixed in outstanding statistics in other categories that demonstrated his versatility at bat. In 1996, Martinez hit .327. In 1997, he hit .330. In 1998, Martinez hit .322 with a league-leading .429 on-base percentage. In 1999, he hit .337, again with a league-leading .447 on-base percentage. In 2000, Martinez hit .324 with 37 homers and a league-leading 145 runs batted in. In 2001, he hit .306 with a .423 on-base percentage and 116 RBIs. It was a tremendous stretch as year after year Martinez showed he owned the plate when he was in the batter's box.

Yet he never made his own case verbally for greatness. It was against his nature to toot his own horn. Once again teammates did the talking for Martinez. "Edgar is probably the most humble of all the great players I've met," said Mariner infielder Bret Boone. "For a guy with his accomplishments, the way he goes about his business, the way he acts, is truly honorable." (Quoted in Edgar Martinez.)

Martinez suffered the usual kinds of injuries that sideline baseball players for extended stretches early in his career, but in 1999 he experienced an obstacle that he feared might bring his playing days to an abrupt end. In May of that year, with the season underway, Martinez went through a period of time when he could not focus on the ball being released from the pitcher's hand and could not see it quickly enough to judge its direction as it approached the plate.

When Martinez was in the minor leagues a visit to an optometrist resulted in him being diagnosed with strabismus. The affliction causes the eyes to become unsynchronized. In Martinez's case that meant his right eye sometimes drifted out and he could focus only his left eye. Complicated by fatigue and aging, the condition typically grows worse. When the 1999 flare-up caught Martinez by surprise at age 36 he believed he might have to retire. The Mariners' trainer Rick Griffin said it was a genuine fear that Martinez might not be able to see a ball that was coming at his head and might be seriously harmed. (Quoted in Rosenthal.)

Although nothing was said publicly about this affliction earlier in Martinez's career, his optometrist, Dr. Douglas Nikaitani, called it "a miracle," that Martinez had achieved so much in a role so dependent on sharp eyesight. "He is basically one-eyed at times," Nikaitani said. The doctor said he also knew of no other Major League players with strabismus. (Quoted in Rosenthal.)

Throughout his career, Martinez said, in addition to his batting practice swings he had to stick to a special routine consisting of 30 minutes of eye exercises before each game in order to be able to compete against throwers with 90 mph stuff.

"I couldn't play at this level without them," Martinez said. The routine helped Martinez keep his eyes working together. What alarmed him in 1999 was the fact that for the first time the eye exercises were failing him. Despite his religious-like devotion to doing them he was still having difficulty judging pitches. He might gauge the release point accurately, but then lose the ball in flight, or misjudge the location altogether. He worried his career might be finished. "I tried everything," he said. "I was doing everything I always did to prepare myself, but still, it wasn't enough." (Quoted in Rosenthal.)

An emergency visit to Nikaitani paid dividends. In a somewhat bizarre trial, Martinez explained how the doctor first threw tennis balls at him requiring the player to react and bat them away, then used martial arts kicking and punching moves that Martinez also had to bat away, all to challenge the hitter's reflexes. To further confuse Martinez, Nikaitani shouted math problems at him. The scene sounded like an out-take from an extreme comedy, but the treatment actually worked. Martinez promptly recorded two multi-home-run games. Two years passed before Martinez told anyone in the media about his complex sight problem and the remedy. "I felt I was improving, back to where I wanted to be again," Martinez said. (Quoted in Rosenthal.)

Martinez remained a top-notch hitter into his late 30s, a time when most players slow down. When asked how he kept up his .324 hitting at age 37, Martinez said, "Older players who survive learn some secrets. When you're young, the season ends and you can take two months off to relax. Now I take one week. When you're older, your body starts to go. You have to do everything you can to fight that. You can't let go." (Quoted in Pearlman.)

At that time, no one outside of the Mariners knew that Martinez's main secret revolved around his eyesight and that the exercises he underwent to fight back went beyond pushups and sit-ups.

A ruptured tendon in his left hamstring in 2002 made Martinez hint at retirement, but he returned to play in 97 games. Then he signed a one-year, $10 million contract for the 2003 season. Looking like his old full-strength self at 40, Martinez batted .294 with 24 homers and 98 RBIs in 124 games. That season he became the Mariners' all-time RBI leader.

On the last weekend of his career, spent entirely in Seattle, Martinez was informed that Mayor Greg Nickels was naming a street after him that is located near Safeco Field. "It blows my mind," Martinez said. "I heard about it earlier today and I thought they were pulling my leg. This is an amazing compliment, really, really nice, and I am honored." (Quoted in Finnigan.)

For his final road trip as a Mariner, the team's airline charter company painted a special message on the side of the plane calling it (at least temporarily), "Edgar Martinez, No. 11." Martinez joked, "Does this mean I get to keep it?" No such luck, though the Mariners did hold a special day for him. (Quoted in Finnigan.)

Martinez retired after the 2004 season, notching 1,261 RBIs in addition to those 309 homers and .312 lifetime average. But only a few weeks later Martinez was honored again—with something more meaningful than his own airplane. He was named the winner of Major League Baseball's Roberto Clemente Award for 2004. The award is presented annually to the player who combines baseball talent and community service. "Clemente was my idol as a child and to get this award is very special to me," Martinez said. (Quoted in Kelley.)

When the designated hitter was created in 1973, Martinez had no idea it would be a position he ever played. That year, Major League Baseball instituted an award for the outstanding DH. After Martinez retired, however, the award was given a new name. As testimony to the work he performed at the position it was renamed The Edgar Martinez Award. The recognition solidified Martinez's stature as the greatest designated hitter.

The only thing remaining is to determine, with Martinez becoming eligible for the first time in 2010, whether or not he will be the first DH elected to the Hall of Fame. Although Martinez appeared in big-league games for 18 seasons, his first three years were almost irrelevant and he did not become a starter until he was 27. Including later injury-diminished years, Martinez had just 12 years when he played full-time. Hall of Fame eligibility revolves around 10 seasons played, so he qualifies, but it is unknown how voters will judge the first superb designated hitter.

"I'm not going to say that I deserve to be there, but I'm not going to say that I don't deserve it," Martinez said near the end of his playing days. "Pitchers are in the Hall and they pitch once every five days. The DH is in the lineup every day." (Quoted in Wilstein.)

And the DH is part of Major League Baseball. Edgar Martinez is the test case for how selectors will view the role, but he made his case.

Further Reading

Edgar Martinez Support for the Hall of Fame, www.abarim.com/bmaigatter.htm (Comments on Martinez collected by Bruce Maigatter.)
Finnigan, Bob, "Mayor names street after Martinez," *Seattle Times*, October 2, 2004.
Keegan, Tom, "Edgar Stands Alone," *New York Post*, October 9, 1995.
Kelley, Steve, "Edgar Martinez receives Clemente Award," *Seattle Times*, October 27, 2004.
Pearlman, Jeff, "Hot to Trot," *Sports Illustrated*, July 17, 2000.
Rosenthal, Ken, "Martinez keeps the hits coming despite eye disorder," *The Sporting News*, April 30, 2001.
Wilstein, Steve, "Martinez could be first DH in Hall of Fame," Associated Press, May 22, 2003.

Pedro and Ramon Martinez

Pedro is always going to be the little brother. He is younger and is smaller physically than Ramon. But both men know the little one is king-sized on the mound, the sibling pitcher who achieved more and hopes for more yet in a career he doesn't want to relinquish.

The Martinez boys have always been close, though, and statistics will never come between them. Growing up in the Dominican Republic, Ramon led the way and Pedro followed, hanging on every word his family idol uttered and watching intently to learn baseball from what he did.

Ramon Martinez was born on March 22, 1968. Pedro Martinez was born October 25, 1971. What were the odds of two youngsters from the same family scraping to get by and surviving to become millionaire major leaguers in the United States? This is the stuff of dreams in the Dominican and the strong right arms of the Martinez brothers made the fantasy come true.

Ramon was born in Santo Domingo, the oldest city in the Western Hemisphere, and Pedro was born in a suburb, a half an hour away, in Manoguayabo. They were raised on the outskirts of the capital city in a family that barely coped financially. Six children (Ramon is the oldest) shared three beds in the household. There were no surplus funds for baseball equipment and the boys, desperate to play ball, did

The dazzling Martinez brothers of the Dominican Republic rose from poverty to star in the majors. Ramon, the elder (seated higher), pitched a no-hitter. Pedro was the greater star and remains active. Twice, with the Dodgers and Red Sox, the siblings shared the same roster. (Dan Levine/AFP/Getty Images)

their own manufacturing. They made balls out of the heads of their sister's dolls, simply ripping off the tops.

The father, Paolino, a school maintenance worker, had played baseball, and when Pedro was small he tagged along with his dad everywhere. But the parents endured a bitter divorce resulting in the clan becoming fatherless. That thrust new responsibility on Ramon and he became a role model for Pedro.

"When I began to play ball, he followed me," Ramon said. "Sometimes I would tell him that he couldn't play with us because we were using a hard ball and he was so little. He would cry. I would try to explain to him that it was danger-ous, but he always wanted to play." (Quoted on Edes.)

The three-year age difference was significant on the diamond during child-hood, but eventually Pedro, despite never growing beyond 5-foot-11 and looking scrawny even during his Major League days at 175 pounds, caught up to his brother.

Ramon was 6-foot-4, a height much likelier to meet with approval from Major League scouts. He also was very light for his size, topping out at perhaps

180 pounds. The pro scouts looking at him in the Dominican thought he would fill out, but he never did. If there were questions about the size of the Martinez brothers in a professional environment, the unavoidable attraction was the power of their arms. Anyone who can throw 90 mph while still in his teens is going to be noticed. Other flaws are likely to be pushed aside. After the radar gun is double-checked, the philosophy becomes, "We can work with him."

Naturally, as the older brother, Ramon drew the attention of the majors first. He joined the Los Angeles Dodgers in 1988 and must have told their scouts that there was another hard-thrower just like him back home and they should go grab him. The Dodgers did so and Pedro reached the majors with the Dodgers, too, in 1992. The brothers were together at the pinnacle of the sport.

There was a good reason for the scouts to listen to Ramon's judgment. In 1990, Ramon finished 20–6 with 12 complete games and a 2.96 earned run average. He struck out 223 batters, second best in the National League and made the All-Star team. It was a fabulous performance coming off two short seasons that stoked fans' appetite for more Ramon Martinez. The single-day highlight occurred in a June game when Ramon struck out 18 Atlanta Braves in a shutout, a mark that tied Sandy Koufax for the team record for K's in one game. "Everyone who walked up there made a right turn," said Atlanta manager Russ Nixon of his players' immediate returns to the dugout from the batter's box. (Quoted in "Martinez joins . . .")

The team knew what it had, saw Martinez's potential from the time he was a member of the Dominican Republic 1984 Olympic team as a 16-year-old. "Ramon is not a surprise," said Dodger vice president Fred Claire. "Ramon did not suddenly jump into the spotlight last year from our standpoint. Literally, since the day that he came into the Dodger organization the projection has been that this is a pitcher who will be a very, very important pitcher for the Dodgers. You look and you just see as much as anything the potential that is there. You see this pitcher with this great body. I mean the long arms, the long fingers, the great ability." (Quoted in Topkin.)

Ramon's fastball was clocked at 96 mph, a blur to many batters. He told sportswriters that his inspiration was hearing from older fans back home what a good player his dad was. "That made me want to play and to be somebody famous," he said. "I really love the game and I really enjoy the game. When I am on the mound I feel very excited and I really enjoy myself when I am pitching." (Quoted in Topkin.)

There was plenty of reason to enjoy himself given the results Ramon got in 1990. The only problem was that the hurler never matched those numbers again. He was a mainstay of the Dodgers' rotation, but he never won 20 games again and was never voted onto another All-Star team. Instead of improving and growing into a perennial star, Ramon had good years and year where he struggled from arm problems. In 1991 he was 17–13 and in 1995 he was 17–7.

On July 14, 1995, Ramon pitched a no-hitter before 30,988 fans at Dodger Stadium, defeating the Florida Marlins 7–0 with nine strikeouts. He walked just one batter, Tommy Gregg, in the eighth inning. Until then Martinez had a perfect game going. After the final out he leapt into the arms of catcher Mike Piazza in celebration. It was a typical emotional outburst of pleasure that Los Angeles spectators appreciated from one of their new favorites.

Some Martinez fans said he retained a child-like joy for the sport, for instance, after a game tossing the ball into the stands to a kid he picked out. But they were misreading the depth of Ramon's memory of an impoverished past. The same young man who took his younger siblings under his wing was still trying to protect them and provide for them once his right wing provided a living. When he made money, the first thing Ramon did was replace the dilapidated family home in the Dominican with a new house. "I thought about buying myself a car or an apartment first," he said, "but then I realize that is not right. I first have to keep the family together. I like the home because it is close to where I am from and because it keeps me close with everybody. My family is where I have my good times." (Quoted in Plaschke.)

When he was healthy, Ramon pitched well and could still hum it, but he seemed fragile and eventually Los Angeles tired of him and did not value his throwing as much as it once did. After spending the first 11 years of his 14-year career with the Dodgers, by 2000 Ramon found himself with the Boston Red Sox.

As Pedro Martinez aged and worked his way through the Dodgers' minor league teams, he never hesitated to credit his big brother for his help. "Ramon was my mom, was my dad, was my friend, my brother," Pedro said. "Everything I needed him to be he was, and he is. And a lot of the reason why I have so much success, it's him." (Quoted in *Baseball Almanac*.) When Pedro was first signed by the Dodgers, he gave Ramon his entire $6,500 signing bonus as a gesture of his fondness and appreciation.

Meanwhile, Pedro was working his own way up to the Dodgers' roster and making a name for himself. He appeared in two games in 1992 and fought his way into the rotation the next season, showing all of the promise in the world with a 10–5 record. But the Dodgers apparently did not have either the patience or the interest in keeping around both Martinez brothers, and in a phenomenal miscalculation dealt Pedro to the Montreal Expos in 1994 for infielder Delino DeShields. The brothers were separated, but in Canada Pedro blossomed into one of the best pitchers in baseball.

He was just 22 and threw a 92 mph fastball despite his comparatively diminutive stature. Martinez also prevented batters from hitting by throwing his fastball inside.

In an era when the pitcher's arsenal had been diluted by officious umpires seeking to prevent them from dusting off hitters, the small Martinez was fearless. He sought to show the sluggers who was boss and who owned the plate. If he hit them, well, so be it. In 1993 and 1994, Martinez nicked 11 batters each season. Some of them complained. Compared to some of the muscular behemoths hauling their lumber up to the plate, Martinez resembled a Little League player. He weighed barely more than 160 pounds before adding a bit of weight later in his career.

"I don't really like to have enemies on other teams," Martinez said. "I'm a friendly man. I don't like to hurt anyone. I'm looking for a living, trying to support myself and my family the best I can. I'm not trying to hurt anybody. I wouldn't like anybody to hurt me so why should I want to hurt someone?" Scare them? Maybe. Or at least make them uncomfortable in the batter's box. What disturbed some baseball people the most was that hitting batters is usually dismissed as a sign of wildness, but Pedro had just about the best control in the sport when it came to being stingy about surrendering bases on balls. "I don't know if he's intentionally throwing at someone's head or not," said Cincinnati coach Merv Rettenmund, "but he's coming up there too often. He's not supposed to do that." (Quoted in Marantz.)

Pedro recorded five straight winning seasons with the Expos and made the National League All-Star team in 1996 and 1997. That year when he finished 17–8 he led the National League with a 1.90 earned run average. A tremendous control artist, Martinez struck out 305 batters while walking just 67. In an explosive hitting season when sluggers were cracking more and more home runs, the opponent's batting average against Pedro was .184. He was otherworldly at times.

No one was happier about Pedro's emergence into a star than Ramon. "I'm very proud of what he's done," older brother said. "And he's not done yet." (Quoted Edes.)

Ramon was correct. Remarkably, many of Pedro's best seasons were ahead of him after a change of scenery. Only a few teams in baseball could meet the star's asking price when he became a free agent, and the Boston Red Sox anted up a huge, multi-million-dollar contract in 1998. The switch to the American League only emphasized Martinez's dominance. During his first season with Boston, Martinez went 19–7 with a 2.89 earned run average and was selected for his first AL All-Star team. A year later he was even better, putting together one of the greatest seasons ever by a starting pitcher. The 1999 Martinez won the Cy Young Award for a second time on the strength of 23–4 work. His winning percentage was an astounding .852, his 313 strikeouts led the league, and so did his 2.07 ERA. He walked just 37 batters all year, nearly a 10–1 strikeout to bases on ball ratio.

Martinez was a marvel in more ways than one. Normally, the flamethrowers who overpower batters with fastballs are big men, standing well over 6 feet and with Major League cabooses and tree trunks for legs to aid their power.

Martinez remains a skinny dude with a whiplash arm. "In 1997 he became the shortest and lightest pitcher ever to strike out 300 batters in a season," *Sports Illustrated* reported. "Last year Martinez became the greatest combination of power and control in the history of the game." (Quoted in Verducci.)

While Martinez's fastball garnered most of the attention, pitching aficionados recognized his slickness in other guises. His other pitches, the curve and change-up, did equal damage in fooling hitters. Bret Saberhagen, a two-time Cy Young Award winner for the Kansas City Royals was finishing his career with the Red Sox when Martinez joined the club. He was agog over Pedro's change-up. "It's a Bugs Bunny change-up," Saberhagen said. "It moves so much. Bugs Bunny is the only one with a change-up that can move like that and he has the help of animators." (Quoted in Verducci.)

As a bonus for Pedro, the Red Sox acquired Ramon for the 1999 season, reuniting the happy brothers. Ramon went 2–1 in limited action that year because of shoulder surgery, but finished 10–8 in 2000. In spring training, *Boston Globe* columnist Dan Shaughnessy said he hoped the pairing of the Martinez brothers would be compared to the Dean brothers, Dizzy and Daffy, who dazzled for the Cardinals in the 1930s. "Heady stuff, no" he wrote. (Quoted Shaughnessy.) The combination was not quite that good, but the brothers both produced. In 2000, Pedro won a third Cy Young Award with an 18–6 record highlighted by a minuscule 1.74 earned run average and 284 strikeouts. His control was as amazing as ever with just 32 walks. Opponents might as well have been carrying toothpicks not Louisville sluggers to the plate against him because they batted a collectively puny .167. At one point in that season the Martinez brothers were scheduled to become the first siblings to start a double-header for the same team in 26 years. But the games against the Cleveland Indians were rained out.

That was Ramon's last good year. He drifted to the Pittsburgh Pirates for a 0–2 season in 2001 and that ended his big-league career with a solid 135–88 record. But Pedro glittered on for the Sox. In 2002 he finished 20–4. During the 2003 American League Championship Series, Pedro became the focal point of a weird incident. The Yankees and Red Sox spilled onto the field for a brawl. Incensed Yankees coach Don Zimmer, then 72, made a beeline for Martinez, who was not even in the game. As the slower man ran at him swinging as if to land a punch, Martinez made like a matador to dodge Zimmer. Then he pushed him slightly. Zimmer fell to the ground harder than expected and it became a cause célèbre to blame Martinez for beating up on an old man even though he did no such thing. Zimmer hurt himself and left in an ambulance. Later he said, "It was not my finest moment and I wish it never happened." (Quoted Zimmer.)

In 2004, Pedro Martinez's 16–9 record helped Boston win its first World Series crown since 1918. It was one of the most popular team-sport victories in the United States in years. The Red Sox defeated the Angels in the first round of the playoffs, became the first team to ever rebound from a 0–3 disadvantage in a comeback over the Yankees, and then swept the Cardinals in the Series. Martinez made a pact with slugger Manny Ramirez to let their hair grow long during the playoffs (much the way hockey players grow playoff beards) and took to flapping their follicles at happy moments. "That's the way we congratulate each other and we thank God for whatever good deed we had done on the field. We do it our own way. That's just Manny being Manny and Pedro being Pedro," Martinez said. (Quoted in McNeal and Veltrop, 128.)

Besides doing his job on the mound every fifth day, Martinez was involved in a strange situation as the celebratory season unfolded. He became friendly with Nelson de la Rosa, a Hollywood actor who was a dwarf, and invited him into the locker room and told the world he was a good-luck charm. De la Rosa, from the Dominican, stood 2-foot-4 and was listed in the Guinness Book of World Records as the world's shortest adult. Eventually Pedro and his pal had a falling out. On a more serious basis, Martinez knew how much long-time Red Sox fans had longed for a title and he desperately wanted to be part of the experience delivering it. "Every day in Boston somebody will tell me, 'My father—or grandfather— wants to see the Red Sox win the World Series just once,' " he said. "I tell them I will try, but I cannot do it by myself. It takes a team." (Quoted in Verducci.)

It did take a team and the Red Sox had the right team at the right time at last. When the Series ended no one celebrated more enthusiastically spraying champagne around the clubhouse than Martinez. If it was possible, the World Series title also made him an even bigger hero in the Dominican. Martinez had long spread his wealth back home. He built clinics, invested in businesses, and helped construct schools, all while winning Cy Young Awards.

"They all want to pitch and they all want to be Pedro and wear his number," said Ruddy Ramirez, one of Martinez's youth coaches. "Pedro is the face that the majority of Dominicans recognize. He's an idol in this country." (Quoted in Red and Quinn.)

Martinez's marriage with the Red Sox ended in divorce after the 2004 season. He joined the New York Mets as a free agent, recorded a fine 15–8 campaign in 2005, but then his body started to break down. Repeated injuries kept him off the mound most of the next few seasons and it looked as if he was bound for retirement in 2008 with a 214–99 mark representing a superb .684 winning percentage.

But Martinez refused to give up. In the summer of 2009 he signed a contract with the Philadelphia Phillies, hoping to coax a few more victories out of his right arm and started 5–0. He appeared in the 2009 World Series and was looking for a new team affiliation for 2010. Even as he rehabbed during his injury-plagued stretch, Martinez tried to give back to the Dominican. He helped with hurricane and tropical storm relief when the island was damaged. He also kept expanding and improving the Escuela Basica San Miguel School for nearly 1,000 students in Manoguayabo that he began funding in 2003. After the 2004 Red Sox World Series win, Martinez donated his entire $223,000 winner's share to the school.

"God has given me so much," Pedro said, "that I can only pay Him back. So many odds I've defeated that my reward for everything is paying back. That's my payback, to help the community." (Quoted in Red.)

At the time Martinez did not know if he would ever throw another pitch in the majors, but he did know that once he was finally retired he would return to the Dominican Republic. There was more to do in his birthplace. A high school, a police station, a library, a health center, and a stadium were all in his plans. He had the money and the blueprint was in his head. His arm had provided well.

Further Reading

Baseball Almanac, www.baseball-almanac.com (Ramon Martinez no-hitter box score).

Edes, Gordon, "Brothers in Arms," *Boston Globe*, April 2, 2000.

"Martinez joins Koufax as Dodger strikeout king," Associated Press, June 6, 1990.

Marantz, Steve, "Pedro Martinez says he has to pitch high and tight to be effective," *The Sporting News*, July 18, 1994.

McNeal, Stan and Veltrop, Kyle, *Curse Reversed* (St. Louis, The Sporting News Books, 2004).

Plaschke, Bill, "Still No Place Like Home," *Los Angeles Times*, February 13, 1991.

Red, Christian, "School That Pedro Built," *New York Daily News*, February 7, 2007.

Red, Christian and Quinn, T.J., "In D.R., Pedro is Daddy," *New York Daily News*, December 5, 2004.

Shaughnessy, Dan, "Brotherly love, Martinez style, warms camp," *Boston Globe*, March 12, 1999.

Topkin, Marc, "Dodgers' Ramon Martinez Chases Dream of Greatness," *Baseball Digest*, July, 1991.

Verducci. Tom, "The Power of Pedro," *Sports Illustrated*, March 27, 2000.

Zimmer, Don, "Zim still pulling no punches," *New York Daily News*, June 27, 2004.

Minnie Minoso

When experts refer to baseball records that will never be topped, they always overlook one. Granted, it is a quirky record, but one worthy of respect and admiration despite the light-hearted manner in which it was established.

A hero to many early Latino players, Cuban Orestes "Minnie" Minoso first played for the New York Cubans in the Negro Leagues, then became the first black player for the Chicago White Sox in 1951. Minoso, a seven-time All-Star, remains an active White Sox ambassador at 87 and there is a statue of Minoso at U.S. Cellular Field. (AP Photo)

Orestes "Minnie" Minoso, the Cuban-born flash who was the first black player to suit up for the Chicago White Sox, is the only man in history to play professional baseball in seven different decades. It is an implausible claim to fame, but in 2003, when Minoso, then at least 77, pulled on a uniform for the St. Paul Saints in the independent Northern League as a designated hitter, he authored unique history.

Minoso broke into professional baseball in the 1940s, advanced to the majors before the decade was out, and continued in the majors through the 1950s and into the 1960s. In 1976, when Minoso's old friend Bill Veeck bought the White Sox for the second time he made his pal a four-decade player. Minoso had eight at-bats with one hit in 1976. In 1980, Minoso had two more at-bats to become a five-decade player.

Although Minoso's flesh was willing, and the opportunity was offered in the 1990s, Major League Baseball officials refused to allow him to play in any league under their auspices. However, Bill Veeck's son Mike, owner of the Saints, stepped up to the plate and invited Minoso to make an appearance for the Minnesota team in 1993. That made Minoso the first ever six-decade player. Finally, a decade later, Minoso made a cameo appearance for the Saints again.

Then, at an age when many cannot stand straight, Minoso got his licks in with that at-bat in 2003. Minoso owns and wears a ring marking his seven decades involved in pro ball. This is certainly a different claim to fame than other ballplayers can make, but it would be short-sighted and incorrect to dismiss Minoso as a mere sideshow under the big top.

Saturino Orestes Arrieta Armas Minoso was born in Cuba in 1922, according to the *Baseball Encyclopedia*, but he insists he is four years younger. A legend in his home country, Minoso also became a star in the United States and many believe he has the credentials to be in the Hall of Fame. Once an unfortunate youngster being raised on a sugar cane plantation by parents living in poverty, Minoso became an orphan at an early age and his upbringing was supervised by two sisters in Havana. Beginning in 1941, the siblings lived in a $7-a-month, one-room apartment. Minoso worked part-time in a cigar-making company as he learned baseball. His first semi-pro team was the Partagas Cigar Factory team. At 16 Minoso became the starting first-baseman.

Swift afoot, with a good glove and a powerful bat, Minoso established himself quickly as a player of many skills. He was especially daring and accomplished on the base paths, taking the extra base on hits, as well as stealing. After three years of seasoning, Minoso's efforts were noticed by one of the top clubs in the Cuban pro league, and the Marianao Tigers signed him.

It was clear immediately that Minoso was traveling in big-time circles. Early in his tenure with Marianao the Tigers were playing Cienfuego, a team that featured one of the all-time Cuban greats Cristobal Torriente. Torriente was at the peak of his fame and was nearing the end of his career. He got Minoso's attention. "Hey, little kid, Minoso!" Torriente beckoned. Torriente saw that Minoso was using a ring on his spikes that added flamboyance to his laces and he disapproved. His advice was that it would be better to respect the uniform. Minoso recalled it as being more of a reprimand, but he listened and ditched the practice. (Quoted in Minoso and Fagen, 22.)

Minoso emerged as a star on his home turf, but he aspired to play baseball in the United States. In the mid-1940s, Major League Baseball was closed to dark-skinned men like Minoso, but he knew he could open up new worlds if the Negro Leagues of Satchel Paige and Josh Gibson took note of his game. Little escaped the ear of Alex Pompez, owner of the New York Cubans, and after baseball's desegregation, one of the most influential Latin talent scouts in history. Pompez liked Minoso's style and in 1945 made the offer the young player hoped for. At 19, Minoso was on his way to the United States to play for the Cubans in New York.

"This was the dream of every black ballplayer anywhere," Minoso said. "I was thrilled and scared at the same time. I had never been out of Cuba." (Quoted in Minoso and Fagen, 26.)

Minoso was enthusiastic about undertaking the adventure of a lifetime but could not have imagined all of the twists and turns his life would take once he committed to a life of baseball in the United States. At the time there was no prospect of Minoso playing in the big leagues. As he headed for New York, Minoso's focus was solely on the Negro Leagues.

As a child of poverty Minoso did not always have enough to eat and he almost never had new clothes. He certainly did not have a distinguished wardrobe as a kid. Once he had money in his pocket Minoso acquired a new habit that became one of his signature traits. Minoso became enamored of flashy clothes and big cars, particularly Cadillacs, and those tastes acquired in New York stayed with him for good. "Some people like to drink," he said. "Others play golf. I liked buying sharp clothes. Sometimes I'd change outfits two or three times a day." (Quoted in Minoso and Fagen, 30.)

Minoso honed his skills with the Cubans as the world changed around him. In 1947, Jackie Robinson broke the color barrier that had prevented black players from competing in the majors since the 1880s and other teams sought black talent. Minoso was an All-Star for the Cubans in 1948 and he was signed by the Cleveland Indians, at the time owned by Bill Veeck. It was not easy for Minoso to crack the lineup of the World Champions, but he saw action in nine games in 1949 before being shunted back to the minors for all of 1950.

In 1951, White Sox general manager Frank Lane, trying to restore long-lost luster to the Chicago club that had been wallowing near the basement of the American League since the 1919 Black Sox Scandal, was swapping live players with the frequency of baseball card trades. He acquired Minoso and the transplanted Cuban found a new home.

Minoso was an instant smash with Comiskey Park fans—literally. He swatted a home run in his first game. That was one way to make a good impression. But Minoso's dashing form on the bases truly convinced Chicago faithful he was a special player. May 1, 1951, the day Minoso's name was first written into the lineup, was also a special occasion for him, the White Sox, Chicago, and Major League Baseball. It marked the debut of the first black man in a White Sox uniform. Minoso does not boast about the appearance, but he has given thought to the significance of his inaugural game and is proud that he took a step forward for race relations.

"Mr. Jackie and Mr. Branch Rickey (general manager of the Dodgers) opened the door to us," Minoso said of breaching the Major League color line. "I don't care for color, position, nationality, beauty, or ugliness. I am the first black player for the White Sox, but it had to be somebody. It is a good thing, but I am not a special person because of that. I paid my price, just like Jackie." (Quoted in Freedman, 127.) Actually, many people in Chicago, where he is revered, do believe that Minoso is a special person, but not only because of his ground-breaking role.

The arrival of Minoso and a couple of other speedster players helped define a White Sox era. Minoso was the front man for the "Go Go White Sox."

Minoso made the All-Star team as a rookie in 1951, his first of seven appearances, led the American League in stolen bases three times, and led the league in being hit by pitches 10 times.

The phrase "taking one for the team" might have been coined for Minoso. One reason he was hit by pitches so often was because he crowded the plate. And Minoso's flashy style might have irked some pitchers. But as the first black man to play for the White Sox, there was also some suspicion that prejudice may have played a role. At times Minoso was hospitalized by fastballs hitting him in the head and he missed long stretches of playing time with occasional injuries. Yet he never backed away in the batter's box and always returned to active play with the same fearlessness.

A few years into his stay in the majors, Minoso, who had the added disadvantage of adjusting to the majors because Spanish was his first language, addressed the race issue. "My first year in big leagues in 1951, one team—I no tell who—always call me names," Minoso said. " 'We hit you in the head, you black____.' I think they try make me afraid. But they stop with names after first year." (Quoted in Miller.)

Minoso grappled with English, but sportswriters at the time made no effort to clean up his phrasing and he resented being made to sound dumb while he tried to improve his knowledge of the language. But as a written record that is how many of Minoso's and his fellow Latino players' thoughts are passed down. Minoso did admit to a New York sportswriter that his tongue could not keep up with his mind. "I know all the words," he said, "but they get stuck here." He pointed to his teeth as he said this. (Quoted in Williams.) That only made it worse if sportswriters seized more upon his accent than the meaning of his words.

At the time of this reflection, Minoso had been beaned by Yankee pitcher Bob Grim and seriously hurt with a concussion. This time, however, Minoso absolved Grim, who visited him in the hospital to apologize, of intent. That pitch was the fifth that had bounced off of Minoso's head in four seasons, but he reiterated his resolve to return as strong as he had been. "I no quit," Minoso said. "I been hit in head eight times, but I rather die than stop playing. Is the best game in the world." The sportswriter quoting Minoso said his dying on the field worried others. "In dugouts around the American League, they're fearful of what may happen next time . . ." (Quoted in Miller.)

For all of the plunkings that left bruisings—in the shoulders, back, forearms, elbows, legs, and feet—Minoso not only survived, but continued to thrive as a star player. Aside from his brief latter years appearances in fresh decades, Minoso spent 17 years in the majors. He compiled a lifetime batting average of .298 and led the AL in triples three times, with a high of 18 in 1954. Minoso also stroked 186 home runs and drove in 1,023 runs. Minoso hit over .300 nine times.

Although he started as a third baseman, Minoso's greatest success in the majors came as an outfielder, where he won three Gold Gloves. He covered large amounts of territory and tried for daring grabs of sinking line drives and tailing away fly balls. As a base-runner Minoso demoralized pitchers by the way he sought to distract them with large leads, stolen bases, and always trying to take an extra base when the ball was in play.

"Minnie beats the opposition so many ways," White Sox mid-1950s manager Marty Marion said. "He's always getting on base, no matter how." (Quoted in Miller.)

Teammates and sportswriters often remarked on Minoso's positive attitude as one of his major attributes. Much like Ernie Banks, Minoso seemed to relish every day at the ballpark, every trip to the plate, every game on the schedule just a little bit more than other ballplayers. Noting a story of how Minoso supposedly gave away a car to someone who admired his wheels, one sportswriter who had pleasant dealings with him over a period of years could not gush enough about his characteristics. He wrote: "About the only thing on which this cheerful, generous, talented fellow has ever placed any value is a starting lineup listing his name." (Quoted in Williams.)

Minoso came up with the Indians, was traded to the White Sox, then in 1957 was traded back to the Indians (unfortunately for him in time to miss the White Sox's first pennant in 40 years), and then in 1960 was shipped back to the White Sox. He played the 1962 season for the St. Louis Cardinals. That was a new experience for Minoso—a journey through the National League. When he joined the Cardinals, Minoso announced that he had purchased a new Cadillac to commemorate the change. "My car had just 8,000 miles on it, but I wanted everything new because I'm in a new league with a new team," Minoso said. (Quoted in Russo.) Alas, by the end of that season, Minoso felt as if he had 8,000 fresh miles on his own odometer, because he had been injured and could appear in just 39 games.

The showing did not influence the Cardinals to retain Minoso's rights and in 1963 he played for the Washington Senators. The Senators, one of the losingest teams in American League history, did not have much to be happy about very often, and when Minoso arrived in the clubhouse for the first time he took issue with the subdued atmosphere. "Hope things aren't always like this," he said. "I hope everybody laughs, because when you're laughing, you're winning." (Quoted in White.) The Senators probably hadn't done much laughing since Walter Johnson's heyday in the 1920s and not even Minoso could alter that.

Although he played in 135 games, Minoso did not have a good season with the Senators, finishing with a .229 average. He was released with the notation that he was 40 years old. The message was clear—Minoso no longer had the goods to play in the big leagues. A man who loved the game so much was not prepared to walk away, however. Minoso got one more chance with the White Sox and was thrilled to have it.

"It is my whole life," Minoso said of his devotion to baseball at the time and his pleasure at being White Sox property again. "Without it, I am nothing at all. I feel like I'm back home again. Now when I hang up my glove, I can do it at home." (Quoted in "Minoso Is . . .")

Minoso was indeed home, but his career was just about over. He appeared in only 30 games in 1964, with a .228 average, and except for the brief "call-ups" for a game or an at-bat far in the distant future, his regular baseball career was over.

By the mid-1960s, sadly for natives of the country whose relatives were stuck on the island, Cuba was no longer hospitable to professional ballplayers. After Fidel Castro took over the government and imposed a Communist dictatorship, Cuba eliminated professional baseball. Only amateur baseball was allowed. Cubans who made their living in the United States could not go home to visit and their families could not come to see them in the United States Minoso did not want to abandon his country. His country abandoned him. So Minoso settled in Chicago, where he continues to live.

For many years, Minoso has maintained a close relationship with the White Sox. He is one of the team's community ambassadors, making public appearances and periodically taking in games at U.S. Cellular Field, the ballpark that replaced old Comiskey Park in 1991. Whether he is wearing sports shirts to the ball game or suits to sports memorabilia conventions to sign autographs, Minoso has retained his reputation as a clothes horse and is usually dashing in appearance.

In tribute to Minoso's stellar playing career, his role as a barrier breaker as the team's first black player, and his close ties to the team, the White Sox erected a life-sized statue of Minoso in September 2004 that stands in the outfield concourse. Minoso is depicted in a batting stance, prepared no doubt to whack the ball for a double. Minoso, said White Sox owner Jerry Reinsdorf, is "probably the most popular player in the history of the franchise. People who never saw him play love him. He has an amazing magnetic personality. He draws people to him." (Quoted in Merkin.)

Minoso's No. 9 jersey was retired in 1983 and a picture of him is displayed on the left-center field wall. Minoso had always been partial to wearing No. 9 wherever he played. It represented an homage to Ted Williams, the Red Sox slugger. "No. 9 also belonged to one of the greatest (Williams)," Minoso said. "And I believe Ted left a few base hits in the No. 9 uniform." (Quoted in Russo.)

Recognition beyond Chicago and Cuba has always come a little bit harder for Minoso, but in 2008 he was awarded the Jackie Robinson Lifetime Achievement Award. The Legacy Award was presented by Major League Baseball and the Negro Leagues Baseball Museum. Minoso always refers to Robinson as

"Mr. Jackie" as a gesture of respect for the pathfinding role that Robinson played in opening the majors to black players from the United States and Latin America. The scope of the award was a reminder that many times in the past when they should have been saying it, not everyone called this ballplayer Mr. Minoso.

Further Reading

Freedman, Lew, *Game of My Life Chicago White Sox* (Champaign, Illinois, Sports Publishing LLC, 2008).

Merkin, Scott, "Minoso Wins Legacy Award," NLB.com October 12, 2007.

Miller, Lou, " 'I Not Afraid,' Says Minnie, Back After 50th Plunking," *Cleveland Press*, July 15, 1955.

"Minoso Is 'Back Home' With White Sox Mates," United Press International, March 22, 1964.

Minoso, Minnie and Fagen, Herb, *Just Call Me Minnie* (Champaign, Illinois, Sagamore Publishing, 1994).

Russo, Neal, "Minoso, Old Man Young, Talks Baseball As Well As He Plays It," *St. Louis Post-Dispatch*, December 12, 1961.

White, Russ, "Minnie's All For Laughs," unattributed newspaper, National Baseball Hall of Fame Library archives, April 4, 1963.

Williams, Joe, "Minoso Is What Cuba Once Was," *New York World Telegram & Sun*, May 16, 1962.

Tony Perez

Tony Perez was one of the caught-in-between Cuban baseball stars. He signed a contract with the Cincinnati Reds' organization in 1960, not long before dictator Fidel Castro proclaimed professional baseball off-limits. Perez was 18 years old and had just graduated from high school. His dream of playing Major League baseball was coming to fruition.

Perez went off to join the Reds, but the "Reds" who ruled the country provided new meaning to the word. It was a Communist revolution and baseball's always significant role in Cuba was reduced to amateur play only. Not only were the big stars from the majors who had journeyed to the island in winter for decades no longer welcome, even the sons of Cuba were not welcome to come home, even for vacation if they kept up their affiliation with a Major League club. Or else they would risk being held indefinitely, their careers gone up in smoke.

Perez was born in Ciego de Avila, Cuba in 1942, and once the Iron Curtain came down he did not know if he would ever see his parents again. He continued his baseball life in the United States, journeying through small minor-league towns, speaking only Spanish before his rise to the Reds for the 1964 season.

Cincinnati Reds slugger Tony Perez was Cuban by birth, but had to leave his native country for good after Fidel Castro took over and banned professional baseball. The future Hall of Famer starred for the Big Red Machine championship teams of the 1970s and slammed 379 home runs in a 23-year career. (AP Photo)

Those who know Perez as the player who grew to 6-foot-2 and 205 pounds and slugged 379 home runs in the big leagues might be surprised to learn that he was a 155-pound shortstop at Violeta Central High School in the Cuban town of Camaguey. He came to the United States with almost no English language vocabulary, proficient only in the words "yes" and "no."

Perez made his first minor league stop in Geneva, New York. There were not a whole lot of waitresses in the upstate New York community who spoke Spanish and could translate the menu. After a while Perez figured out what he would receive on a dinner plate if he ordered chicken. "I ate chicken for a week one time," Perez said in a story that echoes that of many other Latino players who came to the United States in their teens and with no language training. "It was the only word I knew—chicken, chicken, chicken." (Quoted in Stark.)

Minor-league skipper Dave Bristol tutored Perez at Macon in the Sally League in 1963 and told him he was too skinny. That summer Perez worked out hard and hit the dinner table hard. He found good supplies of his favorite foods, meat, rice and beans, and added 40 pounds. He bulked up so much Bristol was astonished when he saw him in spring training. "Tony, you've got to take off some weight," Bristol said in a reversal of his previous instructions. "Dave, make up your mind," Perez answered. (Quoted in Lawson.) Eventually, the hitter found the right balance.

The much bigger Perez made his debut for the Reds in 1964, although he played in just 12 games. By the next season he was getting the majority of time at first base. For 23 seasons, the first 13 and the last three with Cincinnati, Perez shifted between first and third base as a seven-time All-Star while becoming a local icon who ultimately won election to the National Baseball Hall of Fame. Always feared at the plate, Perez distinguished himself as a clutch RBI man. He produced runs. Seven times Perez drove in at least 100 runs in a season and five other times he batted in at least 90. His lifetime RBI total is 1,652.

Cincinnati became a second home for Perez. His upbeat outlook and his steadiness with the bat won him fans easily. Perez and his fans were both ready for his breakout 1967 season when he stroked 26 homers and drove in 102 runs. He was an integral member of a squad of great players that was maturing into one of the greatest teams of all time under manager Sparky Anderson—The Big Red Machine. Perez was a cornerstone, along with Pete Rose, Johnny Bench, and Joe Morgan. The Reds won 108 games and an epic World Series over the Boston Red Sox in 1975, and the next year they repeated with a sweep of the New York Yankees after winning 102 regular-season games.

In 1970, the hard-swinging Perez cracked 40 homers and drove in 129 RBIs, both career bests. By then he was counted on for steady production in both of these statistical categories. That season Perez even awed his own teammates. "There he is, gentlemen, the greatest hitter I've ever seen," said Reds pitcher Wayne Granger. "He's also one of the greatest guys in the world. He'll give you the shirt off his back. I don't want his shirt. I'll just take the homers he hits. I'm sure glad he's on my team." (Quoted in Lawson.)

Perez was on such a hot streak during April, the opening month of the season, that he created new fans and new excitement with the power in his bat. When teammates teased Perez about how he could do so much damage with his bat in a short period of time he joked that was just doing what his four-year-old son Victor told him to do. "I'm just trying to follow Little Victor's orders," Perez said. "It's the same every day. Every day when I head to the park he says, 'Hit a home run, daddy.' " (Quoted in Lawson.) National League pitchers wished Perez wasn't so obliging to his child. The kid was getting spoiled rotten and opposing pitchers' earned run averages were just getting spoiled.

Perez hit 20 or more homers in a season nine times and came close to that mark in three other years. He was always a threat. "Like I said, he's the greatest hitter I've ever seen," Granger said. (Quoted in Lawson.)

Although Perez acclimated well to the United States and to the positive feedback from Cincinnati fans, a part of him always missed Cuba and especially his family. Year after year passed without Perez seeing either his parents or his siblings. More than a decade went by and Perez became an American citizen in October 1971.

Unable to return to Cuba in the off-season, Perez settled in Puerto Rico for many years. He became an adopted son of Santurce, home of the Santurce Crabbers in winter ball, and was treated like a homegrown product. In 1971, the local fans honored Perez with a special night. He was showered with gifts, including a new car, and was so excited by the reception that he called it one of the highlights of his career. "I guess the only thing better than this now would be to win the World Series," he said. (Quoted in Frau.) That was still to come. Perez's team played a double-header that day and he slugged a three-run homer in the opener and a two-run shot in the nightcap.

In November 1972, Perez received word that his application for a visa to visit Cuba for 20 days had been granted. The visa did not permit Perez to bring his wife and two children with him, however.

Gleeful, and conscious of how the Cuban people suffered through shortages of supplies easily available in the United States, Perez packed 17 suitcases for his journey. It wasn't as if he was bringing a new outfit for every day of his trip. He enclosed various gifts, clothes, and medical supplies for his family. Rules stated that Perez's luggage had to be inspected at customs, but the check station was closed for the weekend when he arrived. That cost him a day of seeing his family and when the bags were inspected it cost Perez a whole lot more—a hefty tax for bringing in all of the goods.

His trip continued with a 400-mile train ride from Havana to Santa Violeta. Perez was welcomed by his father Jose Manuel, his mother, Teodora, his three sisters and two brothers, grandparents, and numerous other distant relatives. Many tears were shed during the reunion. Perez said that for a while he and his folks just sat at a table staring at one another. They said, "We're so happy. He's here." A lot of emotion spilled over during the three-week visit. The Cubans marveled at how big Perez was. Perez quietly worried about the frailty of his aging father, then 77. And there was baseball talk with old friends, many of whom asked about the famous major leaguers he knew.

It was difficult to cram a decade's worth of conversations into such a short time, but deep down Perez knew those talks might have to last him much longer. There was no guarantee, no indication, that he would ever return, and there was no hint that his parents and siblings might be free to visit him in the United States. The visit itself acted like an elixir, a rejuvenating sip of life that brought Perez a certain amount of peace. "I am satisfied," he said after returning to the United States from Cuba. "If I never get back, I am satisfied. I have seen them. My mother was speaking to me. She was crying. But she too said she was satisfied. She had gotten to see me." (Quoted in Hertzel.)

It was not easy to make the return journey, retracing his steps, yet Perez was lighter and not only because his baggage was. The tradeoffs were pricey, but he did not question his original decision to play for the Reds over a life of working in a factory or a sugar cane field in Cuba. "It chokes me up. I just can't say. I'm not sorry I came to America and played baseball," Perez said. "They (his family) know I liked baseball and they go along with that." (Quoted in Hertzel.)

It was no joke that baseball had been very, very good to Perez. His success gave him stature in the game and in his community. He was a star in the sport he loved and his Reds club was admired and feared. During his career, Perez played in five World Series, although the only two championships came with Cincinnati. He was not short on World Series jewelry. The Reds' accomplishments and their standing as one of the all-time best teams has stood the test of time and thinking back on the Cincinnati era brings a smile to Perez's face.

"We had eight guys who wanted to go out and play every day and a good pitching staff, good enough for us to win," he said. "And we knew how to play the game to win, do everything we needed to win games. You learned a lot, because you learned from the other guys. You saw guys like Pete Rose, who hustled all the time. If you played for that team, you hustled, too. You had to play the same way he did." (Quoted in King.)

The peer pressure to perform, to work hard at the game, was enormous. Perez was called "Big Dog," by that glittery array of teammates because he delivered. Rose ended up as baseball's all-time hits leader and the only reason he is not in the Hall of Fame is because he admitted to gambling on the sport. Johnny Bench is considered by many to be the best catcher of all and he is in the Hall of Fame. Joe Morgan, still in the game as a broadcaster, compares favorably with the all-time list of second baseman and he is in the Hall of Fame. Manager Sparky Anderson was elected, too.

It took some time, but Perez followed his illustrious teammates into the National Baseball Hall of Fame in 2000. By then he had been retired for 14 years. Supporters frequently noted that he was the leading RBI man in history who was not in the Hall. Perez may have been overlooked for so long because he was surrounded by so much spectacular talent. Gene Mauch, the long-time manager, predicted Perez's Hall inclusion a year before he even left the playing field. "When they induct Tony Perez into Cooperstown, there should be two inscriptions," Mauch said. " 'Respected by all his peers' and 'with a runner on second and two out, he was the best who ever lived.' " (Quoted in Gammons.)

After the 1976 season, Perez, his teammates, and Reds fans were shocked when he was traded to the Montreal Expos. He still had some good years in his bat. Perez spent three years with the Expos and then three with the Red Sox and one with the Phillies before coming full circle back to the Reds. With Montreal,

Perez checked in with two 90-plus RBI seasons and with Boston he recorded his final 100-RBI campaign. When the righty slugger retired with a .279 batting average, he was 44 years old. It became apparent that the Reds' original divestiture was a big mistake. The move did not take into consideration his clubhouse presence and leadership. "His departure was the beginning of the end," said Rose of the break-up of The Big Red Machine and the years of suffering that followed. (Quoted in Gammons.)

Rose reached out to his old cohort when he took over as player-manager. Rose helped grease the way back to Cincinnati for Perez for the last chapter of his career following the Cuban's single year with Philadelphia.

"I saw what he did in Philadelphia," Rose said. "I knew he could still hit, and anyway, as I've said all along, I needed a younger man to platoon with." That comment was to provoke a laugh. The remainder of Rose's thought was far from a joke. "Then, too, think of my position as manager. Here's one of the greatest men who ever played the game. Don't you think I want him around our younger players?" (Quoted in Gammons.)

Perez had an enjoyable return to Cincinnati. Radio broadcaster Marty Brennaman intoned, "The Mayor of Riverfront," each time Perez came to the plate in home Riverfront Stadium. Perez witnessed Rose breaking Ty Cobb's hits record. He made key hits in the clutch. But always there was the lingering question of how long he would play. How long would it be until retirement beckoned? Perez stuck it out for two more seasons, and in the second one hit a remarkable .328 in 72 games. He did not want to strip off the uniform as long as he could coax one more hit out of his bat. The one thing that could turn Perez grouchy was the application of the word "old" in any description that pertained to him.

" 'Old Goat,' " he said, beginning to tick off a list the various ways "old" had been incorporated into those offensive sentences. " 'Old dog.' 'The Old Dog can still do it.' By then he was growling. " 'The old man can still hit home runs.' All of the time it's old man this, old man that. Old, old, old. It's as though people don't pay attention to what I'm doing, but only to how old I am. I get tired of it. It bothers me, but what can you do?" (Quoted in Hoard.) The main thing Perez could do was to march out to home plate and swat another pinch-hit home run. He could make observers think of another number, not his age, but how far he hit the soaring ball.

Perez did not become another Satchel Paige, playing past his 50th birthday. By 1990, when Lou Piniella was in charge of the Reds and they won another World Series, he was a full-time coach. After the 1992 season, Perez was named manager of the Reds. He was in charge of his old team. "I don't talk much, but I can act," Perez said of his soft-spoken image translating to being the boss. "I have to prove myself." (Quoted in "Perez accepts . . .") That's why he received only a one-year contract.

The feel-good hire made Perez the fourth Cuban manager in the big leagues after Mike Gonzalez, Preston Gomez, and Cookie Rojas. The clutch hitter's shift to dugout leader was popular with Reds fans, but Perez never had the same caliber of players to manage as he played with. It was a short honeymoon. The Reds started out 20–24, and mercurial owner Marge Schott gave Perez the heave-ho. There was no patience shown with a first-year manager. The reason Perez said he had to prove himself was because of his lack of managing experience. He never truly got the chance to gain that experience. The team finished 73–89 that season.

Perez got only one more chance to manage. Again it was for a partial season. Perez led the Florida Marlins to a 54–60 record in 2001, but he did have a long-term association with the team as a scout, front office assistant, and coach. The Marlins won two World Series, in 1997 and 2003.

In 2000, after several disappointments and a growing belief it would never happen, Perez was voted into the Hall of Fame. His father had long before passed away, in 1979, but his mother was still alive at 88, still in Cuba, and the event renewed her pride in the distant son who made the oh-so-hard choice of sticking with professional ball over his homeland.

"The greatest man I ever knew," Perez said of his father after he got the word of his Hall election and noted he would never learn of this accomplishment by his son. "All he did was work, work, work for me and my brothers and sisters. There's an emptiness inside me a little bit. It hurts. My parents never saw me play a professional game. It's a shame." (Quoted in Hyde.)

It was a shame for baseball, as well, that there weren't many more Perezes coming along in the pipeline from Cuba. As opportunities expanded for Latin American players from the Dominican Republic, Puerto Rico, and Venezuela, the door remained locked to players from Cuba that were denied the chance to sign with a pro team unless they defected from the Communist regime.

The famous Cuban players of the 1960s and early 1970s were retiring. Minnie Minoso and Luis Tiant were gone. Perez was the last of the stalwarts from his generation with the direct lineage to those who signed pre-Castro. "I was one of the last ones signed. We just ran out," Perez said. "It is a sad thing."

Any journey over the last 20 years and any journey for the foreseeable future for any Cuban baseball prospect will be much longer than the 90 miles from the island to Miami. And any hopeful will be forced to follow Tony Perez's emotional path, leaving loved ones behind to chase a dream.

Further Reading

Frau, Miguel, "P.R. Fans Laud Perez—Tony Repays Favor," *The Sporting News*, January 30, 1971.

Gammons, Peter, "Hall of Famer in the shadows," *Boston Globe*, September 5, 1985.

Hertzel, Bob, "Perez Recounts Homecoming: After 10 Years Of Separation," *Cincinnati Enquirer*, Baseball Hall of Fame Library and Archives.

Hoard, Greg, "The Proud Presence of Tony Perez," *Cincinnati Enquirer*, September 22, 1985.

Hyde, Dave, "Perez's Courage Unique in Hall of Fame," *Florida Sun-Sentinel*, July, 2000.

King, David, "Perez reflects on World Series rings, great jobs, Pete Rose," *San Antonio Express-News*, September 5, 2006.

Lawson, Earl, "Perez Hits HRs to Order—From Son," *The Sporting News*, May 16, 1970.

"Perez accepts Reds' hot seat," Associated Press/United Press International, October 31, 1992.

Stark, Jayson, "Having had four lives, Tony Perez doesn't realize he's getting 'too old,' " *Philadelphia Inquirer*, May 9, 1983.

Vic Power

Most baseball fans would not recognize the name Victor Pellot, but that was the given name of the player who gained fame as a slick-fielding, solid-hitting All-Star first-baseman in the American League during the 1950s. Power was part of his game, but it was not part of his name until he played ball in the United States. For Pellot, becoming Power was much like a rechristening at Ellis Island.

Power's island, however, was Puerto Rico, and he was born in the community of Arecibo in 1927. Power did not grow up with any wealth and his father prevented him from playing baseball at first as a child so he wouldn't ruin his clothes. Power started playing the game at age 13. Power also played a lot of basketball as a kid.

Neither newspapers nor television were available in the Power home, so he did not develop any attachments to prominent Puerto Rican ballplayers of the time. He really had no sports heroes while growing up.

For a few years in the early 1950s it seemed that the hard-hitting Power was likely to become the first black New York Yankee. But those who harbored such ideas were not close enough to the buttoned-down, pin-striped organization that was more conservative than then-Vice President Richard Nixon.

The haughty Yankees had not been in the forefront of desegregating baseball. The prevailing attitude was that the team's source of players was fine as it was

When Puerto Rican Vic Power could not crack the New York Yankees' roster in the 1950s to become the first black Yankee, many felt the reason was prejudice. However, when he got a chance to play first base elsewhere, he was a gem of a fielder. A four-time All-Star, Power hardly ever made an error. (AP Photo/John Lindsay)

because it won the pennant year-after-year and the World Series nearly as often. Higher-ups in the Yankee administration had even been quoted in the media making uncomplimentary remarks about black players. The scuttlebutt was that the Yankees' first black player would not be someone with a thick Spanish accent, who was a flamboyant fielder drawing attention to himself, and who dated white women. This subterranean conversation about Power was fueled by rumor-mongers rather than people holding the facts. Power was indeed seen in public with a lighter-skinned blonde woman—she was his wife, wearing a wig.

"Maybe if I had driven a Volkswagen (instead of the baby blue Cadillac he drove) and told them I was after a big, fat colored girl, they would have said, 'Oh, he's a nice guy, see how beautiful he is!' " Power observed. (Quoted in Burgos, 206.)

Power had the insight to recognize why the stuffy Yankees weren't comfortable with him, even if it was not justified. "His personality was markedly different than that of the quiet, grateful player George Weiss (New York's general manager) wanted the pioneering black Yankee to be," one baseball historian wrote. (Quoted in Burgos, 206.) "The black Puerto Rican ran counter to the genteel black southerner or the corporate player who abided by the rules."

Power joined his first prominent organized team in Puerto Rico when he was 17. He played for Caguas not only as a teenager but kept up the relationship for years. He played 15 years of winter ball for the same club while he was also playing summers in the majors, and he even managed the team for five years. When Power was first noticed by the Yankees he spread the word that he was really born in 1931, making him four years younger and more attractive to a pro club seeking young talent.

The young Power did need a baseball education. He was naïve when he began playing for Caguas, and the young player was duped with a variation of the oldest trick in the book, a variation of the hidden ball trick. Power could thank a veteran first baseman named Alonso Perry from Mayaguez for this burning embarrassment. Power reached first on a single. Perry, making a quick assessment of the young man, said, "Excuse me, I want to clean off the bag." Power stepped off first and was immediately tagged out. "It was a brutal experience," he said. Needless to say, his manager demanded an explanation. "I said that the gentleman had said it with such courtesy. From that I learned that you have to be aggressive." (Quoted in Otto.)

Once signed by the Yankees, Power hit .331 for New York's minor league affiliate in Kansas City and .349 the next year. It was a fairly lonely existence because Power, as the only black player, had few friends on most of his teams. An exception near the end of his stay with the Yankees' organization was Elston Howard, who eventually did become the first black Yankee. The Yankees never called, never even tried out Power with a September call-up. Power hit considerably over .300 during his minor league turns and if he was the property of any other team he would likely have made his Major League debut well before 1954— after being traded to the Philadelphia A's. Power was part of an 11-player trade between the Yankees and the A's, but a review of the names involved show that he was by far the most talented player.

"I knew the Yankees weren't ready to have a Negro player on the big club," Power said. "They had a lot of excuses, like I wasn't ready because I hadn't seen Major League pitchers. I said, 'Let me see one and I'll tell you.' The Yankees just weren't ready." (Quoted in Marazzi.)

Being held down by the Yankees meant that Power was a 27-year-old rookie, although he didn't tell anyone about his true age for some time. In 1954, with

Philadelphia, he became the first Puerto Rican in the American League. Free of the Yankees' shackles, Power stamped his pleasing, outgoing personality on the sport, hit over .300 five times, became a four-time American League All-Star, and won seven Gold Gloves.

"The thing about me is that I love to play," Power said a decade into his career that also carried him to substantial stays with the Cleveland Indians and Minnesota Twins and shorter stops in other Major League cities. "I enjoy myself. I don't think there is anybody that enjoys the game like me. That's why I play so good, because I like to make the plays. I love to be on the baseball field." (Quoted in Isaacs.)

New York sportswriter Stan Isaacs clearly took joy in writing about Power. "There is no pomp or pretense in his speech by Vic Power. He is a colorful man, an ingenuous spirit who not only comes to play, but to cavort, to clown, to bask in the sunshine of acclaim and to put on one of the great shows of baseball." (Quoted in Isaacs.)

The first Latino players in the majors were scattered across teams. Few became stars and many were out of the game quickly. Pre-1947 they were all light-skinned. The next crop of Latino players arriving in the big leagues, the Minnie Minosos and the Vic Powers, made a more significant impact. They brought specific individual styles to the base paths, to fielding their positions. They spoke heavily accented Spanish that put the onus on sportswriters and other listeners to understand what they were saying. These translators of so-called "pidgin" English did not always respond well to the pressure of this task. Latino players whose words were not easily comprehended found it a little bit more difficult to acquire acceptance from the mainstream of American society.

But Power was so outgoing, his demeanor so friendly, his ability to handle his position so superior that he made fans wherever he went—in the stands or among sportswriters. Power might have preferred salsa music (nearly alien to the baseball world at large at the time), but his personality was so infectious that he made you like his music. That was later, though, when he was more mature and played only in big cities.

Power spent several years in the minors before the Yankees freed him. He spent time in Class D ball in Drummondville, Ontario, a member of the Canadian Provincial League, and in small Southern towns. In Canada, he said, his biggest problem was accommodating to those who spoke French—not one of his languages. Even in his early days in the majors, Power was frustrated because he could not always express himself clearly enough to interviewers. He said he was once asked about a specific American League pitcher. He used the phrase "some other pitcher" and it came out as "son of a bitch." Power possessed great self-confidence, though, and he did not let such setbacks worry him. Instead he worked harder at making his English clearer. (Quoted in Krich, 85.)

In other places around the minors, Power had difficulty getting served when he wanted lunch or dinner because he was black. Power said he walked into a restaurant in Florida, took a seat at a table, and was set to order when a waitress told him she couldn't serve Negroes. Power replied, "I don't wanna eat a Negro, I want some rice and beans." (Quoted in Krich, 85.)

Power's stories illustrate the types of obstacles Latino players faced time after time throughout the United States. If someone wasn't trying to hold them back because of their skin color, then facility with English might be a roadblock.

The Yankees did Power a favor by shipping him to the Athletics, who soon moved to Kansas City, and for whom he emerged as a star. But the Yankees disparaged his personality, essentially calling him a clubhouse lawyer or a troublemaker, perhaps to cover their own mistake. "A media blitz by the Yankees accused Power of being stupid, hot-tempered and a showboat," one journalist reported years later. (Quoted in Marazzi.) Also later, when Power was playing for the Twins, someone asked manager Sam Mele about Power's so-called bad reputation. "If he's trouble," Mele said, "I wish we had more trouble like him." (Quoted in Merchant.)

First base is often the position where managers try to hide their weakest fielders. At the least they are expected to stop ground balls hit down the right-field line with their chests and flip the ball to the covering pitcher and to catch their fellow infielders' throws across the diamond. But the best first basemen do much more. They cover the bunt with cat-like quickness. They make those infielders look good by scooping errant throws out of the dirt. And they make the diving stop going to their right to prevent a hard-hit grounder from becoming a base hit. It was performing these beyond-the-basics tasks where Power made his reputation. He knew what he could do and often he made it look easy. Other times Power knew what he was doing was difficult. He might dive in the dirt and come up talking as he did once with the Twins when star right-hander Camilo Pascual, who had lived through many a dark day with the losing franchise in Washington, was on the mound.

A batter got solid wood on a Pascual pitch and the ball shot toward the hole between first and second. Power sprang for the ball and, with full extension as he hit the ground, speared it. Still in the dirt he flipped the ball to Pascual covering first—and made him laugh at the same time. Even as Power was saving the hit he wasn't too busy to talk to the hurler. "That crazy guy," Pascual said later. "While sitting on the ground throwing to me he yelled, 'Camilo, you don't have to worry about these plays anymore.' " (Quoted in Merchant.) Neither Pascual nor any other pitcher with Power behind him in the field had to worry very much.

Infielders weaned on the fundamentals and on coping with the basics of keeping their body in front of the ball and making sure the first baseman was on the base as he threw were sometimes flummoxed by Power's artistry. Unless they had faith in Power from previous viewings, managers fretted about his style that went against the way they were taught. "It is natural for me to catch one-handed," Power said. (Quoted in Merchant.)

Rich Rollins, a solid Twins third baseman of the early 1960s, said working with Power took some getting used to, but he adapted. "He plays so deep that sometimes he arrives at the bag with the ball. When it first happened I didn't know what to do so I fired the throw to an empty bag. But he was there in time. He's saved me at least a dozen errors." (Quoted in Merchant.)

When Power caught a throw that required full extension of his left, glove hand, he followed through with a large sweeping motion, almost like a windmill. At 5-foot-11, the 195-pound Power was not tall for a first baseman, but he still got to more slightly misdirected throws than anyone else. Power said he adjusted his play when he reached the majors, and he admitted to "hot dogging" a little bit on purpose to please the fans.

"As a right-handed first baseman, to make the double play easier, I started catching the ball with one hand," Power said. "They didn't like that too much and the people got mad at me and they even called me a showboat. I talked to Jimmy Dykes, my manager, and I told him that I would catch the ball with two hands and he said, 'Vic, never argue with success.' " So Power stuck with what worked best for him.

"I remember a sportswriter called me a showboat," Power said. "I told him the guy that invented this game, if he wanted you to catch with two hands he would have you wear two gloves. If I was a hot dog, how would I have a .994 fielding average? I noticed the fans liked my style of play. When I was in Minnesota, I caught the last out when Jack Kralick pitched his no-hitter. People were mad at me because I caught the ball one-handed and they thought I would drop the ball. But I knew they (fans) liked that style and I kept playing that way." (Quoted in Marazzi.)

At the plate, Power also displayed a distinctive methodology. As he stared out at the pitcher, the right-handed hitting Power swung the bat back and forth with his left hand like the pendulum of a grandfather clock. That action just made Power look a little bit more menacing at the plate, though his best year hitting home runs came in 1955 when he hit 19. In all, Power swatted 126 home runs during a 12-year Major League career and posted a .284 lifetime average.

Power's hitting was solid, but his fielding always shone. Once witnesses who saw Power dance his way around the first-base bag over and over again got used to his ways, he created a star-laden fan club with members doffing their hats to his fielding prowess.

"He's the best fielding first baseman in the American League," said future Hall of Fame shortstop Lou Boudreau, who also managed the Indians. "Maybe the best in baseball," added Yankees' manager Casey Stengel. (Quoted in Graham.)

Power was a clutch hitter more than a power hitter, a table setter more than a bases clearer. Power was not a very swift runner and did not steal many bases. He stole just 45 in his career overall, but no one can deny he was opportunistic. In a 1958 game, when Power was playing for the Indians against the Detroit Tigers, he stole home plate twice in one game. Any steal of home is rare these days and performing the feat twice in a single game is unheard of. In fact, when Power did so, the act had not been accomplished since 1927, and has not been performed since. For a guy who never recorded double-figure steals in a season it was an unusual achievement. Power had no logical explanation for how he was able to make the plays.

"It was easy," Power said. "I got a good jump." (Quoted in Dolgan.) Clearly, if it was so easy, a few other players might have done the same over the decades.

Power made an acceptable salary for the times, a maximum of $38,000 in a season, but he did not get rich playing Major League baseball. He did have rich experiences, though, memories that he treasured until his death in 2005 at the age of 78.

"We could say that in general baseball was played for personal pride and the dignity of sports," Power said of his era. "The baseball of today, modern baseball, is of a commercial and a monetary nature. How much do I get paid, and I'll play. That has been the big difference. The game we played . . . we went to the playing field to better ourselves every day, to do something new each day. Besides that, we were more complete because of a combination of fielding, running, batting. If you notice, many of today's players are great home-run hitters, but their fielding is a question-mark. Many of them don't run or throw." (Quoted in Otto.)

Long after Power's retirement as an active Major League player, he remained active in the sport he loved. He scouted Puerto Rican players for the California Angels and he operated baseball instructional clinics and schools on his home island. His passion for the sport never waned.

"If I were to come back, reincarnated, I would choose baseball as my main job," Power said in 2001, four years before his death. "It's a great profession." (Quoted in Otto.)

There is every reason to think that if Vic Power is reincarnated he will return to earth in the same role he fulfilled before: a dazzling fielding first baseman.

Further Reading

Burgos Jr., Adrian, *Playing America's Game* (Berkeley, California, University of California Press, 2007).
Dolgan, Bob, "Good glove, better guy for Indians," *Cleveland Plain Dealer*, November 30, 2005.
Graham Jr., Frank, "Power Proves His Case," *Sport Magazine*, August, 1956.
Isaacs, Stan, "Vic and Baseball: Love at First Base," *Newsday*, June 29, 1962.
Krich, John, *El Beisbol* (Chicago, Ivan R. Dee, 1989).
Marazzi, Rich, "The Yankees passed on slick fielding Vic Power," *Sports Collector's Digest*, January 15, 1999.
Merchant, Larry, "The Power of Vic," *Philadelphia Daily News*, June 26, 1962.
Otto, Franklin, National Baseball Hall of Fame Library and Archives recorded interview with Vic Power, November 20, 1991.

Albert Pujols

He was the man of the hour in his home ballpark, the unofficial, honorary host of the Major League Baseball All-Star Game at Busch Stadium in St. Louis in 2009, and the main perk Albert Pujols derived from his role as mainstay star of the St. Louis Cardinals came into play just before the game began.

Pujols, clearly established as one of the two best players of his generation and No. 1 with a bullet in the minds of many, bent into a squat behind home plate as the crowd thundered. It was no everyday pitcher walking to the mound for a ceremonial first pitch. For the moment, Pujols was a first baseman turned catcher. But it was worth it. The southpaw going into his windup on the mound was President Barack Obama. When Obama's left-handed toss bounced a little bit short, Pujols saved the nation's leader from minor embarrassment (and a wild pitch) by blocking the plate.

It was a neat save, as effective as any goalie's stopping the puck in front of the net, and in some ways typified what Pujols has been doing for the Cardinals since he broke into the majors in 2001 as the National League Rookie of the Year. He has been saving games, saving wins, and saving the team with the most astounding hitting feats in baseball history.

No one has ever begun his Major League career with such sustained excellence as Pujols. No injury has interfered. No slump has occurred. For nine straight years Pujols has slugged more than 30 home runs, driven in more than

Considered the best player in baseball today, the St. Louis Cardinals' Albert Pujols, from the Dominican Republic, is a perennial National League All-Star at first base. Pujols has put together the greatest run ever by a player at the start of a career combining annual totals of at least 30 home runs, 100 RBIs, and a .300 average. The slugger has won three Most Valuable Player awards. (AP Photo/James A. Finley)

100 runs, and batted higher than .300. No one in baseball history has matched that feat. Only Hall of Famer Al Simmons had more consecutive seasons of 100 RBIs to begin his career. By 2009, despite Alex Rodriguez's longevity, there were more than a few murmurings that Pujols had supplanted him as the best player in the game.

Jose Alberto Pujols was born January 16, 1980 in Santo Domingo in the Dominican Republic. He was a bit of a late bloomer, not garnering particular notice as a teenager but erupting on the scene dramatically as a full-blown star the moment he arrived in the majors. Pujols and his family moved to the United States when he was 15, and in June 1999 the Cardinals selected him in the 13th round of the amateur draft. It was a vote of confidence in his raw ability but not with such a high pick that his selection implied Pujols would become a major leaguer, never mind a star.

Originally known to baseball scouts as Jose Pujols, the youngster with grand potential fooled experts because he played shortstop in high school. They wondered where he would play in the pros and if his magnificent hitting would translate because he had only used an aluminum bat. Few teams foresaw that he would become a professional star. In Pujols' year of draft eligibility, 401 players were selected before him—which means that every Major League team made a mistake in bypassing him. St. Louis signed Pujols for a $30,000 bonus. These days he is in the midst of a long-term, $100-million contract, and no one suggests he is not worth the money.

Pujols' rise was far more rapid than anticipated. He clobbered Class A pitching in 2000 and by the end of the season was the Most Valuable Player in the Pacific Coast League playoffs. Invited to the big-league spring training camp, the 6-foot-3, 225-pound Pujols dazzled Cardinal management. He was too good to send back to the minors. As a 21-year-old, Pujols was a starter playing in 161 games. His performance as a player unknown outside of the organization and somewhat unheralded within it, was astounding. He slugged 37 homers, drove in 130, and batted .329. The biggest problem was finding the right position for him. Pujols split time between the outfield, third base, and first base, the spot that became his permanent role in the field.

Cardinal officials were delighted, but admittedly a bit overwhelmed by Pujols' early emergence. He was the only one not taken aback by his immediate success. "I'm not surprised at all," Pujols said of his stellar rookie season. "I've played baseball since I was five years old and it was always my dream to be in the major leagues. I've worked hard to get here and I'm working hard to stay. I always felt the talent was there. It's just how hard you work and how much you want to learn." (Quoted in Johnson.)

Pujols came by his hunger to succeed naturally. In the Dominican, Pujols did not know his mother. His father, Bienvenido, struggled to obtain good jobs and left the child care to Albert's grandparents, who were busy raising a gaggle of children, including his siblings and cousins. Pujols' dad moved the family to Independence, Missouri in 1996 and that's where Pujols became Americanized. His baseball education had begun long before. He followed Latino players such as Sammy Sosa and Raul Mondesi in televised games, but he also absorbed information about Latino stars of the past like Roberto Clemente and Tony Perez.

The nearest Major League team to root for was the Kansas City Royals and this city on the opposite side of the state from St. Louis played a key role in his life in many ways. When he was 18, Pujols was hanging out in a Latino dance club in Kansas City when he was attracted to a woman named Deidre. When he found out she was 21, he lied about his age. But he came clean on their first date. Deidre informed Pujols she was the mother of a baby girl with Down syndrome. Many young men would have run the other way, but Pujols embraced the child and the relationship.

Besides his day-to-day courtesy in routine dealings with the press and public, this incident is often cited as an example of Pujols having a good heart and being a caring man. In addition, he and his wife have started a charitable foundation. Right from the start in his relationship with Isabella, the little girl, Pujols was smitten. "She's a real cutie," he said in 2001, "and when I'm not home I miss her every day. I want to be there for her and do the best I can to be a dad. I don't think of it as a responsibility. God has blessed me. He brought my wife and baby my way. I'm very thankful for that." (Quoted in Johnson.)

Pujols played high school ball in Independence and attended Maple Woods Community College in Kansas City for one year. In his first game Pujols not only smacked a grand slam homer, he also executed an unassisted triple play in the field. His season's batting average was .461. He was too good to hang around that level of competition.

During his first nine years in the majors, remarkably, Pujols has almost never had a sustained slump. His slumps are of such short duration that other players might consider them to be off days. He has redefined high-level consistency in a way it has never been recorded in big-league history. Although far from strictly a home-run hitter, Pujols possesses home-run power and, like few hitters before him, can maintain the type of stroke that enables him to punish the ball with long blows but supplement the long-distance strikes with hard-hit singles and doubles. A close look at Pujols' forearms shows why. They are immensely thick and powerful, so sturdy they seem to rival other men's legs.

The late Buck O'Neil, one of the stars of the old Negro Leagues and a pioneer coach with the Chicago Cubs, said he had heard only a few players in his long career produce a certain sound when the bat struck the ball. It went beyond just getting good wood on the ball. Mike Easler, the Cardinals' hitting coach when Pujols joined the team, made a similar comment and suggested that Pujols was one of those few.

"Only a few guys can make that sound," said Easler, from a much later generation than O'Neil. "Willie Stargell, Dave Parker, Dave Winfield, Mike Schmidt. I'm talking about guys like that. The ball just explodes off his bat and he's talented enough that he can take his power swing and make adjustments and go the other way for a base hit." (Quoted in Johnson.)

To say that Pujols made a strong first impression his rookie year is a serious understatement. Everyone wondered if he could keep it up, if he would suffer from a sophomore slump. But Pujols has never faltered or slipped. He has never had a serious injury. He has never had an off-year. He has maintained his level of performance season after season. Discussions now revolve around how great he can be. Each baseball figure, coming from a different perspective, saw different things in Pujols.

"He caught my eye last season as a rookie when, against the Padres, he hit a home run on a three-ball, no-strike pitch—to the opposite field," said future Hall of Famer Tony Gwynn. "Now that was something." (Quoted in *Baseball Almanac*.)

Cardinals' manager Tony LaRussa recognized how fortunate he was to add a player like Pujols to his team. "He is the whole package as far as a player," LaRussa said. "He commits to defense just like he does offense. He has natural talent. He's a young guy, very smart, very tough-minded." (Quoted in *Baseball Almanac*.)

As of the 2009 season, Pujols had become an eight-time National League All-Star. He helped lead the Cardinals to the 2006 World Series championship. In addition to his Rookie of the Year award, Pujols was chosen Most Valuable Player in the NL in 2005 and 2008, and with 47 homers, 135 RBIs, and a .327 average he was the unanimous selection for MVP in 2009. In 2008, Pujols was presented the Roberto Clemente Award for his off-the-field contributions to the community. He won his first Gold Glove Award in 2006 and *The Sporting News* announced that Pujols was chosen as the greatest player in the game today.

By staying healthy and producing year in and year out at an All-Star level, Pujols, at age 29, was taking the measure of all Hall of Famers who came before him when it came to top-notch consistency. *Sports Illustrated* writer Joe Posnanski said, "(Hank) Aaron is the gold standard when it comes to consistency. Pujols, though, is gaining. And that seems to be what drives him: to be great every year." (Quoted in Posnanski.)

That story discussed Pujols' pursuit of perfection. Listening to his wife Deidre talk about Pujols makes it seem possible that he is nearly perfect as a guy, as well as a player. "Talk to him for 10 minutes," she said. "He's an excellent human being— kind, gentle, caring. He's an amazing ballplayer who would never say he's amazing." (Quoted in *Baseball Almanac*.)

Hitting a baseball with regularity is supposed to be one of the most difficult challenges in sports. Pujols has never seemed to struggle with the concept. After making the jump from Class A ball to the Cardinals' lineup in 2001, Pujols hit a home run in his first game in St. Louis. The fans, already intense followers of his surprising progress, gave him a huge ovation. He had to come out of the dugout and take a curtain call.

Although a young player achieving so much so quickly could grow cocky, Pujols endeared himself to fans by being self-effacing and exhibiting a solid work ethic. He never talked about what he had accomplished, only discussed what he hoped to do next—and that was as simple as staying in the lineup and improving game-by-game and season-by-season. Pujols got to the clubhouse four hours before game time and spent the time wisely—preparing. "There are not many players who make it to the big leagues this soon," the young Pujols said. "But it's easier to make it, harder to stay." (Quoted in DiMeglio.)

Not that Pujols had anything to worry about on that front. When he appeared in the Cardinals' lineup, he was there to stay.

Pujols's rookie stats of home runs, RBIs, and average were the best across the board by any newcomer in 51 years. In 2002, his second season, Pujols nearly matched them precisely. In 2003, he led the National League in hits with 212, doubles with 51, and won the batting title with a .359 average. In 2003, 2004, and 2005, Pujols led the league in runs scored. Then he embarked on a stretch of four straight seasons of hitting between 41 and 49 home runs. Pujols has never driven in fewer than 100 runs in a season.

First, Pujols became a star in St. Louis. Then he was recognized as a star around the National League. After a few years he was anointed as one of the top players in the majors. By 2009, Pujols had ascended to the throne of greatest active major leaguer. His start to the 2009 season was almost otherworldly. At one point he led the National League in home runs, RBIs, runs scored, doubles, slugging percentage, and was second in average. Attention on his every at-bat grew. In a cover story for its August 2009 issue, *Baseball Digest* proclaimed, "Albert Pujols: Baseball's Best Player." Such commentary was no longer noted with question-marks but exclamation points. There was no if about it, only a statement of fact. "I don't think there's any question," said Baltimore Orioles manager Dave Trembley. "He's the best player in the game, not only for his tools, but for what he does for the team. He carries the team." (Quoted in Strauss. "Albert . . .")

One reason that Pujols has hit so consistently throughout his career and has avoided lengthy slumps is his ability to swing in exactly the same manner every time up. Gifted with supreme hand speed, he has a solid stance, leaning more weight on his back foot, and an even swing that has been described as graceful, yet powerful. He varies nothing, takes precise cuts, and is rarely tempted to swing at poor pitches. Repetition is a key for Pujols. The Cardinals' video coordinator, Chad Blair, said that watching Pujols' swings over and over on film reveal only the tiniest adjustments being made. He never develops bad habits. Blair called Pujols' swing steadiness "amazing" and said the hitter combines the crispness of form with "desire to be the baddest man on the planet swinging a bat for a living." (Quoted in Habib.)

Although baseball insiders marvel at Pujols' swing, and it is obvious from the time he puts in taking practice swings during the off-season, he tries not to be too obsessive about what he does. "It's whatever I feel comfortable with," he said. "I don't try to be a scientific baseball hitter, or a freaking genius baseball hitter." (Quoted in Habib.) It just works out that way.

It is no surprise that Pujols is a hero to young baseball fans in St. Louis, but he represents more than that to some youngsters. Just as Babe Ruth somehow seemed to hit magical home runs after visiting sick kids in hospitals, Pujols has demonstrated a rare flair to produce big hitting days after being asked to hit home runs for children.

In the early 2000s, the Cardinals introduced a "Buddy Walk in the Park Day" as part of a Down Syndrome Awareness Day. Children are allowed to mingle with players before the game, stroll around the field, and routinely Pujols is asked, "Hit a home run for me." After marrying Deidre, Pujols adopted Isabella, one of three children in his family, so he is keenly appreciative of sharing with the special fans. No hitter, not even Babe Ruth, could ever swat a home run on demand, but in 2006 when the Cardinals bested the Pittsburgh Pirates on "Buddy Walk in the Park Day," Pujols slammed three home runs. "He's better than ever on days like this," LaRussa said of Pujols, who had also hit home runs on two out of four previous Buddy Walk days.

"It's always good to do something special for those kids," Pujols said. "Once in a while the kids will say, 'Hit a home run for me.' It's a special day for those kids, me and my daughter, my family." (Quoted in Goold.)

Pujols's involvement with helping others goes far beyond hitting the home runs that benefit his team and pitchers. He and Deidre created the Pujols Family Foundation to help others. Among other things, the Foundation has contributed to a Santo Domingo orphanage and has donated thousands of dollars worth of baseball equipment to youth programs in the Dominican. Pujols has also supported the Boys and Girls Club of America and the Ronald McDonald House.

Although most of Pujols's baseball career was forged in the United States, he has not forgotten his Dominican roots. Nor has he overlooked the importance of how the role of playing on sandlots in poor neighborhoods served in player development. Pujols was distressed when the Cardinals closed their Dominican baseball complex and was inspired to help continue developing the flow of talent from his native country. "I want to set an example for those kids in the Dominican because I know they look up to me and follow what I'm doing in the game," Pujols said. "That's very important to me. People who have never been there don't know what it's like. It's not easy." (Quoted in Strauss, "Pujols' . . .")

Pujols makes hitting look easy, but he knows life is hard for many. When he received the Roberto Clemente Award in 2008 for his social contributions, it was the fifth time he had been nominated for his community service. "It doesn't matter what you do on the field, it's what you do off the field and the lives you touch," Pujols said when presented with the award in Philadelphia. (Quoted in "MLB honors . . .")

For all that he has accomplished on and off the field, Pujols is still in the middle of his prime years. He continues to excel whether his team is hot or cold. He continues to achieve whether he is at full strength or playing through the pain of a bothersome elbow. He continues to make his mark on baseball by rewriting history and he has never exhibited a cocky attitude or a swelled head. If anything, Pujols continues to be a bit surprised that anyone makes a fuss over him just because he may be one of the greatest baseball players of all time.

"I don't know why people say I'm not supposed to be doing what I'm doing," Pujols said. "I'm just trying to do my job. I'm blessed and I'm glad that I'm blessed." (Quoted in *Baseball Almanac*.)

Further Reading

Baseball Almanac, www.baseball-almanac.com, Albert Pujols Quotes.

DiMeglio, Steve, "Blazing a shortcut to the big leagues," *USA Today Baseball Weekly*, May 16–22, 2001.

Goold, Derrick, "Pujols hits 3 for kids," *St. Louis Post-Dispatch*, September 4, 2006.

Habib, Daniel G., "The sweet stroke of the Cards' Albert Pujols has put him on a home run tear and made him the game's best hitter," *Sports Illustrated*, May 22, 2006.

Johnson, Chuck, "Pujols a Card-carrying star," *USA Today*, May 22, 2001.

"MLB honors Pujols," Associated Press, October 27, 2008.

Posnanski, Joe, "Maybe, Just Maybe, The Most Perfect Player Who Ever Did Live," *Sports Illustrated*, July 13, 2009.

Strauss, Joe, "Albert Pujols: Baseball's Best Player," *Baseball Digest*, August, 2009.

———, "Pujols' affection for Dominican is mutual," *St. Louis Post-Dispatch*, November 28, 2005.

Manny Ramirez

There is little doubt now that Manny Ramirez will rank highly on three of Major League Baseball's all-time lists. After 17 seasons in the big leagues there is indisputable evidence to support all three subjective ratings. The native of the Dominican Republic is surely one of the greatest Latino players of all time. The home-run slugger who is an RBI machine and hits for high average has definitely accumulated National Baseball Hall of Fame numbers. And as each day passes Ramirez rises higher and higher on the list of controversial stars.

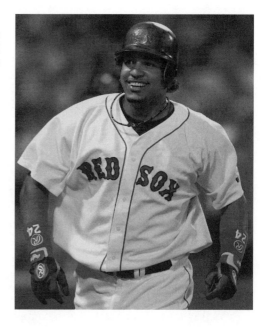

Manny Ramirez may be one of the greatest natural hitters of all time. Although the Dominican star helped the Boston Red Sox to their drought-breaking World Series championship in 2004, and is compiling Hall of Fame-worthy statistics as an out-fielder, he has also faced troubles from a drug-use suspension that could affect how posterity views him. (AP Photo/ Charles Krupa)

During the 2009 season the facts about Ramirez's flakiness, for so long dismissed with the offbeat endearment of "Manny being Manny," took an ugly turn. Early in the season, the player who had become the savior of the Los Angeles Dodgers during the club's late-season 2008 charge and was as popular as any movie actor in Hollywood ran afoul of Major League Baseball's drug program. It was announced that Ramirez flunked a drug test and he was suspended for 50 games. Following his return, it was reported that Ramirez was one of the secret names among 104 players who was listed as failing a drug test for performance enhancing substances in 2003.

Many in and around baseball are justifiably furious about circumstances surrounding the 2003 tests. Before 2003 baseball had no program for administering drug tests and neither steroids nor human growth hormone (common substances used by athletes to better their results) were illegal. The tests in 2003 were implemented primarily as a warning signal. The idea was to gauge how serious usage was. Players were promised that their names would never be linked to drug samples and that the samples would be destroyed. Instead, the samples were retained because of federal intervention. Although the names were suppressed, they began leaking out one by one. Fair or not, the reputation of anyone whose name was reported was tarnished. In Ramirez case, however, it seemed to be a second offense.

The second revelation was a blot on Ramirez's career. And the unhappy developments of 2009 for the first time cast doubts on the possibility of Ramirez's Hall of Fame enshrinement. The drug issues added to Ramirez's image as an enigma. What could not be denied is that for years Ramirez had been an extraordinary hitter with the Cleveland Indians, the Boston Red Sox, and the Dodgers.

Manny Ramirez was born in Santo Domingo in the Dominican Republic on May 30, 1972. However, his family moved to the Washington Heights section of New York City when he was going on 13. The family moved to a neighborhood where many émigrés from their native land preceded them and the language spoken while doing daily business for the most part remained Spanish. Although much of his youth was spent in the United States, Ramirez's first language was Spanish. Ramirez was not a particularly serious student and did not graduate from high school. It was not until after Ramirez was drafted by the Indians (he signed for a $300,000 bonus) and joined their minor-league system that he applied himself to developing his English knowledge.

"Some people say, 'You are a ballplayer, you have money, why do you need a diploma?' " Ramirez said. " 'Why worry about learning English?' It's something I want to do. I want to do it for me." (Quoted in Coffey.)

While the skills needed to absorb tougher courses at George Washington High School were not diligently used by Ramirez as a teenager, he had a visible and extraordinary gift on the baseball diamond that were evident early and propelled him into the Appalachian League as a teenager. Before his twenty-first birthday, Ramirez made his Major League debut with Cleveland. He was a half-time player the next season, 1994, and a star by 1995. That year he slammed 31 homers, drove in 107 runs, and batted .308. By then he was driving a BMW and bought a home in the Cleveland suburbs that enabled him to move his father, mother, and sister to Ohio.

In his first seasons with Cleveland, while feeling his way, Ramirez came off as shy. He smiled often, but did not talk loudly or often. He did display the bad habit of sulking and looking distracted and depressed if he fell into a hitting slump. Major leaguers cannot afford to do that. The at-bats come around too quickly. By his first complete season, Ramirez showed more maturity and patience at the plate and more maturity off the field. Indians general manager John Hart said that reflected just the natural passage of time. "You'll see a big difference in any kid between 18 and 23," Hart said. (Quoted in Coffey.)

Ramirez was a key component in the Indians' rise in the 1990s, a team that added numerous farm-system-raised young players to the lineup with the goal of coming together in their prime at the right time to win a World Series. "I want to prove to everybody I can play," Ramirez said during his breakout 1995 season. "That was my goal coming into this year." (Quoted in Coffey.)

That was a mission accomplished. Ramirez emerged as a coming star and he just built upon the impression after 1995. He quickly became one of the most feared sluggers in the American League, seen as a hitter that pitchers had to throw to with extra caution. Within a few seasons Ramirez's homer total was climbing into the 40s.

"The kid has so much talent, it's unbelievable," said Indians catcher Tony Pena. "He's going to be a superstar." (Quoted in Coffey.)

In many ways Ramirez was still a kid. He was unsophisticated, seemed to play the game with joy, and picked veterans' minds for suggestions on how to improve. During his feeling-his-way lead-up years (22 games in 1993 and 91 in 1994), Ramirez exhibited an endearing, child-like quality. Baseball, it has been said, is really a little boys' game played by men, but it helps to retain some of that little boy in the majors. When Ramirez was treated to an in-season call-up to the Indians for his debut, the first thing he did was telephone his mother, Onelcida, who worked in a dress factory she commuted to in New Jersey. "Mommy," he said, "they called me to the major leagues." (Quoted in Rimer.)

The Ramirez family spread the word about their boy. In the Spanish-speaking enclave, Manny instantly became the talk of the town. These shops were his haunts. Everyone knew who Aristides and Onelcida's boy was and how amazing it was that he had moved so swiftly from high school play to the majors. Even more remarkable, Ramirez was coming to town with the Indians to play New York in Yankee Stadium very soon.

A big fuss was made of Ramirez for his debut in Yankee Stadium. New York City did not export so many baseball players at the time and Ramirez was a home-town novelty who had a name already because of the way he tore up high school pitching so recently. "I miss my friends," Ramirez said when he showed up at one of his favorite restaurants. "I miss my food." (Quoted in Rimer.) Some of that food was fried plaintains, which he devoured as part of a pre-game meal with meringue music playing in the background. Many relatives and friends from the neighborhood, including former high school baseball teammates, jammed into Yankee Stadium to watch Ramirez play later that night.

Ramirez had his own cheering section, with fans chanting, "Manny! Manny! Manny!" It was just the beginning. Soon enough entire stadiums would call his name, though primarily at Jacobs Field in Cleveland, not on the road.

Although there are no readily available published eyewitness accounts, it might be assumed that Olcedia Ramirez also chanted Manny's name once in a while. As his earnings increased, Ramirez bought his parents a new, fancy home in Pembroke Pines, Florida. This is where all of his Major League memorabilia goes. Mom saves the clippings from the newspapers and the trophies from her son's career and puts them on display. One thing that has evidently given her much pleasure are the glowing words—in Spanish—written about Manny in the newspapers in the Dominican Republic as opposed to the New York tabloids'

English version. She gave up her job in a dress factory and Ramirez's father surrendered his job as a livery cab driver when their son used some of his millions of dollars from mushrooming salaries to take care of their needs.

The opulence seemed well-deserved for a family that had struggled to survive financially in New York. The Ramirezes crammed into a dark, sixth-floor tenement apartment and coped with a neighborhood that was welcoming enough on one count because of its Spanish-speaking familiarity but also presented challenges because of drug dealers. While Ramirez's parents and older sister worked, he was able to indulge in playing baseball in the streets. When he swiftly realized it was a game he could be good at, he played all of the time and worked at improving. "I was always in the street playing," he said. (Quoted in Rhodes and Boburg, 54.)

Ramirez could always hit the ball a long distance and it took very little time for him to be noticed as a premier up-and-comer. Even at Little League age he was ferried to games in taxi cabs by older men who wanted to bet on his performance. Usually, they bet on him and usually Ramirez delivered. But as any baseball fan knows, a 1-out-of-3 .333 hitting ratio is tremendous. That means things go south two out of three times. "If you made the last out, or if you made an error, there was a lot of money on the line, and they'd chase you and beat the crap out of you," said Steve Mandl, Ramirez's future high school coach. Mandl indicated this happened to Ramirez once, but Ramirez said he didn't remember it. (Quoted in Rhodes and Boburg, 56.)

A trademark of the 6-foot, 200-pound Ramirez's physical appearance is his dreadlocked black hair held in place by a bandana under his baseball cap when he plays. Another trademark is swinging a deadly hunk of lumber. In 1996, Ramirez improved slightly on his first full season, cracking 33 homers, knocking in 112 runs and batting .309. Was he at his peak? Not quite. In 1998, he slugged 45 homers and knocked in 145, though his average dipped to the .290s. No matter. In 1999, Ramirez smashed 44 homers with a .333 average, but left opponents in awe with his league-leading 165 RBIs. That was the most RBIs in a season by anyone since Jimmy Foxx's 175 in 1938. By then, Ramirez was a nationally appreciated hitting phenomenon.

"His potential is unlimited," said Charlie Manuel, the Indians' hitting coach who later became manager of the Philadelphia Phillies. "Manny has tremendous weight shift, which makes his hands quick to the ball. He's always had tremendous mechanics." (Quoted in Callahan.)

That attribute has been ascribed to Ramirez and hence the application of the old baseball adage, "He can hit falling out of bed." That means people believe he is such a natural hitter that a player could wake up in the middle of the night, stagger to the batter's box, and stroke a hit with his eyes only half-open.

"I don't know how much better he can get," said Indians infielder Travis Fryman. (Quoted in Callahan.)

Ramirez did most of his talking with his bat, preferring to ignore the media on occasion or drive reporters batty with strange answers to questions. He sometimes provided his wrong age, or the wrong age when he moved from the Dominican Republic to New York. As a result, he did not make many friends in the press and that was one reason Ramirez was listed as one of the 10 dumbest players. Mandl, Ramirez's high school coach, said Ramirez is smarter than that but doesn't always listen or concentrate. "That's the way Manny is," Mandl said. "It's hard to tell whether he's not listening to your question or just messing with you." (Quoted in Callahan.)

That was also true at times when Ramirez patrolled right field for the Indians. He periodically made circling under a fly ball an adventure. Later, with the Boston Red Sox, while playing left field at Fenway Park, he displayed the same tendencies and once was beaned on the head by a misjudged fly ball. If Ramirez was bothered by any criticism, or if coming to the plate in pressure situations concerned him in the least, he did not let on. Ramirez usually seemed like the most relaxed man in the ballpark, regardless of situation. "Manny is the single most unpretentious, unassuming guy I've ever met in baseball," said Ray Negron, who had the job of acting as a go-between for the Indians with the club's Latino players. (Quoted in Callahan.)

Although an injury limited Ramirez to 118 games in 2000, he might have been better than ever, cracking 38 homers, driving in 122 runs, and batting .351. That stunning performance was just in time for Ramirez to be a free agent. He wanted so much money—and owners were throwing it around at the time—that it seemed unlikely from the start he would play another game in a Cleveland uniform. The moneybags Boston Red Sox, trying to keep up with the Yankees in the American League Eastern Division, came through. Ramirez signed a boggling, eight-year, $160 million contract. Broken down he was being paid $20 million a season starting in 2001.

Ramirez immediately dispelled any worry that he would let his massive contract be a distraction and stepped right into starhood with the Sox in the same manner he had come through for the Indians. He was also just as erratic in the field. Once teamed with designated hitter David Ortiz, another Dominican slugger, Ramirez helped make the Red Sox offense seem overpowering. However, the baseball spotlight shines brighter in Boston, and the Red Sox wanted Ramirez to be more of a visible leader in the public eye than he wanted to be. He did not adjust smoothly to those demands. "Manny performs best in a relaxed environment," his agent Jeff Moorad said. (Quoted in Chass.) The addition of the naturally gregarious Ortiz, who became a good friend to Ramirez, shifted the lightning rod in 2003.

Until then Ramirez was taking considerable heat in Boston for not running out ground balls and for watching his home runs take flight instead of immediately running the bases. At one point, as if to announce to Ramirez "We don't need this aggravation," the Red Sox put him on waivers. There were no takers for his expensive contract, but it is difficult to believe that the Red Sox would have let him go for nothing.

The Ramirez-Ortiz combination paid a lifetime's worth of dividends in 2004 when the always-the-bridesmaid Red Sox made a fresh run at a World Series title. The year was a highlight for Ramirez in one way. He became a U.S. citizen in May in Miami at the urging of his mother, who had already become a citizen. His next game in Boston he ran out to left field waving a small American flag. The team put an announcement on the Fenway Park video board accompanied by singer Lee Greenwood's "God Bless the USA," song, then followed up by playing Neil Diamond's "America" when Ramirez strode to the plate. "I'm very proud to be an American," Ramirez said. "So now I have to behave better. They can't kick me out of the country." (Quoted in "Boston's . . .")

The season culminated with great joy in Boston. The Red Sox won their first World Series title since 1918. Ramirez sprayed champagne in the locker room and rode in the overwhelming victory parade through the streets of the city. Ramirez led the league with 43 home runs, drove in 130, and hit over .300. That took some of the edge off any anti-Manny feelings. Although Ramirez was not as dominant in 2007 when the Red Sox won a second World Series, he was still a key player with 20 home runs and 88 RBIs.

Relations between Ramirez, his teammates, the fans, and management began to truly sour in 2008. He was still productive, blasting 20 homers in the first 100 games, but Ramirez complained of small ailments and said he was too sore to play. He was worried about his future, with his contract due to run out at the end of the season. Ramirez supposedly shoved the team's 64-year-old traveling secretary to the ground when he could not come up with 16 tickets for a game he sought (an event Ramirez later characterized as a "misunderstanding"). (Quoted in Rojas.) And Boston sports talk radio shows began commenting on him as "a cancer in the clubhouse."

All this was counterproductive to other Manny stories. He made a spectacular catch on the road in left field, running halfway up the wall, then high-fived a fan in mid-play before throwing the ball back into the infield. That left everyone chuckling. He made off-beat, but humorous comments after plays. He made fans laugh again when he had to relieve himself inside the Green Monster, Fenway's left-field wall. When you've got to go, you've got to go. There was a nice moment, too, when he topped 500 career home runs, a statistic that long had ensured immortality in Cooperstown, but as the trade deadline approached at the end of July, speculation was rampant that Ramirez was headed elsewhere.

Ramirez tried to be circumspect in his answers to questions about where he might be playing the next season, but said, "You know, I'm an employee and I will go to any factory that needs me." (Quoted in Rojas.) Hardly a minimum-wage employee, though.

Ramirez was a free agent worker, so he did have some say where he might end up. Not during that season, though. In the end, Red Sox officials pulled the trigger earlier than expected. In a complex trade, the Red Sox acquired outfielder Jason Bay from the Pittsburgh Pirates, and Ramirez became property of the Dodgers. He batted nearly .400 for the Dodgers in 53 games and became an overnight sensation on the left coast. A free agent at the conclusion of the season, Ramirez danced with the Dodgers for months before re-upping for millions of dollars (but less than he wanted) in a calamitous economy.

And then early in the 2009 season Ramirez was banned by Major League Baseball for those 50 games. Somber-looking, he apologized to teammates and owner Frank McCourt, who expressed disappointment. Following the suspension he returned to the LA lineup and began hitting away again, as so few are capable of doing. Then came the shocking news that implicated Ramirez for taking performance-enhancing drugs when he was with the Red Sox. That time he didn't have much to say. There was no punishment for that news. All Ramirez could do to redeem himself was to keep on slugging. Even with 546 home runs and 1,788 RBIs at the end of 2009, his fate was in the hands of others.

Further Reading

"Boston's Ramirez becomes a United States citizen," Associated Press/United Press International, May 12, 2004.
Callahan, Gerry, "Son of Sammy," *Sports Illustrated*, April 5, 1999.
Chass, Murray, "A Shy Ramirez Seeks His Comfort Zone," *New York Times*, December 23, 2001.
Coffey, Wayne, "Washington Heights' Ramirez has Cleveland rockin' again," *New York Daily News*, June 4, 1995.
Rhodes, Jean, and Boburg, Shawn, *Becoming Manny* (New York, Scribner, 2009).
Rimer, Sara, "A Rookie, Yes, but a Neighborhood Hero," *New York Times*, September 4, 1973.
Rojas, Enrique, "Ramirez: I will go to any factory that needs me," ESPN.com, July 4, 2008.

Mariano Rivera

The game was close and the opposing Chicago White Sox had men on base. The manager called to the Yankees bullpen in the eighth inning because he needed someone to put out the brush fire before it spread and consumed the building. There was really only one choice.

Relief specialist Mariano Rivera has recorded more than 500 saves and is on his way to a Major League record. The Panamanian right-hander is 40 and still going as the mainstay of the New York Yankees' bullpen. In many quarters he is regarded as the best closing pitcher of all time. (Ronald Callaghan/Dreamstime)

When the phone rang in the bullpen everyone knew who was being summoned. Mariano Rivera grabbed his blue Yankee warm-up jacket and began jogging from the outfield to the pitcher's mound. Late in the game, with New York protecting a lead, it was Mariano time. He was on his way to his office, not to work eight hours at a desk, but to do what was necessary to fix the trouble. Ordinarily, Rivera was on alert just for ninth-inning work. But sometimes, when the situation was dire and circumstances boosted the importance of a Yankee win, he might be called on for preventive medicine in the eighth. This was one of those times. The White Sox had swept the first three games of a four-game series. If the Yankees lost this one, too, the club would be demoralized and fall out of first place in the American League Eastern Division.

It was up to Rivera to see that this did not occur. He settled into his comfort zone on the mound, zipped a few warm-up pitches at more than 90 mph and took care of the matter. Each time he threw to the plate his left shoulder faced the hitter. He did not use a full windup, just rested the ball in front of his chest as he first bent forward at the waist, then straightened up and whipped the white sphere home. It didn't take long. Rivera mastered the situation, doused the blaze, and finished off the win for the Yankees.

When you are the premier relief pitcher in baseball, perhaps the greatest of all time, your teammates place full confidence in you and you are successful more than 90 percent of the time.

It was mid-summer of the 2009 season when Rivera made this appearance against the White Sox. He was in the twilight of his career as he hurtled toward

40 years old and he ranked second all-time in saves, the statistic most often used to cite the effectiveness of relief pitchers. Only Trevor Hoffman, also still pitching for the Milwaukee Brewers, was ahead of Rivera. But Rivera was younger and likely to catch him prior to retirement. At the rate Rivera was going he might make it to 600 and set a new standard. As of the end of the 2009 season he was up to 526.

"He's something. He's really been something," said White Sox broadcaster and former major leaguer Ken "Hawk" Harrelson of Rivera's accomplishments. While noting how many tremendous relievers have performed in the closer's role, Harrelson said, "He's right there at the top." (Quoted in Harrelson.)

Rivera was born in Panama City, Panama on November 29, 1969. When his skill was noticed he signed with the Yankees for $3,000 in 1990. He broke into the majors with the Yankees in 1995 and never pitched for another team. As the stars of the club came and went in the outfield, the infield, the starting rotation, as the manager of the team and coaching staff changed, Rivera was a constant. He was the fixture in the bullpen, the sure-thing rescuer when the team got into a jam in the late innings.

Rivera's pitching was viewed as producing automatic outs as he shut down opposing hitters—blanking them in the late innings when they harbored illusions of comebacks. His heroics, often under extreme pressure in the playoffs, helped the Yankees win World Series championships in 1996, 1998, 1999, and 2000. Never used as a starting pitcher after his rookie year, Rivera brought a lifetime mark of 482 saves and a 2.29 earned run average into the 2009 season. En route to a 44-save season, he became an All-Star for the 10th time.

Rivera notched his 500th save on June 28, 2009 in a 4–2 victory over the cross-town rival Mets, but when the soft-spoken fireballer was asked how he was going to celebrate the milestone, he looked at his questioners as if they had been imbibing a 12-pack of beer. "I go home," he said. "Simple as that. As quick as I finish, I go home." (Quoted in Cohen.) So much for taking advantage of the late-night pleasures in a city that never sleeps.

The answer was typical of Rivera, a low-key family man who never made headlines in the New York tabloids with brash statements or off-the-field exploits. If Rivera was single in New York his dark good looks, piercing eyes, and thick eyebrows likely would have made him a popular eligible bachelor. He has always been as efficient as a 40-miles-per-gallon automobile and as businesslike as a corporate official. He minded his business, ignored the hullabaloo that sometimes surrounded the Yankees in the world's largest media center, and invested his entire focus on getting opponents out.

Rivera was not the type of guy to toot his own horn, even after recording a significant save like his 500th. Others usually assumed the role of touting how great he was. The role of relief pitchers has changed dramatically since the 1960s when they first assumed true prominence. For decades, pitchers were banished to the bullpen as punishment because they could no longer handle what was seen as the far-more-important job of starting. Sometimes certain circumstances made aging pitchers stars in relief.

In the 1960s, a stud overpowering fastball thrower like Boston's Dick Radatz, nicknamed "The Monster," sparkled for a couple of seasons. Radatz and others who followed him were often called upon to pitch three or more innings, not simply to one or more batter like Rivera and the modern-day closers. They pitched a couple of times a week in a pinch, unlike today's closers who are expected to be on call almost every day. Rivera's workload, only once breaking 100 innings in a season during his Major League career, was different. Frequency was the key element in his availability.

Until the last decade or so few relievers excelled at the role for more than a few years. They often burnt out quickly from overuse. The Yankees have used Rivera only to protect small leads throughout his career. He arrives in a game in a full-fledged pressure situation knowing that a single errant pitch, a single mistake, can cost the team a victory. For 14 years he has almost never made that mistake. In 1999, Rivera was the Most Valuable Player in the World Series. In 2004, he saved 53 Yankee wins. The team won 101 games that summer.

"It's very, very difficult to be consistent year in and year out," said New York shortstop Derek Jeter, a career-long teammate of Rivera's. "He's been consistent every year." (Quoted in Cohen.)

The irony of Rivera's career is that he might be emblematic of the old style—exiled to the bullpen because he wasn't doing a great job as a starter. Rivera seems virtually unhittable to other players, but he did not have a vast repertoire of pitches for a starter who needs at least three to have a solid chance of being a success. In his short relief stints Rivera has made remarkable use of a single pitch, a cutter. In recent years he has added a two-seam fastball. If hitters saw the same stuff over and over in the same game, they might catch up to him. If they see it just once in a while, he is the one in charge—as he has proven. In 2008, an observer broke down Rivera's pitches for the entire season and figured that he threw the cut fastball 82 percent of the time. Empirical knowledge told batters what type of pitch was coming. But they didn't know the location and couldn't pick up the spin, so they still couldn't hit it.

"He's pretty much had one pitch his entire career and he's been dominant," said Yankee outfielder Johnny Damon, who faced Rivera when he played for the Red Sox and Kansas City Royals. "He's been the best at his job for so many years." (Quoted in Botte.)

Like so many other Latino stars, Rivera's childhood was marred by poverty. He used a cardboard baseball glove until his father bought him a real leather glove at the age of 12. He is the son of a Panamanian fisherman and he is quite religious. At one point during his career, Rivera said he planned to retire by 2003, return to Panama, and become a minister. Touched by the terrorist attacks on the World Trade Center in New York of September 11, 2001, when Rivera was named the Rolaids Relief Man of the Year he donated the award to the New York City Fire Department.

Rivera graduated from Pablo Sanchez High School at 16. As a youth he played as much soccer as baseball, but after high school he seemed destined for the life of a fisherman like his dad. His father was captain of his own boat and Rivera worked 12-hour days on the commercial vessel. When he was 19, the 120-foot boat capsized. Rivera had to abandon ship. After this threat to his life, Rivera decided he wanted no part of a fishing career. Baseball emerged as a better option after a Yankee scout spotted him on the mound for a Panamanian team. The Yankees and Rivera were in luck. He was actually an infielder filling in for an injured teammate. When the raw Rivera signed and shipped out to the United States for minor league ball, he had almost no pitching background and was unable to speak English. He learned both disciplines quickly.

Although Rivera is unlikely to ever deliver a speech in English rivaling the Gettysburg Address, his pitching eloquence attained the level of Shakespeare. Players have called his cut fastball the best pitch any hurler has ever thrown, comparing it to a buzzsaw bearing down on them. In all cases, the interpretation of Rivera's skill was taken to mean he was untouchable.

Major League Baseball retired the No. 42 permanently on all teams to honor the contributions of barrier breaker Jackie Robinson as the first black player in the sport in the twentieth century. Rivera had long before quietly selected No. 42 as his jersey number to personally honor Robinson. He was allowed to keep the number and he will be the last player to wear it for any Major League team.

Although Rivera has spent his entire Major League career with the Yankees, things almost turned out differently. In 1995, when he did not show signs of becoming a reliable starter, the team nearly traded him to the Detroit Tigers. Discussions took place between then-New York General Manager Gene Michael and Detroit executive Joe Klein. The deal on the table was Rivera one-on-one for starter David Wells (who eventually became a Yankee anyway and even pitched a perfect game for New York).

Michael hesitated, didn't commit, and didn't call Klein back right away. The Tigers traded Wells to Cincinnati for three players instead. Michael said he couldn't remember exactly why he held off, but thought it was because there had been a jump in Rivera's velocity to the 95 mph level. When Rivera recorded his 500th save, Klein recounted the events and announced to Tiger fans, "I'm telling you, we would have done it." No one can know if Rivera would have become a closer with another team or been installed in the Tigers' rotation. "I'd like to think we'd have thought of it," Klein said. "But he could have been a Hall of Famer as a starter, too. Who knows?" (Quoted in Knobler.)

Years later Michael was relieved, so to speak, that he had not pulled the trigger on that swap, and he still felt Rivera might have been a valuable starting pitcher. "He had a hell of a changeup when he was young," the former New York exec said. "And he had a true slider to go with his fastball. He could have been a starter. Hell, he could have been an infielder, he's such a great athlete. But I think it worked out pretty well for him as a reliever." (Quoted in Harper.) Because immortality beckons for Rivera in Cooperstown, Michael's dry comment is probably accurate.

Rivera made his reputation for always being there for the Yankees, always staying healthy, and always being ready for the call for help. That reliability was tested once in 2004 when a tragedy in Panama grabbed Rivera's attention and threatened to hold him back for the American League playoffs that fall. Two members of Rivera's wife's family were electrocuted in the fishing village of Puerto Caimito while swimming in the pool Rivera owned. An adult cousin of Clara Rivera was cleaning the pool for Rivera while he was in the United States. The man's 14-year-old son was injured unexpectedly when an electrical pole fell into the pool generating the fatal juice. The father jumped in the pool to try to save his boy, but both died.

A saddened Rivera left the Yankees and flew to Panama for the double funeral. "At this moment, my family is my priority," Rivera said to a reporter in Panama. "I stopped thinking about baseball the moment I got on the plane." (Quoted in "Rivera says . . .")

Not everyone in New York believed Rivera would return in time for the opening of a critical playoff series against the Red Sox, and they were concerned whether or not he would be able to put his grief behind him and pitch normally. Manager Joe Torre expressed no doubts. "I think with Mariano, if he's here physically tomorrow, he'll say, 'Give me the ball.' And whether it's 100 percent or 50 percent, it's still going to be damned good." (Quoted in "Rivera says . . .")

The Yankees sent a private plane to Panama to pick up Rivera following the funerals, and he was present for the start of the series and was used in his regular role by Torre.

At no time during Rivera's career has any member of the Yankees publicly or privately doubted the hurler's abilities. The organization has always demonstrated 100 percent faith in his cut fastball. At a time when many teams cut costs by failing to renew even top players' contracts for more than one year, the Yankees always rewarded Rivera's contributions. In 2007, when he was going on 38, some wondered if it was wise to invest in a new long-term deal for Rivera. To do so was counterintuitive. Few relievers in baseball history have maintained Rivera's high-quality longevity and studies of aging pitchers have recorded they suffer extreme drop-offs in performance as they approach and pass 40 years old.

Not only did the Yankees award Rivera a new three-year, $45-million contract in 2007, there has been no reduction in his work load, no concessions to age in the way he is used. He is still The Man in the bullpen, the closer counted on to shut down threats. And he has displayed no signs of advancing age, proving the wisdom of the deal. Throughout his career in the bullpen, Yankee Stadium personnel with a sense of humor have heralded Rivera's march to the mound by playing Metallica's "Enter the Sandman." The hard rock revs up the patrons, but also sends a message to foes. Their bats are about to be put to sleep. The lyrics do imply nightmares are to follow, as well, something hitters going man-to-man against Rivera know well.

In a rarity given his shy personality, Rivera bantered with the media after recording his 500th save. He hinted that there was much more to come in his arm. Even if on that day he trailed Hoffman by 71 saves, he gave the impression he might well be throwing for years beyond Hoffman's retirement.

"You guys are always wondering," Rivera said of reporters asking how long he could go on as a top-flight reliever. "You guys don't learn? Every year's the same thing." (Quoted in Davidoff.)

Rivera was right. Every year was the same thing. His breakout year was 1997 when he collected 43 saves. In the following years Rivera recorded 36, 45, 36, and 50 saves. Injury limited his appearances in 2002 and he posted 28 saves. Then he resumed the normal course of business with consecutive seasons of 40, 53, 43, 34, 30, and 39 saves.

Rivera notched a career low earned run average of 1.38 in 2005, but it was no aberration. In seven other seasons he has recorded seasonal ERAs of below two runs per game. In 2008, presenting convincing evidence that there was nothing frail about his arm, Rivera's ERA was 1.40 in 64 appearances. No wonder he dismissed questions about his future as silly. Those queries will become legit only when he shows signs of slippage.

As a career American League pitcher where the designated hitter takes the hurler's spot in the batting order almost all of the time, Rivera actually seemed to cherish his first career run batted in during his 500th save game. At least he teased reporters about that milestone. "It's my first RBI," he said, making it sound like a bigger deal than the pitching achievement. "I've had 500 saves." (Quoted in Davidoff.)

Some baseball players are so extraordinary at what they do that it doesn't take long to recognize the supreme level of their talent. Rivera is one of them. He has been at the top of the heap of closers for so long that he has worn out other generations of relievers while still ticking. In his case, as in the situations of other superstars, it is a foregone conclusion he will end up in the Hall of Fame. Longevity would be the main question clinging to a reliever, and Rivera is long past putting that issue to rest.

"He's the best ever," said Yankee Jorge Posada, another long-time teammate who has shared the intimacy of Rivera's success many times as his catcher. "There's no doubt about it. There's not going to be another Mariano Rivera out there. Ever. Mariano has meant a lot to me and made my job a lot easier. He's the best ever." (Quoted in Botte.)

Rivera has always had the simple nickname of "Mo" around the Yankees. As he ages and continues to put Hall of Fame numbers on his resume, it's obvious that Mo has a double meaning. In Rivera's case it also stands for "More." There are more saves to come.

Further Reading

Botte, Peter, "Yankee teammates save best praise for Mariano Rivera's milestone," *New York Daily News*, June 29, 2009.

Cohen, Jay, "Rivera adds to legacy as elite closer," Associated Press, June 29, 2009.

Davidoff, Ken, "A lesson learned 500 times: Mo refuses to fade away," *Newsday*, June 29, 2009.

Harper, John, "At start of Mariano Rivera's Yankee career, Gene Michael almost traded him," *New York Daily News*, June 30, 2009.

Harrelson, Ken, WGN-TV, Channel 9 Chicago, Yankees-White Sox broadcast, August 2, 2009.

Knobler, Danny, "Rivera: The trade that never happened," CBSSports.com June 30, 2009.

"Rivera says he will be back for Game 1," Associated Press, October 11, 2004.

Alex Rodriguez

He was a prodigy, a star so luminescent in high school that Alex Rodriguez might as well have had the words "Can't Miss" tattooed across the back of his shoulders. And now, 16 years into his Major League career, it is apparent that one day the player known as "A-Rod" will be mentioned among the all-time greats of the game.

Rodriguez was born in New York, son of Dominican Republic immigrants, on July 27, 1975, and he nearly represented their country in the World Baseball Classic. Indeed, his half-siblings were born in the Dominican. His father Victor ran a shoe store in New York City, but retired when Alex was four, and returned

A major leaguer since he was 18, Alex Rodriguez became a star with the Seattle Mariners, became the highest paid player in history with the Texas Rangers, and in 2009 the New York Yankee third baseman won his first World Series crown. Rodriguez is considered the likeliest prospect to break Barry Bonds' all-time home-run record of 762. (AP Photo/Frank Franklin II)

to their home country for a while before settling in Florida when A-Rod was seven. Rodriguez's parents split up when the boy was nine and he was raised by his mother Lourdes after that. She had to work two jobs to support the family.

Rodriguez said his mother inspired him by working hard. Victor wanted to live in New York, Lourdes in Miami and that was at the root of the split. Rodriguez said he always thought his father would come back, but his parents never reconciled. He tried to convince himself that he didn't miss his father, but he admitted that sometimes he cried over the loss of the other parent in his life.

Always involved in sports, Rodriguez played high school baseball at Westminster Christian in Miami and batted .505 as a senior, an effort that earned him national recognition. He was a particular fan of the New York Mets' Keith Hernandez and Baltimore Orioles shortstop Cal Ripken.

Rodriguez seemed set on competing collegiately for the University of Miami. He rooted for the school's sports teams and signed a letter of intent for a scholarship. When he wasn't swinging for the fences, it was suggested he might play quarterback for the Hurricanes' football team. However, the Seattle Mariners made Rodriguez the No. 1 draft pick in the 2003 amateur draft and he signed a pro contract.

Rodriguez is blessed with a nearly perfect physical specimen of a body for baseball, standing 6-foot-3 and weighing 220 pounds. He has the quickness of a smaller man and the agility to play shortstop at an All-Star level, although he shifted to third base when he joined the New York Yankees.

The youngest player to reach the milestone of 500 home runs (he has 583 now) in a career, Rodriguez is the consensus choice to become the sport's all-time homer leader, someday surpassing Barry Bonds' record of 762.

As property of the Mariners, Rodriguez spent most of 1994 in the minors, but by his 19th birthday that season he got his first taste of big-league ball, appearing in 17 games. Before he was 20 he was a regular for the Mariners and swiftly established himself as a star. Rodriguez played in 48 games in 1995 but by 1996 was a full-time regular. His explosion on the scene that year mesmerized fans. His 215 hits, 36 home runs, and 123 runs batted in were impressive enough, but he led the American League with 141 runs scored, 54 doubles, and a .358 batting average. As an aside Rodriguez stole 15 bases.

That season catapulted Rodriguez into the top realm of players almost instantly. And it was no fluke. Each season he seemed to improve upon the last, whether statistically or in sophistication. In 1998, Rodriguez smacked a league-leading 213 hits and improved upon his personal best for RBIs with 124. Along with Ken Griffey Jr. and Randy Johnson, two certain Hall of Famers, Rodriguez lifted the profile of Seattle baseball at a time when the franchise was in jeopardy. The trio, with a solid supporting cast, energized the region and convinced fans to vote for authorization of a new stadium. The creation of the new ballpark saved the team for the Pacific Northwest.

As a teenage phenom who was not terribly outspoken, Rodriguez seemed like the boy next door. He was transcendently talented and seemed to be the kind of player who would spend a 20-year career with the Mariners. The once-quiet and unassuming young player, however, known for his supremely marvelous play, began to cross the line from sports hero to celebrity figure in 2000.

It was a seller's market for All-Star players when Rodriguez became a free agent and entertained bids for a long-term contract that were almost beyond any economist's imagination. Rather than stick with the Mariners, Rodriguez was wooed by riches previously known only to corporate kingpins. Ultimately, he inked a 10-year, $252-million deal with the Texas Rangers, the richest contract in the history of sports. The announcement rocked baseball's foundations and astonished everyone from players to managers to owners.

If owners worried that this was precedent, a close look at the circumstances indicated Rodriguez was a unique player. He was only 25, in the prime of his career, with a successful track record, and with every chance of fulfilling the 10 years of the contract at a high level of play. In short, no one else brought the same skills and record to the table at so young an age. Given the way the deal was denounced, it did not seem that any other team owner was likely to offer such a payday to any other player.

The clamor began immediately: Is he worth it? Many aspects of the contract boggled minds. Owner Tom Hicks had paid $250 million for the rights to the entire team just three years earlier. "Alex is the only person that deserves this kind of contract," Hicks said. "This transaction is within our budget." (Quoted in Antonen.) Hicks hoped to see his team improve on the field from more than 20 games out of first place and to put more people in the seats.

Although it might not have seemed possible, Rodriguez's performance did hold up his end of the bargain. His first season with the Rangers in 2001 was better than his years with the Mariners. While playing in all 162 games, Rodriguez hit a career-high 52 home runs, knocked in 135, batted .318, stroked 201 hits, scored a league-high 133 runs and stole 18 bases. It was astonishing production. Rodriguez joined Babe Ruth, Hack Wilson, and Jimmy Foxx as the only players to collect at least 50 home runs and 200 hits in the same year. Yet because of weak pitching, Texas was not transformed into a pennant contender.

Similarly, no one could blame Rodriguez for any Ranger faults in 2002, either. He led the American League in homers with 57, the second of three straight seasons he would lead in that category. He also led the AL in RBIs with 142 and hit .300. For all of that the Rangers were a last-place team and Hicks began talking about starting all over with young players surrounding Rodriguez. Hicks concluded that his dream of presiding over a championship team by 2004 was dead. Raves for A-Rod's play read like the notices on a smash Broadway show.

"If he's not already one of the greatest shortstops ever, he's on a short list with (Cal) Ripken," said Rangers manager Jerry Narron. (Quoted in Newhan.)

The context for Narron's observation was his being asked if Rodriguez was the best shortstop of all time. Los Angeles Angels manager Mike Scioscia chimed in on the same theme. "I don't think you'll get much argument that he's the best player in the game," he said. "He's probably the most complete player I've ever seen. He can hurt you in so many ways. By the time he's finished his offensive numbers are going to fly by guys who played what are considered to be the most traditional power positions." (Quoted in Newhan.)

Others took note that the Mariners had spent wisely, using the money they had not bestowed on Rodriguez, and had improved as a team since he departed, while the Rangers floundered. Fans and sportswriters appalled at the price of horse flesh gave nods to Rodriguez's greatness, but held him up as a poster boy for what was wrong with pro sports. He was seen as evidence that salaries had run amok. Rodriguez resented the implications he was a bad guy for seeking the best deal he could.

"It hurts me when people want to equate me with what's wrong with the game I love," Rodriguez said. "I put myself in position, through dedication and hard work, to be rewarded, and suddenly, I'm a villain. A lot of skeptical people thought I'd fail. Last year wasn't easy, but I'm proud of the way I handled it, being able to build on the consistency I'd established over previous years." (Quoted in Newhan.)

It is perhaps more difficult for a single baseball player to improve a team's performance by himself than in any other major American team sport. A LeBron James can uplift his basketball team, using just five players on a court at the same time, with his efforts. A Sidney Crosby can uplift his hockey team, using just six players on the ice at the same time. Even professional football, with its 22 starters and special teams, a quarterback or superstar running back can have more of a single-handed effect on a game than one of a team's nine baseball starters (unless it's a pitcher having a special day).

Rodriguez was so spectacular during the 2002 season—when his 52 homers broke Ernie Banks's record for most four-baggers by a shortstop—that there was considerable support for him to win the Most Valuable Player award despite Texas' last-place finish. However, because the Rangers were so awful that year much of Rodriguez's brilliance went unseen on the national level. As the season drew to a close, *Sports Illustrated* headlined a story about Rodriguez in Texas with the phrase, "The Lone Ranger." (Quoted in Verducci.) Once again an article suggested that Rodriguez was the best player in baseball.

Still working hard to improve his play, Rodriguez did not want to be accused of letting his team down, of letting his money go to his head. He knew how lucky he was to reap the benefits of the largest contract of all. "I have enough (money) to last forever," he said. "Not one day goes by when I don't remind myself of how grateful I am for those who came before me over the last 25 years." (Quoted in Verducci.)

In 2003, once again showing that he could rise above his team's poor play, Rodriguez cracked 47 home runs, drove in 118 runs, scored a league-high 124, posted the American League's best slugging percentage of .600, and led the league in fielding average at .989. Rodriguez became the first player in American League history and the second in Major League history (Andre Dawson was the other), to claim an MVP award while competing for a last-place team.

Although Rodriguez never did suit up for the University of Miami, in 2003 he donated $3.9 million to the school for renovation of the baseball field. The name was changed to Mark Light Field at Alex Rodriguez Park. In 2004, Rodriguez was declared an honorary alumnus of the school.

Soon enough—way before the 10-year contract was completed—Rodriguez was an alumnus of the Rangers, too. Despite Hicks's optimism, it turned out that Rodriguez's salary was not really within the Rangers' budget. A baseball team needs more than one star to win. Texas had no luck finding adequate pitching and with so much money tied up in Rodriguez's contract, had little success recruiting other valuable free agents. Hicks's spending dried up. The A-Rod-Rangers love affair quickly showed signs of disintegrating.

Rodriguez wanted to play for a winner and Hicks wanted out from under Rodriguez's contract so he could afford to build a winner. An attempt to trade Rodriguez to the Boston Red Sox fizzled, but then he was shipped to the New York Yankees for Alfonso Soriano and Joaquin Arias. Rodriguez said New York was his favorite city in the world.

The trade to the Yankees altered Rodriguez's life in ways he may never have imagined. He went from producing superstar numbers under the radar to having every move he made—at the ballpark, on the street, at a nightclub—reported and magnified by the fiercely competitive hungry-to-break-any-tidbit-of-gossip tabloids the *New York Post* and *New York Daily News*. Rodriguez could easily have become sick of seeing his conveniently shortened A-Rod nickname in the tabloids. The nickname was bestowed by Mariners broadcaster Dave Niehaus and Rodriguez trademarked it. He just couldn't keep it out of the headlines.

If the move to New York enhanced Rodriguez's national profile and enhanced his chance of winning a World Series, the transformation of Rodriguez from ballplayer to celebrity was complete. There was no such thing as having a bad day at the office and walking away from it quietly. There was no such thing as marital struggles and having those problems play out in the quietude of his own living room.

A photographer spotted Rodriguez emerging from a nightclub with a blonde woman not his wife and snapped a picture. The photo appeared in the *Post* with the headline, "Stray-Rod." Rodriguez's wife, Cynthia, showed up at Yankee Stadium wearing a tank top with obscenities written on it. The *Post* headline? "Mrs. A-Rod Is A Bronx F-Bomber." The initial mystery woman was later identified as a stripper.

Rodriguez and his wife eventually split up, providing more fodder for the tabloids. Apparently, Rodriguez dated, had an affair with, or simply shared milkshakes with Madonna, with that information, too, being emblazoned all over the headlines. An affair between the two was denied. More recently, Rodriguez has dated actress Kate Hudson. They have also been photographed together, with photos in the tabloids.

Back on the playing field, Rodriguez has not been controversy free, either. In 2004, Rodriguez joined the Yankees and was shifted to third base because the shortstop role was controlled by future Hall of Famer Derek Jeter. Once again, Rodriguez put together a superb all-around statistical season with 36 homers and 106 RBIs. Almost from the moment that he arrived in New York, though, Rodriguez has been under increased scrutiny and faced exponentially more criticism than he ever did in Seattle or Texas. Although no one can argue with the case built by his stats, Rodriguez sometimes suffered critiques suggesting he is not a clutch player.

Rodriguez answered back in 2005 with a season of virtually heroic proportions. He led the American League with 48 home runs and 124 runs scored. He batted .321, drove in 130 runs and won his second Most Valuable Player award. The Yankees won the American League East title but did not win the World Series. Falling short was blamed on A-Rod by some.

"I stunk," he said bluntly of his play during the New York loss to the Angels in the Division Series playoff. "My only regret is that toward the end I got a little anxious and expanded the strike zone a little bit. I'm a target, a player that the other team doesn't want to beat them. I was very prepared for the playoffs. It just didn't work out. Sometimes that happens." (Quoted in Verducci.)

By then, Rodriguez was starting to understand that anything he got involved in—baseball or his personal life—was going to be dissected in the media. "When you don't have news, I realize now that everything I do—whether it's true or not—becomes a big story," he said. (Quoted in Feinasand.)

Winning his second MVP award, denoting his excellence over the long season, thrilled Rodriguez. He said he did not know what his chances were given the monster slugging season David Ortiz had for the Red Sox. "This award is very special to me," Rodriguez said. "First, doing it in a Yankees' uniform is unbelievable. Second, to win it twice in three years, knowing how hard this game can be, it's what I strive for every year. I strive to be consistent and this shows that I am." (Quoted in Feinasand.)

Rodriguez has said his mother is his biggest influence, but he also had help along the way from others and when he won major awards like the MVP he often reflected on their assistance. Eddie Rodriguez, supervisor of the baseball program at the Boys and Girls Club of Miami, was a hands-on helper with the game. So was Rich Hofman, Rodriguez's high school baseball coach. And Rodriguez described Lou Piniella, his Mariners' manager, as being "like an uncle or a father. He's the greatest teacher I've had as a pro." (Quoted in Feinasand.)

Year after year Rodriguez produced awesome statistics. Then came 2007, when he topped himself in several ways. A-Rod smashed a league-leading 54 home runs and led the AL with 156 RBIs and 143 runs scored while batting .314. Rodriguez was unstoppable from the first pitch to the last and was voted his third MVP award. In an event that garnered even more attention, Rodriguez also slammed the 500th home run of his career. The blast was recorded on August 4, in a Yankee Stadium game against the Kansas City Royals. The first-inning homer was smacked off of pitcher Kyle Davies. The shot made Rodriguez the youngest player to reach the milestone at 32 years, 8 days.

"I thought when I hit it initially, with the path of the ball, it would definitely go foul," Rodriguez said. "It means the world. To do it at home and to wear this beautiful uniform that I appreciate and I respect so much, it's special. New York's a special place. I've had my trials and tribulations here in New York. I've learned from them. A day like today kind of brings it full circle and maybe there's a happy ending for me somewhere." (Quoted in White.)

Just how happy an ending Rodriguez would find in New York was up in the air for a while. Under the terms of his long contract with Texas, Rodriguez could become a free agent again in 2007. He did so. Although there was a great deal of media speculation, Rodriguez re-upped with the Yankees with a fresh, 10-year deal worth $275 million. He was still the highest paid player of all time.

Rodriguez's future, stature, and legacy all came into question during a complex 2009 season that at times was a living nightmare for the player. Rodriguez, who withdrew from the initial World Baseball Classic, intended to play for the Dominican Republic in the second event. However, he underwent surgery to remove a cyst and learned that he was also suffering from a torn labrum in his right hip. Rodriguez missed the Classic, spring training, and the first month of the regular season.

While Rodriguez was sidelined, *Sports Illustrated* reported that he was one of the 104 major leaguers who tested positive for performance-enhancing drugs in 2003. At the time, as part of its first step into drug testing, Major League Baseball promised anonymity to players to participate and also promised the tests would be destroyed because there was no penalty for drug use at the time. Instead, the tests were preserved and some players' names have been leaked to the media one by one. Rodriguez admitted using steroids from 2001 to 2003, feeling he was under "an enormous amount of pressure to perform." (Quoted in Rieber.)

When Rodriguez returned to the Yankee lineup, his hitting stroke was off and his overall game was below par. Yet he gradually returned to top form as the weather warmed. However, as he traveled around the league, Rodriguez faced shouts of "Cheater!" from some fans. Although Rodriguez's prior baseball conduct had been exemplary and the tests were supposed to remain anonymous and carried no punishment, it was not clear how the incident would affect Rodriguez's long-term image.

Still, Rodriguez, a 12-time All-Star who has won 10 Silver Slugger Awards as the best hitter at his position, is a rare three-time MVP. In 2009, he was a key figure as the Yankees returned to World Series championship form and he could become the all-time home-run champ. His performance-enhancing drug lapse may yet be forgiven.

Further Reading

Antonen, Mel, "A-Rod gets $242 million and a new address in Texas," *USA Today*, December 12, 2000.
Feinasand, Mark, "A-Rod discusses MVP award," MLB.com November 14, 2005.

Newhan, Ross, "The Best Ever?" *Los Angeles Times*, June 19, 2002.

Rieber, Anthony, "Wait over in a New York minute," *Newsday*, August 5, 2007.

Verducci, Tom, "The Lone Ranger," *Sports Illustrated*, September 9, 2002.

White, Paul, "Before He Was A-Rod," *USA Today Sports Weekly*, February 16–22, 2005.

Ivan "Pudge" Rodriguez

The catcher can be the cornerstone of team greatness. He is the rock guarding home plate with his body. He is the soother of pitchers' jitters. He signals the fielders how many are out. He guns out the base stealers trying to embarrass his team. And sometimes he just slugs his club to victory.

Another word for catcher is "backstop," and while the term has fallen out of favor, it remains accurate. No position on the diamond is more challenging and less appreciated. No other player's body takes as much physical abuse. In a generally benign sport where contact is at a minimum, the catcher takes the brunt of it and by squatting into position pitch after pitch, play after play, straining his knees, his career is often shortened.

Ivan "Pudge" Rodriguez of Puerto Rico has caught more games than any player in history, a record he set with his 2,227th appearance behind the plate in June 2009. The long-time star has been a star backstop for the Texas Rangers, Florida Marlins, Houston Astros, and Detroit Tigers and has been an All-Star 14 times. (AP Photo/Tony Gutierrez)

In many ways the catcher is the mudder of the lineup, the sacrificer of his own skin to save his team a run here or there. Foul tips crack against the small areas of bare skin not protected by shin guards, face mask, and chest protector, the so-called "tools of ignorance." There is a better chance at the end of each game that the catcher's uniform will be dirtier than anyone else's.

The catcher is warrior as baseball player and no one in the current generation of receivers better fits that description than Ivan Rodriguez. Although setting the mark got some attention during the summer of 2009, it didn't stick in fans' brains the way batting averages and home run statistics do. It is guaranteed, though, to stay in Pudge Rodriguez's mind. On June 17, Rodriguez, wearing the uniform of the Houston Astros, appeared in his 2,227 game as a catcher, setting a new Major League record. The milestone surpassed the old record set by Hall of Famer Carlton Fisk.

Rodriguez was 19 when he broke into the majors with the Texas Rangers in 1991. After stints with the Florida Marlins, Detroit Tigers, and briefly the New York Yankees, he started his nineteenth Major League season in Houston at age 37. He brought a .301 lifetime average, 295 home runs and 1,217 RBIs with him. Most remarkably for a catcher with so much wear and tear on his joints, he showed little signs of slippage.

The record for longevity was a long time coming. Fisk played for 24 seasons. Rodriguez caught more games per season on average—and wasn't finished yet. "It's been a long time," Rodriguez said. "But I'm still feeling the same way (as) when I was 19. I love this game. I love what I do." (Quoted in "Ex-Tiger . . .")

Rodriguez burst onto the scene with the Rangers, establishing very quickly that his catcher's mitt was flexible and attracted bouncing pitches and foul pop-ups like a magnet. In only a handful of seasons it became clear that Rodriguez was the finest catcher of his generation and would be mentioned in the same sentence as the all-time greats.

In what was seen as a curious move at the time, Rodriguez was criticized for jumping to the Marlins for a one-year $10 million contract. It was felt he did not care about winning. But Rodriguez proved to be the glue that helped lead the Marlins to a World Series crown in 2003. When he signed a fresh, rich contract with the Tigers, they were the worst team in baseball. Rodriguez helped carry Detroit into a World Series.

"He's a very proud guy," said Tigers manager Jim Leyland when Rodriguez set the catcher's game mark. "Obviously, he's going to the Hall of fame where he deserves (to be)." (Quoted in "Ex-Tiger . . .")

Rodriguez is the most decorated catcher of the last few decades. He needs a trophy room as large as a three-car garage to hold his baubles. A 14-time All-Star, Rodriguez was awarded the 1999 American League Most Valuable Player award. Winner of seven Silver Slugger awards as the best hitter at his position, Rodriguez is also the winner of 13 Gold Glove awards as the best fielder at his position. His rocket arm helps him mow down one of the highest percentages of attempted base stealers among catchers. Don't mess with Pudge on the base paths or you will take the long, slow trudge back to the dugout with your head down.

Just like other catchers, Rodriguez suffers from black and blue marks where balls strike his flesh, bent back fingers where foul tips crush his nails, and aching toes where his pitchers' low throws clip his body. But generally Rodriguez has been durable and not suffered the type of long-term serious injuries that could affect his production. He topped 100 games caught in 15 seasons (with two more of 90-plus) and twice caught at least 150 of his team's 162 games in a season. His career high was 153 games caught with Texas in 1993. Few major leaguers catch more than 130 games in a season. "To be able to play so many games behind the plate, it's unbelievable," Rodriguez said. (Quoted in "Ivan . . .")

Ivan Rodriguez was born in Manati, Puerto Rico on November 27, 1971. Rodriguez stands 5-foot-9, but when he reached the majors weighing 195 pounds he still retained some of his baby fat. Hence, the nickname "Pudge." And it was no matter to baseball aficionados if long ago the moniker was also applied to another star catcher, Carlton Fisk.

Rodriguez began playing baseball as a youth in Vega Baja under the tutelage of his father Jose and older brother Jose Jr. The boys' baseball bats were sticks and their baseballs were jumbled together round lumps of tape. It was the best they could do to approximate the sport's basic equipment given the family's limited financial means. That status did improve as Rodriguez's mother Eva Torres became a career elementary school teacher and his father worked as an electrician. The finances took a quantum leap when Rodriguez erupted into high school stardom and began attracting professional scouts to his games.

Jose, the father, was a tough taskmaster on the field, regularly pointing out mistakes to Ivan and, showing that he was difficult to please, he continued his picayune criticisms long after his son became a star where the best baseball in the world is played. "He's on top of me all of the time," Rodriguez said 13 years into his Major League career. "My father always tells me the truth. First of all, he hates it when I'm hitting and I swing at the first pitch. And if I'm trying to hit a ball that's out of the strike zone, he gets mad at me." (Quoted in Barnas.)

Rodriguez has enough confidence to cope with the second-guessing, and as a respectful son he lets his dad have his say. After all, no one knows his swing better, so he might be able to pick up a flaw long distance more readily than a team hitting coach watching Ivan in the batting cage up close. "He (Jose Sr.) tells me, 'You're a great hitter,' " Rodriguez said. " 'Let the pitcher work a little bit.' " (Quoted in Barnas.)

Over the years, Rodriguez certainly did make pitchers sweat many a time, but in the beginning, when the Rangers made him a teenaged starting catcher they were mostly focused on what he could do for them as a fielder and with an arm as strong as a bazooka. Rodriguez solidified his place in the game right away as a rookie by throwing out 48.6 percent of attempted base stealers. That elicited "Wow" reactions from baseball people. Even sneakier was the Rodriguez bold rocket throw to first base to pick off base runners. The combination of the two skills virtually froze opposing runners in place near the bag. No statistics were kept to determine how many runners failed to advance from first to third or who failed to score from first because their fear of Rodriguez's arm strength kept them virtually rooted in place as the pitcher went into his windup and made them leave late from first on a hit.

The Rangers did not want to make Rodriguez their big-league catcher when he was still 19. They wanted him to get more seasoning in the minors. But his performance forced management to give him the job. In spring training of 1991, manager Bobby Valentine tried to put the brakes on the runaway optimism that was pushing Rodriguez ever higher, ever faster. "For a 19-year-old his tools are very good," Valentine said. "But he has to develop attributes that a catcher needs to perform at the Major League level. He needs to understand and learn the game a little bit better." (Quoted in Sullivan.)

Valentine was talking about the know-how and seasoning that comes with experience and translates into firmness and sound advice to pitchers. As it so happened, Rodriguez's education took a month or so. There was no denying his talent and value and the rookie ended up catching 88 games that season. The cannon arm distinguished Rodriguez from the start and caused any rough edges to be overlooked. "It's not so much what he can do for your pitcher, but what he does to the opposing manager," said Texas pitching coach Tom House. "A guy with that arm who gets rid of the ball that quickly can intimidate the opposing manager and make him think twice about having runners try to steal." (Quoted in Sullivan.)

Rodriguez's fielding skills got him to the majors more quickly than expected, but his batting talents matured and propelled him into the top echelon of all-around catchers in history. Eight seasons he hit 19 or more home runs. Ten times he hit .300 or more. Rodriguez's finest all-around season with Texas came in 1999. During his Most Valuable Player award season Rodriguez whacked 35 homers, drove in a career high of 113 runs, stole an outrageous (for a catcher) 25 bases, and batted 332. In 2004, the Puerto Rican batted a career best .334 for the Tigers.

When discussions about the best catcher in baseball history focus on names from the past, most voters lean toward Johnny Bench, the icon of the Cincinnati Reds, as the greatest fielder. Also a fine hitter, Bench doesn't quite measure up to Yogi Berra of the Yankees and Roy Campanella of the Dodgers for all-around power. Each was a three-time Most Valuable Player. Bench, however, won 10 Gold Gloves at catcher, the gold standard for receivers until Rodriguez came along. Rodriguez matched Bench's total in 2002. On that occasion Bench spoke out about Rodriguez's capabilities: "At least I'm tied with him for a while," Bench said. "He'll be going past me this year. That's great. I'm proud of him and what he's done for catching. There are only eight or 10 catchers who have really distinguished themselves. They come along once a decade." (Quoted in Fay.)

Rodriguez did zoom past Bench in Gold Gloves won. He is not retired, but he may have peaked as his career winds down. Bench led the National League in RBIs three times, but his lifetime batting average was just .267, far short of Rodriguez's. Bob Boone, another superior receiver, who won seven Gold Gloves, said Bench and Rodriguez share the best-ever honors. "As far as throwing and hitting, Rodriguez is the best of all-time," Boone said. "But he can't touch Bench's power. They're both kind of the standard bearers as far as scouting." (Quoted in Fay.)

It was natural that looking for a role model at his position as a youngster Rodriguez focused on Bench as his choice. Bench was everything Rodriguez wanted to be. Bench retired eight years before Rodriguez reached the big leagues, but a couple of years into Rodriguez's career with Texas the Rangers were playing the Reds during spring training in Florida and Bench was there. Rodriguez introduced himself. "He was always my favorite when I was growing up," Rodriguez said. "He was the one I wanted to be like." (Quoted in Fay.)

Many aspire to such lofty levels, but few can thrust themselves into the discussion of the best ever. Rodriguez remained with the Rangers through the 2002 season, the mortar of the franchise. But when his contract was up before the 2003 season, making him a free agent, he had suffered a couple of injuries and was pushing 32. There were suggestions that the injuries had permanently slowed Rodriguez and that he would never be the same as he was. The team was going nowhere and it just didn't look like such a great investment to give Rodriguez a long-term deal worth many millions of dollars to stick around.

Surprising baseball observers and negotiating for what he was worth, Rodriguez signed a one-year deal with the expansion Florida Marlins for $10 million. He said he would prove his value on the field—and he could take advantage of being a free agent again the next season. The Marlins were coming off a 2002 season with a 79–83 record and the year before that they were 10 games under .500. And before that, after dismantling the 1997 World Series champion, they were even worse. Some believed Rodriguez was taking the money and ignoring the chance to play for a winner.

Instead, a remarkable thing happened. With a gaggle of lower-paid young players waiting to break out, and with savvy manager Jack McKeon at the controls, Rodriguez made the Marlins winners. They won 91 games and the National

League wild-card birth. The Chicago Cubs were on their way to their first Series appearance since 1945 when they imploded, and the Marlins defeated the allegedly cursed Cubbies in seven games. The Cubs express jumped the tracks. "This is where every player wants to be, the World Series," Rodriguez said. "We did it. And nobody was expecting us to be in the playoffs, anyway, and we ended up winning 91 games in the regular season and then beating two great teams in the playoffs, the Giants and the Cubs." (Quoted in Burris.)

Rodriguez was at the vortex of the action all season. He played in 144 games, batted .297, stroked 16 homers, drove in 85 runs, and stole 10 bases while providing leadership to a young team. In the National League Division Series against San Francisco, Rodriguez hit .353. In the National League Championship Series against the Cubs, Rodriguez batted .321 and set an NLCS record with 10 RBIs. "I prepared myself to play a great season and I thank God I did it," he said. "I'm very happy." (Quoted in Burris.)

He got happier still. The surprises kept on coming as the Marlins then toppled the New York Yankees in the Series. It was one of the most surprising triumphs in Major League history. Rodriguez was the key cog, the wise veteran who helped show the young players what winning was all about. It was a slap in the face to all of the teams that ignored him as a free agent, an "I told-you-so-season" of magnificent proportions. "Pudge, he's back to his All-Star status again," said McKeon. "He's playing remarkably well. He's been a take-charge guy, a leader of the ball club." (Quoted in Baxter.)

Rodriguez did not act surprised about the season he turned in. He had felt all along that his fluke injuries were temporary setbacks, not career finishers. He had now showed everyone else that was true, too. "I've heard about the injuries a million times over the last year-and-a-half or two," Rodriguez said. "But when you believe in yourself and you work hard and you prepare yourself in spring training for playing a full, healthy season, everything is possible." (Quoted in Burris.) It was a double mission accomplished for Rodriguez. Not only did he show his skills were intact, but he won a World Series crown for the first time in his life. Both the Marlins and Rodriguez chose wisely in their brief marriage.

Rodriguez, his wife Maribel, and his three children, had always been a tight-knit family. Going into the playoffs in October 2003, Rodriguez made a pledge to his 11-year-old son Dereck. "If we win the World Series," he told the boy, "we're going to walk around the bases, and we're going to get down on our knees and pray." (Quoted in Barnas.)

After the Marlins bested New York in six games, ending the Series in Yankee Stadium, there was bedlam, a celebration for a while. Fans did not linger at Yankee Stadium, however. Their team had lost. They exited to the parking lots and the subway. When it was quiet, Rodriguez led Dereck back out to the scene of the triumph. They slowly walked the bases, stopping at each one to bend down and kiss the bags. At home plate they paused longer, to kiss the platter and to pray, as promised. Rodriquez was so very grateful.

When the hubbub subsided, when Miami was through celebrating its World Series title, and it became clear that the club was going to shed payroll and would not be a serious player to keep Rodriguez for several years and bunches of dollars, he went back to business. He was a much more desirable free agent in the autumn after 2003 than he had been in 2002.

Strangely, the best offer, the most intriguing offer, came not from one of baseball's most established teams. Once again an unlikely bidder surfaced in the mix. The Detroit Tigers, flirting with being the worst team in history in 2003 with a 43–119 record (just one loss shy of the New York Mets' 120 defeats in 1962), wanted Rodriguez. They were on the upswing, team officials told Rodriguez. Young players were blooming. They were prepared to fork over a rich contract and thought that Rodriguez could do for the Tigers what he had done for the Marlins—like Moses lead them to the Promised Land. Rodriguez signed a four-year, $40 million deal.

And darned if the Tigers and Rodriguez didn't nearly manufacture the instant replay. No one expected it, and it took a little bit longer, but the Tigers reached the Series in 2006 with Rodriguez in the lineup. They couldn't culminate the dream, though, losing to the St. Louis Cardinals. The Tigers couldn't sustain their rise, either, and when they began faltering they traded Rodriguez to the Yankees in 2008. At 37 he still had enough left to become a starter for the Astros in 2009.

No matter how it is defined, the end is around the corner for Rodriguez, certainly after another season or two. When he walks away, Ivan Rodriguez will likely be acclaimed as the greatest catcher of all time. Even Johnny Bench thinks the kids of tomorrow will emulate Rodriguez. "There'll be other kids who watch the way he catches," Bench said. "There will be better catchers who come along. That's the way it should be." (Quoted in Fay.)

Torch passed, from Bench to Rodriguez, or perhaps to someone, somewhere in the United States, Puerto Rico, or the Dominican Republic who is just trying out his first catcher's mitt right now.

Further Reading

Barnas, Jo-Ann, "The Power of Pudge: He credits his father for success and his son shares in it," *Detroit Free Press*, April 5, 2004.

Baxter, Kevin, "The Marlins' $10 million bargain," *Miami Herald*, October 30, 2003.

Burris, Joe, "Nice catch for Marlins," *Boston Globe*, October 18, 2003.

"Ex-Tiger Ivan Rodriguez sets record for catching," Associated Press/United Press International, June 18, 2009.

Fay, John, "Reds great Bench 'proud' of Pudge," *Cincinnati Enquirer*, June 11, 2002.
"Ivan Rodriguez breaks records for games caught," Associated Press, June 18, 2009.
Sullivan, T.R., "Catchy Situation," *Fort Worth Star-Telegram*, March 13, 1991.

Sammy Sosa

When he tapped his heart, everyone knew Sammy Sosa loved them. When he did his little hop at the plate, not showing much of a vertical leap in a basketball sense, but merely as an indicator of his enthusiasm, everyone knew the Chicago Cubs' outfielder had just knocked a home run over the Wrigley Field wall. When he blew kisses to the sky, everyone knew Sosa was sending them special delivery to his mother in the Dominican Republic, who was likely watching on TV.

At his best, Sosa smashed home runs with the frequency of all but a handful of players in the history of Major League baseball. In 1998, when he engaged in a knockdown, drag-out race to break Roger Maris's then-61 home-run mark with Mark McGwire, it was Sosa's 100-watt smile and playful demeanor that won over the nation and hauled McGwire along for a good-time ride.

Many said that the home-run battle that culminated with McGwire's then-record 70 homers, and Sosa's 66 (but a Most Valuable Player award for leading the Cubs into the National League playoffs), virtually saved baseball from indifference and cynicism following a prolonged strike.

Although outfielder Sammy Sosa hit most of his home runs with the Chicago Cubs, the Dominican smasher launched his 600th blast with the Texas Rangers in 2007. Sosa is the only player to hit 60 or more homers in a season three times and he ranks sixth on the all-time home-run list. Sosa retired in 2009. (AP Photo/Tony Gutierrez)

The impoverished shoeshine boy from the Dominican Republic was hailed as one of the saviors of the game. He was beloved in his home country, wildly popular in his adopted city, and even casual fans across the United States knew his name and expressed pleasure in watching Sosa come to bat and revel in his moment in the spotlight.

Fans identified with Sosa because he looked like he was having fun every minute of every game. He built a following with fantastic hitting exploits and at a time when home runs ruled the sport he was royalty. Although the entire focus of spectators and baseball insiders now look upon the home-run era of the last decade with suspicion because of the use of steroids and other performance-enhancing drugs (though none were banned at the time because baseball had no drug-testing program), Sosa's massive home-run numbers stand as records for the Cubs and represent some of the highest single-season and career totals in Major League history.

In his 18-year career with the Texas Rangers, Chicago White Sox, Baltimore Orioles, and mostly the Cubs, Sosa collected 609 home runs, 1,667 runs batted in, with a .273 batting average. He is the only player to clout 60 or more home runs three times in a season. He smashed his 66 in 1998, 63 in 1999, and 64 in 2001.

Sosa left the Cubs after the 2005 season, no longer as welcome in the clubhouse as he had been following an incident with a corked bat, leaving the team early in the season's final game, and showing signs of wear in his swing. He sat out 2006, but returned to the game the next year for a last hurrah with the Rangers, his first team. On June 20, 2007, he cracked his 600th career homer—in a game against the Cubs.

"Getting my 600th home run against the Cubs and my first team was the Texas Rangers," he said, "it's like everything clicked. My emotions, I don't know what they are." (Quoted in "Sosa becomes . . .") Likely a bit confused since his finest years were all with the Cubs.

Sammy Sosa was born November 12, 1968, in the community of San Pedro de Macoris. In recent years San Pedro has become the highest per capita supplier of Major League baseball talent. Young people with grand ambitions, shoddy equipment, but a gaggle of role models like Sosa are the town's major export. Sosa, who always maintained an opulent home in the Dominican while he was playing (throwing lavish birthday parties for himself), was a pull-himself-up-by-his-bootstraps success story. He wallowed in poverty as a youth, hustling customers with his shoeshine business (making 35 cents a pair), hustling on the baseball diamond with only the rudiments of proper gloves and bats.

Among some of the early talented players from San Pedro de Macoris who percolated to the surface and broke through in the majors are Rico Carty, Joaquin Andujar, George Bell, and Pedro Guerrero. During Sosa's prime there were approximately 125,000 people living in the city. But it has a small-town feel and most people at least recognize one another. A major leaguer is a hero and none was bigger than Sosa, who came from so little. He was a boy whose father died when he was six years old and was raised by a mother, Lucrecia, or Mireya, whom he idolizes for her sacrifices.

Speaking of the neighborhood ballpark where he got his start in baseball, Sosa said, "There is great poverty in my country and it surrounds this park. I used to shine shoes near here. I used to live near here in a one-bedroom house with dirt floors and no plumbing. Those kinds of dwellings have not disappeared with the passage of time. The people who are always waiting for me at the park in San Pedro live that way today. These are my people." (Quoted in Sosa and Breton, 16.)

Even after he became a Major League star, Sosa returned home for much of the winter and regularly revisited the shabby park that gave him a boost as a youngster, working out there regularly before spring training. He did stay in touch with the people, his old neighbors, and his admirers. He also gave back to them through a charitable foundation he started and in organizing relief efforts when a hurricane ravaged the Dominican.

Many of Sosa's earliest memories revolve around hardship and hard work. Sammy and his brothers Luis and Jose washed cars for small change. His mother sold lottery tickets and cooked for other people. He and his brothers shared shoes and clothing. Although he liked baseball and was given his first glove by a family friend at 13, Sosa said his first sporting ambition was to become a professional boxer. He admired the handiwork and fast fists of Sugar Ray Leonard, Thomas Hearns, and Marvin Hagler, world champions and worldwide figures during Sosa's boyhood. Sosa's mother put the kibosh on that career choice, however.

Instead, Sosa applied himself to baseball. He improved, but gradually, and was not seen as a young prospect. Overlooked in his home area at first, when Major League scouts flooded the Dominican, Sosa gained some attention and, soon enough, a contract. He had not grown into his 6-foot, 190-pound frame yet, and he had some rough edges, but the talent scouts saw potential in Sosa's swing.

Sosa got looks, but no deals from the New York Yankees, New York Mets, Toronto Blue Jays, or Montreal Expos. Omar Minaya, who years later became the general manager of the Mets, is the one who singled out Sosa as a potential pro. The Rangers gave Sosa a $3,500 signing bonus and he made his professional debut in 1986 with the club's Gulf Coast rookie team, batting a respectable .275. "At that stage of his life, Sammy was a very happy person," Minaya said. "There was a lot of positive energy in his smile and his mannerisms. He was a focused kid with an eagerness to understand this new culture that he had been thrown into." (Quoted in Sosa and Breton, 74.)

It took three years for Sosa to reach the majors. It was a brief stay with the Rangers before he was shipped to the White Sox. In 1990, Sosa became a regular with the Sox. He hit 15 home runs and drove in 70 runs in 153 games. By 1992, after showing little improvement, Sosa had been traded to the Cubs. And it was on the North Side of Chicago, not the South Side, where his career blossomed.

By 1993, Sosa was a first-rate hitter and by 1995 he was a superstar. That season he mashed 36 home runs, accumulated 119 RBIs, and even stole 34 bases. Sosa was named to his first All-Star team in 1995 and was selected to six more. Three times he led the National League in games played, three times in runs scored, twice in home runs, and twice in RBIs.

Sosa had his own cheering section in right field at venerable Wrigley Field and made nice with the fans when he came out to field his position. He may have played his salsa music a little bit too loudly to suit some in the clubhouse, but it was pretty much Sosa's clubhouse by the late 1990s. He was on a roll, swatting home runs with the regularity of a short-order cook flipping pancakes.

Between 1995 and 2004, Sosa put up the following annual home-run statistics: 36, 40, 66, 63, 50, 64, 49, 40, and 35. During the 1998 season Sosa hit 19 home runs in the month of June, a single-month record. "I'm not going to lie to you," Sosa said during his June hot streak that was hotter than the weather, "I'm in my zone right now." (Quoted in Muskat, "Sosa picks . . .")

Sosa was constantly working on slowing down his tendency to swing too fast with Cubs' hitting coach Jeff Pentland. Every day they talked for 10 minutes solely about going slowly. The teacher was having almost as much of a blast as the pupil. "He is the most physically talented player I've ever worked with," Pentland said. "And I've worked with (Barry) Bonds and (Gary) Sheffield. All I've tried to do is get him (Sosa) on the right path." (Quoted in Muskat, "Sosa picks . . .")

That summer Sosa cracked one homer that sailed not only out of play, but out of Wrigley, landing across the street on one of the famous rooftop fan-viewing area apartment buildings. The travel distance was estimated to be 460 feet, or in need of a pilot and flight attendant.

Although it sometimes seemed so, not every hit Sosa got was a homer. Between 1995 and 2003 Sosa knocked in at least 103 runs in nine straight seasons. He led the National League with 158 RBIs in 1998 and with 160 in 2001.

Waves of adulation followed and not only on Waveland Avenue outside Wrigley. The National League record for home runs in a season stood at 56 since 1930 when Hack Wilson, another Cub, also set the single-season record of 191 RBIs. Never had the Americas seen such an outburst of slugging as produced by Sosa and the St. Louis Cardinals' McGwire as they unleashed their onslaught on the single-season homer record.

When Babe Ruth was revolutionizing baseball with his singular blasts in the 1920s, the Yankee right-fielder hit 60 home runs in 1927. That remained the all-time record until 1961 when Maris, another Yankee right-fielder, smashed 61.

The McGwire-Sosa duel was reminiscent of the 1961 chase that pitted Maris against his teammate Mickey Mantle, who, stalled by injury at the end of the season, finished with 54.

McGwire was established as a home-run threat almost from the moment he stepped into a batter's box in the majors. As a rookie in 1987 he clouted 49 homers. In 1996, he hit 52. McGwire's 1997 season was split between Oakland and St. Louis, but his combined total was 58. If anyone was going to challenge Maris's record in 1998, it figured to be McGwire.

"Pressure? Pressure was when I was a child and I didn't know where my next meal was coming from. Pressure was shining shoes for a living. This is base-ball. I love baseball!"

—Dominican Sammy Sosa in 1998 when he was trying to break Roger Maris's home-run record. (Quoted in Breton, Marcos, *Home Is Everything: The Latino Baseball Story* (Cinco Puntos Press, El Paso, Texas (2002), 17.)

He did so, but Sosa's homer-for-homer matching of McGwire elicited unexpected drama. McGwire seemed to bristle about all of the attention focused on the feat during the first half of the season, but when it became a two-man race Sosa's bubbly personality was a balm. Sosa was so gracious, so fun-loving, that if McGwire had not begun sharing hugs and smiles with the Chicago slugger (especially when their teams played one another), he would have been perceived as a grumpy old man.

Certainly baseball purists who enjoyed the hit-and-run were not all overjoyed at what baseball had become with its hit-and-duck style, but the turnstiles clicked, and regular-season baseball games involving McGwire and Sosa approached the level of rock-concert excitement. By mid-September 1998, reporters from dozens of media organizations were trailing the men around the country, waiting for them to hit another home run with the eagerness of someone anticipating the announcement of a cure for cancer.

When each player stroked his 62nd homer, and thereby both surpassing Ruth and Maris, the Associated Press summed up the competition as "the greatest home-run derby of all time" stoking "one of baseball's most unforgettable summers." (Quoted in "All Tied . . .")

After a dramatic, 11–10 Sunday afternoon victory over the Milwaukee Brewers when Sosa hit his 61st and 62nd blasts in the fifth and ninth innings, teammates hoisted Sosa on their shoulders and paraded him around Wrigley Field. Fans cheered and chanted, calling out "Sam-mee! Sam-mee!" At one point, they caused a six-minute delay in play as they showered the field with whatever was handy. It was a little bit like celebrating a hat trick in a hockey game, only instead of a chapeau the average fan tossed a paper cup.

"It's unbelievable," Sosa said. "It was something that I can't believe I was doing. It can happen to two people, Mark and I." One of the two homers that day covered 480 feet. The applauding fans demanded three curtain-call acknowledgments from Sosa, and he broke down in tears. "I don't usually cry," he said, "but I cry inside. I was blowing kisses to my mother. I was crying a little bit. I have to say what I did was for the people of Chicago, for America, for my mother, for my wife, for my kids, and the people I have around me. My team. It was an emotional moment." (Quoted in "All Tied . . .")

When Sosa hit his 63rd homer of the year in San Diego, it was caught by a fan from Tijuana, Mexico, who returned it to the slugger. Fabian Perez Mercado gave the ball back to Sammy, but not before he kissed it and asked his wife and two children to bless the ball the same way. "Viva Dominican Republic!" said Mercado as he watched his two-year-old son hand Sosa the ball. "Viva Mexico! Viva baseball!" Sosa was stunned by the warmth of his reception. "It is amazing he comes to me with all his family and he gives me the ball and also makes everybody kiss the ball first," Sosa said. (Quoted in "Happy fan . . .") The Mercado family did not go home empty-handed. In exchange, the fans were given five baseball caps, a bat, two gloves, and two jerseys, all autographed by Sosa, and seven tickets to each of the Padres' first-round home playoff games.

In the end, McGwire passed Maris first. He paid his respects to the late Maris' family members seated in the stands, and scooped up his own son, acting as the Cardinals' batboy, with a hug. He finished the season with 70 home runs, a new record. Sosa finished with 66. Sosa led the Cubs into the NL playoffs. The Cardinals fell short. That helped Sosa claim the MVP award over McGwire.

Late in the baseball season, the Dominican Republic was attacked by a powerful hurricane named Georges, which produced devastating damage. Soon after the playoffs, Sosa returned home to San Pedro de Macoris and was greeted by thousands of people who awaited his five-hour-late arrival while standing in the mud as a light rain fell. Humbled and overwhelmed by the monster crowd, Sosa broke down in tears. "I'm crying for happiness," he said. "I'm a person touched by God. I feel happy and honored that my people are on their feet, waiting for me. I am happy and proud to be Dominican." (Quoted in Muskat, "Sosa's homecoming . . .")

Before his season had even ended, Sosa had created a foundation to funnel money into his hurricane-ravaged homeland. The act only added to the nation's embrace of him. President Leonel Fernandez declared a national holiday when Sosa came back to the Dominican. No stranger to major leaguers in their midst, the outpouring of love for Sosa exceeded that lavished on any other pro athlete there. Even Alfredo Griffin, a one-time Major League shortstop, believed that. "He brings happiness to the country," Griffin said of Sosa. "This makes people forget about their problems and enjoy life." (Quoted in Muskat, "Sosa's homecoming . . .")

Sosa's concern over the plight of Dominicans left homeless by the hurricane manifested itself in several ways. In November of that year Sosa visited Japan as part of an eight-game baseball tour where he was greeted as a conquering hero. But he extended his stay to negotiate a deal with the Japanese government for prefabricated homes to be sent to the Dominican Republic. "A lot of people don't have houses," Sosa said. (Quoted in Hill.)

The year was an astonishing tour de force for Sosa, professionally, individually, and as a coming out party to the United States. He was at the top of his game, and he was appreciated and even loved by his fans.

Although there was no Act II chase per se, Sosa's 1999 on-field performance was nearly equally phenomenal with 63 home runs, 141 RBIs, and a .308 average. He remained an All-Star-caliber player for several more years. He was collecting roughly $13 million a year as a pitchman for products in addition to his $10 million salary, but as baseball's slowly evolving war on drugs took shape and Congress became involved in inquiries, some of Sosa's reputation was tarnished.

McGwire's image was severely damaged by his refusal to speak candidly before Congress; he became a virtual recluse, and five years into retirement received little support for his Hall of Fame candidacy, something previously considered foregone. Only in 2010 did he re-emerge, becoming a hitting coach for the Cardinals. During the same federal hearing Sosa replied that Spanish was his first language and his English was not always good enough for him to understand questions. It was not his finest hour.

By 2008, although he indicated he still wanted to play, Sosa could not find an active roster job and in 2009 he retired. After that announcement, it was revealed by unnamed sources in a media report that Sosa had tested positive for a performance-enhancing drug in 2003. That test, administered as a warning by Major League Baseball before it adopted a new drug-restrictive policy, was supposed to remain confidential as the sport gauged its level of drug problems, and the tests were supposed to be destroyed.

Instead, the news might have diminished Sammy Sosa's reputation sufficiently to cause one of the greatest hitters of his generation and an icon to Dominicans to be left out of the Hall of Fame. It is too soon to tell how Sosa's candidacy will be received when he first becomes eligible on selectors' ballots in 2012, but if his 609 homers and his devotion to his fellow countrymen are overlooked it will be a sad denouement to a glittering career.

Further Reading

"All Tied at 62," Associated Press, September 14, 1998.
"Happy fan returns No. 63 to grateful Sosa," *USA Today*, September 18, 1998.
Hill, Thomas, "Going to bat for homeless," *New York Daily News*, November 13, 1998.
Muskat, Carrie, "Sosa picks up power pace by slowing swing tempo," *USA Today*, June 23, 1998.

———, "Sosa's homecoming: Tears, cheers for city's 'great gift,' " *USA Today*, October 21, 1998.

"Sosa becomes fifth player to blast 600 home runs," Associated Press, June 20, 2007.

Sosa, Sammy and Breton, Marcos, *Sosa: An Autobiography* (New York, Warner Books, 2000).

Luis Tiant

Pitching coaches covered the eyes of young hurlers when Luis Tiant took the mound. Not because it was painful to watch him fool batters, strike out hitters, and win games, but because they didn't want any protégés popping up mimicking the Cuban thrower's style.

It is safe to say that there has never been anyone else quite like Tiant when it came to delivering the ball to the plate. Unlike the majority of pitchers (some of whom did possess a textbook style for teaching), Tiant did not stare in at the plate, rear back, and fire. His motion was much more complicated. When he went into his delivery he actually turned his back to the plate, tilted his head back, looked up at the sky, then spun around, and heaved. Some thought it was amazing that he didn't trip on the rubber and fall to the front of the mound every time he pitched, but Tiant got the job done. And he got the job done better than most.

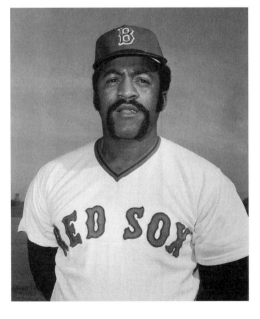

A star pitcher with the Cleveland Indians and Boston Red Sox, the Cuban-born Luis Tiant followed in the footsteps of his talented hurling father. Luis Sr. was prohibited from trying out for the majors, however, because of his dark skin color. The younger Tiant was a master of control who relied on many different types of deliveries to fool batters during a 19-season career. (AP Photo)

The only child of a famous Cuban pitcher with the same name, Tiant was allegedly born in Marianao in 1940 (though there were always rumors about his true age). His mother was named Isabel and his father Luis pitched from 1926 to 1948, not only on the island, but for the Negro Leagues' New York Cubans. Raised in the tradition of serious Cuban baseball, the younger Tiant was stamped as a star at an early age. By 1957, Tiant, the son, was making good wages playing in the Mexican League and for the Havana Sugar Kings in the AAA International League.

Tiant, though, was one of the Cubans who came of age at an inconvenient time to test the majors. Cuban baseball is nearly as old as the game in the United States and top players in the island nation flocked to the States when the gates opened with integration of the majors. Such a flood of great players likely would have continued and indefinitely helped to fuel the Latino revolution in the majors that has been populated by Dominicans, Puerto Ricans, and Venezuelans. However, the takeover of the government by Fidel Castro doomed the long-term relationship between Cuba and the United States and the relationship between up-and-coming Cuban baseball players and the majors. Distrustful of Castro's proclamations that he was implementing a Communist society, the International League moved the Havana franchise to New Jersey. After 1961, Castro slammed the door, refusing to allow his citizens free access to professional baseball in the States. He ordered the cessation of play-for-pay in Cuba and steered the country's passion for the game into amateur international competition instead.

Tiant and many other young Cubans with baseball talent were caught in the middle. They could either abandon their dreams of playing Major League baseball or abandon their homeland and their families. Tiant was one of those torn by being forced to make such a difficult decision. He opted to continue his career in the Cleveland Indians organization and, as a result, went years without seeing his parents.

No one foresaw that United States and Cuban relations would remain so chilly for so long. A half century later there has yet to be normalization of diplomatic relations between the Western Hemisphere neighbors and the only way for top-flight Cuban baseball talent to make a living in the pros is to defect, usually while an international tournament is taking place in a neutral country. Some 50 years after Castro decreed that the borders were closed to professional baseball players—going in either direction—younger generations of stars face the same type of dilemma Tiant faced before he broke in with Cleveland in 1964.

Tiant met his wife while pitching in Mexico and planned to bring her to Cuba to meet his parents in the summer of 1961. He spoke on the phone to his dad and told him his plans. Tiant Sr., reading the political winds in Cuban, and recognizing his son might never get back to the United States to play ball, shocked the young man by telling him not to come home. "Luis," he said, "stay in Mexico. Don't come home. There's nothing for you here now. Stay where you are and make a good life for your family." (Quoted in Fitzgerald.) It was a nudge that hurt, but Tiant listened and stayed away. He became an exile.

Tiant was a very sad exile, to be sure, but he was someone who tried to make a new life in a new country. As he pursued his career, Tiant had to contend with the pain of missing his parents. In the mid-1970s, when he was an established player, Tiant could still break down crying in anguish because his parents were prisoners on his home island and he was outside the bars looking in.

"How much longer?" he said. "It's been 15 years since I've seen them. All my life I gave them the best I could and all they wanted was what was good for me. My father's 70 now and he's not well. Yet he still works in a garage down there and here I am living like this (in comparative luxury) and I can't even send him a dime for a cup of coffee. He doesn't know my wife. He doesn't know my children." (Quoted in Fitzgerald.)

This was the great regret of Tiant's life. He had found success, he had accomplished many things that could make his parents proud, yet he could not share things with them. He lived with the hope that one day things would change and the family would be reunited. In the meantime, he tore up the American League.

Tiant was a mature pitcher on arrival in the majors. His rookie year he went 10–4 for the Indians with a 2.83 earned run average. That won him a permanent spot in the Cleveland rotation. For the next three seasons Tiant was a staple as a starter, but his success rate was stuck at about 50 percent. In 1968, when he was chosen for the first of three All-Star games, Tiant was dazzling. His record was 21–9, but his ERA was a microscopic 1.60. It was an astonishing mark, one so good that batters had almost no chance of hitting safely against him. The performance elevated Tiant to a new elite status.

In mid-season, before 21,135 paid witnesses in Cleveland's Municipal Stadium, Tiant turned in a one-game effort that typified his magical season. It was July 3 and it happened to be a day his teammates weren't hitting very well against the visiting Minnesota Twins. Tiant shrugged off the lack of run support and just kept throwing, confusing batters with his off-speed specialties, making their eyes blur with his fastball. Inning after inning sped by and it became apparent that Twins hitters were only going to put wood on the ball by accident.

In the fifth inning, Tiant struck out the side. In the eighth inning he did likewise. The game passed beyond the regulation nine innings into the 10th. Tiant struck out the side in the 10th, as well. Finally, the Indians pushed across a run and Tiant was the winning pitcher in a 1–0 game. Catcher Joe Azcue, also a Cuban, was someone Tiant could thank in Spanish when his battery mate drove in the game-winner. Tiant struck out 19 men, at the time the most ever in an extra-inning game. Tiant scattered six hits and, at that point in the season, with a 13–5 record, his ERA was a ridiculously low 1.11. "That was my best game ever," Tiant said. (Quoted in Schneider, "My Finest . . .")

By at least one measurement, it was everybody's best game ever. The old record for strikeouts in extra innings was 17, held by Dazzy Vance and Rube Waddell, a couple of guys whose prime seasons pretty much pre-dated even Tiant's father's.

Azcue was not only Tiant's catcher with Cleveland, he was an admirer. Tiant possessed one of the most diverse repertoires of any pitcher. He could throw the ball fast or slow and fool batters. His off-beat delivery disguised his release point and he could vary his motion to further create chaos. At his best, like that July day in 1968, Tiant's arsenal was too much for even the best hitters. In some ways, Tiant was all smoke and mirrors, brilliant at deception even when his best stuff wasn't clicking.

"Tiant had a backup curveball," Azcue said. "It never broke. His change-up was so-so. But he had pinpoint control and could bring it at about 95 miles an hour. And he had a hell of a move to first base. He liked to talk to the hitters. He'd say, 'Hit it baby.' " (Quoted in *Baseball Almanac*.) Most of the time they couldn't.

Pitchers must have confidence, but every once in a while a dose of reality gets mixed into their thought process. Even the best of throwers wake up on the wrong side of the bed and come to the mound out of sorts sometimes. No one is going to finish 20–0 with a 0.00 ERA. Tiant understood this and had an endearing way of explaining in his Spanish-accented English how the pitcher-batter confrontation unfolded. "If I am luckee, I kille them," he said. "If I no am luckee, they kille me." (Quoted in Schneider, The Sporting . . .) And there you have it. That is as blunt as any pitcher can get.

Tiant was not always a master of mysterious deliveries. His style was fairly straightforward until the 1968 season. He began experimenting with more and more moves designed specifically to flummox batters. The goal was to disrupt their concentration. The piece de resistance was jerking his head to the side just as he threw. "It is something I started to do this year," he said. "I know it bothers me when I am batting. The first time I do it was against California. I forget who is batting, but I know it bother him. The motion depends on how I feel. Sometimes I do nothing but throw the ball. You can't use the motions too much or they will get used to it." (Quoted in Schneider, The Sporting . . .)

The remarkable thing given Tiant's phenomenal earned run average is that he lost at all. But the Indians were not hitting and it cost him. In 1968, Denny McLain of the Tigers won 31 games, the first time any pitcher broke the 30 mark in more than 30 years and the last time it has happened. He felt Tiant should have been right there with him challenging for the American League lead in wins. "Luis and I would each be fighting for 30 wins if we had our kind of hitting to go with his kind of pitching," McLain said. (Quoted in *Baseball Almanac*.)

It was a dream season for Tiant, but after his sudden ascension, things went haywire. The tricky pitcher of 1968 couldn't get the ball over the plate in 1969. His luck ran out with Cleveland when injuries contributed to him finishing 9–20. Impatient, or believing that Tiant's one year was a fluke, the Indians gave up on him and traded him to the Twins. Tiant went 7–3 in 1970 in Minnesota, but that was a cameo. A fractured scapula led to his release in 1971 and there were suggestions that Tiant's career was over.

Instead, it was resurrected in Boston after a grim 1–7 1971 season. In less than a year, Tiant was the toast of the town. Red Sox fans fell in love with him and his quirky motions, pitches, and facial hair, the mustache and hair trim surrounding his upper lip and sides of his mouth and they chanted "Loo-ee! Loo-ee!" every time he pitched. Tiant went 15–6 in 1972 with a stunning 1.91 ERA, and 20–13 in 1973. In 1974, he went 22–13 and was an All-Star again.

Tiant was also going bald and gaining weight but no one seemed to care. It just added to his charm because he looked more and more like Joe Everyman. Another of Tiant's many distinctive trademarks was smoking a big cigar after he won a game. He brandished a stogie with the same aplomb as Groucho Marx and was even photographed in the locker room, his chest bare, or soaped up in the shower, puffing on the cigar. For a guy who had the reputation of keeping teammates loose in the clubhouse it was just another identifiable trait that appealed to his fans.

Seemingly washed up abruptly in the early 1970s, within two seasons of his departure from Cleveland, Tiant was again one of the most dominant forces in the American League; the anchor of the Red Sox rotation, he took the ball every fourth day and never wanted to relinquish it to a reliever. Few kept close track of pitch counts in that era, but Tiant's numbers regularly ballooned as high as 140 or more in a game. He didn't care. He just wanted to keep throwing till the game was over.

"Nobody can tell me anything about this game," said Tiant in 1974, sounding like a grizzled veteran. "I've seen it all. I've seen the good times and the bad. I've been up and down and everything I've learned comes to this: Win. When you win everything is OK. When you win, you make money. But you can't play baseball just for money. The money is important if you want to live right, but you've got to love what you're doing, too." (Quoted in Horgan.)

Tiant won and won big for the Red Sox, a team that had seemingly had a shortage of reliable starting pitching for decades. "If a man put a gun to my head and said I'm going to pull the trigger if you lose this game, I'd want Luis Tiant to pitch that game," said Red Sox manager Darrell Johnson, who didn't have to face such drastic choices, but selected Tiant for big gigs anyway. (Quoted in *Baseball Almanac*.)

By 1975, Tiant was a hero in Boston, beloved for his victories, but also his personality and, yes, that inimitable style. Only occasionally did Tiant speak of the heartache of being a Cuban exile and the hardship of not seeing his parents. After quiet, behind-the-scenes maneuvering spearheaded by U.S. Senator Edward Brooke of Massachusetts, in the summer of that season Tiant's parents were granted what was supposed to be a three-month visa to visit the United States. On a hot August night at Fenway Park, Luis Tiant Sr., a man denied a chance to play Major League baseball because of his dark skin, walked to the mound alongside his son to throw out a ceremonial first pitch in front of 32,086 fans granting him a standing ovation.

A couple of days before that heart-warming moment, the Tiants had an emotional reunion at Boston's Logan Airport, though not one in privacy. Mobs of reporters and supporters greeted Luis Sr. and Isabel's plane. The two men, who had not seen one another for a decade-and-a-half, embraced. "Don't cry," said Luis Sr. "The cameras will see you." Luis Jr. didn't mind and said so. He let his emotions run free. On the mound, Luis held his father's coat as the older man went into his windup. The ball sailed toward home plate. "Tell 'em I'm ready to go five," the one-time star pitcher whispered. (Quoted in Fitzgerald.)

In 1975, when Tiant finished 18–14, the Red Sox made it to the World Series for the first time in eight years. However, they were chasing their first world championship since 1918. The opponent was Cincinnati's Big Red Machine, regarded as one of the top teams of all time. In the first game of the Series, at Fenway Park, Tiant threw a six-hit shutout as the Sox won, 6–0. Tiant's parents got to see him soak up the glory. Although the Red Sox did not break their Series jinx, Tiant won the fourth game, too. After the game he dipped his right arm and elbow in a bucket of ice and fired up his traditional cigar.

Tiant's parents never returned to Cuba. They remained in the United States. Only 15 months later, Luis Tiant Sr., who had been ailing, passed away. Stunningly, Isabel Tiant died suddenly in her sleep three days later. They were both 71 years old and were buried side by side in Massachusetts as their only son grieved. Tiant felt fortunate that after being deprived for so long of their mutual affection, the trio was able to spend so much time together during the final year-plus of his parents' lives.

The pitcher had one more great season for the Red Sox in 1976, going 21–12 and making the All-Star team again. In 1977 Tiant finished 12–8 and in 1978 he was 13–8. In a shocking move, the New York Yankees, Boston's main rival, swooped down and signed the free agent Tiant in 1979. He put up a 13–8 record again and he was greatly missed by Red Sox players and fans. "Luis was the heart, the heart of our pitching staff," said Boston Hall of Famer Carl Yastrzemski. "They have torn away our heart." (Quoted in Whiteside.)

Yet after his first positive season in New York, the aging Tiant, who turned 42 just after his final 1982 Major League season, lost his stuff. After 19 seasons, Tiant retired with a 229–172 mark. He still dreamed of a comeback as late as 1985, but soon was occupied by off-the-field baseball connections.

Over the ensuing years, Tiant scouted for the Yankees, worked as a minor league pitching coach for the Red Sox, Chicago White Sox, the Los Angeles Dodgers, and took over the baseball program at NCAA Division III Savannah College of Art & Design.

After residing in Mexico for a while, Tiant returned to Massachusetts. Tiant was inducted into the Boston Red Sox Hall of Fame—another honor from the team that most appreciated him—and the Hispanic Heritage Baseball Museum Hall of Fame. In 2009, a documentary about Tiant, his family, and his roots in Cuba, was released called, *The Lost Son of Havana*.

In the half century under Castro's rule, Luis Tiant was one of many such Cuban sons.

Further Reading

Baseball Almanac, www.baseball-almanac.com, Luis Tiant Quotes.
Fitzgerald, Joe, "Luis Tiant can tell you the real story of Cuba," *Boston Herald*, November 6, 1983.
Horgan, Tim, "Luis Tiant—All Man," *Boston Herald-American*, June 12, 1974.
Schneider, Russ, " 'My Finest Game' Says Tiant After 19-Whiff Effort," *The Sporting News*, July 20, 1968.
———, "Lucky Luis? Modest Hurler Tiant Thinks So," *The Sporting News*, August 3, 1968.
Whiteside, Larry, "Loss of Tiant 'Tears Out Heart' of Red Sox," *The Sporting News*, November 2, 1978.

Fernando Valenzuela

Fernandomania!

That was the phenomenon during the summer of 1981 that swept through the United States like a goofy, uplifting epidemic. Fernando Valenzuela was the new hula hoop, the new craze. A left-handed pitcher from Mexico who turned his eyes to the sky when he threw a humdinger of a fastball that baffled hitters and who charmed listeners when he shyly tried to explain how he was able to get everyone out for his Los Angeles Dodgers.

Fernando Valenzuela, an unheralded southpaw from Mexico, burst onto the baseball scene for the Los Angeles Dodgers in the spring of 1981. Named Rookie of the Year and Most Valuable Player, Valenzuela became a hero in his home country. He was also responsible for a phenomenon called "Fernandomania" throughout the United States because of his brilliant pitching. (Focus on Sport/Getty Images)

Valenzuela burst on the Major League scene unexpectedly, with little heralding or fanfare, yet seemingly fully formed as an unhittable ace who belied his youth (just 20!) after making a quiet, 2–0 debut as a late-season call-up in 1980. He was unorthodox but dominating. He was fresh box office for a team located where the largest segment of Mexican-Americans lived and was close enough to Mexico itself to serve as a conduit to the masses in that Central American nation.

Easy-going, soft-spoken in Spanish (he needed a translator for his post-game chats), Valenzuela was lionized virtually overnight when he made a fast start on the mound in the spring of 1981 by winning his first eight decisions in masterful style. He was almost too good to be believed, statistically, and seemed like a character from nearby Hollywood's central casting.

The 5-foot-11, 195-pound Valenzuela, who was a little roly-poly around the middle, giving him even more of a common man connection, was born in Navoja, Mexico in 1960. He grew up in a large family where the luxuries of life were more likely to be pictured in magazines than in the home. Valenzuela was one of seven sons and 12 children raised by his father Avelino and mother Hermenegilda in the village of Etchohuaquila. Populated with a couple of dozen adobe huts, the community is 20 miles from Obregon, a city located 350 miles south of the U.S. border that at the time had 65,000 people.

Valenzuela's father was making $92 a month working as a farmer on government land. Garbanzo beans and sunflower seeds were the crops harvested. Avelino was helped by his sons, most of whom continued to play baseball on a local club team. Only Fernando, the youngest, showed the type of talent that carried him north to the big-time with the Dodgers. The apparent secret of Valenzuela's success, beyond his work ethic and aptitude, was an urgent fastball and a confusing screwball. The screwball is rarely mastered, an exception being its most famous proponent, Hall of Famer Carl Hubbell, but Valenzuela made the pitch thrown with the opposite wrist turn of a curveball work for him.

Part of the story that reporters seized on was the unlikely rise of Valenzuela from poverty and living in a dusty village with few conveniences. The young pitcher did not paint grim pictures, but he was blunt in assessing the family lifestyle. "We were poor, but we always had food on the table and clothes on our backs," he said. (Quoted in Yates.)

Nobody saw the degree of Valenzuela's brilliance coming down the pike, not even after his 2–0 start as a 19-year-old. But when four of his first five victories were shutouts and he was cruising along with an unfathomable 0.20 earned run average, Valenzuela became more popular than ice cold beer on a 90-degree day. At a point of inexperience in his career when Valenzuela figured to be nervous like other rookies, he was striking out National League hitters at the rate of one per inning and few could get the bat on the ball to hit safely. Oh yes, and often Valenzuela knocked out several hits at the plate. Was there nothing this upstart couldn't do?

Within a month of his holding down full-time employment in the majors, Valenzuela collected nicknames like some young fans collected baseball cards. Among them were: Senor Cero, Mr. Zero; El Neveria, The Icebox; and El Gordo de Oro, The Golden Fat Man. The latter implied that Valenzuela might be even better if he lost some weight.

On days when Valenzuela's turn rolled around in the pitching rotation, fans flocked to ballparks to see him throw. This was true on the road, as well as at Chavez Ravine where Valenzuela's emergence stoked Mexican-American pride and made the team even more popular in that Latino community. During one shutout performance after Valenzuela walked back to the dugout, the home fans rose and gave him a sustained standing ovation. He was bewildered and had to be pushed into view to tip his cap to the crowd. "This never happens in Mexico," Valenzuela said. "I didn't know what to do." (Quoted in Yates.)

This adulation poured forth overnight, instantly elevating Valenzuela's profile from that of an everyday rookie to one of the most famous people in the United

States. That was because he was no everyday rookie, putting up pitching records during his first weeks in the majors that had never been matched by any other big-league beginner. Fans took to wearing sombreros and Mexican blankets as signs of solidarity with the pitcher.

If Valenzuela had toiled only in the little sandlot park without walls or comfortable seating near his home he might never have made it to California. Ironically, the Spartan facility is called "Dodger Stadium South" in Etchohuaquila. But by 17, Valenzuela was pitching in the professional Mexican League. Dodgers' scout Mike Brito, the club's legendary bird-dog talent sniffer in Latin America, found his man.

> *"Going through `Fernandomania' was an experience. It wasn't just in Los Angeles. Every city we went into they wanted to see Fernando pitch."*
>
> —Former Dodgers manager Tommy Lasorda on the excitement when Mexican Fernando Valenzuela was a rookie. (Quoted in *Beisbol—The Latin Game*, movie, lead producer Alfonso Pozzo, 2007.)

"We barely got him," Brito said. "The Yankees, Pirates, Cubs and Mariners were all after him, but because I saw him first, we got him." (Quoted in Yates.) They got him for a $120,000 payment to his Mexican League club, an organization that surely was the first to identify Valenzuela's value on the mound.

Brito saw raw ability. A year later, at Class A Lodi, pitching guru Bobby Castillo taught Valenzuela the screwball. It was so screwy that it worked and swiftly catapulted the southpaw to the majors and into the international spotlight. Valenzuela did not so much work his way through the minors as leap-frog over various classifications and look so good doing it that coming out of spring training the Dodgers felt they had to keep him despite his youthfulness. No one was more stunned by public reaction to his feats, however, than Valenzuela himself. "I'm overwhelmed by the attention I am getting," he said. "And I'm getting a little mentally tired of it all, you know. I feel kind of dizzy." (Quoted in Yates.)

Who could blame him? It was a great ride and if no one else seemed to understand it, Valenzuela recognized that he was not going to go undefeated. "There will be games when I don't last one inning," he said. "I'm ready for that because a person can never win all the time." (Quoted in Shah and Contreras.)

As it so happened, like the astronauts who flew to the moon, Valenzuela did eventually come back to earth. Just like every other player who ever reached the majors, he was not perfect. But he kept up his good work in a strike-shortened season and finished with a 13–7 record accompanied by a 2.48 earned run average. He led the National League with 192 1/3 innings and 180 strikeouts.

Valenzuela began the season 8–0, making him the talk of the sport. It took until mid-May for him to lose a game, 4–0 to the Phillies, while surrendering just three hits, and he handled it maturely. "I knew sooner or later I would lose a game," he said. "I'm not sad." (Quoted in "Time for . . .")

Not only was Valenzuela selected as the NL rookie of the year, he won the Cy Young Award emblematic of the best pitcher in his league. The innocence of Valenzuela was on display again when he said he didn't know who Cy Young was—the winningest pitcher in baseball history. "Seeing this is my first year in the major leagues, I don't know much about him," Valenzuela said. "But he must be something special for baseball." (Quoted in "Fernando Edges . . .")

It was no shock that Valenzuela had claimed the prestigious award. The topic had been raised with him by sports reporters during the season. Not only didn't he know about the pitcher who won 511 games, he didn't know about the award. When someone asked Valenzuela if he thought he had a chance to win it as a rookie, he said, "What is that?" A sportswriter standing in the background yelled back, "Never mind trying to explain. In 30 years, they'll be calling it the Fernando Valenzuela Award." (Quoted in Spander.)

Although that did not occur, it did seem that the young man had the world at his feet. In his second season, Fernando won 19 games, and he won a career high of 21 in 1986. By 1983, the Mexican native who had never dreamed of such riches as a youth in his remote village was making $1 million a year, up from the $45,000 rookie wages of 1981. During a 17-season career, Valenzuela won 173 games and lost 153. Injuries held him back from matching his debut season, but he was a six-time All-Star.

One thing that became apparent during Valenzuela's electric start was that he was a role model for all Latinos, not just Mexicans. Fans in countries of Central and South America that appreciated baseball fell in love with Fernando even faster than U.S. fans. By 1981, Major League games were routinely broadcast in Spanish in several overseas markets, and the influential radio commentators helped build Valenzuela's reputation across the Americas, as well as authors of the written word. His screwball was the foremost element in his popularity, but the picture painted of a round-cheeked, dark-haired somewhat chubby thrower with youthful looks, a shy demeanor, a polite countenance, and a habit of looking to the heavens on his tosses contributed to an image popular everywhere the sport was followed.

"Most of the Latin American baseball countries are following him wherever the Dodgers go," said Pablo Nunez of Agence France Presse. "Venezuela, Peru, Ecuador, Colombia, all the Central American countries are extremely interested in Valenzuela and his pitching performances," said Luis Uncal of Voice of America. "Our Latin American points are taking everything we can provide on Valenzuela," said Luis Suarez of the Associated Press. (Quoted in Los Angeles Dodgers . . .)

Depending on the source, Valenzuela kept piling up nicknames. The Dodgers sometimes referred to him as El Toro in press releases. That stemmed from a contest the team conducted. El Toro—The Bull. Others termed the attention engulfing

Valenzuela "Fernando Fever." The frenzy of appreciation was real, though. The Dodgers tried to capitalize immediately by ordering 35,000 bumper stickers, 15,000 pennants, and 10,000 dolls, all featuring Valenzuela. When a newspaper sought comment on this, the reporter could not get a straight answer from the non-English-speaking Valenzuela. The small item noted that Valenzuela could only say, "food, beer, and lite beer" in English. "He just smiles a lot," the story said. (Quoted in "Go go . . .")

After the first blush of mania, Valenzuela settled down into becoming merely a reliable, solid pitcher with brushes of greatness on a given day for the Dodgers. In the 1986 All-Star game, Valenzuela struck out five American League players in a row, including Cal Ripken Jr. and Don Mattingly. One of the other strikeout casualties was Ted Higuera, another Mexican pitcher who that same season also won 20 games. Ironically, Valenzuela's performance tied a record set by Carl Hubbell, the Hall of Fame screwball artist in the 1934 All-Star game. Hubbell's victims were all Hall of Famers, including Babe Ruth and Lou Gehrig.

"I feel nervous before the game, kind of excited," Valenzuela said. "But once I get out there on the mound, then I am very comfortable. That is where I like to be. I don't worry about the crowd or the situation. I like to pitch." (Quoted in Blinebury.)

Valenzuela remained with LA through the 1990 season—a year during which he tossed a no-hitter at the St. Louis Cardinals—and then with his stuff faltering, the Dodgers released him, costing him $2 million. It was an ignominious and shocking fall. The phone did not ring any time soon, either. Valenzuela had to wait months until the California Angels picked him up. In-between he worked out to stay in shape at the same kind of small, out-of-the-way sandlot where he first played the game in back in Mexico. He was emotionally hurt being sent into exile by LA, but refused to give up. It was a poignant time.

"You find out who cares about you," Valenzuela said. "It is good to find this out. The more I think about what happened to me, the more I do not understand it. The Dodgers could use me. Anybody could use me." (Quoted in Plaschke.) He insisted his arm was OK.

It took some time before Valenzuela showed flashes of his earlier self. He won eight games for the Baltimore Orioles in 1993 with 10 losses, but he got better as he regained his equilibrium with five wins in a row. He was only 32. At one point Valenzuela had given up just two earned runs in 32 2/3 innings. A *Washington Post* columnist suggested that if he won one more game "Fernandomania" might again sweep the land. "O's fans will carry him around the Inner Harbor in a chair," the story said. (Quoted in Kornheiser.)

Valenzuela missed the game after he saw little action in 1991 and nearly went back to playing in the Mexican League again in 1992. He never took his eyes off the prize, however. He always hungered to play in the majors again and was glad he got the chance with Baltimore. "Baseball is in my heart," he said. "It's always fun for me, whenever I pitch, wherever I pitch." (Quoted in Kornheiser.)

The warm welcome in Baltimore did not last long. In 1994 Valenzuela drifted to Philadelphia for a lost season. In 1995, whatever seemed to be bothering his arm, or interrupting his clear view of the sky, evaporated and Valenzuela went 8–3 for the San Diego Padres. In 1996, continuing to reverse his skid, he compiled a 13–8 record in San Diego. Valenzuela last pitched in the majors for the Padres and Cardinals in 1997, his final season record a combined 2–12.

The end was subdued for a man who emblazoned his name and pitching mannerisms across the United States in such dramatic fashion. Major League baseball lost sight of Valenzuela for a while, but he never lost sight of baseball. He went home to Mexico and kept on pitching. Just a few months after he wrapped up his brief stay with the Cardinals, Valenzuela resumed throwing in the same winter league where he made his debut as a 16-year-old, where he had been discovered by Mike Brito so long before.

"I needed to keep playing," he said. "I am Mexican. I wanted to put on a good show in front of my people." (Quoted in Llosa.)

It wasn't a one-shot deal, though. Valenzuela kept on pitching in Mexican winter league games. When one contract ran out he signed another. The general feeling was that the caliber of hitters Valenzuela faced was equal to the AAA minors in the United States. Rosters also included players with Major League experience trying to work their way back to the top. So good results meant Valenzuela was still throwing pretty well for a guy encroaching on his mid-40s. Indeed, in 2005, at age 45, Valenzuela went 4–2 in limited action. As he had said to a reporter years earlier, he always had fun wherever he pitched. In 2006, Valenzuela's oldest son, 24-year-old Fernando Valenzuela Jr. joined him on the Mexicali Aguilas. The older Valenzuela's fastball had certainly lost some zip, but because his specialty had always been control and hitting the corners of the plate that impacted his game only in a limited way. He could still fool hitters. Unlike some of those other players with high hopes, Valenzuela was playing to please himself and to please some of his old fans who remembered the good old days with the Dodgers in Los Angeles.

"It's the opportunity for me to give something to the people," Valenzuela said. "Whatever I have left to give them, in return for all of the support the people have given me. At this point in my career, in the new Millennium, to hear people cheering in the stands about baseball and about what you've achieved, it keeps you going." (Quoted in Smith.)

Brito, Valenzuela's old friend and mentor, the man who first saw the potential in the young southpaw, was still scouting in Mexico. Although Valenzuela was not the first Mexican star in the United States, Brito believes he had the most impact for future generations. "Fernando is a warrior. He never gives up," Brito said.

"And the people love him. Before him, the Mexican players didn't have any ambitions. After they saw the success of Fernando Valenzuela, then all of Mexico wanted to play in the big leagues. He opened the door." (Quoted in Smith.)

The door that long before seemed shut to Valenzuela with the Dodgers following his release also swung open again in 2003. The team made amends and, in mid-season, Fernando Valenzuela, the comet once shooting across the Pacific Coast sky, was back in the fold. Not to pitch this time but merely to talk. Valenzuela joined the club's Spanish-language broadcast crew. This time he would tell about the exploits of others.

Further Reading

Blinebury, Fran, "Fernando joins great Hubbell on strikeout list," *Houston Chronicle*, July 16, 1986.

"Fernando Edges Seaver in N.L Cy Young vote," *San Francisco Chronicle*, November 12, 1981.

"Go go Fernando," *Chicago Tribune*, May 14, 1981.

Kornheiser, Tony, "Fernando: Star in the Remaking," *Washington Post*, July 20, 1993.

Llosa, Luis Fernando, "Mania Man," *Sports Illustrated*, June 30, 2003.

Los Angeles Dodgers game press box media notes, May 7, 1981.

Plaschke, Bill, "Till Next Time," *Los Angeles Times*, May 12, 1991.

Shah, Diane K. and Contreras, Joe, "The Most Happy Rookie," *Newsweek*, May 11, 1981.

Smith, James F., "Winter Wonder," *Los Angeles Times*, December 30, 2000.

Spander, Art, "The Mexican Cy Young," *San Francisco Chronicle*, May 29, 1983.

"Time for Fernando's Hideaway," *San Francisco Examiner*, May 19, 1981.

Yates, Ronald, "Fans, players beating path to Valenzuela," *Chicago Tribune*, May 3, 1981.

Omar Vizquel

He makes the plays at shortstop that leave fans blinking. They can't believe what they have just seen as Omar Vizquel ranges far to his right, somehow throws his body in front of a hard-hit grounder, then twists his torso to throw to first base and nip a runner crossing the bag.

Vizquel makes the unbelievable seem commonplace. He makes the extraordinary seem routine. But he adds his own dash and spice to the maneuvers that have set him apart as one of the great shortstops of the modern generation. Outgoing, gregarious, fun-loving, and talkative, Vizquel not only adores roaming the infield, but flashy moves come naturally to him. He might barehand a ball or flip a behind-the-back pass to a teammate covering second base. The moves all seem instinctive, not premeditated.

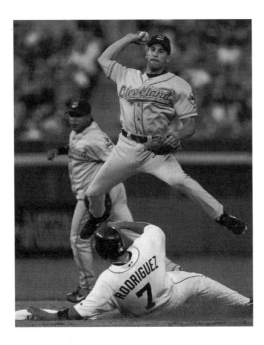

Omar Vizquel made his mark with the Cleveland Indians as another great Venezuelan shortstop, but played superbly wherever he went. An 11-time Gold Glove winner, Vizquel made three All-Star teams and was still playing in the majors in 2010 at the age of 43, serving as a player-coach for the Chicago White Sox. (AP Photo/Duane Burleson)

Some accuse Vizquel of being a showboat, playing up his slick grabs and tosses out of ego, but Vizquel has always maintained that he does what he does on the baseball diamond to get the ball to its destination as swiftly as possible. Like a point guard who throws pinpoint bounce passes or tosses the basketball over his shoulder while looking the other way, Vizquel has great court sense and a special instinct that permits him to make plays that others cannot. As long as the ball gets where it's supposed to go to make an out, who can find a beef with the method of delivery?

"You see, a hot dog would be if I did all that because I was trying to show up my teammates, trying to make me look good at the expense of someone else," Vizquel said. "I do all of those things only for one reason. Because I like to have fun and baseball is supposed to be about having fun." (Quoted in Olson.) And getting people out. Vizquel has always more than held up his end on that responsibility—getting to grounders he has no right to reach, preventing singles through the infield with his diving stabs, and throwing out runners with his quarterback-powerful arm.

A linear descendent of Chico Carrasquel, Luis Aparicio, Davey Concepcion, and Ozzie Guillen, Vizquel is another great Venezuelan shortstop making his mark in the majors with acrobatic fielding ability. He was born in Caracas April 24, 1967; in 2009, at the age of 42, ancient for a middle infielder, Vizquel was still holding down the fort for the San Francisco Giants before moving on to the Chicago White Sox for the 2010 season.

Much like his ballyhooed predecessors who played the key infield spot, Vizquel did not come from a background of wealth. Most of his youth was spent playing baseball on rocky fields that were never manicured or smoothed. The tricky hops batters hit helped Vizquel develop his reflexes and get his glove on the bad bounces. The skill translated to professional ball, even though the fields are made of artificial turf or are cared for by groundskeepers with the souls of hair stylists.

Vizquel knew his baseball history and recognized the big-name shortstops from Venezuela who performed so spectacularly in the majors before him. They were his idols. When Vizquel first joined a youth team at home his father insisted that he wear No. 17. That was to honor Carrasquel. "Shortstop is the position of choice in Venezuela," Vizquel said. When he was old enough to pick his own number, however, Vizquel selected No. 13, a tribute to Concepcion. Carrasquel and Aparicio were more names in a history book to him. Concepcion he actually saw play. "Americans sometimes ask me about wearing an 'unlucky' number," Vizquel said. "In Venezuela, we don't think that way. It's just another number." (Quoted in Vizquel and Dyer, 37–38.)

With his own flair, Vizquel made it more than just another number. He performed so well that kids who came along later wanted to wear No. 13 to be like Omar.

Although he did not start out playing on well-groomed fields, Vizquel's family was much better off financially than many of his teammates and Major League contemporaries from Latin America. The son of an electrician and a stay-at-home mom, Vizquel said the clan was "middle class," though not in the higher income bracket of American middle-class families. He describes himself as a toddler terror when he was young. Vizquel said he first got into trouble for depositing the family cat in the washing machine, and he had the nickname "Earthquake" because he was always running around and shaking things up. He called himself "a smart ass" in school and a student who rarely studied. But Vizquel said he also kissed up to his friends' parents so they didn't know what type of devil he really was. (Quoted in Vizquel and Dyer, 25, 26, 28.)

One of Vizquel's hobbies was listening to American rock and roll and watching American TV shows. However, they were all translated into Spanish. It wasn't until years later that he realized that "Tom and Jerry" cartoons, "Sesame Street," "Superman," and "Batman and Robin" were not homegrown television shows. "I almost died when I found out "Sesame Street" wasn't made in Venezuela," he said. When Vizquel moved to the United States as a minor leaguer, he turned on the TV set and saw all of the same shows he grew up with and was stunned. "They were all speaking English!" Vizquel said. "I couldn't believe it. I swore Zorro was Venezuelan." (Quoted in Vizquel and Dyer, 46.) It was like discovering there was no Santa Claus or Easter Bunny.

For all of his naïveté about American popular culture's translation to Venezuela, Vizquel was aware that baseball was imported from the United States. But he also realized at a young age that Venezuela was different from most Central and South American countries in its embrace of his favorite sport. Soccer rules in that part of the world, especially in neighboring countries like Brazil, where Pele was the most famous player in the world.

"You need to understand that baseball is king in Venezuela," Vizquel said. "In most Latin countries baseball is popular, but soccer is even more popular. Not so in Venezuela, where soccer is a distant second." (Quoted in Vizquel and Dyer, 36.)

Baseball didn't care if Vizquel knew who Big Bird was or if could sing along with his favorites like Led Zeppelin, Kiss or Van Halen in English, not as long as he could pluck those grounders and complete an accurate throw across the infield. He was only 17 when his parents gave permission to Vizquel to sign a contract with the Seattle Mariners. Nobody got rich at the dining room table that day. Vizquel's signing bonus was $2,500, and the deal called for bonuses of $500 each time he moved up a notch through the minor-league chain.

Still a teenager, Vizquel looked even younger. He stood 5-foot-9 and although he later filled out at 175 pounds, he was scrawny and did not yet resemble a professional athlete. In 1984, Major League clubs were not as sophisticated in preparing Latino players for the United States as they are now. Vizquel was not old enough to drink or vote, and he spoke no English when the Mariners shipped him to Butte, Montana, for 15 games of rookie ball that summer.

If Vizquel knew anything about the Rocky Mountains or the "Cowboy Way" it was because Oscar the Grouch had taken a vacation out West during "Sesame Street." Vizquel said he knew exactly one word of English when he arrived in Butte: "Eggs." Whenever he went out to eat he ordered eggs. He didn't know how to order scrambled or sunny-side-up. Every question he was asked at the table he answered, "Eggs." This would not be a nutritionist's dream diet. "My cholesterol level must have been 400," Vizquel said. Vizquel graduated from a neighborhood café where he was a regular, but looked upon as somewhat of an object of curiosity, to a Denny's. Denny's had illustrated menus. Huge step up. "I could just point to the food I wanted," Vizquel said. (Quoted in Vizquel and Dyer, 45.)

Vizquel was lucky to have other Latino teammates so he could chat in Spanish, but he became determined to learn English as swiftly as possible. It was not long before he was conversant in the language and over time became comfortable speaking English and making jokes in his second language. Vizquel's glove spoke a universal language. He could make plays at short that few could master. At times he was compared to future Hall of Famer Ozzie Smith, another flashy player who could make the impossible probable. Like Smith, though, Vizquel was a weak hitter at the beginning of his career. After a tour-of-North-America minor-league swing that lasted until 1989, Vizquel got a chance to show his stuff in Seattle. He played 143 games, but could hit only .220. It took until the second half of the 1990 season for Vizquel to become a full-time major leaguer.

In 1991, Vizquel led American League shortstops in fielding for the first of four times. With the Cleveland Indians in 1998, Vizquel was chosen as an AL All-Star for the first of three times. Through practice, repetition, and listening to instruction, he made himself into a better hitter, astounding observers with a career high .333 mark in 1999. That was Vizquel's only .300-plus season among his 20 years in the majors through 2009. But Vizquel was always appreciated more for his dazzling glove work. He won 11 Gold Gloves between the 1990s and mid-2000s, at one point he collected nine in a row.

"I'll never be recognized as a great hitter," said Vizquel, who took a very respectable lifetime batting average of .273 into the 2010 season. "I'm not a bad hitter. But the main reason I'm in the big leagues is because of my defense." (Quoted in Robbins.)

Fans enjoy spiffy plays, but teammates are more concerned with outs going up on the scoreboard. If a guy makes a great play, they will be the first to acknowledge it, but if a guy botches a play unnecessarily, he's going to hear about it. With luck it won't cost his team a run or a game, but the ribbing will come no matter what. Catch and throw—that is the role of the infielder. Vizquel makes the hardest plays, but teammates have not been above warning him to make the simple ones. "It's pretty to see," said former Indians third baseman Matt Williams of some of Vizquel's sparkling moves, "although if he drops it I reckon we're all going to strangle him." (Quoted in Olson.)

It was not clear if Williams was joking or not, but Vizquel's true admirers were those who shared the middle infielding job. They know how difficult it is to get to hard-hit balls that seem out of reach, to catch them, spin, and make an on-target throw. The best infielders reach grounders that few others can. Their range helps define their prowess. Their swiftness and instincts on where to play a batter might save hits at a critical moment while a less accomplished player might just watch as a grounder zips through the infield.

"Amazing," said one-time Indians second baseman Carlos Baerga. "He makes me jealous." Said Indians coach Buddy Bell, a six-time Gold Glove-winning third baseman: "He's got the best instincts I've ever seen. He's very intelligent and he positions himself very well." (Quoted in Robbins.)

Vizquel was never shy, but it took time to adapt to the United States as he absorbed English. Once entrenched in the Mariners' infield, he took advantage of being a big leaguer by letting his wild side show through his purchases. At one point he drove a yellow Porsche, and he owned a companion same-colored suit. That might have made him the only person in the United States to wear an outfit that compared to the San Diego Chicken's. There was that purple-and-yellow suit, too. Perhaps Prince had the only other one. In addition to being a music lover, Vizquel also took up painting. That made him an artist on two fronts—with a glove and a brush.

Vizquel began oil painting in 1994, while with Cleveland. He invested in a good set of paints and equipment and started honing his skills. He reached the point later in his career when he painted two hours a day when his team was at home.

"It was a late-blooming thing," Vizquel said. "I never had it in my mind. For some reason it got to me. I liked art, but I never thought about doing anything. It's awesome. I just enjoy it so much. You never know what kind of talents you have. You have to experiment. Sometimes something cool comes out of it." (Quoted in "Shortstop Finds . . .") No one is ever going to confuse Vizquel with Picasso, but then no one was going to give Picasso a huge free-agent contract to play shortstop, either.

Perhaps wondering if Vizquel would ever become half the hitter he was as a fielder (he did), the Mariners traded the Venezuelan shortstop to the Indians for two players in 1993. Vizquel joined the Indians at a time when they were being built into the franchise's best team in decades. The farm system produced. The general manager made trades. By 1995, the Indians looked like the best team in baseball. In a strike-shortened season they finished 100–44. Cleveland won its first American League pennant in 41 years.

Dominant teams are usually teams having fun. What's not to like when you come to the ballpark almost certain you are going to win? But the Indians set some kind of high-water mark for high jinks, according to Vizquel. They had so much fun together they could have been a situation comedy. The way Vizquel describes the season the most outrageous players set shoelaces on fire for a hot foot, made holes in drinking cups so teammates would get splashed, stuck wads of bubble-gum on unsuspecting teammates' caps or uniforms, and sneaked around lathering telephones and towels with shaving cream. "We were having a blast," Vizquel said. (Quoted in Vizquel and Dyer, 96.)

The Indians had a blast all season long—until the World Series. The Indians had to beat Vizquel's old team, the Mariners, to advance to meet the National League winner, which they did. They felt certain they would defeat the Atlanta Braves for the Indians' first championship since 1948, but they did not.

"Although the loss stung, given our high expectations," Vizquel said, "the pain passed relatively quickly. In 1995, I was happy to simply have gotten to a World Series. A lot of great players never do." (Quoted in Vizquel and Dyer, 114.)

The Indians returned to the World Series in 1997, though they hadn't played nearly as well during the regular season. Matched against the Florida Marlins, a recent expansion team, the Indians were confident of victory. However, they lost in seven games, with the Series-ending defeat going 11 innings. The second time around Vizquel was distraught. He jetted home to Venezuela for an out-of-touch journey into a jungle with his brother and some friends. The nature getaway included a visit to Angel Falls, a 1,000-foot waterfall. The escape lasted nine days and then he hung out with wife Nicole and son Nico, banishing thoughts of baseball from his mind as soon as he could stop brooding over the loss. He was reinvigorated by spring training.

By the mid-1990s, Vizquel was an established star. In Venezuela his breathtaking fielding compared favorably in fans' minds with that of his illustrious predecessors. He was hitting at the big-league level and was recognized with Gold Gloves and All-Star-game appearances. Traditionally, throughout baseball history, shortstops have been graded the most leniently when it comes to hitting. Vizquel's skills were a match for those of the generations before, but it was his misfortune to come along when the American League fielded its greatest group of hitters ever at the position. Because Alex Rodriguez, Derek Jeter, and Nomar Garciaparra outslugged and out-hit him, Vizquel was sometimes squeezed off of All-Star teams altogether.

This was an unprecedented era and Vizquel realized what he was up against with Jeter leading the Yankees to World Series crowns, with Rodriguez leading the league in homers, and Garciaparra leading the league in batting. A dozen years into his career, Vizquel could only hope that his sparkling record in the field would be remembered by Hall of Fame voters when his playing days were over. "Right now, that's like a dream," Vizquel said in 2001. "I just hope that my numbers are recognized by the time I retire." (Quoted in Livingstone.)

Known as a light hitter when he first set sail in the majors, Vizquel established a milestone during a 2004 game that put him in the company of Rodriguez, Garciaparra, and Jeter as a hitter and surprised even him. In a late August game against the Yankees (which the Indians won by a remarkable 22–0 score), Vizquel cranked out six hits. That tied a record for most hits in a nine-inning game and was the Yankees' worst lost ever. He even got the at-bat needed for an attempt at a seventh hit, but flied out to right field in the ninth inning. "Of course the seventh hit was on my mind," Vizquel said. "It was weird. When I went to the plate some of the Yankee fans were giving me a standing ovation." (Quoted in Hoynes.)

After the 2004 season, the Indians blew up the team, discarding old reliables for fresh faces. Vizquel joined the San Francisco Giants. He had clearly lost a step, but could still play big-league shortstop, if not with the same daring.

In his waning years, Vizquel added to his legacy. In the spring of 2008, Vizquel became the majors' all-time leader in games played at shortstop. In June 2009, when Vizquel notched his 2,678th hit, it made him the Venezuelan with the most hits in the majors. He had surpassed all of the other shortstop greats, the heroes of his youth. It was a pretty special accomplishment for a guy who came to the majors more than two decades earlier with the rap of "good-field, no-hit." Time and Omar Vizquel's perseverance, still going strong as he signed with the Chicago White Sox for the 2010 season, proved the world wrong.

Further Reading

Hoynes, Paul, "22–0! Omar's 6 hits ignite a Bronx bombardment as Tribe deals Yanks record-setting rout," *Cleveland Plain Dealer*, September 1, 2004.

Livingstone, Seth, "Indians' Vizquel finds beauty in glovework," *USA Today*, May 1, 2001.

Olson, Lisa, "Omar not relishing hot dog," *New York Daily News*, October 3, 1987.

Robbins Liz, "Vizquel's glove boosts Tribe," *Cleveland Plain Dealer*, July 23, 1995.

"Shortstop Finds Outlet in Paints and a Palette," Associated Press, July 17, 2005.

Vizquel, Omar, and Dyer, Bob, *Omar!* (Cleveland, Gray & Company Publishers, 2000).

Part III

Seventy-five More Significant Latin American Baseball Figures

Bobby Abreu

A native of Turmero, Venezuela, Abreu, born March 11, 1974, is one of the steadiest hitters in the majors today. He broke into the big leagues in 1996 with the Houston Astros and carried a .299 lifetime average into the 2010 season, his second with the Los Angeles Angels. A two-time All-Star, Abreu has good power and won the Home Run Derby at the 2005 All-Star game. That season he also won a Gold Glove for his outfield play. Versatility has been a hallmark of Abreu's game, with his on-base percentage of 40 percent combining with his home-run power to show off all-around hitting skills. In 1999, Abreu batted a career high .335. Abreu has seven 100-plus RBI seasons and his career best for homers is 31 set in 2001. Although the appendage has not followed him to the United States, Abreu has an odd nickname. In Spanish he is called "El Comedulce," which means "candy eater." It was actually his father Nelson's nickname and when he died, Abreu suggested that fans keep the name in use with him.

Very popular wherever he has played, Abreu devoted himself tirelessly to charitable events when he played for the Phillies. For the 2003 and 2004 seasons, Abreu created a section in the ballpark for "Abreu's Amigos" and purchased $10,000 worth of tickets to games on Friday nights for children. Abreu also paid for the young fans' team jerseys, concessions, and met with them on the field before the games. Abreu was the Phillies' nominee for Major League Baseball's Roberto Clemente Award for community service. During the 2008 season with the New York Yankees, his new team, Abreu, who had begun his own charity, "Abreu's Finest," made donations to the Police Athletic League to supply sporting goods to kids.

Ruben Amaro Sr. and Ruben Amaro Jr.

Both Ruben Amaros spent years with the Philadelphia Phillies, the team's only father-son combination. Ruben Sr. was born in Vera Cruz, Mexico on January 6, 1936 and broke into the majors with the St. Louis Cardinals in 1958 as a shortstop. His father, Santos Amaro, played ball in Mexico for 25 years during the summer and played in Havana, Cuba, his home, during the winter. Ruben Sr. played 11 years in the majors and batted .234. Son Ruben Jr., was born in Philadelphia, February 12, 1965, and followed his dad into the majors in 1991 with the California Angels. But he also spent five years with the Phillies.

Ruben Sr. was noticed by pro scouts while competing in the Pan American Games for Mexico in 1954 after he had also lettered in college soccer in Vera Cruz. He quit school against his father's wishes, but promised his father it would be worth it. He was never a true star, but always steady, although he did win a Gold Glove at short in 1964. Fielding was Ruben Sr.'s calling card. It was not easy in the beginning, especially when Amaro played minor-league ball in Texas and was treated roughly because of his skin color. Ruben Sr. proved his savvy and became a Phillies coach before becoming a Mexican League manager.

Ruben the younger had many advantages his father did not. Ruben Jr. attended Stanford University and his success there made it easier to get noticed by pro scouts. At 5-foot-10 and 175 pounds, he was physically almost identical to his father, but Ruben Jr. played outfield. However, he hit like an infielder—just .235 in eight seasons. Like his dad, Ruben Jr. learned from everything going on around him and is currently the general manager of the Phillies, after serving for 10 years as an assistant. Amaro, who is Jewish and Hispanic, is the second Latino general manager after Omar Minaya of the Mets.

Sandy Amoros

Outfielder Edmundo "Sandy" Amoros, a native of Havana, Cuba, was born January 30, 1930, and arrived in the majors in 1952, at a time when Latin American players were just beginning to get more chances to play. The Brooklyn Dodgers had led the way with integration of African American players and had no concerns about adding a dark-skinned Latino to the mix. Amoros got into 20 games in 1952 and continued to receive more playing time for the next few years. Amoros saw his most action in 1955 while playing in 119 games; his highest average was .277 in 1957. Amoros's fielding gained him opportunities on a roster filled with sluggers.

Amoros's singular claim to fame—and the reason why he is remembered fondly by Brooklyn fans—was a critical catch he made in the 1955 World Series. Playing left field in the seventh game against the New York Yankees after being inserted for defensive purposes in the sixth inning, Amoros sprinted a great distance toward the fencing on a ball sliced by Yogi Berra. Running full out, Amoros speared the ball in the glove on his right hand just into foul territory. He swiftly fired a throw to shortstop Pee Wee Reese, who relayed the ball to Gil Hodges at first base, catching Yankee runner Gil McDougald for a double play. It was the key sequence in the Dodgers' 2–0 victory. The win gave Brooklyn its only World Series triumph before moving to Los Angeles and Amoros's catch has been hailed

Sandy Amoros's biggest moment of fame in the majors occurred in the seventh game of the 1955 World Series when he speared a curving foul pop near the left-field stands off the bat of the Yankees' Yogi Berra. The Brooklyn Dodgers won the game and their only Series in New York. Amoros, from Cuba, played seven years in the majors with a .256 average and after facing many difficulties died in 1992. (Mark Rucker/Transcendental Graphics, Getty Images)

ever since as one of the greatest ever in the Series. "I still receive a lot of letters," Amoros said in 1989. (Quoted in "Amoros Dies . . .") Amoros played seven years in the majors and appeared in three World Series with the Dodgers. He retired in 1960 with a .255 average. Amoros died of pneumonia at 62 in 1992 and had previously lost a leg to diabetes.

Further Reading

"Amoros Dies Of Pneumonia," Associated Press/United Press International, June 28, 1992.

Joaquin Andujar

Born December 21, 1952 in the Dominican Republic, the fire-balling right-hander was one of the early stars who helped to put his hometown of San Pedro de Macoris on the baseball map. The community has sent a huge number of players to the majors, establishing an unprecedented pipeline to the pros. Andujar was a high-profile player from the start with the Houston Astros in 1976. In addition to possessing the pitching skills necessary for success, he was cocky and loud and showed a temper. A four-time All-Star, Andujar struggled as a youth to make the grade. He was raised by grandparents in poverty. "I was so poor, I didn't have shoes," he said. (Quoted in Nevius.)

Andujar blossomed with the St. Louis Cardinals. His first big year was 1982 when he finished 15–10. In 1984, Andujar won 20 games for the Cardinals, tops in the National League that season, and he led the NL in innings pitched, as well, with 261 1/3. Andujar's off-field explosiveness, saying too much, too often, produced more attraction than his on-field play, however, including refrains that he did not receive the recognition he deserved.

"They make me out to be a stupid clown," Andujar said of his frequent contretemps with the media. (Quoted in Hummel.) In 1985 he won 21 games. In 13 seasons, Andujar finished with a 127–118 record. Later, as he grew more mature, Andujar realized he had only hurt himself with blowups at umpires that got him in trouble with baseball officials and earned him enmity from some fans. "Past is past," Andujar said near the end of his career, years after saying he was "born macho." (Quoted in Goldstein.) After retirement in 1988, Andujar returned to the Dominican and threw himself into providing opportunities in youth baseball programs and provided notable assistance when the island nation was harmed by a hurricane.

Further Reading

Goldstein, Alan. "Today, Andujar is one mellow Dominican," *Baltimore Sun*, August 21, 1986.

Hummel, Rick. "Sport Interview: Joaquin Andujar," *Sport Magazine*, September, 1985.

Nevius, C.W. "Andujar: A Misunderstood Pitcher With 'Too Much Blood,'" *San Francisco Chronicle*, date obscured, National Baseball Hall of Fame Library archives.

Luis Arroyo

Born in Penuelas, Puerto Rico on February 18, 1927, Arroyo had a short, but productive career in the majors, mostly as a relief pitcher. He made his debut with the St. Louis Cardinals in 1955, got off to a hot start, making the All-Star team, and finished 11–8 as a rookie. Arroyo, whose nickname was "Yo-Yo," specialized in throwing a nasty screwball. However, he could not find a home for long in the National League, bouncing from St. Louis to Pittsburgh to Cincinnati. He discovered his calling in the bullpen when he landed with the New York Yankees in 1960 and pitching coach Johnny Sain fine-tuned his mechanics. As a reliever Arroyo went 5–1 with a 2.89 earned run average for the AL champs. When the tight seventh game of the World Series was rolling to a conclusion, Arroyo was warming up. Instead, Casey Stengel brought in Ralph Terry and the Pirates' Bill Mazeroski hit one of the game's most legendary home runs. "I had confidence I could get Mazeroski out," Arroyo said later. (Quoted in Marazzi.)

The next season Arroyo emerged as a star. He dominated in relief, going 15–5 with 29 saves and a 2.19 ERA. The phenomenal season helped the Yankees steamroll to another pennant. The colorful Arroyo, who showed a preference for wearing Panama hats and smoking cigars that seemed as long as baseball bats, was named the top reliever in the American League that year. Yankee fans loved Arroyo's style and when he came into a game they chanted, "Loo-ee! Loo-ee!" Arroyo ran into arm trouble the next season, and he was out of the majors for good by 1963, retiring with a 40–32 record. Still, Arroyo was chosen for the Latin American Baseball Hall of Fame in 2002.

Further Reading

Marazzi, Rich. "Arroyo was Yanks' relief ace in epic '61 season," *Sports Collector's Digest*, May 17, 1996.

Bobby Avila

After he won the 1954 American League batting title with a .341 average, Cleveland Indians' second baseman Bobby Avila was recognized and hailed on the streets of Mexico during his off-season visits. Born in Vera Cruz, Mexico on April 2, 1924, Avila was the first player from his country to win a Major League batting crown. Until he uncovered his skill with a bat and glove, Avila aspired to become a bullfighter. Instead, he became a three-time All-Star and spent his life in baseball.

Avila said he nearly joined the Brooklyn Dodgers instead of the Indians, spurning an offer that was $1,000 less. If he had taken that deal, Avila said he would have been stuck on the bench behind Jackie Robinson. Fortunately, he came to the Indians when All-Star Joe Gordon was winding down his career. "Gordon did more for me than anyone in baseball," Avila said. "I was a kid of 20 in a strange land and I didn't know my way around." (Quoted in Gutierrez.)

After an 11-year career that ended in 1959 with a .281 lifetime average, Avila returned to Mexico. He continued to play in the Mexican League and in 1960 showed he still had pop left in his bat by hitting .333 with 125 RBIs. When he ceased playing, Avila became an owner of more than one Mexican League team over the years. Eventually, he became commissioner of the league and was even elected mayor of his home town. "Everybody knows who Avila was in Mexico," said Fernando Valenzuela, the Mexican pitcher who came to the majors a generation later. "He was an inspiration, of course, for Mexican ballplayers to follow to the States and play in the major leagues." (Quoted in Finch.) Avila died at age 78 in 2004.

Further Reading

Finch, Paul. "Matter of $1,000 Once Stopped Avila From Becoming A Dodger," *Los Angeles Times*, March 15, 1962.

Gutierrez, Paul. "Bobby Avila, 78; First Mexican to Win Major League Batting Crown," *Los Angeles Times*, October 28, 2004.

Carlos Baerga

Dazzling with a glove, Baerga made heads turn when he fielded second base for the Cleveland Indians after being brought to the majors in 1990. Also a solid hitter, Baerga, who was born in Santurce, Puerto Rico on November 4, 1968, was a three-time All-Star before retiring in 2005. Baerga compiled a lifetime .291 batting average. A chatterbox who played the game of pool with equal ferocity to his baseball game, Baerga led the Indians in commentary and showed surprisingly effective bat work for a middle infielder when he hit between .312 and .321 four consecutive years. "When you swing at a pitch, you must swing with passion," Baerga said. (Quoted in Lidz.) Baerga accomplished a unique feat in a 2003 game with the Indians. He became the only switch-hitter to belt home runs from both sides of the plate in one inning.

Early in his career, Baerga was off to a start that would have ranked him among the best-hitting second-basemen of all time. Then he suffered injuries and missed games. He eventually admitted spending too much time partying and going out for late-night drinks. When he joined the New York Yankees late in the 1996 season and started fresh with them in spring training of 1997, Baerga said he had changed his life. "I don't drink anymore," he said. "I came back to the church." He called himself "a born-again Christian." (Quoted in Smith.)

Baerga became an Evangelical Christian and helped convert two other prominent athletes, boxers Alex Sanchez and Felix Trinidad, to his church.

Baerga became a baseball broadcaster upon retirement, doing some national TV work on game-of-the-week coverage, but also handling a large slate of games in Spanish.

Further Reading

Lidz, Frans. "Slick with the Stick," *Sports Illustrated*, April 4, 1994.
Smith, Claire. "Baerga Turns New Leaf in His Life Style," *New York Times*, February 21, 1997.

Jorge (George) Bell

At times Bell was one of the best sluggers in the American League. He was born October 21, 1959 in San Pedro de Macoris, Dominican Republic, one of the earliest homegrown players from the legendary town that produces so many major leaguers. In the 1970s, when Bell was discovered, the Toronto Blue Jays operated just about the most sophisticated tryout system for young Dominican players. Bell was the cream of the crop, and he made his debut with the big club in 1981 and matured into a three-time All-Star in a 12-year career as an outfielder and designated hitter.

Bell displayed prodigious power—in 1987 cracking 47 home runs and accounting for an American League-leading 134 RBIs while hitting .308. That year he won the AL Most Valuable Player award. Most of Bell's career was spent with the Blue Jays, but Bell also achieved his final All-Star berth with the Chicago Cubs and played two seasons with the Chicago White Sox. Bell might have accomplished more in his career, but he always seemed at odds with reporters, umpires, fans, or team management. Bell claimed to be misunderstood and said he was really a nice guy. Yet he did not react well to being booed after committing an error in a situation that became magnified when he told reporters that those fans could place a kiss on his derriere.

Bell was frequently angered because he felt he did not receive the recognition he deserved for his hitting. Bell announced that he felt he should be considered one of the superstars of the sport and that elite group was the only category of players anyone had a right to match him up against. And then he said he didn't care about any of that, leaving fans with a very mixed message.

Carlos Beltran

Born April 24, 1977 in Manati, Puerto Rico, Beltran was the American League Rookie of the Year in 1999 for the Kansas City Royals. An exciting talent, he can run, hit, hit with power, and cover ground in the outfield. A five-time

Carlos Beltran, an outfielder from Puerto Rico, made a mark with the Kansas City Royals and Houston Astros and now plays for the New York Mets. A one-time rookie of the year and an adept base-stealer, Beltran is a four-time All-Star who also owns a Gold Glove and captured a Silver Slugger Award as the best hitter at his position. (AP Photo/Kathy Willens)

All-Star by 2009, and a three-time Gold Glove winner, Beltran has been a hotly pursued property during his career, earning multi-million-dollar deals with Kansas City, Houston, and the New York Mets. During his first seven seasons, Beltran had smacked more than 20 home runs five times and knocked in at least 100 runs four times. In his first six years as a full-time player, Beltran always stole a double-figure number of bases, with a high of 41 in 2003.

When Beltran joined the Mets in 2005, he spoke about the grand tradition of center fielders in New York baseball history, from Joe DiMaggio to Mickey Mantle with the Yankees and Willie Mays with the Giants. "I know there are a lot of expectations of me and I will do the best I can," Beltran said. "I like to run down balls and dive and make catches." (Quoted in Johnson.) Beltran's raw talent had long before caused him to be likened to the best in the game. Buck O'Neil, a shrewd judge of ability in his long career in the Negro Leagues and as a Major League scout and coach, compared Beltran to Mays. O'Neil got to see the youthful Beltran at the start of his Royals stay. "(Willie Mays), that's who young Beltran reminds me of," O'Neil said. "He's got everything Willie had . . . hit, run field, and throw. He's so smooth you think he might be loafing." (Quoted in "Buck O'Neil . . .")

Further Reading

"Buck O'Neil sees Willie Mays in Carlos Beltran," Associated Press, March 22, 2000.
Serby, Steve. "Serby's Q&A with . . . Carlos Beltran," *New York Post*, January 16, 2005.

Hiram Bithorn

The 6-foot-1, 200-pound right-hander was the first Puerto Rican to play Major League baseball when he broke into the big leagues with the Chicago Cubs in 1942. Bithorn was born March 18, 1916, in Santurce, Puerto Rico, of Dutch parents. As a Cubs rookie, Bithorn went 9–14 in 38 games, mixing starting and relieving assignments. He posted a solid 3.68 earned run average in 171 1/3 innings. The Cubs already knew Bithorn was durable. In 1937, while pitching for Norfolk in the minors, Bithorn won the first game of a double-header in the evening. The second game ran very long into the night and when his manager needed relief help in the 13th inning, he had no one else to put in but Bithorn. The game ended in the 15th with Bithorn again the victor.

In his second year with the Cubs, Bithorn was a huge success, going 18–12 as one of their key starting pitchers. He recorded an exceptional ERA of 2.60 and tossed a league-leading seven shutouts. Bithorn did not know that his career peaked with that season and he was out of the majors for the next two seasons because of World War II.

Returning to the big leagues in the post-War era, Bithorn went 6–5 for the Cubs with a 3.84 earned run average in 1946. He concluded his Major League career in 1947 with the White Sox, appearing in just two games that year. Bithorn was pitching in winter ball in Mexico in 1951 when he was shot to death by a police officer who was convicted of his murder. Bithorn was only 35. In 1962, when a shiny new ballpark was built in Puerto Rico, it was named Hiram Bithorn Stadium to honor the pioneer. The nearly homeless Montreal Expos played part of their home schedule there in 2003 and 2004 before becoming the Washington Nationals.

Bobby Bonilla

The powerful hitting outfielder was born in the Bronx, New York on February 23, 1963, to a Puerto Rican family. A six-time All-Star who gave the Pittsburgh Pirates extra punch in a lineup featuring Barry Bonds, Bonilla produced six seasons of 20 or more home runs and four seasons of 100 or more RBIs that were hallmarks of his versatile game. Dangerous on the bases, as well, Bonilla had 257 steals in a 16-year career. In 1991, Bonilla clubbed a National League-leading 44 doubles and also stole 43 bases. The combination of hard hitting and swift feet made him difficult to pitch to and challenging to defend. Los Angeles Dodgers' Hall of Fame manager Tommy Lasorda summarized that point: "He's very, very impressive, not just as a power hitter, but an all-around player. He can do a lot of damage in a lot of directions." (Quoted in Hubbard.)

During his younger years and in his heyday with the Pirates between 1984 and 1988, Bonilla also played in the Puerto Rican winter league. Bonilla was a bona fide star with the Pirates when the franchise was still going well. But he was also a symbol of the club's impending problems when his salary demands couldn't be met after the team came close to going to the World Series. "This stuff about Pittsburgh being a small market and a team that can't afford to keep its players is bull," Bonilla said. (Quoted in Castellano.) Then he signed a five-year, $29 million contract with the New York Mets in 1992. Twice an All-Star in New York, Bonilla never quite lived up to the Big Apple hype before moving on to Baltimore and other teams for short stays before his 2001 retirement. His career numbers were very solid: 287 homers, 1,173 RBIs, 1,084 runs scored, and a .279 average.

Further Reading

Castellano, Dan. "Bonilla's last games as Pirate leave him with bad memories," *Newark Star-Ledger*, March 15, 1992.

Hubbard, Steve. "Thrift found a gem in Scandinavia," *Pittsburgh Press*, May 15, 1988.

Pedro Borbon Sr. and Pedro Borbon Jr.

Pedro Sr. was born in Mao, Dominican Republic on December 2, 1946. Pedro Jr. was born in Mao, Dominican Republic on November 15, 1967. The older Borbon broke into the majors in 1969 with the California Angels, but spent most of his 12-year Major League career with the Cincinnati Reds. His lifetime record was 69–39 and he amassed 80 saves. After a slow start he blossomed in time to be a relief contributor to the Big Red Machine teams of the mid-1970s. Borbon was 11–4 in 1973, 10–7 in 1974, and 10–5 in 1977.

For a few years mired in the minors at Indianapolis, making only cameo appearances in Cincinnati, Borbon displayed superb control and high-quality pitches in practice. But he couldn't replicate it in a game. After manager Sparky Anderson offered several upbeat lectures, Borbon looked more comfortable on the mound. "How can I expect Borbon to have confidence in himself if I don't show I have confidence in him?" Anderson said. (Quoted in Lawson.) It worked. Borbon also proved entertaining to sports writers. Once, he stepped onto the mound, turned to face center field in Fenway Park, and heaved the ball over the wall. He said he did it on a dare. He once earnestly explained that his grandfather was 136 years old—the oldest man in the Dominican. No one believed him.

Pedro Jr. was also a reliever. He came up with Atlanta in 1992 and earned a World Series ring with the Braves in 1995. His lifetime record was 16–16 with six saves in parts of nine Major League seasons. Borbon said he didn't know if he could live up to his father's career. "I was kind of intimidated by my dad because I was afraid I would fail and not become the same quality of player he was. He never forced me to play. I did it on my own." (Quoted in Rains.)

Further Reading

Lawson, Earl, "Confidence Makes Reds' Borbon a Winner," *The Sporting News*, January 13, 1973.
Rains, Rob, "Dad tries comeback, son sits out," *Baseball Weekly*, date missing, National Baseball Hall of Fame Library archive.

Miguel Cabrera

Miguel Cabrera is a young player whose career is still a work in progress, but is trending toward superstardom. Born April 18, 1983 in Maracay, Venezuela, Cabrera has completed seven seasons in the majors, and has won a World Series ring with the Florida Marlins and led the American League in home runs with the Detroit Tigers in 2008 with 37. He routinely knocks in more than 100 runs (107 in 2009), and bats over .300 as a sound first baseman. He is already a four-time All-Star selection.

Already in love with baseball, Cabrera gained more motivation when he was cut from the Venezuelan national team. It didn't take long for him to grow into a Major League star after that, and Florida only parted with him because the Marlins wanted to cut payroll and Cabrera was going to be a free agent. After five seasons with Florida, Cabrera signed an eight-year, $152-million deal with the Tigers. Constantly improving, Cabrera is growing into one of the best players in baseball and the deal acknowledged that. "He is part of our foundation now," said Detroit general manager Dave Dombrowski. (Quoted in "Cabrera . . .")

Sturdily built at 6-foot-2 and 240 pounds, Cabrera is physically imposing. But he is light-hearted and comes across as friendly and loose, as if he doesn't take anything too seriously. When a reporter asked Cabrera who he would invite to a dream dinner party, he said aside from his parents he would like to sit around the table with Vladimir Guerrero, Manny Ramirez, and Albert Pujols. "Guess what we're talking about all night?" he said. "Hitting. And we're probably talking until breakfast." (Quoted in "20 questions.")

First baseman Miguel Cabrera is the current cornerstone of the Detroit Tigers. Cabrera, of Venezuela, is considered one of the top young power hitters in the sport day. Turning 27 at the beginning of the 2010 season, Cabrera was already a four-time All-Star. He was the 2008 American League home-run champ with 37. (AP Photo/Tim Sharp)

Further Reading

"20 questions with Miguel Cabrera," MiamiHerald.com, July 10, 2005.
"Cabrera finalizes eight-year, $152.3M deal with Tigers," ESPN.com, March 25, 2008.

Bert Campaneris

One of the outstanding shortstops of his time, Dagoberto "Campy" Campenaris was born March 9, 1942 in Pueblo Nuevo, Cuba. He made his Major League debut in 1964 with the Kansas City Athletics and spent 19 years in the big leagues with a .259 average. His quick hands aided him in the field and his quick feet aided him on the base paths. A six-time All-Star, Campaneris led the American League in stolen bases six times. He recorded a high of 62 steals twice, in 1968 and 1969, and had 649 thefts in his career.

Although Campaneris's style of play endeared him to teammates, he spoke almost no English when he joined the A's and had few Spanish speakers to converse with. Initially, he referred to stealing bases as "robo de bases." (Quoted in McGuff.) The shortstop on the A's' 1972, 1973, and 1974 World Series champs, Campaneris collected 2,249 hits in his career. During a 13-inning game in 1965, Campaneris played all nine positions. He pitched the eighth inning and surrendered one run in the 5-3 late-season loss. "He won't kill you with the long hit—although he might," said Mets manager Yogi Berra. "But he'll hurt you in a dozen other ways." (Quoted in Grimsley.)

Campaneris stood 5-foot-10 and weighed 160 pounds. In his dreams he saw himself as a home-run hitter. In reality, he knew it wasn't so. "I'm no banjo hitter," Campaneris said, "but I'm no hero, either. Many times I wish I could be a big hitter like Hank Aaron or Willie Mays. But I must be satisfied with what I've got." (Quoted in Grimsley.)

Further Reading

Grimsley, Will. "It's Campy's Night," Associated Press, October 7, 1974.
McGuff, Joe. "Campaneris Thrills Kaycee Fans With Exploits as Bandit," *The Sporting News*, July 31, 1965.

Buck Canel

Born Eloy Canel in Buenos Aires, Argentina on March 4, 1906, and better known as "Buck," the sportswriter and broadcaster was an influential Spanish-language journalist who enjoyed a lengthy career. He was honored posthumously with the Ford Frick Award for outstanding broadcasting by the National Baseball Hall of Fame in 1985. Canel, who died April 7, 1980 from emphysema, was of Scottish-Hispanic heritage but an American citizen. His first newspaper job was with the *Staten Island Advance*, in New York, but in 1927 he joined the Associated Press and was posted to Latin America. He spent years writing for AP and a French news agency, but was broadcasting baseball by the 1930s. To much of the Spanish-speaking Americas, Canel was the voice of the World Series.

Canel's broadcasts were heard throughout the Caribbean, and Hall of Famer Tony Perez said Canel's calls of the game were his first exposure to the World Series as a boy in Cuba. One of Canel's signature phrases was, "Don't go away—this game is really getting interesting." (Quoted in Hall of Fame . . .) Canel also settled into a long-time role of handling New York Yankee radio broadcasts in Spanish.

Canel was present for an English-language press conference in 1959 when Fidel Castro took over Cuba. Castro recognized Canel and began speaking Spanish. Afterward, Canel said that Castro was critiquing Milwaukee manager Fred Haney's handling of his pitching staff in the 1958 World Series. Later, while Canel was dining with Castro, he turned down sugar (the island's staple crop) for his coffee and the new Cuban leader accused him of an anti-Cuban gesture. Canel eyed the bearded Castro and, referring to the sponsor of his Series broadcasts, said, "I'll take sugar when you shave with Gillette." (Quoted in Hall of Fame . . .)

Further Reading

National Baseball Hall of Fame press release, February

Jose Canseco and Ozzie Canseco

When he was younger, Jose Canseco was renowned for his power hitting as an outfielder and designated hitter. Later, no longer quite so popular, there was no denying Canseco's influence on the game. Born in Havana, Cuba on July 2, 1964, with his twin brother Ozzie (also briefly a major leaguer), Jose Canseco burst on the Major League scene in the mid-1980s with the Oakland A's. He and another young power-hitting muscleman named Mark McGwire became known as "The Bash Brothers." A six-time All-Star during his 17-year career, and the 1988 American League Most Valuable Player, Canseco clubbed 462 home runs. That year he became the first major leaguer to hit 40 home runs and steal 40 bases in the same season. He twice led the American League in homers and three times blasted at least 40—42 in 1988, 44 in 1991, and 46 in 1998.

Occasionally making controversial news for exploits with fast automobiles and fast women, Canseco bulked up and became a huge physical specimen, spreading at least 240 pounds on his 6-foot-4 body. Although hoping to continue his quest for 500 career homers, Canseco could not hook on with another team following the 2001 season and announced he was writing a tell-all book. He penned a best-seller that exposed baseball's drug culture and its reliance on steroids and other performance-enhancing drugs—Canseco admitted that he took the drugs himself and said he injected others. Canseco helped spark an investigation, and fans, players, owners, and the sports' administrators were dismayed as information about famous players leaked out name after name. Post-baseball, Canseco tried acting and boxing, but also got into trouble with the law for trying to illegally import a fertility drug.

Cuban-born Jose Canseco, whose family fled the island because of a distaste for Communism, hit 462 home runs in a long career that included stops with the Oakland A's, Texas Rangers, and Boston Red Sox. Canseco earned far more attention, however, by turning the spotlight on the use of steroids in baseball in a best-selling book. He also has made numerous electronic media appearances detailing his and others' use of performance-enhancing drugs. (Ronald C. Modra/ Sports Imagery/Getty Images)

Ultimately, Canseco's fine career, with six years knocking in more than 100 runs, including 1988 when his 124 RBIs led the AL, was overshadowed by his confession of drug use and his implication of others made him persona non grata in baseball.

Rene Cardenas

A multitasking journalist for more than half a century, Rene Cardenas's words and voice are appreciated throughout Latin America. He has been a baseball broadcaster and newspaper reporter and adapted to the Internet. A native of Nicaragua, Cardenas got his journalistic start in Managua, the nation's capital, as a 16-year-old.

After four years of double duty writing for newspapers and broadcasting sports, Cardenas was hired by *La Prensa*, the Spanish-language newspaper, to cover sports in the United States. When the Dodgers moved West, from Brooklyn to Los Angeles, Cardenas became the first Spanish-language broadcaster for a Major League team. He held the position from 1958 to 1961. He picked up more work, broadcasting the All-Star game and World Series and in 1962 moved to the new Houston Astros as Spanish-language broadcaster, a role he continued in until 1975.

Between 1976 and 1979 Cardenas lived in Nicaragua, serving as sports editor of *La Prensa*. He returned to the United States; in 1982, he went to Los Angeles to become part of the Dodgers' broadcast coverage staying until 1998. Since then Cardenas has broadcast on various stations, been writing for Houston Astros publications, and started his own web site. Cardenas is a member of the Nicaraguan Baseball Hall of Fame and the Hall of Fame of the National Museum of U.S. Hispanic Heritage.

Cardenas was with the Dodgers in their early Los Angeles days and remembered how "Dodgertown," the club's spring training home in Vero Beach, first struck him. "I remember how cold they (barracks) were," he said, "how dark they were, how mysterious they were. But we had a great time, because we loved baseball, so it didn't matter where we were sleeping as long as we were looking at those fantastic baseball stars that the Dodgers had in those years."

Further Reading

Walter O'Malley Official Web Site, www.walteromalley.com.

Rico Carty

Probably the earliest notable to come out of San Pedro de Macoris, Dominican Republic, Carty was born September 1, 1939 and made it big with the Milwaukee and Atlanta Braves. Carty made the Major League club's roster for good in 1964 and hit an eye-opening .330 as a rookie. In 1970, moving with the team to Atlanta, Carty batted .366, to lead the National League. That was his only All-Star season, but Carty wielded a dependable bat for many years.

Carty also hit .310, .326, and .342 in the 1960s. Never known as a huge slugger, nonetheless Carty accumulated 204 homers in his 15-year career with a high of 31 in 1978 when he split the season between Toronto and Oakland. His 99 RBIs that year were the second most in his career to the 101 of 1970. Carty seemed destined for even bigger things, but injuries and illness cost him. He caught tuberculosis and missed the entire 1968 season, spending 163 days in a hospital, and a knee injury sidelined him for the entire 1971 season. Carty said in neither case did he ever worry that his career was over. "I will always hit," he said. "God has given me that talent." (Quoted in "Carty's Creed . . .")

Although Carty admitted he almost quit baseball as a youth because he couldn't find a position to play, his bat kept him going. While he did not make the millions that players who came later did, Carty's baseball salary left him well off after an early life in his poor Dominican community. Once he had money, Carty became a dapper dresser and even purchased 25 pairs of shoes in one shopping spree. "I like shoes," he said of a $600 splurge. (Quoted in Minshew.)

Further Reading

"Carty's Creed: Born to Hit," Associated Press, June 25, 1972.
Minshew, Wayne. "Shoe Salesman in Deep Shock; Carty Buys 25 Pairs at a Clip," *The Sporting News*, July 22, 1967.

Vinny Castilla

Born July 4, 1967 in Oaxaca, Mexico, Castilla made his first showing in the majors with the Atlanta Braves in 1981. A 16-year major leaguer, Castilla was a two-time All-Star, a solid hitter who at his best was one of the elites in the game in a given year. Castilla played with seven big-league teams, but starred with the Colorado Rockies.

The hard-hitting third baseman hit more than 30 homers in a season six times, and he led the National League in RBIs with 131 in 2004. Castilla was always a fan favorite in Colorado dating back to being one of the original players on the 1993 expansion club. Castilla blasted 40 home runs in 1996, 40 in 1997, and 46 in 1998. In 1998 he drove in a career high 144 runs. Castilla returned home to play winter ball early in his career and maintained his popularity in Mexico. "He's like the president out there," Rockies teammate Curtis Goodwin said of Castilla after sharing a winter of play in Mexico with him. "People love me over there," Castilla said. "I love them, too." (Quoted in Lopez.)

Castilla wrapped up his Major League career in 2006 with 320 home runs, 1,105 runs batted in, and a .276 average. But at 39 he played for Mexico in the 2007 Caribbean Series. "When the players from the other countries hugged me after the game, I couldn't hold back the tears," Castilla said. "I felt very emotional and proud for all my accomplishments." (Quoted in "Vinny Castilla . . .") Castilla did not stay out of baseball long. He took a job as a special assistant to the Rockies' general manager and managed Mexico's national teams in the 2007 Pan American Games and the 2009 World Baseball Classic.

Further Reading

Lopez, Aaron J. "Vinny Castilla Is Jordan of Mexico," Associated Press, March 1, 1999.
"Vinny Castilla retires from baseball after 16 seasons and one final win with Mexico," Associated Press, February 7, 2007.

Cesar Cedeno

When he was young and a raw talent, some scouts thought Cedeno might become one of the greatest all-around players of all-time. Manager Leo Durocher predicted he would be the next Willie Mays. Cedeno, born February 25, 1951, in Santo Domingo, Dominican Republic, did not reach those heights, but he was definitely a star who accomplished much. He made his Major League debut in 1970 at age 19. In a 17-year career, the swift Cedeno batted .285 with 199 home runs, 959 RBIs, and 550 stolen bases. A four-time All-Star in the 1970s and a five-time Gold Glove winner, he almost never made an error in the outfield.

The 6-foot-2, 195-pound Cedeno was fast and strong, but he was injury prone and was haunted for a time by an incident where a girlfriend with him in a hotel room was killed by a gun that discharged. The player was found guilty of involuntary manslaughter in the Dominican, but was fined only $100. The penalty was levied after the prosecution asked for the charges to be dismissed for lack of evidence. Cedeno's great promise was on display early in his career when he batted .320 in 1972 and 1973, but he did not maintain that level. Six times Cedeno stole more than 50 bases and he was as fluid as running water in the outfield.

Cedeno coped with various injuries and high expectations. Alternately he was compared to Mays and Roberto Clemente, but he bristled at the suggestions and said, "I am Cedeno." (Quoted in Mendelson.) Given Cedeno's final statistics that would have been just fine for most players. In the years since his retirement in 1986, Cedeno has stayed active in winter league baseball in Venezuela and the Dominican and worked as a coach in the Washington Nationals' organization.

Further Reading

Mendelson, Abby. "Whatever Happened to Cesar Cedeno?" *Baseball Quarterly*, Winter, 1978–79.

Davey Concepcion

Born June 17, 1948 in Aragua, Venezuela, the lanky, 6-foot-1, 180-pound infielder was a featured player in two special baseball lineages. Davey Concepcion was part of the great tradition of Venezuelan shortstops starting with Chico Carrasquel, and he was one of the regulars in the lineup of the Big Red Machine, the Cincinnati Reds' powerful teams of the 1970s. In a glittering, 19-year career between 1970 and 1988—all of it with Cincinnati—Concepcion was a nine-time National League All-Star.

Concepcion's major connections make him part of Major League lore. The line of star Venezuelan shortstops began with Carrasquel, continued with Luis Aparicio, and ran through Concepcion, all inspirations for younger generations back home. With the Reds, Concepcion formed a superb double-play combination with Hall of Fame second baseman Joe Morgan and wielded a surprisingly strong bat for a middle infielder. His lifetime average was .267 and he batted .280 or higher eight times. He also had a career high 16 homers in 1979 when he drove in a career high 84 runs. For the Reds, Concepcion constituted an additional weapon with his 321 career steals.

"When you play against him you realize he is a very good player, but you don't realize how great he is until you see him day in and day out," said John McNamara, the Reds' manager in the early 1980s. (Quoted in "Davey . . .") Concepcion won five Gold Gloves and earned two World Series championship rings with the Reds.

In 2007, the Reds retired Concepcion's No. 13 uniform in a ceremony at the Great American Ballpark, and the flashy shortstop broke down in tears. "I can't speak, but I'm going to try," he said. "This microphone is the hardest part of my baseball career. Baseball was very easy, this is very hard." (Quoted in McCoy.)

Further Reading

"Davey 'Heart' of Reds," Cincinnati Reds scorebook, 1982.
McCoy, Hal. "Concepcion gets emotional as Reds retire No. 13," *Dayton Daily News*, August 26, 2007.

Jose Contreras

Born December 6, 1971 in Las Martinas, Cuba, Contreras is representative of some of the top Major League ballplayers who had to defect from Communist-ruled Cuba to play professionally. One of Fidel Castro's decrees after becoming dictator put an end to the free flow of Cuban baseball stars to the United States. They were required to stay home and play for the national team in amateur competitions such as the Pan American Games and the Olympics. Any player who sought to make a living at the game had to escape from the island.

One of the greatest of all Cuban amateur pitchers, the right-handed Jose Contreras fled his home county in 2002. Contreras signed with the New York Yankees, later helped the Chicago White Sox win the 2005 World Series and began the 2010 season with the Philadelphia Phillies. (AP Photo/Amy Sancetta)

For years, the 6-foot-4, 225-pound Contreras represented his country with dignity. But as he passed 30 and realized he would never test himself against the best regularly, Contreras defected in Mexico. He surfaced in Miami in October 2002, and at a news conference said he did so because "This is where they play the best baseball." (Quoted in Farrey.) Contreras had to leave his wife and two daughters behind and risked imprisonment if caught, but he became a free agent and signed with the New York Yankees for the 2003 season. He obtained a four-year, $32 million contract.

Contreras spent parts of two pretty fair seasons with New York, going 7–2 and 13–9, but was traded to the Chicago White Sox in 2004, where he blossomed in time to lead the Sox staff with a 15–7 mark. The team won its first World Series in 88 years in 2005 with Contreras starring. Up and down in performance after that, Contreras suffered an Achilles tendon tear late in the 2008 season and it was considered potentially career-ending. Contreras made a remarkably swift recovery and had several special moments on the mound in 2009, but seemed to lose his stuff near the end of the year, again putting his career in jeopardy. When banished to the bullpen, Contreras had a 70–62 Major League record, and he was then traded to the Colorado Rockies.

Further Reading

Farrey, Tom. "Cuban pitcher wants to be free agent," MLB.com, October 10, 2002.

Jose Cruz Sr. and Jose Cruz, Jr., Tommy and Hector Cruz

Born August 8, 1947 in the fishing village of Arroyo, Puerto Rico, father Jose was an outfielder for 19 years, all but one of them in the National League. Son Jose was born April 19, 1974, in the same Puerto Rican community. He has been trying to extend a career that began in 1997 and mostly has played in American League outfields. Jose Sr. was chosen for two All-Star teams and was a solid contributor and very popular player for the Houston Astros, a team that retired his number.

Tommy, one of Jose Sr.'s brothers, born in 1951, played in just seven Major League games over two seasons in the 1970s with a .000 average. Hector, born in 1953, played nine seasons in the National League and hit .225.

Jose Cruz played in 2,353 games, accumulated 2,251 hits, stroked 165 home runs, knocked in 1,077 runs, and batted .284. He topped .300 six times. Cruz was also a slick base stealer, with a high of 44 in a year and a total of 317 steals lifetime. He was a good front-of-the-order man and collected more than his share of walks. Cruz was underrated and he knew it and felt it. "Half the people in America get me mixed up with that guy (Julio Cruz) who plays second base for the White Sox," he said. "I just try to do my job, help my team win, and as far as publicity goes, I just let my statistics talk about me." (Quoted in Stark.) Jose Sr. is a member of the Hispanic Heritage Baseball Museum and Hall of Fame, managed in the Puerto Rican winter league, and has spent 11 years as a coach with the Astros.

Jose Jr. was a heralded player at Rice University, but never developed the consistency of his father. He has a .247 lifetime average while drifting between nine different teams. "It definitely has been quite the roller-coaster career," he said. (Quoted in Forman.)

Further Reading

Forman, Ross. "Baseball runs in the family for Jose Cruz Jr.," *Sports Collector's Digest*, June 11, 1999.
Stark, Jayson. "Jose Cruz: The Big Leagues' Most Unheralded Star," *Baseball Digest*, August, 1985.

Mike Cuellar

Born in Santa Clara, Cuba on May 8, 1937, Cuellar, in his prime, was one of the top pitchers in the American League. In a 15-year Major League career, he won 185 games and he posted four seasons of 20 or more wins. He also won 18 games in a season twice. Cuellar won the 1969 Cy Young Award with the Baltimore Orioles with a 23–11 record and a 2.38 earned run average. In many ways the southpaw was even better the next year when he finished 24–8. That led the American League in wins and winning percentage (.750). Cuellar was also tops with 40 starts and 21 complete games that year.

Capturing the Cy Young (shared with Denny McLain that year) was a milestone for Cuellar—he was the first Latin-American winner of the prize signifying the top pitcher in the league for a year. Cuellar was known for throwing a devastating screwball and of being part of one of the best rotations of all time in 1971, sharing Orioles' starting duties with Jim Palmer, Dave McNally, and Pat Dobson. That group was one of only two foursomes to win 20 games for a team in the same season. Known as a player who kept his teammates loose in the clubhouse, Cuellar received the nickname "Crazy Horse."

Cuellar was a four-time All-Star. As one of the Cuban pitchers who came to the United States before Castro's coup, Cuellar moved to Florida after his retirement. Besides his screwball, Cuellar, who did not have the speed in his arsenal of many top starters, also fooled batters with his change-up. Cuellar was a durable innings eater in the rotation, as well, throwing between 246 and 297 innings in a season eight times. Cuellar died at age 73 in 2010.

Carlos Delgado

Born June 25, 1972 in Aguadilla, Puerto Rico, age and injuries are starting to catch up to the hard-hitting Delgado. But he still has enough pop left in his bat to reach some serious slugging milestones before he retires. Seventeen years into a sterling career that has lit up pitchers for the Toronto Blue Jays and New York Mets, Delgado is still one of the most feared hitters in the game today. Already the holder of the most home runs by any Puerto Rican, Delgado is closing in on the cherished milestone of 500 with 473 taters. He has 2,038 hits and his RBI total is 1,512, another superior mark.

Delgado broke into the majors briefly in 1993 when he was still a catcher, but the Blue Jays quickly converted him into a first baseman. Delgado has smacked more than 40 home runs in a season three times and has hit at least 30 homers 11 times. A top-notch RBI producer, Delgado led the American League with 145 in 2003 and has driven in at least 100 nine times. Three other times he has topped 90. On September 25, 2003, Delgado gained a share of the Major League record for home runs in one game: He hit four in a 10–8 victory over Tampa Bay.

A pacifist by nature, Delgado has protested against militaristic situations on many occasions. As an anti-war activist, when ballparks in the United States

Slugger Carlos Delgado, a long-time star mostly with the Toronto Blue Jays, is closing in on 500 home runs after 17 years in the big leagues. The Puerto Rican first baseman is a two-time All-Star and three-time Silver Slugger Award winner. Delgado tied the record of four home runs in a game in 2003. (AP Photo/Matt Houston)

began playing "God Bless America," Delgado disappeared down the tunnel to his team's clubhouse. It was a quiet protest, though eventually it was noticed and fans began shouting, "USA! USA!" at him. Delgado felt he must take the action because he thinks the U.S. invasion of Iraq "is the stupidest war ever." (Quoted in Walker.) When a dispute arose over the continued use of a U.S. naval base in Vieques, Puerto Rico, Delgado also protested the continued presence of the ships. "You're dealing with health, with poverty, with the roots of an entire community," he said, "both economically and environmentally. This is way bigger than just a political or military issue." (Quoted in Baker.)

Further Reading

Baker, Geoff. "Citizen Carlos," *San Juan Star*, July 3, 2004.
Walker, Ben. "Blue Jays' Delgado Protests War in Iraq," Associated Press, July 21, 2004.

Bobby Estalella (grandfather) and Bobby Estalella (grandson)

Born April 25, 1911 in Cardenas, Cuba, the older Estalella was an outfielder who played nine seasons of Major League ball starting in 1935. When he jumped to the fledgling Mexican League in the 1940s, he was suspended by

Commissioner Happy Chandler, but later reinstated. The second Bobby Estalella is the grandson of the original. He was born in Hialeah, Florida on August 23, 1974 and spent nine seasons in the majors as a catcher, mostly as a backup starting in 1996.

The older Estalella stood 5-foot-9 and weighed 180 pounds. Heralded in the minors when he led his league in home runs and hit far north of .300, Estalella had an ungainly running form, but always did the job with the bat. A solid, but not spectacular RBI man, he hit for a quite respectable .282 average during his career with the Washington Senators and Philadelphia Athletics. However, when he returned to the majors after a four-year absence in the Mexican League in 1949, Estallela played only another handful of games. He was a hero, though, in Mexico. In 1935, when Estalella broke into the majors, the barrier banning dark-skinned Americans was in full effect. Much later it was explored in a Spanish-speaking publication that Estalella might well have been the first black ballplayer in the twentieth century. But that remained murky territory. Estalella spoke little English when he joined the Senators but gradually educated himself, and much later he specifically identified himself as Latino, not black.

The second Estatella knew little about his grandfather's career until, at the age of 13, he discovered a 1930s baseball card portraying him. That was an inspiration and the younger Estalella did make the majors with the Phillies, the first of six teams he spent time with in compiling a .216 average.

Tony Fernandez

Born June 30, 1962 in San Pedro de Macoris in the Dominican Republic, the town that grows baseball players the way other communities grow fruit, Fernandez made his Major League debut with the Toronto Blue Jays in 1983 and spent 17 years in the big leagues, recording a .288 batting average. A marvelous fielder, Fernandez twice led the American League in fielding percentage and once led the National League in fielding as a first-rate second baseman.

Fernandez was best known for his association with the Blue Jays—he was on their 1993 World Series championship team—and was employed by the club four different times. Fernandez also played a season in Japan, making him a rare three-country player. Fernandez was a five-time All-Star and a four-time Gold Glove winner in 2,158 games. Fernandez swatted a playoff home run to help the Cleveland Indians win a pennant, but his making a crucial error helped prevent the Indians from winning a World Series. At certain times, Fernandez expressed concern about how Latino ballplayers were viewed. "They say racism is over," he said.

"I don't know about that. I think because we are from so-called Third World countries, some people label us as having bad attitudes. What is a bad attitude? It's telling the truth." (Quoted in Beaton.)

More dangerous with his feet than his muscles, Fernandez was a sterling lead-off hitter who stole at least 10 bases 11 times. Despite traveling great distances, Fernandez never forgot his home. He started a foundation to help underprivileged children in the Dominican in 1995. Fernandez was also very active in providing financial assistance and his own labor to hurricane relief efforts in the Dominican in 1998, and he oversees a religious retreat on the island. "I've had many thrills and highlights," said Fernandez, who retired in 2001. (Quoted in Moriah.)

Further Reading

Beaton, Rod. "Reds' Fernandez: Latino players don't get treated fairly," *USA Today*, May 12, 1994.
Moriah, David. "Steady personality keeps Fernandez in the game," *Sports Collector's Digest*, January 15, 1999.

Ed Figueroa

Born October 14, 1948 in Ciales, Puerto Rico, Figueroa enervated his home island in 1978 as he notched his first (and only) 20-victory season for the New York Yankees. Figueroa was a fixture on the news as Puerto Ricans watched eagerly each time his turn in the rotation arrived. The excitement revolved around pride in their own seeking to become the first Puerto Rican to achieve that 20-win milestone. In 1976, Figueroa came close, finishing 19–10. "I've come this far and I want to make it," Figueroa said that time. "It's something I've been thinking about it all season. Winning 20 will be a big thing for me." (Quoted in Foley.)

Even though he was informed so many TV sets back home were tuned it to watch him twirl for the Yankees, Figueroa ended that season short of his goal. In 1978, he came through, finishing 20–9. "It means so much to me and the people of Puerto Rico," said Figueroa when he took his first crack at the mark. (Quoted in Foley.) Three decades later, Figueroa remains the only Puerto Rican hurler with a 20-win season on his resume.

Figueroa broke into the majors with the California Angels and despite a 16–13 record his second season, the right-hander was packaged in a trade to the Yankees. Wearing a thick mustache, Figueroa was easily recognized, but did most of his talking with his fastball. In eight seasons with four American League teams he compiled a record of 80–67 with a 3.51 earned run average. Figueroa's longevity was cut short by military service with the Marines in Vietnam on the front end and by injuries on the back end. He was just 33 when he retired.

Further Reading

Foley, Red. "Puerto Rico Eyes Figueroa's 20-Bid," *New York Daily News*, September 29, 1976.

Julio Franco

Born August 23, 1958 in Hato Mayor, Dominican Republic, Franco was a true wonder of the game, not officially retiring until he was 49 years old. Franco broke into the majors in 1982 and played his last game in 2007. He retired early in 2008 after winter ball in Mexico. He began his career as a shortstop with the Phillies, shifted to second base, where he had his greatest success with the Cleveland Indians and Texas Rangers, and had late-in-career success with the Atlanta Braves in the early 2000s.

Periodically, when Major League clubs termed Franco too old, he landed in Japan (two separate seasons), or Mexico (two separate seasons), and in South Korea. In 1998, at age 40, Franco batted .423 in 93 games in Mexico. With a lifetime average of .298, with 2,586 hits, 173 home runs, and 1,194 runs batted in, Franco recorded a fine set of big-league statistics. In 1991, the 6-foot, 190-pounder batted .341 and won the American League batting title for the Rangers. Franco was a three-time All-Star (winning the MVP award in the 1990 game), and five times won the Silver Slugger award as the best hitter at his position.

In 2006, Franco was asked if he was an inspiration to middle-aged men, but offered a serious reply: "Kids need more leadership right now." One way he stayed young, Franco said, was by eschewing fried foods and eating healthy. "What nature produces," he said, "I eat. Doesn't matter how horrible it tastes." (Quoted in Serby.) In 2004, Franco became the oldest regular position player in Major League history when he was the Braves' first baseman. He was the last player active who was born in the 1950s. Along the way he became the game's oldest player to pinch run and to hit a grand slam.

Further Reading

Serby, Steve. "Serby's Sunday Q&A with Julio Franco," *New York Post*, June 25, 2006.

Andres Galarraga

"The Big Cat" was born June 18, 1961 in Caracas, Venezuela. The powerfully built, 6-foot-3, 235-pound first baseman started playing in Venezuela as a 16-year-old, then enjoyed a 19-year Major League career as a player popular for his offensive stats and his friendly demeanor. While hitting .288 with 399 home runs and 1,425 runs batted in, Galarraga also overcame a bout with cancer. A bone in his lower back was afflicted.

Greeted as a hero upon his visits to Venezuela and beloved by his teammates, Galarraga made friends wherever he played. "Nobody in baseball will say anything bad about the guy," said Braves third baseman Chipper Jones. "He's a great teammate." (Quoted in Beaton.)

A five-time All-Star with the Montreal Expos, Colorado Rockies, and Atlanta Braves, Galarraga earned two Gold Gloves, two Silver Slugger awards, and the National League Comeback Player of the Year award in 2000 after he missed the entire 1999 season with non-Hodgkin's lymphoma. "The worst part is not to be in uniform," said Galarraga when he realized he would miss the whole season. But he was feeling upbeat compared to learning his diagnosis. "I felt like I'd die the next two or three days," he said. (Quoted in Beaton.)

The illness came back in November 2003, but so did Galarraga in 2004, though he played only briefly with the Angels before retiring at age 43. "Playing has been a part of my life for so long, but I just felt this was the right time to give a younger guy a chance to play," he said. (Quoted in "Big Cat . . .")

Further Reading

Beaton, Rod. "Galarraga says support 'makes me feel so strong,' " *USA Today*, March 18, 1999.
"Big Cat retires at 43 years old," Associated Press, March 30, 2005.

Nomar Garciaparra

Born July 23, 1973 in Whittier, California, of Mexican heritage, Garciaparra began his career with the Boston Red Sox in 1996 with a short warm-up for a stupendous official rookie season of 1967. He had been an All-American at Georgia Tech, but no one expected Garciaparra to burst upon the scene so dramatically. The young shortstop became American League Rookie of the Year by hitting 30 home runs, driving in 98, batting .306 and collecting 209 hits. He had a league-leading 11 triples and even stole 22 bases.

A Mexican American who once drove in 10 RBIs in a game for the Red Sox, Nomar Garciaparra was the 1997 American League Rookie of the Year. Garciaparra won two batting titles for Boston, but fell out of favor with management in a contract dispute and was shuffled off to the Chicago Cubs in 2004 despite five All-Star appearances for the BoSox. Injuries have slowed his career and led to his retirement in 2010. (AP Photo/Elise Amendola)

Fans at Fenway Park chanted "Noh-mahr!" Garciaparra picked up two batting titles while hitting .357 and .372, respectively, in 1999 and 2000. Garciaparra was a six-time All-Star, but a variety of injuries interfered with his career. The best hitting shortstop in team history was a crowd favorite and Garciaparra and the team's fan base were shocked when he was dealt to the Chicago Cubs while hitting .321 in 2004 because his contract was expiring.

From there Garciaparra became a free agent and joined the Los Angeles Dodgers, but then he shifted from team to team and fought off injuries that diminished his performance. He retired in the spring of 2010 as a Red Sox with a lifetime batting average of .313. Known for his lengthy, fidgety ritual with his batting gloves and bat each time he stepped into the batter's box, Garciaparra also made headlines when he married U.S. Olympic soccer star Mia Hamm. Growing up, Garciaparra joked that his baseball hero was Bugs Bunny. He remembered watching a cartoon of the peripatetic rabbit fielding every position. He thought it was pretty cool; still does. In 2005, while walking near Boston Harbor, Garciaparra dove into the water and rescued two women, fulfilling the hero role off the diamond.

Juan Gonzalez

Born October 20, 1969 in Arecibo, Puerto Rico, the slugging outfielder won the American League Most Valuable Player award twice with the Texas Rangers, in 1996 and 1998, and was a three-time All-Star. A slugger who crunched 434 homers lifetime, the 6-foot-3, 220-pound Gonzalez had a powerful build. Known for his prodigious blasts, one of Gonzalez's nicknames was "Juan Gone." At his best, Gonzalez terrorized pitchers. He led the AL in homers with 43 in 1992 and with 46 the next year. In 1998, Gonzalez led the league with 157 runs batted in. That same season he clouted 45 home runs and 50 doubles.

Life was not always quiet around Gonzalez. He was divorced three times and in the early part of his career was outspoken about his likes and dislikes after coming to the mainland in 1986 and adjusting to cultural differences. He feuded with the media and was frustrated when injuries disrupted his seasons. As Gonzalez matured, there was more focus on his game. He developed a friendship with George W. Bush when Bush was managing partner of the Rangers and later, when Bush inhabited the White House, he twice invited Gonzalez for visits. "I think I have found peace of mind," Gonzalez said. (Quoted in Caldwell.)

A six-time Silver Slugger award winner and winner of the Home Run Derby at the 1993 All-Star game, Gonzalez finished with a .295 batting average and 1,404 RBIs. Near the end of his career, Gonzalez struggled with back problems. Just when he thought he had that licked, he suffered a serious hamstring tear and retired in 2005. His name was mentioned as someone suspected of taking performance-enhancing drugs, but nothing was proven. Gonzalez denied ever taking steroids.

Further Reading

Caldwell, Dave. "Juan on Juan," *Dallas Morning News*, May 13, 1996.

Vladimir Guerrero and Wilton Guerrero

Born February 9, 1976 in Nizao, Dominican Republic, Vladimir Guerrero is regarded as a free swinger who can hit any type of pitch. Wilton was born October 24, 1974 in Don Gregorio, Dominican. By 2009, and then playing with the Los Angeles Angels, Vladimir had recorded 13 seasons of hitting at least .300, all but one of his Major League campaigns. Remarkably consistent, Guerrero became a star with the Montreal Expos and has continued to be a top-notch hitter with the Angels. The 2004 American League Most Valuable Player, Guerrero hit .345 in 2000 and has regularly hit in the .320s.

An eight-time All-Star who reached 407 home runs in 2009 and who is on his way to 3,000 hits as long as he stays healthy, Vladimir Guerrero was a critical piece of the offense for the Angels as they won five American League Western Division crowns in six years starting in 2004, before joining the Texas

Rangers in 2010. Guerrero joined the Angels in 2004 as part of a $70 million deal. Vladimir also passed 1,300 career RBIs in 2009. During the 1999 season, Vladimir put together a 31-game hitting streak and in a 2003 game he hit for the cycle against the Mets. Wearing his hair in dreadlocks is a Vladimir trademark as is saying little about his achievements, particularly because he speaks only limited English.

Wilton Guerrero broke into the majors with the Dodgers in 1996 and played eight years as a second baseman and utility infielder. His lifetime average was .282. The Guerrero brothers teamed up to build a modern grocery store in Don Gregorio, a community of 19,000 people, a factory manufacturing concrete blocks, and opened a hardware store. They provide the employment base for their home area. "I feel a sense of responsibility, especially with Latino fans," Vladimir Guerrero said. (Quoted in Shaikin.)

Further Reading

Shaikin, Bill. "The Angels' $70 Million Homebody," *Los Angeles Times*, February 14, 2004.

Guillermo (Willie) Hernandez

Born November 14, 1954 in Aguada, Puerto Rico, Hernandez achieved the ultimate when he was named winner of the Cy Young Award and the Most Valuable Player award in leading the Detroit Tigers to the American League pennant and a World Series title in 1984. Hernandez appeared in 80 games, all in relief, finished with a 9–3 record and 32 saves and a 1.92 earned run average. Hernandez was the go-to guy, the late-inning rescue man.

It was a year so special that Hernandez could not single out just one great memory. "Almost the whole season," he said made for a highlight. "When you have success and you go out to the field and have a great time, those things you never forget." (Quoted in Sipple.) Hernandez blew just one save all season. That year he made the first of his three All-Star teams, too. Hernandez pitched for 13 years in the majors and had a 70–63 record with 147 saves and a 3.38 ERA, all between 1977 and 1989 with the Chicago Cubs and the Tigers.

The 1984 campaign stood out. "I knew he was going to be good," Tigers manager Sparky Anderson said. "I told everyone we traded for a premier relief pitcher, but I didn't know he was going to be this good." (Quoted in Gage.) Hernandez said winning the Cy Young and MVP was hard to believe. "It was like

I have another win, like winning the World Series again," he said. "I feel very proud of myself. I know the people in Puerto Rico feel very proud." (Quoted in "Hernandez . . .")

Further Reading

Gage, Tom. "A.L. Pitcher: Tigers' Hernandez Was Nearly Perfect," *Detroit News*, October 29, 1984.
"Hernandez seventh pitcher to win MVP," Associated Press, November 7, 1984.
Sipple, George. "Hernandez: All those games are unbelievable," *Detroit Free Press*, July 8, 2005.

Orlando Hernandez and Livan Hernandez

Orlando claimed to be born October 11, 1965 in Villa Clara, Cuba and was famously nicknamed "El Duque" for his magnificent hurling with the Cuban national team. Some claimed he was older, however. Livan was apparently born February 20, 1975 in the same town. The half-brother pitchers are Cuban defectors who escaped Fidel Castro's law against playing professionally. When he signed with the New York Yankees in 1998 as a free agent, Orlando told a story of fleeing Cuba in a 30-foot fishing boat that braved the waves of the Atlantic. Details of the flight to freedom were later questioned but not disproved. The half-brothers became a symbol in the United States of the repressive Castro regime and the political tensions between the two Western Hemisphere countries.

With his distinctive high leg kick (with the left leg almost folded in half), Orlando took New York by storm. He went 12–4 in 21 starts in 1998 and made the American League All-Star team in 1999 with a 17–9 record. That year he was MVP of the American League Championship Series. Hernandez, who compiled a 90–65 record in 10 seasons, was a member of three Yankee World Series titlists and won a fourth championship with the Chicago White Sox in 2005. "He's a warrior," the Yankees' premier reliever Mariano Rivera said of "El Duque." (Quoted in Kepner.)

Although younger than Orlando, Livan defected in 1995 and was a member of the 1997 World Series-winning Florida Marlins. He won the MVP award in the National League Championship Series that year and the MVP award in the World Series. A two-time All-Star, Livan was still in the majors in 2009 and had a 156–151 career record as he finished up the season with the Washington Nationals.

A one-time Cuban amateur and Olympic star with a quirky delivery that recalls Luis Tiant's moves, Orlando Hernandez lived a dream by winning four World Series titles with the New York Yankees. He was the Most Valuable Player of the 1999 American League Championship Series. Hernandez retired after the 2007 season with 90 big-league wins. (AP Photo/Osamu Honda)

Further Reading

Kepner, Tyler. "Hernandez: The Pinstripes Make the Man," *New York Times*, July 12, 2004.

Teddy Higuera

For a time, fans thought Higuera was the second coming of Fernando Valenzuela. They even looked alike. Born in Los Mochis, Mexico on November 9, 1958, Higuera made a big splash with the Milwaukee Brewers for a few seasons, but had his career cut short by injury. Like Valenzuela, Higuera threw left-handed. Like Valenzuela, he had a portly rather than a sculpted look to his physique. He was listed at 5-foot-10, 178 pounds, but still featured a low 90s mph fastball.

After breaking into the Mexican League at 20, Higuera became an even more popular figure back home when he worked his way into the Brewers' starting rotation as a 26-year-old rookie in 1985. His unexpectedly swift rise produced a 15–8 season with a 3.90 earned run average. His knack for winning earned him many accolades despite his inexperience. Higuera was not even a favorite to make the final roster that season. "The big thing about Teddy is he is very composed on the mound," said Brewers coach Tony Muser. "He's never been intimidated about where he's pitched or certain hitters. His composure and the way he's handled himself on the mound have been a big part of his moving up the ladder so quickly." (Quoted in Covitz.)

Higuera improved quickly. In 1986 he made his only All-Star team and finished 20–11 with a 2.79 ERA. Higuera went 18–10 in his third season and 16–9 in his fourth. Back and ankle injuries reared up in 1989, with Higuera limited to 22 starts and a 9–6 record. A torn rotator cuff in 1991 effectively ended his career. Attempts to come back proved futile, and Higuera had to retire prematurely after nine seasons with a 94–64 career record. Higuera remains a significant figure in Mexican baseball today after coaching with the national team in the World Baseball Classics and pre-Olympic qualifying tournament.

Further Reading

Covitz, Randy. "Brewers rookie looks like a winner," *Kansas City Times*, June 5, 1985.

Jaime Jarrin

Jarrin is the Spanish-speaking Vince Scully for Los Angeles Dodgers' fans who in some quarters is called "The Golden Voice." Born December 10, 1935 in Quito, Ecuador, Jarrin is the Dodgers' representative to the Latino community in the city of Angels and has been since 1959. Growing up in Ecuador, Jarrin knew he wanted to be a broadcaster and got his start in radio at age 16. When he came to the United States in 1955, however, he had never seen a baseball game.

Jarrin's timing was right. He settled in Los Angeles ahead of the Dodgers, who moved west for the 1958 season. With foresight, Jarrin's station went after the Spanish-language rights and nabbed them. For the first several years, Jarrin did not travel on the road with the team, instead re-creating the action in the studio as many other English-speaking stations did with their home teams around the majors. From 1962 to 1984, Jarrin never missed a Dodgers' game, more than 4,000 in all. During that time period he gained prominence by acting as the official team interpreter for Fernando Valenzuela at the height of his fame. Jarrin broke his own streak by choosing to broadcast the Summer Olympics in Los Angeles in 1984.

A master of all other sports, as well (particularly boxing and its title bouts), Jarrin received the highest honor a baseball broadcaster can receive in 1998 when he was awarded the Ford Frick Award from the Baseball Hall of Fame and was inducted into the broadcast wing of the Hall. He was the second Hispanic broad-caster, after Buck Canel, to be singled out for that recognition. "Jaime Jarrin is a real treasure for the Dodgers and baseball fans around the world," said then-Dodgers' owner Walter O'Malley in 1998. (Quoted in Los Angeles . . .)

Further Reading

Los Angeles Dodgers press release, February 2, 1998.

Julian and Stan Javier

Born August 9, 1936 in San Francisco de Macoris, Dominican Republic, Julian Javier played 12 of his 13 Major League seasons with the St. Louis Cardinals. Born January 1, 1964, son Stan (named after Julian's teammate and friend Hall of Famer Stan Musial), broke into the majors in 1984 and played 17 seasons as an outfielder for several teams.

Julian was a table-setter, reaching base on singles and walks for the 1964 and 1967 champion Cardinals, and waiting for the team's power hitters to utilize his speed and drive him in. A two-time All-Star, Julian had a lifetime batting average of .257. He was a prominent starting fixture at a time when there were a limited number of Latino players in the majors. He signed for a mere $500 bonus when he joined the Pirates organization in 1956. Javier was also a rare player who wore glasses. Julian had worn the number six his whole life and when someone teased him about the Cardinals giving him 25, Javier said, "I think somebody else on this club has got six," he said. (Quoted in Hershkowitz.) That numeral was Musial's.

Stan Javier inherited his father's speed and stole 246 bases in his career. He also won a world championship as a member of the 1989 Oakland A's. Stan's lifetime average was .269. In an odd distinction, Stan Javier hit the first inter-league home run while playing for the San Francisco Giants against the Texas Rangers when Major League baseball adopted its new policy in 1997. Both Javiers have stayed active in the sport in the Dominican. Stan was general manager of the 2006 and 2009 Dominican teams in the World Baseball Classic. Julian founded a kids league now called the Roberto Clemente League and an expansion winter ball franchise.

Further Reading

Hershkowitz, Mickey. "Julian Javier Is Key to Cardinal 'Jopes,' " *Houston Post*, April 29, 1962.

Andruw Jones

Born April 23, 1977 in Willemstad, Netherlands Antilles, Jones is the first player from his country to reach the majors. A superstar with all-around ability, the 6-foot-1, 240-pound Jones electrified Atlanta Braves fans with his raw tools. The 1998 campaign represented Jones's breakthrough. As a starting center fielder he swatted 31 home runs, drove in 90, and stole 27 bases. That year began a string of 10 straight 20-homer seasons, including 2005 when Jones smashed a National League-leading 51 and also led the league with 128 RBIs.

"I've likened him to a comet streaking across the baseball (landscape)," said Braves general manager John Scheurholz before Jones reached the big club. "He is a superbly gifted player and ready to be a productive major leaguer." (Quoted in Winston.) At the time, Jones was just 19 and was recognized as the Minor

Andruw Jones was a wunderkind, bursting upon the unsuspecting baseball fan out of The Netherlands Antilles. Jones broke into the majors for the Atlanta Braves in 1996 and has been a five-time All-Star and 10-time center field Gold Glove winner. Jones' stats have showed premature signs of age lately, but he was trying to make a comeback with the Chicago White Sox in 2010. (AP Photo/Gregory Smith)

League Player of the Year. It didn't take long for Jones to draw comparisons to Willie Mays. He destroyed the opposition with his bat and made diving catches in the outfield, playing the same position as Mays. "He's the greatest I've ever seen," said teammate Greg Maddux, a pitcher destined to become a Hall of Famer. (Quoted in Kernan.)

Never a hitter for average, Jones five times knocked in at least 100 runs for the Braves and had four other seasons when he topped 90. Jones was a five-time All-Star and won 10 Gold Gloves. He played on Atlanta's 1996 and 1999 World Series teams. However, in 2007, after showing an abrupt decline in production, Jones signed as a free agent with the Dodgers. Jones reported overweight and eventually had knee surgery, and washed out in Los Angeles. In 2009—still just 32—he tried to rejuvenate his career with the Texas Rangers and joined the Chicago White Sox in 2010.

Further Reading

Kernan, Kevin. "Mates: Andruw is just a-Mays-ing," *New York Post*, July 3, 2000.
Winston, Lisa. "There are few like Andruw," *USA Today Baseball Weekly*, September 25/ October 1, 1996.

Roberto Kelly

Born October 1, 1964 in Panama City, Panama, Kelly was one of the rare major leaguers from his home country. Kelly broke into the majors in 1987 with the New York Yankees and played 14 big-league seasons while hitting .290. At various times Kelly displayed a mix of skills. He led the American League by playing in all 162 games in 1990 and was a two-time All-Star—with the Yankees and Cincinnati Reds.

The biggest challenge Kelly had in 1988 and 1989 was winning a job with the Yankees while Panama suffered with political upheaval. He ran up large phone bills trying to stay in touch with his wife, daughter, parents, and grandparents while trying to make the New York roster out of spring training in 1988. At home following the 1988 season, Kelly had a cocked gun placed to his head by military loyalists of dictator Manuel Noriega. One of the soldiers recognized Kelly as a ballplayer and prevailed on the others to let him go. "I was barely breathing," Kelly said. "There wasn't much going through my head except that I thought I was going to die." (Quoted in Kay.)

Despite all of his worries, Kelly batted .302 in 1989, the first of five .300 seasons. Kelly had some problems in the field, however, with two high-profile misses of fly balls that clunked him on the head; those mistakes had long life spans because of instant replay. "I try not to bring it to the park with me," Kelly said of Panama's woes. (Quoted in Spencer.) After retirement, Kelly became a minor-league manager in the San Francisco Giants' system and then joined the big club as a coach.

Further Reading

Kay, Michael. "Surviving Panamania," *New York Daily News*, date missing, National Baseball Hall of Fame Library archives.
Spencer, Lyle. "Kelly's Heart Back In Panama," *New York Post*, May 19, 1989.

Hector Lopez

Born in Colon, Panama on July 7, 1929, Lopez was the first player from his country to become a starting player in the majors when he joined the Kansas City Athletics in 1955. For the Yankees, Lopez was the third outfielder, alongside center fielder Mickey Mantle and right-fielder Roger Maris on the 1961 Yankees World Series title team that some call the best ever. Lopez also played on the 1962 Series champs and was part of five pennant winners in New York during his 12-year career that ended with a .269 average.

With Kansas City in 1958, Lopez hit three home runs in one game against the Washington Senators. He hit 136 homers in his career. Lopez was inspired to become a baseball player after watching the Yankees' Phil Rizzuto and the Brooklyn Dodgers' Jackie Robinson play when both teams conducted spring training in Panama in 1947. Lopez's finest hitting seasons were for the A's. In 1959, when he split his time between Kansas City and New York, Lopez clouted 22 homers, drove in 93 runs and hit .283.

Lopez hit a three-run homer and drove in seven runs in the five games of the 1961 World Series against Cincinnati. He enjoyed the winning, but didn't enjoy being shuttled around from position to position. "In '60 they had me playing here, there and everywhere," Lopez said. "I guess that's what they thought was best for the ball club, to be an all-around ballplayer." (Quoted in Sacucci.) Lopez's longevity in the majors inspired a younger generation of Panamanian players, but in 1969 he quietly became a barrier breaker of a different sort. Named manager of the Texas Rangers' International League team in Buffalo made Lopez the first black manager of an AAA team, six years before the majors had their first black manager.

Hector Lopez, from Panama, was a solid outfielder for the New York Yankees in the early 1960s alongside Mickey Mantle and Roger Maris and also contributed at third base. Overshadowed by many of his glittering teammates during the Yankees Dynasty run, Lopez was the first black manager at the AAA level when he took over the Buffalo Bisons in 1969. (Rogers Photo Archive/Getty images)

Further Reading

Sacucci, Fluffy. "Hector Lopez: Integral part of Big Pinstripe Machine," *Sports Collector's Digest*, November 9, 1990.

Javy Lopez

Born November 5, 1970 in Ponce, Puerto Rico, Lopez was a distinguished catcher mostly with the Atlanta Braves. He broke into the majors in 1992 and played 15 seasons, retiring in 2006. A three-time National League All-Star, Lopez's best year was 2003 when in only 129 games he smacked 43 home runs, drove in 109 runs, and batted .328. That set a new single-season record for home runs by a catcher. Lopez's slugging percentage was .687 that year.

Lopez tried to continue his career for two years beyond 2006, but he appeared to lose the pop in his bat and the snap in his arm. His lifetime totals are an impressive .287 average with 260 home runs and 864 RBIs. Lopez was part of the Braves' 1995 World Series title team and he won the National League Comeback Player of the Year award in 2003 after batting just .233 in 109 games in 2002. In 1996, Lopez was the MVP of the National League Championship Series when he hit .542. "That's what you want to do," Lopez said, "come through when your team needs you most." (Quoted in Beaton.)

Just one of the many stars on Atlanta's pitching-rich winning teams, Lopez moved more into the public eye after the World Series championship. Making a sports card show appearance, Lopez discovered he had a new generation of female fans who viewed him as a rock star or movie star. He was a family man, though. Lopez expressed sorrow in being cut from the Braves' roster and forcing his hand on retirement. "It's just that the hitting wasn't there and unfortunately I didn't throw the guy out on the stealing attempts," he said. "That's a concern. I don't blame them." (Quoted in "Longtime . . .")

Further Reading

Beaton, Rod. "Lopez hits .542 for MVP," *USA Today*, October 18, 1996.
"Longtime catcher ends career after getting sent down," SI.com, March 22, 2008.

Felix Mantilla

Born July 29, 1934 in Isabela, Puerto Rico, Mantilla was primarily a backup short-stop and infielder during his 11-year career that began with the Milwaukee Braves in 1956, though he reached new individual heights near the tail-end of his career with the Boston Red Sox. Mantilla was a part-time starter and fill-in on Milwau-kee's World Series teams of 1957 and 1958, and he scored the winning run in the 13th inning after Pirates hurler Harvey Haddix lost his 12-inning perfect game in 1959.

During his time with the Braves, Mantilla roomed with Hank Aaron on the road. He found a new group of fans in 1962 when he was lost to the new New York Mets in the expansion draft. Proving it wasn't his fault, Mantilla hit .275 in 141 games for the team described as the worst in the modern baseball era. Better known for his glove than his stick, Mantilla still batted .261 lifetime and in his one All-Star season with the Red Sox in 1965 he hit 18 home runs, drove in 92 and batted .275. In 1964, Mantilla cracked a career high 30 homers with Boston.

His unexpected prowess with the bat ensured that the Red Sox would find a place in the starting lineup for Mantilla, a problem for most of his career.

In fact, even after swatting the 30 dingers in 1964, Mantilla arrived in 1965 spring training unaware of where he would play. "Nobody knows," Mantilla said when a reporter asked him. "That's a secret every year. This winter I played some first base in Puerto Rico." (Quoted in Claflin.) Indeed, although second base was his true home, Mantilla found himself at first base for part of that year.

Further Reading

Claflin, Larry. "'65 RBI Champ, Handyman's Torrid Tempo No Surprise to Hub Fans," *Boston Record-American*, June 12, 1965.

Jose Mendez

Born March 19, 1887 in Cardenas, Cuba, the dark-skinned Mendez was a star pitcher with Cuban and American teams featuring black players, because skin color made him unwanted in the majors. Manager of the famed Kansas City Monarchs from 1920 to 1926, Mendez was elected to the National Baseball Hall of Fame in 2006. Mendez, who stood 5-foot-8 and weighed 170 pounds, was a right-hander who began pitching in 1908 and toured the United States with the Cuban Stars and other teams until 1914.

Although statistics were not always reported and recorded, in 1909 Mendez was said to compile a 44–2 record as a barnstormer. J. L. Wilkinson, later the Hall of Fame owner of the Monarchs, sponsored a touring team called the All-Nations Stars and Mendez pitched for that club between 1912 and 1917. He then suffered a serious arm injury and switched to shortstop for a couple of seasons. Mendez was just as dominating a pitcher when he threw in Cuban leagues' ball. With the Monarchs in the 1920s, Mendez regained his form. Acting as player-manager it was reported that he won about 70 percent of his games and helped carry the Monarchs to three straight pennants between 1923 and 1925.

There were reputable witnesses to Mendez's excellence, notably Hall of Fame manager John McGraw, who expressed regret that he couldn't sign the pitcher for his New York Giants because he was black. "(If) Mendez was a white man (McGraw) would pay $30,000 for his release. (He is) sort of Walter Johnson and Grover Cleveland Alexander rolled into one." (Quoted in Hall of Fame . . .) Mendez died October 31, 1928 in Havana, but nearly 80 years later was selected for inclusion into the Hall of Fame after a special committee was convened to investigate nominees among black players shut out of the majors before 1947.

Further Reading

Baseball Hall of Fame press release, January 23, 2006.

Omar Minaya

Born in the Dominican Republic on November 10, 1958, Minaya became the first Hispanic to become a Major League general manager in 2002 when he joined the Montreal Expos. In 2004, Minaya returned to the New York Mets, where he served his front office apprenticeship, as general manager of that club, a job he currently still holds. Although he was born in the Dominican, Minaya's family moved to Queens in New York when he was eight years old. He retained the Dominican attitude toward baseball, though. Reflecting what has become evident to the world, Minaya said baseball is in the blood of Dominicans, who find the sport almost as essential as taking their next breath.

Minaya dreamed of becoming a Major League baseball player and was drafted by the Oakland Athletics in 1978. He played in the minors, in Italy, and in the Dominican, but could not reach the majors. Injuries finished his playing career and Minaya joined the Texas Rangers as a scout in 1985. After about a decade, Minaya went to work for the Mets' front office, rising to assistant general manager his first time around with the team. When he got the top job, Minaya was determined to bring the Mets a World Series title. Given an expansive budget, Minaya made headlines by signing Pedro Martinez, Billy Wagner, Carlos Delgado, and Carlos Beltran to beef up the roster.

Life with the Mets did not go smoothly for Minaya in 2008 and 2009 as the team faltered, partially due to an epidemic of injuries. Minaya was embroiled in the controversial firings of manager Willie Randolph and vice president for development Tony Bernazard and an unseemly argument with a New York sportswriter.

Bengie, Jose and Yadier Molina

The Catching Molina Brothers sounds like a circus act, but it is a Major League dynasty of sorts, with all three natives of Puerto Rico holding down backstop jobs in the big leagues simultaneously. Bengie was born July 20, 1974 and plays for the San Francisco Giants. Jose was born June 3, 1975 and plays for the New York Yankees. And Yadier was born July 13, 1982 and plays for the St. Louis Cardinals.

All three Molinas are renowned for their fielding capabilities and another trade-mark is a strong throwing arm. Bengie carries the biggest stick at the plate.

The trio was heavily influenced by father Benjamin, who is the all-time hits leader in Puerto Rican amateur league play, as well as a tool manufacturer in a factory. At times when the boys were young, the family was so poor that the kids had just one meal a day, but still the dad took his sons out to play ball every night. The players' success stems from their father, Bengie said. "It's because of all the hard work he did," he said. (Quoted in Foster and Shaikin.)

All three catchers are sturdily built receivers, with Bengie and Yadier listed at 5-foot-11 and 225 pounds and Jose listed as 6-foot-2 and 245 pounds. Bengie broke into the majors in 1998 with the Angels, but his best hitting years en route to a life-time average of .276 have come with the Giants where he has had home-run seasons of 19, 19, and 16, and he drove in a career high 95 runs in 2008. After a brief trial with the Chicago Cubs, Jose joined his brother on the Angels before moving on to the Yankees in 2008. His lifetime average is .235. Yadier joined the Cardinals in 2004 and has twice played in the World Series for St. Louis. His average is .269.

Further Reading

Foster, Chris, and Shaikin, Bill. "City of Brotherly Gloves," *Los Angeles Times*, October 17, 2002.

Willie (Guillermo) Montanez

Born on April 1, 1948 in Catano, Puerto Rico, Montanez played parts of 14 seasons in the majors, starting in 1966 and ending in 1982. He was a career .275 hitter with 139 home runs and 802 RBIs and was a dazzling fielder after moving to first base from the outfield. Montanez' career fielding percentage was a superlative .992. Montanez possessed a strong arm, posting 15 assists one season in the outfield, and led National League first basemen in assists three times.

An All-Star with the Atlanta Braves in 1977, Montanez's peak hitting years were between 1975 and 1977 when he topped .300 each season. Montanez was traded nine times during his career. Montanez was likely victimized by his image as a showboat in some of those transactions. Always displaying his joy at playing the game, Montanez acquired the derogatory label of being a "hot dog." He milked his home runs by jogging around the bases at a very slow pace. In an even showier gesture, when Montanez caught infield flies he grabbed the ball in a swift move with his glove and then shifted the ball to his hip in imitation of a gunslinger holstering his pistol. Many laughed, but others resented the flair.

A colorful slugger from Puerto Rico, Willie Montanez broke into the majors in 1966 for the Los Angeles Angels and played for 14 seasons. Montanez bounced around to many teams. It was suggested that he faced prejudice from owners who wanted him to conform and play conservatively, but Montanez, partially at the urging of other Latino players, refused to buckle under and preserved his own style. (AP Photo/Ray Stubblebine)

Montanez hit 30 home runs and drove in 99 as a rookie with the Philadelphia Phillies in 1970—and introduced his individualistic style immediately. He always said he wasn't trying to upstage anyone but was merely showing off his pleasure in being on the field. Veteran Jose Pagan offered advice to the young Montanez. "Be yourself," Pagan said. "The fans should not expect Willie to change the way he plays the game. To change, just because someone thinks you are showing off would be a big mistake." (Quoted in Kelly.)

Further Reading

Kelly, Ray. " 'Don't Give Up Your Rituals,' Pagan's Sermon to Montanez," *Philadelphia Bulletin*, date missing, National Baseball Hall of Fame Library archives.

Manny Mota

The king of pinch hitters was born February 18, 1938 in Santo Domingo, Dominican Republic. Mota, always a great hitter, proved it time and time again with the Pittsburgh Pirates and primarily the Los Angeles Dodgers in a 20-year career spanning 1962 to 1982. A lifetime .304 hitter, Mota batted at least .300 in 11 seasons, though some of those were very short seasons when his only action was coming off the bench cold in the late innings to pinch-hit. He collected 150 pinch hits, at the time of his retirement, a Major League record.

Mota broke into the majors with the Giants, hit .332 for the Pirates in 1967, and in 1969 was the first player taken in the expansion draft by the Montreal Expos. He was dealt to the Dodgers after 31 games and spent the rest of his career with L.A. The last few years Mota played he was a late-season activation and spent most of his time coaching. By 2009, Mota had been with Los Angeles as a coach for 30 seasons. A 1973 All-Star, Mota was part of two Dodger teams that won World Series. In 1976, the Dodgers held a special Manny Mota Day to honor him. Mota was greatly appreciated in Los Angeles. "Manny's popularity in this city is second to none," said former Dodger manager Tommy Lasorda. "The people love him." (Quoted in Johnson.)

An accomplished batting tutor, Mota was not boastful about his own skill. "I don't consider myself a good hitter," he said once. "I consider myself a lucky hitter, a guy who tried to hit everything down. The other thing is I watched where they played me. You see, I was always mentally prepared in any situation." (Quoted in Johnson.)

Further Reading

Johnson, Terry. "A Conversation with Manny Mota," *Dodger Blue*, July 15, 1983.

Tony Oliva

Tony Oliva was a hitting machine, churning out hits with more frequency in his prime than anyone in the American League. Born on July 20, 1940 in Pinar del Rio, Cuba, the left-handed swinger was the league's Rookie of the Year in 1964 and was an eight-time All-Star for the Minnesota Twins. Oliva made his Major League debut in 1962 and played his entire 15-year career for the Twins. He won one Gold Glove, but was slowed by knee injuries (he had six surgeries) near the end of his career, forcing him to become a designated hitter. Oliva captured batting titles in 1964, 1965, and 1971 and compiled a career average of .304.

When Oliva won the Rookie of the Year award and the batting title in the same season, he was the first player to do so.

Oliva led the American League once in runs and for five seasons in hits, twice topping 200 in a year. Oliva displayed steady power, usually hitting more than 20 homers in a season, and he led the AL in doubles four times. Oliva clubbed 220 homers in his career and drove in 947, twice collecting more than 100 RBIs in a season. Many baseball fans believe he should be in the Hall of Fame, and he was chosen for the Twins' team Hall of Fame in 2000.

Twins teammate Zoilo Versalles equated Oliva with the best in history. "He is the new Ty Cobb," Versalles said. (Quoted in Pepe.) An expatriate, Oliva has visited his family in Cuba over the years, but kept his home in Minnesota. "It's always been a special place for me," he said. "Everybody has treated me so nice. The winters are cold, but I learned to stay inside." (Quoted in Colston.)

Further Reading

Colston, Chris. "Oliva's hot bat warmed Minnesota," *USA Today Baseball Weekly*, August 27/September 2, 1997.

Pepe, Phil. "They Call Tony Oliva the New Cobb," *New York World Telegram & Sun*, May 22, 1964.

Luis Olmo

Born August 11, 1919 in Arecibo, Puerto Rico, Olmo arrived in the majors in 1943 with the Brooklyn Dodgers at a time when few Latino players got the big-league call. An outfielder who played in 57 games that season, Olmo debuted with a .303 rookie average. Olmo came right to spring training from Puerto Rican winter ball and had also previously been the Most Valuable Player and batting champ of the Piedmont League.

The son of a carpenter who said he hated the English lessons required in school, Olmo dreamed of becoming a prominent pitcher. Then he snapped his right arm throwing the javelin and became a position player. Well aware of the limited appreciation of Latino players at the time, Olmo said there were many other top ballplayers in Puerto Rican unknown on the U.S. mainland. "The only reason you haven't heard of many Puerto Ricans in the majors is that our best players are colored," Olmo said. (Quoted in Turkin.)

The 5-foot-11, 190-pound Olmo was a solid hitter. In 1945 he batted .313 with 10 home runs, a league-leading 13 triples and 110 runs batted in. However, Olmo became enmeshed in controversy when the Mexican League dangled large salaries and began raiding American teams to improve its caliber of play. Amidst some confusion, Olmo jumped and then was one of the majors' players slapped with a lengthy suspension. "If I have made a mistake, I do not know it yet," Olmo said during the 1947 season. (Quoted in Holmes.) Eventually, the Mexican League's high aspirations faltered and Olmo was reinstated in the majors. He ended his six-year career with two seasons on the Boston Braves roster after one more year in Brooklyn and recorded a .281 lifetime average.

Further Reading

Holmes, Tommy. "The Corner Catches Up With Lou Olmo," *Brooklyn Eagle*, February 26, 1947.
Turkin, Hy, "All About Olmo," *New York Daily News*, March 17, 1943.

Magglio Ordonez

Born January 24, 1974 in Caracas, Venezuela, Ordonez is an all-around slugger who has starred as an outfielder with the Chicago White Sox and Detroit Tigers and who won the 2007 American League batting title with a .363 average. The 6-foot, 215-pound Ordonez has 13 years in the big leagues and is still going strong. His resume includes 277 home runs, 1,145 RBIs, and a lifetime .312 average.

A six-time All-Star and three-time winner of the Silver Slugger award at his position, "Maggs" for four straight years clubbed 30 or more home runs and drove in at least 100 runs with the ChiSox before a knee injury at the end of his contract made him expendable. He had highs of 38 home runs, 135 RBIs and a .320 average in 2002. Promising that he was fully healed from his injury problems, Ordonez signed a lucrative long-term contract with the Tigers starting in 2005. "I don't want to talk about my knee anymore," Ordonez said. "I look forward to showing everyone that I'm healthy." (Quoted in Latham.) He proved that doctors took good care of him by bouncing back with characteristic production, adding three more 100 RBI seasons. Ordonez was a cornerstone signing for Detroit as it rebuilt from dismal years.

In 2006, Ordonez helped the Tigers reach the World Series. He was at his best in 2007, inspiring Detroit manager Jim Leyland to say, "The best single-season performance I've ever seen." (Quoted in "Hitman . . .") Ordonez's batting title was the first for a Tiger since 1961, and he was just the second Venezuelan (after Andres Galarraga) to win a crown. Venezuelan President Hugo Chavez telephoned his congratulations.

Further Reading

"Hitman: Pitchers had little chance stopping Magglio Ordonez in 2007," *Detroit News*, December 28, 2007.

Latham, Krista. "Ordonez super signing for '05," *Detroit Free Press*, February 8, 2005.

David Ortiz

Ortiz is affectionately known as "Big Papi" in Boston where he stars as a designated hitter for the Red Sox. Born November 18, 1975 in Santo Domingo, Dominican Republic, Ortiz really is large. He stands 6-foot-4 and his weight is listed as 240 pounds. When the five-time All-Star follows through with his powerful left-hand swing the ball often is propelled out of Fenway Park and out of sight. In his 13th season in 2009, Ortiz passed 300 career home runs and 1,000 career RBIs.

Signed as a free agent in 2003 after being let go by the Minnesota Twins, Ortiz has been one of the most popular players in Red Sox history. He is admired for his upbeat personality, community service (in Boston and the Dominican), and towering home runs. Ortiz's 54 home runs in 2006 is the club record, and he was a key figure in the Red Sox' World Series triumphs of 2004 and 2007. Touted as the greatest clutch hitter in the fabled history of the franchise, Ortiz said, "There have been so many great players here. I never sat down to think about that, but if they feel that way, I appreciate it." (Quoted in Shaughnessy.)

The immense David Ortiz, who is listed at 6-foot-4 and 230 pounds, is called "Big Papi." The Dominican native is a hero in Boston where he performs yeoman community service and has set the Red Sox single-season homer record of 54. A full-time designated hitter, Ortiz has the record for most DH homers and owns four Silver Slugger Awards. (AP Photo/Winslow Townson)

When the new Yankee Stadium was being built, a workman with Red Sox sympathies buried an Ortiz jersey in the concrete as a jinx. The Yankees dug it up. It was then auctioned off, raising more than $175,000 for charity. In 2009 Ortiz's name emerged on a list of players who might have flunked a Major League baseball drug test in 2003. He denied any wrongdoing and most people seemed to give him the benefit of the doubt. When he hits home runs, Ortiz points skyward with both index fingers in a gesture of remembrance for his deceased mother.

Further Reading

Shaughnessy, Dan. "For end results, he's their man," *Boston Globe*, September 7, 2005.

Jose Pagan

Born May 5, 1935 in Barceloneta, Puerto Rico, Pagan broke into the majors with the San Francisco Giants in 1959 and split his 15-year career as an infielder between the Giants and Pirates. A solid player who provided leadership for other Latino players, Pagan led the National League in fielding at shortstop in 1962 with a .973 mark. Scouted from the sandlots of his hometown, Pagan was brought to the Giants training camp in 1955 along with another Puerto Rican standout—Orlando Cepeda. At the time he was considered a hotter prospect.

The 5-foot-9, 160-pound Pagan impressed more with his glove than his bat, and he had a career average of .250. He was a clutch hitter in the 1962 World Series—his best batting show on a large stage. The Giants could not overcome the Yankees, however. In 1971, with the Pirates, Pagan came out on the winning side. His double in the eighth drove in Willie Stargell with the winning run in the Series' last game. A utility infielder in his final days as a player, Pagan was also an extraordinary pinch-hitter, hitting .452 in the role in 1969 in 42 tries. "You don't get to play often," he said, "but when you do, you must be ready. You must make good instantly. You're really under pressure all of the time." (Quoted in Biederman.)

Always regarded as a savvy player, Pagan worked as a Pirates coach between 1974 and 1978 after retiring as a player. As a player, Pagan gave sage advice to young Latin players trying to adjust to the ways of the United States and he was brought back as a Pirates coach to tutor infielders in the fine points of fielding.

Further Reading

Biederman, Les. "Super Handyman Jose Pagan Earns Pirate Plaudits," *Pittsburgh Press*, January 18, 1969.

Rafael Palmeiro

Born September 24, 1964 in Havana, Cuba, Palmeiro put up Hall of Fame-caliber numbers for the Chicago Cubs, Texas Rangers, and Baltimore Orioles in a 20-season career. His total of 3,020 hits and 569 home runs put him among the elite players who have ever seen Major League action and the 3,000-hit mark and 500-homer milestone ordinarily would ensure automatic selection to the Hall. In addition, his 1,835 RBIs places him 14th on the all-time list.

Palmeiro's hallmark was putting together consistently fine seasons rather than overpowering ones. Even when he smashed his 500th career homer with the Rangers in 2003, Palmeiro showed no emotion as he ran the bases, head down, as fireworks filled the sky above him. "I've never been a guy who does any look-at-me-stuff," he said. "I'm not fancy." (Quoted in Elliott.) Palmeiro was a four-time All-Star and led the American League in hits with 191 in 1990 and in runs with 124 in 1993. He recorded six .300 seasons en route to a .288 lifetime batting average. Palmeiro exceeded 40 homers in a season three times and he notched 10 seasons of 100 or more RBIs with high marks of 148 in 1999 and 142 in 1996.

After putting together a highly esteemed record, Palmeiro's achievements were discredited and his reputation besmirched when he was fingered by a number of sources as a user of performance-enhancing drugs. Late in the 2005 season, Palmeiro

Rafael Palmeiro has not played in the majors since 2005 after 20 seasons mainly with the Texas Rangers and Baltimore Orioles. The Cuban slugger has Hall of Fame statistics with 569 homers, 1,835 runs batted in and a lifetime batting average of .288. He was a four-time All-Star. However, Palmeiro was suspended for failing a steroid test near the end of his career and future honors are uncertain. (AP Photo/Donna McWilliam)

released a public statement indicating, "I am here to make it very clear that I have never intentionally used steroids, Never. Ever. Period." (Quoted in Baltimore Orioles . . .) And after denying such use before Congress, Palmeiro disappeared from the game and the public eye. Whether or not Palmeiro will find the backing he needs for the Hall of Fame when he becomes eligible is open to question.

Further Reading

Baltimore Orioles press release, August 1, 2005.
Elliott, Josh. "Raffy Joins the Club," *Sports Illustrated*, May 19, 2003.

Camilo Pascual and Carlos Pascual

Renowned for throwing a vicious curveball, Camilo Pascual was an outstanding American League pitcher for 18 years, but he suffered from poor run support with the losing Washington Senators. Born January 20, 1934 in Havana, Cuba, Pascual mustered a record of 174–170. A five-time All-Star with the Senators and the Minnesota Twins, Pascual had a career earned run average of 3.63.

The right-hander's support woes were evident in 1961 when he finished 15–16, but had an AL high eight shutouts. Pascual compiled a 20–11 record in 1962 and a 21–9 record in 1963, despite missing 30 days with injuries in each of those seasons. He led the American League in strikeouts three times and in complete games three times. Older brother Carlos, born March 13, 1931, pitched in just two games for the Senators in 1950 and had a record of 1–1.

Camilo Pascual's last big-league appearance was in 1971 with the Indians. He tried to make a comeback as a relief pitcher in 1973 by showing his stuff in Venezuela, but never made it back to the majors. In his prime, Pascual took special pride in making his curve unhittable for the majority of batters. Hall of Famer Ted Williams said he thought Pascual had the best curveball in the league. Pascual said he learned his curve from Adolfo Luque, the Cuban who was the first Latin-American Major League star. Luque coached Pascual into throwing the pitch completely overhand, but he also couldn't succeed as a one-pitch pitcher. "I used to throw as hard as I could for almost six innings," Pascual said, "but I couldn't go nine innings and win games. I learned to win on days I didn't have my curve." (Quoted in Nichols.)

Further Reading

Nichols, Max. "Camilo's Curve Sharper Than Ever," *The Sporting News*, April 2, 1966.

Tony Pena and Tony Francisco Pena

Born June 4, 1957 in Monte Cristo, Dominican Republic, the elder Pena followed an outstanding catching career with an impressive leadership career. Pena introduced himself to the majors with the Pittsburgh Pirates in 1980 and was best known for his extraordinary fielding and stunningly strong arm. In 1988 with the St. Louis Cardinals, he led the National League in fielding percentage at .994. A year later he was slightly better, again leading the league at .997.

Pena was one of the many Dominicans who achieved Major League success despite scuffling in poverty as a youth with no advantages starting out. "I was out in the back yard playing every day," Pena said. "No shoes, half-naked. We used to make a glove out of soap boxes. Fold it, make a hole in the back and go out and play. We'd climb a tree with a machete, cut a piece of wood and make a bat. Then we used to get old socks from my mom and dad to make a baseball. We wrapped them with tape." (Quoted in Kaegel.)

In his 18-year career, the tobacco-chewing Pena, who loved indulging in rice and beans, was a five-time All-Star and seven times (with the Pirates, Cardinals, and Boston Red Sox) he caught more than 140 games in a season, a huge work load by today's standards. He was a four-time Gold Glove winner. In 2002, Pena became manager of the Kansas City Royals and won the American League manager of the year award in 2003 when the Royals recorded their first winning season in eight years. Pena's son, Tony Francisco Pena, made it to the majors with the Atlanta Braves in 2006, and he became the Royals' shortstop the next season. Poor hitting led the younger Pena to turn to pitching.

Further Reading

Kaegel, Dick. "Dominican managers make history," *Kansas City Star*, June 25, 2002.

Juan Pizarro

Born February 7, 1937 in Santurce, Puerto Rico, Pizarro had a career of highs and lows that defied anticipation, primarily with the Milwaukee Braves and Chicago White Sox. Touted as a mesmerizing fastballer, but someone who produced inconsistent results, Pizarro was legendary in the Puerto Rican winter league. In parts of 18 Major League seasons he compiled a 131–105 record.

Luis Olmo, then scouting for the Braves, signed Pizarro. Pizarro's first season in the majors was 1957, the year Milwaukee won the World Series. For a few years, Pizzaro teamed with Warren Spahn, one of his childhood heroes, but the pitching-rich Braves didn't use him very often. In 1961, with the White Sox, Al Lopez coaxed a 14–7 year out of Pizarro, his first double-figure victory season. In 1963, he was 16–8 and in 1964 he was 19–9, his finest performance in the United States. Although he played another decade in the United States, Pizarro never hit double figures in wins again.

Off the field, Pizarro was often uncommunicative and a loner despite his knowledge of English. Teams asked him to skip winter ball, but he did not. During one season in Puerto Rico, Pizarro posted a 19-strikeout game, a no-hitter (the first in his league in four years), and a one-hitter. He always impressed winter spectators, but also admitted he spent more time at horse races than working out. Lopez felt Pizarro was worn out by the end of the summer season. "Nobody can pitch the year 'round and not get tired at some time or another," said the Sox manager. (Quoted in Munzel.) Although he had moments of glory, Pizarro's best pitching was probably done at home where he was most comfortable. After retirement, Pizarro returned to Puerto Rico to work for the government—teaching baseball to youngsters.

Further Reading

Munzel, Edgar. "Sinking White Sox Blame Winter Ball For Pizarro's Skid," *Chicago Sun-Times*, October 3, 1969.

Alex Pompez

A great facilitator, Pompez opened doors to Latin American players to compete in the United States, first with Negro Leagues teams that he owned called the Cuban Stars and the New York Cubans. Although he worked with organized crime figures in his younger days, Pompez was an influential man in his sport and was elected to the National Baseball Hall of Fame in 2006. Born in Key West, Florida, the son of Cuban immigrants, on May 14, 1890, Pompez provided United States playing forums for such stars as Martin Dihigo and Minnie Minoso.

Later, after fleeing to Mexico and avoiding prosecution as a numbers runner for mobster Dutch Schultz, Pompez acted as a go-between in the 1950s for such Latino players as Orlando Cepeda and Felipe Alou during a 25-year connection with the San Francisco Giants. He scouted and suggested the Giants sign Monte Irvin and Willie Mays, and he signed Willie McCovey. Alou said Pompez's reputation spread throughout Latin America as a talent spotter for the Giants. "The big door of the Dominican was opened by Pompez," Alou said. "It's not only the talent that he brought in, it was a relationship. Anywhere and everywhere they played baseball—Panama, Colombia, Venezuela, Puerto Rico, Cuba—Pompez was a legend." (Quoted in Brown.)

Pompez, who died on March 14, 1974, stayed close to his guys as they worked their way up through the team's minor-league organization, and stood up for them with the organization. He gave advice to Latino players struggling to adjust to the United States and advice to the Giants on how to smooth their relations with players who might have felt misunderstood. "He did so much for us, the Latin and black ballplayers," Cepeda said. "He was a father for all of us. He really looked after us. He was there for us." (Quoted in Brown.)

Further Reading

Brown, Daniel. "Pompez helped open doors for Latinos in major league baseball," *San Jose Mercury News*, August 2, 2006.

Aramis Ramirez

The hard-hitting third baseman for the Chicago Cubs was born on June 25, 1978 in Santo Domingo, Dominican Republic. A steady hitter, the 6-foot-1, 215-pound Ramirez is also a solid third-sacker. Although his 2009 season was disrupted by a shoulder injury, Ramirez still batted .317. After 12 seasons in the majors, Ramirez had seven seasons of 20 or more homers and six seasons of 100 or more RBIs on his record.

Picked up in a 2003 mid-season trade with the Pittsburgh Pirates, Ramirez quickly made himself a fixture with the Cubs and signed a long-term deal. In 2006 he put up career highs in home runs (38) and RBIs (119). A two-time All-Star, Ramirez has brought stability to the most erratically staffed position in the Cubs lineup. In a 30-year period between 1973 and 2003, following Ron Santo's 13-year tenure on the job, the Cubs employed 97 third basemen. With Ramirez on the roster, the position is locked in concrete. "There have been 100 third basemen?" Ramirez said when he was just 25 and putting his roots down. "I know the history. Hopefully, I can change all of that." (Quoted in Nightengale.)

The son of a doctor and an accountant, Ramirez dreamed of becoming a pro basketball player, but realized there were no Dominicans in the NBA. He was only 16 when he signed a pro contract with the Pirates' organization and 19 when he made his Major League debut in 1998. Ramirez's All-Star selections represent steady improvement. He committed a Major League high 33 errors in 2003. As a hitter, however, he has recorded two three-homer games and in the 2003 playoffs smacked four homers and knocked in 10 runs. Ramirez is closing in on 300 career homers and 1,000 RBIs.

Further Reading

Nightengale, Bob. "Ramirez finds home at Wrigley," *USA Today Sports Weekly*, June 2–8, 2004.

Pedro Ramos

Ramos was better than his record and his life was crazier than he bargained for when he left Cuba to work for the Washington Senators. Born April 28, 1935 in Pinar Del Rio, Cuba, Ramos ran almost as swiftly as he pitched. He was a starter for years and then excelled as a relief pitcher. In 1956, Ramos went 12–10 for Washington. But the Senators were so bad that it was difficult for him to post a winning record, going 12–16, 14–18, 13–19, and 11–18. With the Minnesota Twins, Ramos went 11-20. He led the American League in losses four times. Twice during that stretch, however, he led the American League in starts and once in innings pitched.

Despite struggling with a lousy team, Ramos enjoyed himself. He had an outgoing personality and was called "the Gay Caballero." Growing up on a tobacco farm with cows and horses he learned to ride. Ramos wore 10-gallon cowboy hats and loved Western movies. He tooled around in a white convertible Charger (carrying Western novels in the trunk) and reveled in the single life. "I love the Lone Ranger," Ramos said. "I'm just a poor country boy from Cuba, but I'm not a hillbilly." (Quoted in Flanagan.)

After coping with disappointments as a starter, Ramos's career was resurrected in 1964 when the New York Yankees made him a reliever. The late-season acquisition ripped off eight saves. He recorded 19 in 65 and in 1966 he had 13 in 52 appearances. He became a key figure in helping the Yankees to the '64 pennant. Much later, Ramos served time in prison for drug possession. "I made a mistake and I learned my lesson," he said. "I tell kids to stay away from bad stuff." (Quoted in Vecsey.)

Further Reading

Flanagan, Barbara. "Ramos Is Kooky Cavalier," *Minneapolis Tribune*, April 16, 1961.
Vecsey, George. "The Gift of Freedom," *New York Times*, December 24, 1982.

Edgar Renteria

One of only a handful of players from Colombia to make the majors, the sharp-fielding, solid-hitting Renteria is a hero in his home country, one of the Latin American nations where soccer is still the sports fan's greatest passion

Shortstop Edgar Renteria, who has played for many teams, including the Boston Red Sox (above), is the first competitor from Colombia to play in a World Series. Renteria has been selected for five All-Star teams and has been honored with two Gold Gloves and three Silver Slugger Awards. (AP Photo/Gregory Bull)

instead of baseball. Born August 7, 1976 in Barranquilla, Colombia, the five-time All-Star opted for a sport less traveled. Still, Renteria gets national attention in Colombia via television. The 6-foot-1, 200-pound two-time Gold Glove winner is a .288 lifetime hitter in 14 seasons, but his biggest hit was cheered when he drove in the game-winning run in the 1997 World Series for the Florida Marlins.

There is some interest in baseball in Colombia, although when Renteria stroked his winning hit it was reported that some fans rooting for him shouted "Goal!" Renteria played in local youth leagues in Colombia, and to help the family Renteria and his six siblings sold candy, fried pork rinds, and raffle tickets. There is recognition in the local media that Renteria made it in the big-time and that he represents his country well. Even at the worst times during Colombia's 1990s drug wars involving the Medellin cartels, he returned home in the off-season and eschewed bodyguards. The fourth Colombian in the majors, Renteria was joined by Orlando Cabrera, another shortstop, later in 1997.

In the 2004 World Series, Renteria suited up for the St. Louis Cardinals and Cabrera wore the colors of the Boston Red Sox, giving the Series a strong local angle. "It's exciting," Renteria said. "In Colombia, they've already won because one of us will be the champion." (Quoted in Crouse.) It was Cabrera. Late in the 2009 season, Renteria clouted one of the biggest hits of his career—a grand-slam homer that pushed his San Francisco Giants into National League wild-card playoff contention.

Further Reading

Crouse, Karen. "Two shortstops unite violence-torn nation," *Palm Beach Post*, October 27, 2004.

Jose Rijo

There were moments when Jose Rijo seemed headed for greatness. Born May 13, 1965 in San Cristobal, Dominican Republic, Rijo, who once was married to legend Juan Marichal's daughter, had an unhappy debut with the New York Yankees as a 19-year-old, going 2–8. He emerged as a potential star with the Cincinnati Reds in 1988, going 13–8. In 1990, his record was 14–8 and he was the Most Valuable Player in the World Series. A year later his 15–6 led the National League in winning percentage—.714. He was 15–10 in 1992 and 14–9 in 1993. Off to a great start in 1994, Rijo made his only All-Star team.

Then it all fell apart for the 6-foot-2, 200-pound hurler. Shoulder and arm miseries set in and surgeries followed. Beginning in 1995, aborted returns, interrupted by five operations didn't pan out. He hadn't thrown a pitch in the majors after the age of 30 when he should have been entering his prime. Rijo returned to the Dominican and started a baseball academy. In 2001, six years after retiring, realizing his arm no longer hurt, Rijo launched an unlikely comeback with the Reds.

Rijo re-appeared like an apparition, making good out of the bullpen in 13 showings. "My arm feels good," Rijo said. "Two innings, two days off. One inning, one day off. My arm will get stronger." (Quoted in Eradi.) His ERA was 2.12. "He really is a miracle," said Reds pitching coach Don Gullett. (Quoted in DiMeglio.) In 2002, Rijo got into 31 games and finished 5-4, but his earned run average shot up and that was it. In 2005, Rijo was inducted into the Reds' Hall of Fame.

Further Reading

DiMeglio, Steve. "Reconstructed and rejuvenated," *USA Today Baseball Weekly*, April 24–30, 2002.
Eradi, John. "After six years, finally Rijo returns," *USA Today Baseball Weekly*, August 22–28, 2001.

Francisco Rodriguez

His nickname is "K-Rod" because of the way he so routinely strikes out batters. Rodriguez, born January 7, 1982 in Caracas, Venezuela, is easily identifiable by the smoke he throws and the thick goggles he wears for protection.

Signed by the Angels as an undrafted free agent 16-year-old, Rodriguez suffered arm problems that turned him from a starter to a reliever. He introduced himself to the world at age 20 in electrifying fashion in the 2002 playoffs. A late-season call-up who had not won a regular-season game, Rodriguez won five post-season games to become an instant hero as the Angels won the World Series.

A virtual unknown, Rodriguez's emergence made front-page news in the papers in Venezuela. As a youth, Rodriguez took bets on horse racing in order to fund his school supply purchases. He barely knew his mother, and his birth father deserted him when he was four. A grandmother raised him. In off-seasons he visits his old neighborhood but not his parents.

He has only improved since his World Series debut. Carefully nurtured by the Angels, Rodriguez became a full-time closer in 2005 and saved an American League-leading 45 games. In 2006, Rodriguez saved a league-leading 47 games with a 1.73 earned run average. In 2007 he saved 40 games. Then came Rodriguez's monumental 2008 performance. Appearing in an AL-leading 76 games, he saved a Major-League record 62 games. Rodriguez got results in a hurry. As he went onto the free agent market, he had accumulated 587 strikeouts in 451 2/3 innings behind a 93 mph fastball and a sharp curveball. After the season, free agent Rodriguez signed a three-year, $37-million contract with the New York Mets. A four-time All-Star, Rodriguez has set records every step of his career as the youngest reliever to achieve 50, 100, and 200 saves.

Cookie Rojas

Rojas's father wanted him to be a doctor. Rojas wanted to be a baseball player. Born March 6, 1939 in Havana, Cuba, Rojas won the argument, first joining the Havana Sugar Kings, starting his advance in the minors in 1956, and then breaking into the majors in 1962 with the Cincinnati Reds. In a 16-year career as a second baseman, Rojas was a five-time All-Star with the Philadelphia Phillies and the Kansas City Royals, becoming the rare player to represent both leagues in the mid-season contest. He recorded a lifetime average of .263 and led his league in fielding three times.

Rojas fielded .987 for the 1968 Phillies, .991 for the 1971 Royals, and .987 for the 1974 Royals. He twice hit .300. During one of Rojas's All-Star games, he was put in to pinch-hit for league-leading batter Rod Carew. "I got booed like hell," said Rojas, who said Carew had a pulled muscle. (Quoted in "Catching up ...") Rojas hit a home run to give the AL the lead in the game.

Cookie Rojas was a slick second baseman for the Kansas City Royals after leaving Cuba for good once Fidel Castro shut down hometown professional baseball. A long-time coach who also managed, Rojas was respected for his savvy knowledge of the game. Rojas was a five-time All-Star. (AP Photo/Ron Frehm)

His accomplishments were due to hard work. "Cookie played like he practiced," said former Angels' manager Gene Mauch. "He was always very well-prepared. He had average speed, marginal power and marvelous hands." (Quoted in Newhan.) Rojas became the third Cuban-born manager when he took over the California Angels in 1988 after nine years in the organization. It turned into a one-year gig when the team finished with a 75-79 record. Rojas also managed one game for the Florida Marlins in 1998, but he spent several years coaching with different teams, including acting as third base coach and infield instructor for the Marlins.

Further Reading

"Catching up with Royals Hall of Fame second baseman Cookie Rojas," KansasCity.com, July 13, 2003.

Newhan, Ross. "Cookie: With Grit and Intelligence, He Became a Top Player; Will Angers Give Him Full Chance?" *Los Angeles Times*, May 23, 1988.

Manny Sanguillen

A three-time All-Star catcher for the Pittsburgh Pirates, Sanguillen was born March 21, 1944 in Colon, Panama. Renowned during his 13-year career for swinging at any pitch he could reach—and successfully hitting it safely for a .296 lifetime average—Sanguillen is also remembered for his joy in approaching life. A major contributor to the Pirates World Series triumphs in 1971 and 1979, Sanguillen made his Major League debut in 1967 and, except for one season with the Oakland A's in the middle of his career, stayed with the Pirates until 1980.

As the 1971 Pirates swept to the World Series crown, Sanguillen contributed 11 hits and a .379 average. In the 1979 Series, Sanguillen had one game-winning hit. A close friend of Roberto Clemente's, Sanguillen's anguish at the loss of the Puerto Rican hero in a plane crash in 1972 was evident when he skipped Clemente's funeral to dive repeatedly into the ocean in search of his body. A four-time .300 hitter, Sanguillen's career high was .328 in 1975. Sanguillen is the only player in Major League history to be traded for a manager—he was swapped to Oakland for Chuck Tanner in 1977.

Although he acknowledged his reputation as someone not very discerning at the plate, it was noted that Sanguillen didn't strike out much. "Everybody calls me a free swinger," he said. "I swing at any pitch I think I can handle. But any ball I swing at I follow the ball through with my eyes, so that's what happens, especially when I have two strikes." (Quoted in Smith.) Sanguillen maintains his connection with the Pirates and their fans today; at each home game he sets up "Manny's BBQ" to sell his favorite eats, pose for photos, and sign autographs.

Further Reading

Smith, Ken. Transcript, National Baseball Hall of Fame interview, March 23, 1974.

Johan Santana

One of the premier pitchers in baseball today, Santana was born March 13, 1979 in Tovar, Venezuela. A two-time winner of the American League Cy Young Award (2004 and 2006), Santana broke into the majors in 2000 with the Minnesota

Twins. Before signing with the New York Mets as a free agent for the 2008 season, Santana led the AL in strikeouts three times, earned run average twice, and in wins once. In his first season with the Mets, Santana led the National League in innings pitched and ERA. He is a four-time All-Star and a Gold Glove winner.

Santana has a lifetime record of 120–60. At the start of the 2004 season, following elbow surgery and problems with his mechanics, the 6-foot, 200-pound southpaw didn't even know if he would be in the Twins' rotation. By the end of the season he was making national news in Venezuela. The announcement of his winning the Cy Young was that huge. "A lot of people are going crazy," Santana said. "It's a big thing. It's on the news, national TV." (Quoted in Sheldon.)

Off-seasons, Santana retreats to Tovar, the small town in Venezuela where he grew up and is raising his own family. But he began worrying about the increasing violence in his country, and the increase in kidnappings. "You do things for yourself, and for your family to support them, then people want to take advantage of you," Santana said. "I don't think it's right." (Quoted in Farrey.) Santana makes the effort to do right—paying for chemotherapy treatments for a sick Venezuelan child, replacing police department motorcycle parts, buying a needed fire engine for Tovar. His six-year, $137.5-million contract with the Mets makes that possible. His 2009 season ended early with concerns, though, when Santana had surgery on his throwing elbow.

Further Reading

Farrey, Tom. "Not safe at home," ESPN.com, September 27, 2004.
Sheldon, Mark. "Santana captures AL Cy Young," MLB.com, November 11, 2004.

Benito Santiago Jr.

Born March 9, 1965 in Ponce, Puerto Rico, Santiago experienced a 20-year career in the majors between 1986 and 2005 as an excellent catcher who made five All-Star teams and won three Gold Gloves. Praised for his cat-like quickness behind the plate during his early years with the San Diego Padres, Santiago was a near-99 percent fielder during his career, including posting a .997 league-leading mark with the Philadelphia Phillies in 1996. His trademark was attempting to nab base stealers by throwing from his knees.

The 1987 National League Rookie of the Year, Santiago recorded a 34-game hitting streak. It remains the longest hitting streak by a catcher. Santiago's lifetime average was .263 and he hit 217 home runs and drove in 920 runs. "Every day that I play baseball is a lovely thing," Santiago said. "My favorite thing about spring training is just waking up in the morning and knowing I'm going to play baseball. I love everything about it, actually." (Quoted in Kovacevic.)

The biggest challenge the usually upbeat Santiago faced occurred in 1998 when he was property of the Toronto Blue Jays. He was in a serious off-season automobile accident in Florida, crashing his yellow Ferrari into a tree, and participated in just 15 games that season. At the time doctors wondered if he would walk again. Among Santiago's injuries were a fractured pelvis, a wrecked right knee, and loss of blood. He was lucky enough to have the accident close to a hospital. "Thank God the hospital was just down the block," Santiago said. (Quoted in Miech.) Santiago's surprising recovery was so complete he made one of his All-Star teams with the Giants in 2002, was still able to throw from his knees, and walk without a limp.

Further Reading

Kovacevic, Dejan. "Playing baseball never gets old for Santiago," *Pittsburgh Post-Gazette*, March 6, 2005.
Miech, Rob. "All-Star Santiago defies odds," *USA Today*, date missing, National Baseball Hall of Fame Library archives.

Tony Taylor

Born December 19, 1935 in Central Alara, Cuba, Taylor made his Major League impression with his fast feet and fast hands. His feet accounted for 234 stolen bases. His hands accounted for 19 years as primarily a second baseman. Taylor played in 2,195 games and collected 2,007 hits while batting .261. He made the National League All-Star team in 1960. Although he broke into the majors with the Chicago Cubs in 1958, Taylor was most closely identified with the Philadelphia Phillies.

Lonely in a minor-league outpost in Texas where he muddled through by pointing at food on menus and uttering "OK," his only English-language word, Taylor revealed on Tony Taylor Night in Philadelphia that he almost abandoned his quest for the majors. He was ready to scamper back home, but needed $72 for transportation. "I looked in my pocket," Taylor said. "I had only $62, so I stayed"—and changed his life. (Quoted in "Lack of . . .")

For all of his flash with the glove, Taylor worked hard (with the aid of Cubs coaches) to make himself an acceptable Major League hitter. After retiring, Taylor coached with the Phillies and Marlins. In 2002, he was selected to become part of the Phillies' team Wall of Fame, receiving the Phillies' Latin Legends Award. "My first day here I got a couple of hits and got a standing ovation," Taylor said.

"And from that day on I thought I'd be in Philadelphia the rest of my life." (Quoted in Carchidi.) Not quite, but he has always been associated with Philadelphia, even when also being inducted into the Hispanic Heritage Baseball Museum Hall of Fame in 2004.

Further Reading

Carchidi, Sam. "Tony Taylor honored as Phils' Latin Legend," *Philadelphia Inquirer*, July 18, 2002.
"Lack of $10 Made Star Out of Taylor," *The Sporting News*, March 23, 1970.

Miguel Tejada

A six-time All-Star who emulated and was inspired by Iron Man Cal Ripken Jr., Tejada became a star all-around shortstop like his hero. Born May 25, 1976 in Bani, Dominican Republic, Tejada's tracking of Ripken went so far as to put together his own streak of consecutive games. Tejada's milestone topped out at 1,152 games in a row. Tejada made his Major League debut with Oakland in 1997, became a regular in 1998, and a star in 1999. In 2004, Tejada signed a six-year, $72 million deal with the Baltimore Orioles.

The 2005 All-Star game MVP, Tejada played in all 162 games of the season six times. "My last day off, I don't really remember it," Tejada said in 2007 after his streak ended. (Quoted in Christensen.) He went on the disabled list for a fracture in his arm. Tejada has eight seasons with at least 20 home runs (four with 30) and six seasons with 100 or more RBIs. In 2004, Tejada knocked in a tremendous 150 runs to lead the American League. He also has recorded five .300 seasons. Tejada helped the A's make three straight playoff appearances and he won the 2002 AL Most Valuable Player award. Tejada's jump to the losing Orioles surprised many and despite professing love for the city, he ultimately returned to Houston.

Like many of his contemporaries, Tejada ran afoul of baseball's new drug testing program; even worse, early in 2009, he pled guilty to misleading Congress in sworn testimony about performance-enhancing drugs. Tejada received a sentence of 100 hours of community service, unsupervised probation, and a $5,000 fine. Uncontradicted was a statement that Tejada bought human growth hormone but did not use it. He apologized for lying, saying, "I learned a very important lesson." (Quoted in "Tejeda sentenced . . .")

Miguel Tejada possesses a mix of slick-fielding talent and is a damaging hitter who mans third base for the Baltimore Orioles. The Dominican infielder is a six-time All-Star and won the American League Most Valuable Player award in 2002. In 2005, Tejada was the MVP of the All-Star game. (AP Photo/Chris Gardner)

Further Reading

Christensen, Joe. "O's pick up Tejeda, credibility," *Baltimore Sun*, December 15, 2003.
"Tejeda sentenced to year's probation," Associated Press, March 26, 2009.

Cristobal Torriente

One of the most underpublicized great players of the game, Torriente was a Negro Leagues star who played between 1914 and 1932 and whose achievements with the Chicago American Giants, the Kansas City Monarchs, the Atlanta Black Crackers, and other teams were recognized in 2006 when he was elected to the National Baseball Hall of Fame. Born November 16, 1893 in Cienfugos, Cuba, Torriente was only 44 when he died in New York in 1938 from tuberculosis and the effects of alcoholism.

A .335 lifetime hitter, Torriente liked to play hard on the field and off of it; living it up in nightclubs at night, he reported to the park grumpy enough to get into arguments with team management. He won two league batting titles in the United States and hit .352 in Latino winter leagues. Torriente was not considered for Major League play because he was black. New York Giants manager John McGraw wanted to sign the light-skinned Torriente, but could not pull off the charade because the talented Torriente's giveaway was tightly curled hair. "If I should see Torriente walking up the other side of the street," said C.I. Taylor, a Negro Leagues manager and official, "I would say, 'There walks a ballclub.' " (Quoted in Shatzkin.)

Torriente batted .432 in 1920, drove in seven runs in a game, and at 5-foot-9 and 190 pounds was a player who could run, hit, throw, field, and hit with power. Partial to jewelry, Torriente wore bracelets on his wrist when he stepped up to the plate, and he shook them when targeting the fences. "He did everything well," said Martin Dihigo, another Cuban Hall of Famer. "He fielded like a natural, threw in perfect form, (and) he covered as much field as could be covered. As for batting, he went from being good to being something extraordinary." (Quoted in Hall of Fame release.)

Further Reading

National Baseball Hall of Fame press release, February 23, 2006.
Shatzkin, Mike. (editor), *The Ballplayers: The Ultimate Baseball Biographical Reference*, excerpt sheet, National Baseball Hall of Fame Library archives.

Cesar Tovar

Tovar was a get-on-base-any-way-I-can type of guy, whether that meant taking one for the team and getting hit by pitches or smacking triples. Born July 3, 1940 in Caracas, Venezuela, Tovar, whose nickname was "Pepito," died from pancreatic cancer on July 14, 1994 in Caracas. Tovar broke into the majors with the Minnesota Twins in 1965 and spent 12 seasons in the big leagues, retiring in 1976 with a .278 lifetime average.

Among Tovar's notable achievements were hitting a league-leading 13 triples and 36 doubles for the Twins in 1970 when he batted .300, clouting a league-leading 204 hits in 1971 when he hit .311, and leading the American League in being hit by pitches with 14 in 1972. In a game for the Twins on September 22, 1968, Tovar joined Bert Campaneris as one of just two ballplayers to play nine positions in a Major League game. Two other American Leaguers have since joined them on that short list. Campaneris was on the field when Tovar matched him in a game against Oakland. Remarkably, Tovar broke up five different pitchers' attempts at no-hitters, recording the only hit in a game against them all.

Just 5-foot-9 and weighing 155 pounds, Tovar was durable. Because of a schedule quirk in 1967 he appeared in 164 games. That year Boston's Carl Yastrzemski won the Triple Crown and AL MVP Award. Yaz was one vote shy of unanimous selection and that vote went to Tovar. Although playing nine positions in a single game was a gimmick, Tovar routinely shifted positions for the Twins. As long as he was in the lineup, he was happy. "When the manager asks if I play," he said, "I say all right. Maybe I have to die to say no." (Quoted in "Cesar Tovar . . .") Unfortunately, Tovar died way too young at 54.

Further Reading

"Cesar Tovar: One-Man Show," Minnesota Twins game program, date missing, National Baseball Hall of Fame Library archives.

Manny Trillo

In the great tradition of Venezuelan middle infielders, Trillo was a four-time All-Star second baseman and won three Gold Glove awards. Born December 25, 1950, Trillo, who was nicknamed "Indio," left his biggest footprints with the Philadelphia Phillies. Trillo was part of the Phillies' 1980 World Series champs and was the Most Valuable Player in the National League Championship Series that year as the club won its first pennant in 30 years and its first title in 65 years. "Manny is the best defensive second baseman I have ever played with—or against," said Phillies' teammate Pete Rose. (Quoted in Brady.)

Trillo broke in with the Oakland Athletics in 1973, but spent quality time with the Chicago Cubs, as well as the Phillies, during his 17-year Major League career that ended in 1989. In 1,780 games, Trillo had a lifetime batting average of .263. He also led the National League in fielding with a .994 percentage in 1982. Trillo was an All-Star with three different teams and in both leagues, with the Cubs, Phillies and Cleveland Indians.

In 1982, Trillo played 89 straight errorless games at second base, two shy of the record. When he made an error on a ground ball on July 31, it had been 109 days and 479 chances since he recorded a miscue. The official scorer admitted it was a close call and he reviewed it on video three times and conferred with others. Trillo was not upset by the call. "I'm not mad at the scorer," he said after the game against the Cubs. "I think I should have handled that ball. The ball hit right in the heel of my glove. In my mind it was an easy ground ball. I'll just start again." (Quoted in Brady.)

Manny Trillo was a marvelous second-baseman primarily for the Chicago Cubs and Philadelphia Phillies, as well as other teams during a 17-season career. Venezuelan Trillo, a four-time All-Star and winner of three Gold Gloves, at one time held the record for most consecutive errorless chances in a row at second base. He also won two Silver Slugger Awards. (AP Photo)

Further Reading

Brady, Frank. "To Err Is Rare for Trillo of Phillies; It is His First in 89 Games," *New York Times*, August 1, 1982.

Zoilo Versalles

Born December 18, 1939 in Velelado, Cuba, Versalles broke into the majors with the Washington Senators in 1959 and moved with the team to Minnesota, where he emerged as a top-flight player. A two-time All-Star and two-time Gold Glove winner at shortstop, Versalles's greatest triumph was being named American League Most Valuable Player in 1965 when he batted .319 and led the AL in runs scored with 126, doubles with 45, and triples with 12. It was the third straight year he led the league in triples.

A lifetime .242 hitter in 12 Major League seasons, Versalles went into decline after his great performances of the mid-1960s. He was popular with the Twins and acquired the nickname of "Zorro," which he did not particularly embrace. Versalles was always homesick for Cuba, though his father and uncle joined him living in Minnesota, where he raised four daughters. The Twins, who won the pennant and advanced to the World Series, were at the top of their game in 1965. Versalles was proud of winning the MVP, but said, "Every man on this team was the most valuable. We have a lot of ballplayers good enough to win this award." (Quoted in Nichols.)

Although portrayed as a happy-go-lucky guy when he was playing and the Twins were losing, Versalles encountered hard times later in life. After retirement in 1971, Versalles suffered from various health problems and in 1995 he separated from his wife. He collected workmen's compensation due to an injury suffered working for an airline and late in his life was having such a difficult time financially the Twins set up a bank account for him. Versalles was only 55 when he was found dead in his Bloomington, Minnesota home on June 9, 1995. In 2006, Versalles was inducted into the Twins Hall of Fame.

Further Reading

Nichols, Max. "At Zoilo's House, Everyone's Happy!" December 4, 1965.

Ozzie Virgil Sr. and Ozzie Virgil Jr.

Born May 17, 1933 in Monte Cristo, Dominican Republic, Ozzie Sr. broke into the majors in 1956 with the New York Giants, but notably became the first black player in Detroit Tigers history in 1958. A backup throughout his career, Ozzie Sr. was a third baseman and catcher for 324 games spread over nine seasons with a .231 average. The 6-foot, 175-pounder actually attended high school in the Bronx, New York after his family moved to the United States when he was 13. Ozzie Sr.'s landmark debut with the Tigers took place in a game against the Washington Senators in Briggs Stadium in Detroit. He went five-for-five and received a standing ovation from Tiger fans. "It felt special," said Virgil. "I loved Detroit. They were such good people. They treated me nice." (Quoted in Henning.)

Detroit was the next-to-last team in the majors to integrate and the development was front-page news in the *Detroit Free Press* when Ozzie Sr. was called up from the Tigers' Charleston, West Virginia farm team and it was announced he would play third base on the night of June 6, 1958.

Among the many Dominicans following in Ozzie Sr.'s path was his son Ozzie Jr. Ozzie Jr. played one game for the 1980 Phillies in his debut season, but spent 11 years in the majors and made two All-Star teams. Born December 7, 1956 in Mayaguez, Puerto Rico, Ozzie Jr.'s batting average was .243 and in 1994 he led the National League in fielding with a .994 percentage. Ozzie Sr.'s pioneer role is what the clan is best remembered for. That's why there is an "Osvaldo Virgil National Airport" in the Dominican. "Everybody in the Dominican Republic knows he was the guy who opened the door," said Ramon Santiago, a later major leaguer. (Quoted in Henning.)

Further Reading

Henning, Lynn. "Virgil's legacy stronger than ever," *Detroit News*, June 17, 2008.

Bernie Williams

An accomplished guitarist, Williams was a superior center fielder for the New York Yankees and lauded as the second-best Puerto Rican outfielder after Roberto Clemente. Born September 13, 1968 in San Juan, Williams was a five-time

A solid-as-a-rock New York Yankee centerfielder from Puerto Rico, Bernie Williams was a four-time Gold Glove winner and a five-time All-Star. Williams' had a lifetime of batting average of .297. He is also an accomplished musician, excelling as a classically trained guitarist of great versatility. (AP Photo/Elise Amendola)

All-Star, a four-time Gold Glove winner, and a fixture on four Yankee World Series championship teams during his 16-year Major League career that culminated with a .297 batting average.

The athletic 6-foot-2, 205-pound Williams (who was a teenage track and field quarter-mile star) broke in with the Yankees in 1991 and played his entire career for the club. His .339 average in 1998 won the American League batting title and in 2000 the superb fielding Williams played 141 games without making an error—he fielded 1.000. Williams, who was too young to see Clemente play, did not compare himself to the all-time great. A student of classical guitar who in 2009 played "Take Me Out to the Ballgame" at Yankee Stadium, Williams was jokingly asked if he would rather sleep with a baseball bat or his guitar. Williams chose the guitar. "At least I can play the guitar if I wake up in the middle of the night," he said. (Quoted in Serby.)

Although not identified especially as a power hitter, the switch-hitting Williams clouted 287 homers in his career, including 30 in 2000, and drove in a career high 121 runs the same year en route to 1,257 lifetime RBIs. Near the end of his career, Williams was asked if he would like to be one of the rare players who spent his entire playing time with one team and to retire with the Yankees. "Absolutely," he said. "It would be an absolute honor." (Quoted in Serby.) Williams did retire as a member of the Yankees in 2006.

Further Reading

Serby, Steve. "Serby's Sunday Q&A with Bernie Williams," *New York Post*, June 26, 2005.

Appendix A

Hispanic Heritage Baseball Museum Hall of Fame

In 1999, a San Francisco Bay area entrepreneur got an idea. Gabriel "Tito" Avila created the Hispanic Heritage Baseball Museum Hall of Fame. Designed to honor the greatest baseball figures of Hispanic heritage, the non-profit organization does not have a building, but it has a presence in cyberspace. The museum also mounts traveling exhibits to baseball events and Major League cities.

In part the Hall of Fame's mission statement reads: "Dedicated to the recognition of the contributions made to baseball by Hispanic players. The Hispanic Heritage Baseball Museum is committed to preserving the history and profound influence that Hispanic players have had on 'America's Favorite Past Time.' Our primary purpose is to provide a center where displays of Hispanic baseball history will educate visitors on the true meaning of diversity, as exemplified in sports. The museum will be built on donations from corporate sponsors, private donors, and fund-raising activities."

Avila remains the driving force behind the museum and hall. The vice-president of the board of directors is Amaury Pi-Gonzalez, who is the voice of the Oakland A's Spanish broadcasts. Also a member of the board is Puerto Rican star Orlando Cepeda.

The museum has been amassing memorabilia and features traveling exhibits. Each year in the city of the Major

"Without the influx of Latin players, we certainly wouldn't have 30 Major League teams. So they've been a great boon to our game, its growth in franchises, as well as in quality of play."

—Roland Hemond, special assistant to the president of the Arizona Diamondbacks. (Quoted in Wendel, Tim and Villegas, Jose Luis, *Far From Home*, National Geographic Society Books, Washington, D.C., 2008, 90.)

League Baseball All-Star game an event is held called "Fan Fest." The Hispanic Heritage Hall had an exhibit at the Fan Fest in connection with the 2008 All-Star game at Yankee Stadium and brought its exhibits to Major League towns like Phoenix, Houston, Miami, and Arlington, Texas.

The first inductees into the Hispanic Heritage Hall in 2002 were Cepeda, a star with the hometown Giants and St. Louis Cardinals; Minnie Minoso, the Cuban who was the first black player for the Chicago White Sox; Tito Fuentes, the 13-year Major League infielder (mostly with the Giants), who was born in Havana, Cuba; and Ted Williams.

Williams's was the most surprising name on the list. Although never identified as being of Hispanic heritage during his playing days between 1939 and 1960 with the Boston Red Sox, Williams's mother was of Mexican origin.

During his long and magnificent career with the Boston Red Sox, Ted Williams was known as "The Splendid Splinter." He was also known for saying that his goal was to become the greatest hitter who ever lived. He broke in with the Red Sox in 1939 and played his entire career with the franchise, retiring in 1960 with a .344 lifetime batting average and 521 home runs. Williams hit .406 in 1941 and no one at the time was willing to predict that he would be the last man to ever hit .400 in the majors. But no one has topped the barrier since.

And no one during Williams's career ever thought of him as Latino. Williams was born in San Diego, California on August 30, 1918. His father was named Samuel and that was Williams's middle name. Samuel was of Welsh and English background. The ball-playing Theodore Samuel Williams was named after Teddy Roosevelt, but outside of sportswriters who referred to him as "Teddy Ballgame" sometimes, Williams was almost universally known as Ted. Initially, Williams was christened Teddy, but his first name was formally changed to the more dignified Theodore.

Williams's mother was named May Venzor, and although she was born in El Paso, Texas, she was of Mexican heritage. All of Williams's maternal ancestors were of Mexican descent, and the lineage cited in Williams's later years leading up to his death in 2002 referred to him being of Mexican heritage. Tracing the family history, Williams was related to Pascual Orozco, a famous Mexican revolutionary general. Of his Mexican heritage, Williams said, "If I had had my mother's name, there is no doubt I would have run into problems in those days (growing up because of) the prejudices people had in Southern California."

Williams discussed his Mexican heritage in the book he wrote with John Underwood in 1969 called "My Turn At Bat." But throughout all of his years in the big leagues, Williams spoke little, if at all, about his Mexican background. He neither denied it nor glorified it in the newspaper reports written during his career.

Danny Williams, Williams's brother, who died in his late 30s from leukemia, was not a baseball player but had a reputation as more of a neighborhood troublemaker. He, more than Ted, had a complexion and visage that recalled their Mexican heritage. Ted Williams more resembled their father, and Danny their mother. "Danny Williams looked Mexican," one biography of Ted Williams stated.

Williams had a nephew, also named Ted, and during the debate over whether or not the player should be on the Latino ballot, he spoke out. "He (Ted) never made a point of letting it be known," the younger Williams said. "He didn't promote it. He was very friendly with our Mexican relatives on a private basis, but sometimes he shunned them in public because he didn't want it to be known. His mother led an Anglo life in San Diego. My father loved to repeat things that my uncle (Williams) said, and one of them is that he called the family in Santa Barbara 'The Mexicans,' kind of lovingly."

A Boston author with a deep background in writing about the Red Sox wrote a book about Williams's youth, and he said that Williams's uncle, Saul Venzor (his mother's brother and a Mexican), tutored him in the fundamentals of baseball and that the ballplayer visited his grandmother in Santa Barbara who spoke primarily Spanish. Relatives who felt disrespected by Williams at times, however, said they believed then-Red Sox general manager Eddie Collins "told him to turn his back on his background and not acknowledge that part of the family."

For some, another surprising name on the list of Hispanic Heritage Museum inductees is Dickie Thon. You can't always tell a player by his birth certificate. A casual glance at Thon's biography is misleading. He was born in South Bend, Indiana on June 20, 1958. The community in the heartland of the United States is best known as the home of the University of Notre Dame.

There is a Notre Dame connection in Thon's life, but he did not grow up in Indiana. Two weeks after Thon was born his family moved back to its real home—Puerto Rico. His father had just completed a college degree, which ended the family's stay in the state.

The Thon roots in baseball go back quite far in Puerto Rico. Dickie's grandfather Freddie Thon was a top player on the island and a long-time manager. His father, also named Freddie, was considered a Major League prospect, but after signing a contract suffered an arm injury that ruined his promise. Brother Frankie Thon played in the minors and in Puerto Rico, was a scout in the United States, and was a winter league manager.

Dickie Thon played 15 Major League seasons with the California Angels, Houston Astros, Philadelphia Phillies, and other teams. He was selected for the 1983 National League All-Star team and had a career .264 batting average. Thon's career was severely hampered after he was hit by a pitch in 1984. A ball thrown by Mike Torrez crushed the orbital bone around Thon's left eye and he was never quite the same again.

Late in the 2008 season prior to a game at Yankee Stadium, the sell-out crowd of more than 50,000 fans stood and applauded a frail, yet vigorous Latino man who played baseball long before they were all born but never spent a moment in the major leagues.

The man's name was Emilio "Millito" Navarro, and as of September 18 of that year he was 102 years old and considered the oldest living professional baseball player. Due to turn 103 the next week, Navarro was on the Yankee Stadium mound to throw out the first pitch in a game against the Chicago White Sox.

Navarro was being honored as the first Puerto Rican to play in the Negro Leagues and spoke mostly in Spanish to reporters and players as he was shepherded around by Felix Lopez, the Yankees' senior vice president. As part of the special occasion, Navarro, who had never been inside Yankee Stadium, was accompanied by his son, grandson, and great-grandsons. Several Yankees sang "Happy Birthday" to him as early delivery of a birthday cake was made.

Navarro was born in Ponce, Puerto Rico in 1905. As a youth he was too poor to pay his way into the local ballpark, so he attended his first game by climbing a fence. The manager of the home team saw him and invited Navarro to play. After that, baseball was his life.

"I mean, 103, that's ridiculous," said third baseman Alex Rodriguez. "He does not look that old. I mean, he was doing push-ups or something a few minutes ago."

Navarro was a middle infielder for the New York Cubans in 1928 and 1929 with a batting average of .337 and also played professionally in the Dominican Republic and Venezuela. His career lasted from 1928 to 1948. He said it was a thrill for him to be at Yankee Stadium. "This is a dream for me," he said, "and I feel like I'm in heaven."

Wearing a Yankees' jersey, Navarro was presented with a commemorative bat. To demonstrate that he was in good shape—at least for someone his age—Navarro touched his toes five times. It wasn't quite push-ups, but it was a pretty limber demonstration. When Navarro was asked what the main difference was between players of his day and the modern player he said, "Dinero" or money. To emphasize his point, Navarro rubbed his thumb and forefinger together.

Navarro said that he made $25 per game in the Negro Leagues after making $2 or so in semi-pro ball in Puerto Rico. "When I played, I met many people who loved me for my whole life," he said, "so even though I didn't have too much money, I was always happy."

After his playing days, Navarro returned to Puerto Rico and founded a baseball team called the Ponce Lions. For 20 additional years, Navarro played, coached, and ran the operations of the club. In 2005, the Puerto Rican Senate passed a resolution of recognition for Navarro's contributions to the game and to his home island. Eventually, Navarro was inducted into the Puerto Rican Sports Hall of Fame and the Hispanic Heritage Baseball Museum.

"I know that a lot of great things happened in this place," said Navarro in reference to Yankee Stadium's years of hosting World Series games, "but for me, this will always be the greatest day. This is a great pleasure for me. No matter my age, I am the man who is enjoying this day the most."

Navarro was 104 as the 2010 baseball season began.

Members of the Hispanic Heritage Baseball Museum and Hall of Fame

Sandy Alomar
Felipe Alou
Matty Alou
Luis Aparicio*
Billy Berroa[#]
Buck Canel[#]
Bert Campaneris
Rene Cardenas[#]
Rod Carew*
Orlando Cepeda*
Roberto Clemente*
Jose Cruz
Martin Dihigo*
Alex Fernandez
Tito Fuentes
Alfredo Griffin
Lefty Gomez
Preston Gomez
Amaury Pi-Gonzalez[#]
Jaime Jarrin[#]
Tony LaRussa
Al Lopez*
Hector Lopez
Juan Marichal*
Edgar Martinez
Minnie Minoso
Jose Mendez*
Orlando Mercado
Manny Mota
Emilio Navarro
Tony Perez*
Alex Pompez*
Rafael (Felo) Ramirez[#]

Jackie Robinson*
Cookie Rojas
Diego Segui
Tony Taylor
Dickie Thon
Luis Tiant
Cristobal Torriente*
Alex Trevino
Fernando Valenzuela
Ted Williams*
Omar Vizquel

*Also members of the National Baseball Hall of Fame in Cooperstown, New York.
Broadcasters

Appendix B

Twelve Young Hispanic Players to Watch

Asdrubal Cabrera, Cleveland Indians shortstop. Born November 13, 1985 in Puerto La Cruz, Venezuela, Cabrera is 6 feet tall and weighs 170 pounds. He saw his first Major League action in 2007. A switch-hitter, Cabrera had a breakout season in 2009, hitting .308. His most memorable feat on the diamond occurred on May 12, 2008 when Cabrera became the 14th player in Major League history to record an unassisted triple play. The magical play occurred during the fifth inning of the second game of a doubleheader against the Toronto Blue Jays at Progressive Field.

Robinson Cano, New York Yankees second baseman. Born October 22, 1982 in San Pedro de Macoris, Dominican Republic, Cano broke into the majors in 2005, quickly becoming the Yankees' starting second baseman. In 2006, the year he was named to his first American League All-Star team, Cano batted .342 and he has almost always kept his average over .300. Robinson was named after legendary player Jackie Robinson.

Fausto Carmona, Cleveland Indians pitcher. The 6-foot-4, 220-pound right-hander was born December 7, 1983 in Santo Domingo, Dominican Republic. Carmona suffered through a painful 2006 rookie year, going 1–10, but bounced back in 2007 to finish 19–8 and help lift the Indians into the playoffs. Known for throwing a good slider, Carmona also possesses a 97-mph fastball.

Johnny Cueto, Cincinnati Reds pitcher. Born February 15, 1985 in San Pedro de Macoris, Dominican Republic, Cueto is a right-handed pitcher listed at 5-foot-10 and 185 pounds and says the slightly built Pedro Martinez is his role model. Cueto joined the Reds' rotation as a rookie in 2008 and finished 9–14. In his Major League debut, Cueto was perfect through five innings and was the first Reds pitcher since 1900 to strike out 10 batters in his first game. Cueto pitched for the Dominican in the 2009 World Baseball Classic.

Adrian Gonzalez, San Diego Padres first baseman. Gonzalez, born May 8, 1982 in San Diego, California, is of Mexican heritage. His parents are Mexican and as a youngster Gonzalez lived in Mexico for 12 years. Gonzalez played for Mexico in the 2006 and 2009 World Baseball Classic. He has blossomed into one of the top sluggers in the National League with highs of 36 home runs and 119 RBIs in 2008. A two-time All-Star, Gonzalez won his first Gold Glove in 2008.

Francisco Liriano, Minnesota Twins pitcher. Born October 26, 1983 in San Cristobal, Dominican Republic, the 6-foot-2, 225-pound southpaw is regarded as a player with a world of potential. Liriano made a handful of appearances for the Twins in 2005, but in 2006 he made a huge splash in the American League. Liriano finished 12-3 with 144 strikeouts in 121 innings and a 2.16 earned run average. However, Liriano has had arm woes since and his future is murky.

Kendry Morales, Los Angeles Angels of Anaheim, first baseman. Morales was born June 20, 1983 in Fomento, Cuba. A sensation as he moved up through the ranks with Cuba's amateur teams, Morales reportedly tried to defect eight or more times to play professional baseball before being successful in 2004. Morales had been suspended from Cuban national team play in retaliation for his several attempts to flee the island. Morales worked his way through the Angels' minor league system, earning sporadic playing time with the big club until he took over as the full-time first baseman in 2009.

Hanley Ramirez, Florida Marlins shortstop. Considered a rising superstar, Ramirez won the 2009 National League batting championship with a mark of .342. It was his third full-season mark over .300. Born December 23, 1983 in Samana, Dominican Republic, Ramirez is 6-foot-3 and weighs 195 pounds. Ramirez played the first few games of his Major League career with the Red Sox, but has been a cornerstone of the Marlins. He was named 2006 National League rookie of the year and is a two-time All-Star.

Jose Reyes, New York Mets shortstop. The slick-fielding Reyes was born June 11, 1983 in Villa Gonzalez, Dominican Republic and has been with the Mets since 2003, his first game coming the day before his 20th birthday. Reyes has led the

National League in at-bats three times, in hits (with 204 in 2008) once, in triples twice, and in stolen bases three times. His best year for stolen bases was 2007 when he swiped 78. Reyes is already the Mets' all-time leader in triples and stolen bases. Reyes competed for the Dominican in the 2006 and 2009 World Baseball Classics. He is also known for his colorful wiggles and dances in the Mets' dugout.

Pablo Sandoval, San Francisco Giants, third baseman. A switch-hitter who packs power in his 5-foot-11, 245-pound frame, Sandoval emerged as a sensation during the 2009 season. Born August 11, 1986 in Puerto Cabello, Venezuela, Sandoval was a free agent when he hooked up with the Giants. His speedy development surprised officials and his sophistication at the plate was a boon to the team after he reached the majors in 2008. Popular for his humor in the clubhouse and crowd-friendly behavior and light-hearted demeanor, Sandoval was nick-named "Kung Fu Panda," based on a cartoon character in a children's movie. In 2009, he finished second in National League hitting at .330.

Geovany Soto, Chicago Cubs catcher. Soto was the National League Rookie of the Year in 2008 when he appeared in 141 games, batted .285, and stroked 23 home runs. He was also selected for the All-Star game. The 6-foot-1, 230-pound receiver was born on January 20, 1983 in San Juan, Puerto Rico. After backstopping the Cubs to the playoffs with a division title in 2008, Soto encountered several problems in 2009. Soto strained an oblique muscle that sidelined him for a long period, and it was announced that he tested positive for marijuana at the World Baseball Classic. He was banned from international play for two years.

Carlos Zambrano, Chicago Cubs pitcher. Regarded as one of the purest talents in the game, the 6-foot-5, 250-pound Zambrano has pitched a no-hitter and been selected for three National League All-Star teams, but he has not shown the type of consistency the Cubs are seeking. Born June 1, 1981 in Puerto Cabello, Venezuela, Zambrano, probably the best hitting pitcher in the majors, has won 105 big league games, but has also had several run-ins with managers and management. His potential remains untapped.

Appendix C

Latin Americans in the National Baseball Hall of Fame

In 2009, the National Baseball Hall of Fame in Cooperstown, New York mounted a tribute to Latin American baseball stars and the roots of the sport in neighboring countries called "Viva Baseball!" It was a symbolic act that demonstrated the importance of the Latin American ballplayer to the United States' national pastime. Once, players from Latino countries were shunned, either because of their dark skin color, or they were slow to be accepted because their first language was Spanish. Now they were being celebrated.

The Hall pointed out that at the start of the 2009 Major League season some 29 percent of the players on opening day rosters were of Hispanic heritage. The exhibit and the statements of officials at the Hall took special note of the growth in the number of players flocking to big-league teams from the Dominican Republic, Mexico, Puerto Rico, and other Latino nations and ports of call.

"Over the last 30 years, perhaps nothing has impacted baseball more than the rise of the Latino star and the number of Latino players making important contributions to the game today," said Hall President Jeff Idelson. (Quoted in Hall release May 23.)

The exhibit was unveiled with funding help from the Chicago White Sox, the Kansas City Royals, a number of individuals, and some Cooperstown businesses. It features 150 artifacts of Latino involvement in the game. Opening on May 23, 2009, it was announced that "Viva Baseball!" would be a permanent display at the Hall.

One of the most dramatic items on display is a baseball from an 1871 game in the United States in which Cuban Esteban Bellan played. The first Latino chosen for the Hall of Fame was Roberto Clemente in 1973. The five-year waiting period after retirement was waved following his tragic death in an airplane crash while trying to deliver emergency supplies to earthquake devastated Nicaragua. Other Latino Hall of Famers are Cubans Tony Perez, Martin Dihigo, Cristobal Torriente, and Jose Mendez. Luis Aparicio represents Venezuela, Juan Marichal represents the Dominican Republic, Rod Carew represents Panama, and Orlando Cepeda represents Puerto Rico. That number should expand greatly in the coming years as the current-day stars from Latin American countries retire.

Cepeda was present for the opening of the exhibit. "To be here today, we went through some obstacles and we are very, very pleased," Cepeda said. "I am proud to be Puerto Rican and grateful to the Hall of Fame for this wonderful day." (Quoted in Hall release May 23.)

Idelson noted how the best Latin American players have been inspirations for the youngsters in their home countries or communities. "Latin American players have made a tremendous impact on our National Pastime," he said. "Two generations of Latin American youngsters have grown up idolizing players like Juan Marichal and Orlando Cepeda." (Quoted in Hall release May 9.)

Further Reading

National Baseball Hall of Fame press release, May 9, 2009, www.baseballhalloffame.org.
National Baseball Hall of Fame press release, May 23, 2009, www.baseballhalloffame.org.

Appendix D

Roberto Clemente Award

The Latino baseball star who engenders the greatest respect among the Hispanic players who came after him is Roberto Clemente. With his 3,000 hits, phenomenal fielding skills, his concern for other Latin players, his pride in being Hispanic, his devotion to community and charity, and his untimely death on a mercy mission, Clemente is the icon that stands above all others.

Major League Baseball waved the five-year waiting rule for election to the National Baseball Hall of Fame after Clemente's death in a plane crash while attempting to transport food and medical supplies to earthquake-torn Managua, Nicaragua on December 31, 1972. Clemente was voted in immediately.

But the administrative arm of baseball went beyond that accommodation. In 1971, the sport's governing body began singling out and rewarding the off-the-field contributions of its players. The Commissioner's Award was introduced. Upon Clemente's death, however, the name was changed to the Roberto Clemente Award. The award is given annually to a player that "best exemplifies the game of baseball, sportsmanship, community involvement and the individual's contribution to his team."

Each year one nominee is put forth from each of the 30 Major League teams and then a panel of baseball luminaries vote on the winner. The winner is announced on national television during the World Series.

Winners of the Roberto Clemente Award

1971 Willie Mays, San Francisco Giants

1972 Brooks Robinson, Baltimore Orioles

1973 Al Kaline, Detroit Tigers

1974 Willie Stargell, Pittsburgh Pirates

1975 Lou Brock, St. Louis Cardinals

1976 Pete Rose, Cincinnati Reds

1977 Rod Carew, Minnesota Twins

1978 Greg Luzinski, Philadelphia Phillies

1979 Andre Thornton, Cleveland Indians

1980 Phil Niekro, Atlanta Braves

1981 Steve Garvey, Los Angeles Dodgers

1982 Ken Singleton, Baltimore Orioles

1983 Cecil Cooper, Milwaukee Brewers

1984 Ron Guidry, New York Yankees

1985 Don Baylor, New York Yankees

1986 Garry Maddox, Philadelphia Phillies

1987 Rick Sutcliffe, Chicago Cubs

1988 Dale Murphy, Atlanta Braves

1989 Gary Carter, New York Mets

1990 Dave Stewart, Oakland Athletics

1991 Harold Reynolds, Seattle Mariners

1992 Cal Ripken, Jr., Baltimore Orioles

1993 Barry Larkin, Cincinnati Reds

1994 Dave Winfield, Minnesota Twins

1995 Ozzie Smith, St. Louis Cardinals

1996 Kirby Puckett, Minnesota Twins

1997 Eric Davis, Baltimore Orioles

1998 Sammy Sosa, Chicago Cubs

1999 Tony Gwynn, San Diego Padres

2000 Al Leiter, New York Mets

2001 Curt Schilling, Arizona Diamondbacks

2002 Jim Thome, Cleveland Indians

2003 Jamie Moyer, Seattle Mariners

2004 Edgar Martinez, Seattle Mariners

2005 John Smoltz, Atlanta Braves

2006 Carlos Delgado, New York Mets

2007 Craig Biggio, Houston Astros

2008 Albert Pujols, St. Louis Cardinals.

2009 Derek Jeter, New York Yankees

Further Reading

Roberto Clemente Award winners, www.mlb.com.

Bibliography

Abarim.com, www.abarim.com/bmaigatter.htm, Edgar Martinez Support for the Hall of Fame site.

"All Tied at 62," Associated Press, September 14, 1998.

"Amoros Dies Of Pneumonia," Associated Press, June 28, 1992.

Anderson, Dave. "In Old Cuba With Dihigo And Lasorda," *New York Times*, March 23, 1999.

———. "Say It Ain't So, Fidel," *New York Times*, March 25, 1982.

Antonen, Mel. "A-Rod gets $242 million and a new address in Texas," *USA Today*, December 12, 2000.

———. "Roberto Alomar gives credit to sibling for baseball career," *USA Today*, October 10, 1997.

"Aparicio Likes AstroTurf on White Sox Park Infield," *The Sporting News*, September 20, 1969.

Arangure, Jr., Jorge. "New world of hope awaits Chapman," *ESPN The Magazine*, August 12, 2009.

———. "Top Cuban prospect defects," *ESPN The Magazine*, July 3, 2009.

Baker, Geoff. "Citizen Carlos," *San Juan Star*, July 3, 2004.

Baltimore Orioles Press Release, August 1, 2005.

Banks, Ernie. "Ernie Banks Rates Clemente Toughest Star He Ever Faced," *Chicago Tribune*, July 6, 1968.

Barnas, Jo-Ann. "The Power of Pudge: He credits his father for success and his son shares in it," *Detroit Free Press*, April 5, 2004.

Baseball Almanac.com, http://www.baseball-almanac.com.

"Baseball's Best Hitter Tries for Glory," *Time Magazine*, July 18, 1977.

Baxter, Kevin. "The Marlins' $10 million bargain," *Miami Herald*, October 30, 2003.

Beaton, Rod. "Reds' Fernandez: Latino players don't get treated fairly," *USA Today*, May 12, 1994.

———. "Baseball cracks down on underage signings," *USA Today*, February 8, 2000.

———. "Galaragga says support 'makes me feel so strong,' " *USA Today*, March 18, 1999.

———. "Indians sign up Cuban pitcher for record $14.5 million," *USA Today*, November 8, 1999.

———. "Lopez hits .542 for MVP," *USA Today*, October 18, 1996.

Beisbol—The Latin Game, Major League Baseball Presents, 2007.

Biederman, Les. "Bat King Matty—The Man Everybody Knows," *Pittsburgh Press*, March 25, 1967.

———. "Clouter Clemente Popular Buc," *The Sporting News*, September 5, 1964.

———. "Dolph Luque Had Temper To Match Fine Curve," *Pittsburgh Press*, July 7, 1957.

———. "Hitting in Daylight (.411 Versus .302) Best For Clemente," *Pittsburgh Press*, March 11, 1962.

———. "Latin Player Faces Many Tough Barriers in U.S., Roberto Says," *The Sporting News*, September 5, 1964.

———. "Super Handyman Jose Pagan Earns Pirate Plaudits," *Pittsburgh Press*, January 18, 1969.

"Big Cat retires at 43 years old," Associated Press, March 30, 2005.

Bjarkman, Peter C. *Baseball With A Latin Beat*. Jefferson, North Carolina, McFarland & Company, Inc. Publishers, 1994.

———, "Martin Dihigo: Baseball's Least-Known Hall of Famer," Elysian Fields Quarterly, Spring, 2001.

Blinebury, Fran. "Fernando joins great Hubbell on strikeout list," *Houston Chronicle*, July 16, 1986.

Bloom, Barry. "Alomar, As In All-Star," *Sport Magazine*, March, 1991.

———. "Favorite Son," *Sport Magazine*, May, 1998.

Boone, Roderick. "Yankees honor 102-year-old former ballplayer," *Newsday*, September 19, 2008.

"Boston's Ramirez becomes a United States citizen," Associated Press, May 12, 2004.

Boswell, Thomas. "Cuban Baseball: The Only Way of Life, Marriage of a People and a Game," *Washington Post*, April 30, 1978.

Botte, Peter. "Yankee teammates save best praise for Mariano Rivera's milestone," *New York Daily News*, June 29, 2009.

Brady, Frank. "To Err Is Rare for Trillo of Phillies; It is His First in 89 Games," *New York Times*, August 1, 1982.

Breton, Marcos. *Home Is Everything: The Latino Baseball Story*. El Paso, Texas, Cinco Puntos Press, 2002.

Broeg, Bob. "Matty Alou: The Talking Mouse Who Soared At the Plate," *St. Louis Post-Dispatch*, August 29, 1968.

Brown, Daniel. "Pompez helped open doors for Latinos in major league baseball," *San Jose Mercury News*, August 2, 2006.

"Buck O'Neil sees Willie Mays in Carlos Beltran," Associated Press, March 22, 2000.

Burgos, Jr., Adrian. *Playing America's Game*. Berkeley, California, University of California Press, 2007.

Burris, Joe. "Nice catch for Marlins," *Boston Globe*, October 18, 2003.

Caldwell, Dave. "Juan on Juan," *Dallas Morning News*, May 13, 1996.

Callahan, Gerry, "Son of Sammy," *Sports Illustrated*, April 5, 1999.

Carchidi, Sam. "Tony Taylor honored as Phils' Latin Legend," *Philadelphia Inquirer*, July 18, 2002.

Carew, Rod and Berkow, Ira. *Carew*. New York, Simon & Schuster, 1979.

Carmona, Emilio. "Clemente Once Hit 10 Homers in One Game," *San Juan Star*, June 26, 1960.

"Carty's Creed: Born to Hit," Associated Press, June 25, 1972.

Castellano, Dan. "Bonilla's last games as Pirate leaves him with bad memories," *Newark Star-Ledger*, March 15, 1992.

CBSSports.com, www.cbssports.com.

Cepeda, Orlando and Fagen, Herb. *Baby Bull: From Hard Ball to Hard Time and Back*. Dallas, Texas, Taylor Publishing Company, 1998.

Chapin, Dwight. "Cepeda can't get to first in post-baseball life," *San Francisco Examiner*, May 22, 1988.

Chass, Murray. "A Shy Ramirez Seeks His Comfort Zone," *New York Times*, December 23, 2001.

———. "Clemente's Dream: A Utopian Sports City," *New York Times*, October 21, 1971.

Christensen, Joe. "O's pick up Tejada, credibility," *Baltimore Sun*, December 15, 2003.

Christine, Bill. "Clemente Reveals Close Call With Kidnappers," *Pittsburgh Press*, August 22, 1970.

———. "Matty Magic," *Pittsburgh Press*, June 18, 1969.

Cincinnati Reds Scorebook, 1982.

Claflin, Larry. " '65 RBI Champ, Handyman's Torrid Tempo No Surprise to Hub Fans," Boston Record-American, June 12, 1965.

Coffey, Wayne. "Washington Heights' Ramirez has Cleveland rockin' again," *New York Daily News*, June 4, 1995.

Colston, Chris. "Oliva's hot bat warmed Minnesota," *USA Today Baseball Weekly*, August 27/September 2, 1997.

Condon, David. In the Wake of the News Column, *Chicago Tribune*, July 6, 1957.

Covitz, Randy. "Brewers rookie looks like a winner," *Kansas City Times*, June 5, 1985.

Crouse, Karen. "Two shortstops unite violence-torn nation," *Palm Beach Post*, October 27, 2004.

Current Biography.

Daley, Arthur. "The Cuban Curver," *New York Times*, July 14, 1957.

Daniel, Dan. "Fox, Aparicio Rated Greatest by Al Lopez," *New York World Telegram & Sun*, August 24, 1959.

Davidoff, Ken. "A lesson learned 500 times: Mo refuses to fade away," *Newsday*, June 29, 2009.

Dellios, Hugh. "Venezuela Wild About Sox," *Chicago Tribune*, October 22, 2005.

Dillon, Sam. "Beisbol, Si! But Can U.S. Players Drink the Water?" *New York Times*, March 31, 1999.

DiMeglio, Steve. "Blazing a shortcut to the big leagues," *USA Today Baseball Weekly*, May 16–22, 2001.

———. "Reconstructed and rejuvenated," *USA Today Baseball Weekly*, April 24–30, 2002.

Dodger Blue, Los Angeles Dodgers' Team Publication, July 15, 1983.

Dolgan, Bob. "Good glove, better guy for Indians," *Cleveland Plain Dealer*, November 30, 2005.

Donnelly, Joe. "Alou Bridged the Gap For Latin Americans," Newsday, September 8, 1971.

Dozer, Richard. "Veeck Eyes Cuba for White Sox Talent," *The Sporting News*, October 23, 1976.

Durslag, Melvin. "A stroke of genius," *TV Guide*, September 3, 1977.

Edes, Gordon. "Brothers in Arms," *Boston Globe*, April 2, 2000.

Eisenberg, Jeff. "Venezuelan major leaguers take protective measures," *Riverside Press-Enterprise*, May 20, 2007.

Elliott, Josh. "Raffy Joins the Club," *Sports Illustrated*, May 19, 2003.

Encyclopedia of World Biography. "Alex Rodriguez," www.notablebiographies.com.

Eradi, John. "After six years, finally Rijo returns," *USA Today Baseball Weekly*, August 22–28, 2001.

ESPN news services, "Tejada admits to being two years older than he had said," April 18, 2002, www.espn.com.

"Ex-Pirates Scout Howie Haak Dies," Associated Press, February 28, 1999.

"Expos' Martinez reaping success," Associated Press, August 8, 1987.

"Ex-Tiger Ivan Rodriguez sets record for catching," *Detroit Free Press*, June 18, 2009.

Fainaru, Steve. "Revolutionary: playing for the love of the game," *Boston Globe*, December 3, 1995.

Fay, John. "Reds great Bench 'proud' of Pudge," *Cincinnati Enquirer*, June 11, 2002.

"Feeney, Charles. "They've Stopped Calling Matty 'Lucky Alou,' " *The Sporting News*, August 2, 1969.

"Fernando Edges Seaver in N.L. Cy Young vote," *San Francisco Chronicle*, November 12, 1981.

Finch, Paul. "Matter of $1,000 Once Stopped Avila From Becoming A Dodger," *Los Angeles Times*, March 15, 1962.

Finnigan, Bob. "Mayor names street after Martinez," *Seattle Times*, October 2, 2004.

Fitzgerald, Joe. "Luis Tiant can tell you the real story of Cuba," *Boston Herald*, November 6, 1983.

Flanagan, Barbara. "Ramos Is Kooky Cavalier," *Minneapolis Tribune*, April 16, 1961.

Foley, Red. "Puerto Rico Eyes Figueroa's 20-Bid," *New York Daily News*, September 29, 1976.

"For the Alous, a Father-Son Reunion Comes in Giants Uniform," Associated Press, March 6, 2005.

Forman, Ross. "Baseball runs in the family for Jose Cruz Jr.," *Sports Collector's Digest*, June 11, 1999.

———. "Little Looie," *Sports Collector's Digest*, June 28. 1991.

Forreo, Juan. "Cultivating a Field of Dreams," *Newark Star-Ledger*, July 5, 1998.

Foster, Chris and Shaikin, Bill. "City of Brotherly Gloves," *Los Angeles Times*, October 17, 2002.

Frau, Miguel. "P.R. Fans Laud Perez—Tony Repays Favor," *The Sporting News*, January 30, 1971.

Freedman, Lew. *Game of My Life: Chicago White Sox*. Champaign, Illinois, Sports Publishing LLC, 2008.

Frizzell, Pat. "No. 200 Restores Marichal's Wide Grin," *The Sporting News*, September 12, 1970.

Gage, Tom. "A.L. Pitcher: Tigers' Hernandez Was Nearly Perfect," *Detroit News*, October 29, 1984.

Gammons, Peter. "Hall of Famer in the shadows," *Boston Globe*, September 5, 1985.

"Go go Fernando," *Chicago Tribune*, May 14, 1981.

Goldstein, Alan. "Today, Andujar is one mellow Dominican," *Baltimore Sun*, August 21, 1986.

Goldstein, Richard. "Howie Haak, Baseball Pioneer in Latin America, Dies at 87," *New York Times*, March 1, 1999.

Goold, Derrick. "Pujols hits 3 for kids," *St. Louis Post-Dispatch*, September 4, 2006.

Graham, Frank. "Adolpho Luque Is Dead?" *New York Journal-American*, July 17, 1957.

———. "Power Proves His Case," *Sport Magazine*, August, 1956.

Greenstein, Teddy. "Guillen shoots from hip in HBO interview," *Chicago Tribune*, February 5, 2006.

———. "White Sox name Ozzie Guillen their latest manager," *Chicago Tribune*, November 3, 2003.

Gregory, Sean. "Arturo Moreno," *Time Magazine*, August 13, 2005.

Grieve, Curley. "Matty Ready To Go; Leg Gets Doc's OK," *San Francisco Examiner*, May 12, 1962.

Grimsley, Will. "It's Campy's Night," Associated Press, October 7, 1974.

Gross, Milton. "Cepeda Grows Up; He's Starting to Act Like A Team Man," *Pittsburgh Press*, July 2, 1961.

———. "Death Threat to A Batting Champion," *Sports Today*, August, 1971.

"Guillen 'like the king of Venezuela,'" *Albany Times-Union*, October 31, 2005.

"Guillen gives back to ravaged homeland," Associated Press, February 25, 2000.

Gutierrez, Paul. "Bobby Avila, 78; First Mexican to Win Major League Batting Crown," *Los Angeles Times*, October 28, 2004.

Habib, Daniel. "The sweet stroke of the Cards' Albert Pujols has put him on a home run tear and made him the game's best hitter," *Sports Illustrated*, May 22, 2006.

Haft, Chris. "High-Kicking Excellence," *San Jose Mercury News*, May 18, 2005.

"Happy Fan returns No. 63 to grateful Sosa," *USA Today*, September 18, 1998.

Harper, John. "At start of Mariano Rivera's Yankee career, Gene Michael almost traded him," New York Daily News, June 30, 2009.

Harrelson, Ken. WGN-TV, Chicago. Chicago White Sox versus New York Yankees, August 2, 2009.

"He Had The Touch of Royalty," *Newsday*, January 2, 1973.

Henning, Lynn. "Virgil's legacy stronger than ever," *Detroit News*, June 17, 2008.

"Hernandez seventh pitcher to win MVP," Associated Press, November 7, 1984.

Hershkowitz, Mickey. "Julian Javier Is Key to Cardinal 'Jopes,'" *Houston Post*, April 29, 1962.

Hertzel, Bob. "Perez Recounts Homecoming After 10 Years of Separation," *Cincinnati Enquirer*, National Baseball Hall of Fame Library archives (date missing).

Hill, Thomas. "Alou: Teams want white managers," *New York Daily News*, May 22, 1999.

———. "Going to bat for homeless," *New York Daily News*, November 13, 1998.

Hispanic Heritage Baseball Museum Hall of Fame.com.

"Hitman: Pitchers had little chance stopping Magglio Ordonez in 2007," *Detroit News*, December 28, 2007.

Hoak, Don and Cope, Myron. "The Day I Batted Against Castro," *Sport Magazine*, June, 1964.

Hoard, Greg. "The Proud Presence of Tony Perez," *Cincinnati Enquirer*, September 22, 1985.

Hoffer, Richard. "Heeeere's Ozzie!" *Sports Illustrated*, April 6, 1992.

Holmes, Tommy. "The Corner Catches Up With Lou Olmo," *Brooklyn Eagle*, February 26, 1947.

Holway, John B. *Black Diamonds*. Westport, Connecticut, Meckler Books, 1989.

———. Josh and Satch, Westport, Connecticut, Meckler Books, 1991.

Horgan, Tim. "Luis Tiant—All Man," *Boston Herald-American*, June 12, 1974.

Hoynes, Paul. "22-0! Omar's 6 hits ignite a Bronx bombardment as Tribe deals Yanks record-setting rout," *Cleveland Plain Dealer*, September 1, 2004.

Hubbard, Steve. "Thrift found a gem in Scandinavia," *Pittsburgh Press*, May 15, 1988.

Hummel, Rick. "Sport Interview: Joaquin Andujar," *Sport Magazine*, September, 1985.

Hyde, David. "Perez's Courage Unique in Hall of Fame," July, 2000. *Florida Sun-Sentinel*, National Baseball Hall of Fame Library archives (day missing).

Hyman, Mark. "Will Martinez and Montreal Mix?" *Baltimore Sun*, June 26, 1986.

Isaacs, Stan. "Vic and Baseball: Love at First Base," *Newsday*, June 29, 1962.

"Ivan Rodriguez breaks record for games caught," Associated Press, June 18, 2009.

ivoryTowerz.com. "Fidel Castro, Baseball Writer," March 16, 2009, www://ivorytowerz.com.

Jacobson, Julie. "Yankees show former ballplayer, 102, a great time," September 19, 2008.

Jamail, Milton H. *Venezuelan Bust, Baseball Boom: Andres Reiner and Scouting on the New Frontier*. Lincoln, Nebraska, University of Nebraska Press, 2008.

Johnson, Chuck. "Alomar sons deepen roots in baseball," *USA Today*, July 13, 1990.

———. "Bell confident he'll eventually earn respect," *USA Today*, June 26, 1990.

———. "Pujols a Card-carrying star," *USA Today*, May 22, 2001.

Kaegel, Dick. "Dominican managers make history," *Kansas City Star*, June 25, 2002.

KansasCity.com. "Catching up with Royals Hall of Fame second baseman Cookie Rojas," July 13, 2003. Kansas City Star, www.kansascity.com.

Kay, Michael. "Surviving Panamania," *New York Daily News*, National Baseball Hall of Fame Library archives (date missing).

Keegan, Tom. "Edgar Stands Alone," *New York Post*, October 9, 1995.

Kelley, Brent. *Voices From the Negro Leagues*. Jefferson, North Carolina, McFarland & Company, Inc. Publishers, 1998.

Kelley, Steve. "Edgar Martinez receives Clemente Award," *Seattle Times*, October 27, 2004.

Kelly, Ray. " 'Don't Give Up Your Rituals,' Pagan's Sermon to Montanez," Philadelphia Bulletin, National Baseball Hall of Fame Library archives (date missing).

Kepner, Tyler. "Hernandez: The Pinstripes Make the Man," *New York Times*, July 12, 2004.

Kernan, Kevin. "Mates: Andruw is just a-Mays-ing," *New York Post*, July 3, 2000.

King, David. "Marichal is a man of many hats," *San Antonio Express-News*, April 11, 2004.

———. "Perez reflects on World Series rings, great jobs, Pete Rose," *San Antonio Express-News*, September 5, 2006.

Klein, Alan M. *Sugarball: The American Game, The Dominican Dream*. New Haven, Connecticut, Yale University Press, 1991.

Klein, Frederick. "Carew: Master thief of home," *Wall Street Journal*, May 14, 1980.

Kornheiser, Tony. "Fernando: Star in the Remaking," *Washington Post*, July 20, 1993.

Kovacevic, Dejan. "Playing baseball never gets old to Santiago," *Pittsburgh Post-Gazette*, March 6, 2005.

Krich, John. *El Beisbol: The Pleasures And Passions Of The Latin American Game*. Chicago, Ivan R. Dee, 1989.

"Lack of $10 Made Star Out of Taylor," *The Sporting News*, March 23, 1970.

Lamey, Mike. "Carew Wins Support as Possible .400 Swatter," *The Sporting News*, July 12, 1969.

Lang, Jack. "Guillen named AL's top rookie," *New York Daily News*, November 27, 1985.

Latham, Krista. "Ordonez super signing for '05," *Detroit Free Press*, February 8, 2005.

Lawson, Earl. "Confidence Makes Reds' Borbon a Winner," *The Sporting News*, January 13, 1973.

———. "Perez Hits HRs to Order—From Son," *The Sporting News*, May 16, 1970.

Leonard, Buck and Riley, James A. *Buck Leonard: The Black Lou Gehrig*. New York, Carroll & Graf Publishers, Inc., 1995.

Lidz, Franz. "Slick with the Stick," *Sports Illustrated*, April 4, 1994.

Livingstone, Seth. "Indians' Vizquel finds beauty in glove work," *USA Today*, May 1, 2001.

Llosa, Luis Fernando. "Mania Man," *Sports Illustrated*, June 30, 2003.

Lopez, Aaron J. "Vinny Castillo is Jordan of Mexico," Associated Press, March 1, 1999.

Los Angeles Dodgers Press Box Notes, May 7, 1981.

Los Angeles Dodgers Press Release, February 2, 1998.

Lott, John. "Another level; As Roberto is honoured by Blue Jays, the star hopes fans forgive an old mistake," *The National Post*, April 4, 2008.

Lowell, Mike and Bradford, Rob. *Deep Drive*. New York, Celbra Books, 2008.

MacDonald, Ian. "Heeding Expos' Call for Arms," *The Sporting News*, September 12, 1988.

Maraniss, David. *Clemente: The Passion and Grace of Baseball's Last Hero*. New York, Simon & Schuster, 2006.

Marantz, Steve. "Pedro Martinez says he has to pitch high and tight to be effective," *The Sporting News*, July 18, 1994.

Marazzi, Rich. "Arroyo was Yanks' relief ace in epic '61 season," *Sports Collector's Digest*, May 17, 1996.

———. "The Yankees passed on slick fielding Vic Power," *Sports Collector's Digest*, January 15, 1999.

"Marichal's induction hailed in 2 countries," Associated Press, August 2, 1983.

"Martinez Attains Perfection in L.A.," Associated Press, July 29, 1991.

"Martinez could be first DH in Hall of Fame," Associated Press, May 22, 2003.

"Martinez joins Koufax as Dodger strikeout king," Associated Press, June 6, 1990.

"Martinez surpasses mark in Marichal's home," *USA Today*, August 11, 1998.

McCollister, John. *The Good, The Bad & The Ugly, Pittsburgh Pirates*. Chicago, Triumph Books, 2008.

McCoy, Hal. "Concepcion gets emotional as Reds retire No. 13," *Dayton Daily News*, August 26, 2007.

McDonald, Jack. " 'Nothing Wrong With Cepeda's Eyes,' Says Medic After Exam," *San Francisco Examiner*, November 10, 1962.

———. "Those Bad Pitches Look Too Juicy for Jesus Alou to Resist," *The Sporting News*, April 2, 1966.

McGuff, Joe. "Campaneris Thrills Kaycee Fans With Exploits As Bandit," *The Sporting News*, July 31, 1965.

McHugh, Roy. "Matty Alou Goes By His Own Book," *Pittsburgh Press*, April 10, 1969.

McNeal, Stan and Veltrop, Kyle. *Curse Reversed*. St. Louis, Sporting News Books, 2004.

Mendelson, Abby. "Whatever Happened to Cesar Cedeno?" Baseball Quarterly, Winter, 1978–79.

Mercer, Sid. National Baseball Hall of Fame Library archives, unattributed newspaper, January 5, 1937.

Merchant, Larry. "The Power of Vic," *Philadelphia Daily News*, June 26, 1962.

Meyers, Bill. "Teams woo Hispanic fans," *USA Today*, September 29, 1997.

MiamiHerald.com. "20 questions with Miguel Cabrera," July 10, 2005, www.MiamiHerald.com.

Miech, Rob. "All-Star Santiago defies odds," *USA Today*, National Baseball Hall of Fame Library archive (date missing).

Miller, Lou. " 'I Not Afraid,' Says Minnie, Back After 50th Plunking," Cleveland Press, July 15, 1955.

Minnesota Twins Game Program, circa 1960s (date missing).

Minnie, Minoso and Fagen, Herb. *Just Call Me Minnie*. Champaign, Illinois, Sagamore Publishing, 1994.

"Minoso Is 'Back Home' With White Sox Mates,' " United Press International, March 22, 1964.

Minshew, Wayne. "Shoe Salesman in Deep Shock; Carty Buys 25 Pairs at a Clip," *The Sporting News*, July 22, 1967.

MLB honors Pujols," Associated Press, October 27, 2008.

MLB.com.

Montville, Leigh. Ted Williams: The Biography Of An American Hero." New York, Doubleday, 2004.

Moriah, David. "Steady personality keeps Fernandez in the game," *Sports Collector's Digest*, January 15, 1999.

Moton, Tom. "Unanimous vote names Alomar best rookie," November, 1990. The National, National Baseball Hall of Fame Library archives (day missing).

Mullin, John. "Guillen playing to rave reviews; Humor, wisdom boosts manager's stock as a leader," *Chicago Tribune*, March 22, 2004.

Munzel, Edgar. "2,000 Hits for Looey, Still a Chisox Pillar," *The Sporting News*, May 31, 1969.

———. "Sinking White Sox Blame Winter Ball For Pizarro's Skid," *Chicago Sun-Times*, October 3, 1969.

Murphy, Jack. "Gomez' Visit to Cuba Includes Chat With Castro," *The Sporting News*, February 21, 1970.

Muskat, Carrie. "Sosa picks up power pace by slowing swing tempo," *USA Today*, June 23, 1998.

Muskat, Carrie. "Sosa's homecoming: Tears, cheers for city's 'great gift,' " *USA Today*, October 21, 1998.

National Baseball Hall of Fame Library archives, National Baseball Hall of Fame archives, March 28, 1940.

National Baseball Hall of Fame Press Release, February 23, 2006.

National Baseball Hall of Fame Press Release, February 28, 1985.

National Baseball Hall of Fame Press Release, January 23, 2006.

National Baseball Hall of Fame Press Release, May 23, 2009.

National Baseball Hall of Fame Press Release, May 9, 2009.

Nevius, C.W., "Andujar: A Misunderstood Pitcher With 'Too Much Blood.' " *San Francisco Chronicle*, National Baseball Hall of Fame Library archives (date obscured).

Newhan, Ross. "Cookie: With Grit and Intelligence, He Became a Top Player; Will Angels Give Him Full Chance?" *Los Angeles Times*, May 23, 1988.

———. "The Best Ever?" *Los Angeles Times*, June 19, 2002.

———. "The King of the Caribbean," 1990, *Los Angeles Times*, National Baseball Hall of Fame Library archives (date missing).

Newman, Bruce. "Home Suite Home," *Sports Illustrated*, June 8, 1992.

———. "Return of the Native," *Sports Illustrated*, December 31, 1991/January 6, 1992.

"Nicaraguans cheer Martinez," *USA Today*, July 30, 1991.

Nichols, Max. "At Zoilo's House, Everyone's Happy!" *Minneapolis Tribune*, December 4, 1965.

Nichols, Max. "Camilo's Curve Sharper than Ever," *The Sporting News*, April 2, 1966.

———. "Rookie Rod Carew Stakes Out Claim to Twin Keystone," *The Sporting News*, March 25, 1967.

Nightengale, Bob. "Ramirez finds home at Wrigley," *USA Today Sports Weekly*, June 2–8, 2004.

Nigro, Ken. "Dennis Martinez Is O's Hit," *The Sporting News*, June 27, 1981.

———. "Martinez' Turnaround Is Eye-Popping to O's," *The Sporting News*, February 28, 1981.

O'Neil, John "Buck" and Wulf, Steve, and Conrads, David. *I Was Right On Time*. New York, Simon & Schuster, 1996.

Olson, Lisa. New York Daily News. "Omar not relishing hot dog," *New York Daily News*, October 3, 1987.

Orr, Jack. "Cepeda's For Real," *Sport Magazine*, October, 1958.

Ortiz, Jose De Jesus. "Lying about age not uncommon for Dominican baseball players," Houston Chronicle, May 4, 2008.

Otto, Franklin. Transcript of Interview with Jose Santiago, National Baseball Hall of Fame, November 19, 1991.

———. Transcript of Interview with Vic Power. National Baseball Hall of Fame, November 20, 1991.

Pearlman, Jeff. "Hot to Trot," Sports Illustrated, July 17, 2000.

Pepe, Phil. "Alomar Glad to Do His Bit For Friend He Seldom Saw," New York Daily News, March 19, 1975.

———. "They Call Tony Oliva the New Cobb," New York World Telegram & Sun, May 22, 1964.

———. "Yanks Built Their High Rise Upon a 'Sandy' Foundation," New York Daily News, September 21, 1974.

"Perez accepts Reds' hot seat," Miami Herald, October 31, 1992.

Petition for inclusion of Martin Dihigo in the Baseball Hall of Fame, National Baseball Hall of Fame and Library archives, July 20, 1974.

Pittsburgh Pirates, Roberto Clemente Night Program, July 24, 1970.

Plaschke, Bill. "Still No Place Like Home," Los Angeles Times, February 13, 1991.

———. "Till Next Time," Los Angeles Times, May 12, 1991.

Posnanski, Joe. "Maybe, Just Maybe, The Most Perfect Player Who Ever Did Live," Sports Illustrated, July 13, 2009.

———. The Machine. New York, William Morrow, 2009.

Price. S.L. "War of the Words," Sports Illustrated, February 20, 2006.

Rains, Rob. "Dad tries comeback, son sits out," Baseball Weekly, National Baseball Hall of Fame Library archives (date missing).

———. Albert The Great. Champaign, Illinois, Sports Publishing LLC, 2005.

Red, Christian. "In D.R. Pedro is Daddy," New York Daily News, December 5, 2004.

———. "School That Pedro Built," New York Daily News, February 7, 2007.

Regalado, Samuel O. Viva Baseball: Latin Major Leaguers and Their Special Hunger. Champaign, Illinois, University of Illinois Press, 1998.

Rhodes, Jean and Boburg, Shawn. Becoming Manny. New York, Scribner, 2009.

Ribowsky, Mark. Don't Look Back: Satchel Paige in the Shadows of Baseball. New York, Simon & Schuster, 1994.

———. The Power and the Darkness, New York. Simon & Schuster, 1996.

Rieber, Anthony. "Wait over in a New York minute," Newsday, August 5, 2007.

Rimer, Sara. "A Rookie, Yes, but a Neighborhood Hero," New York Times, September 4, 1993.

"Rivera adds to legacy as elite closer," Associated Press, June 29, 2009.

"Rivera says he will be back for Game 1," Associated Press, October 11, 2004.

Robbins, Liz. "Vizquel's glove boosts Tribe," *Cleveland Plain Dealer*, July 23, 1995.

Roberts, Howard. "Tiny Tormentor." *Chicago Daily News*, National Baseball Hall of Fame Library archives (date missing).

Robinson, Joshua and Schmidt, Michael S., "Nationals' G.M. Resigns as Scandal Deepens," *New York Times*, March 1, 2009.

Roderick, Joe. "End of a Giant Journey," *Contra Costa Times*, May 3, 1999.

Rogin, Gil. "Happy Little Luis," *Sports Illustrated*, May 9, 1960.

Rosenthal, Ken. "Martinez keeps the hits coming despite eye disorder," *The Sporting News*, April 30, 2001.

Rubin, Bob. "Cuban relives big-league baseball ties," *Miami Herald*, March 28, 1999.

Ruck, Rob. *The Tropic of Baseball: Baseball in the Dominican Republic*. Lincoln, Nebraska, University of Nebraska Press, 1999.

Rumill, Ed. "Boyer calls Alou, 'most underrated,' " *Christian Science Monitor*, August 21, 1967.

Russo, Neal. "Minoso, Old Man Young, Talks Baseball As Well As He Plays It," *St. Louis Post-Dispatch*, December 12, 1961.

Sacucci, Fluffy. "Hector Lopez: Integral part of Big Pinstripe Machine," *Sports Collector's Digest*, November 9, 1990.

Sanchez, Jesse, "Hall honors Mexican greats," MLB.com, January 7, 2004.

———, "History of baseball in Mexico," MLB.com, January 7, 2004.

Sandomir, Richard. "When Marichal and Spahn Dueled for a Game and a Half," *New York Times*, July 2, 2008.

———. "Who's a Latino Baseball Legend?" *New York Times*, August 26, 2005.

Sandoval, Ricardo. "Monterrey making pitch for baseball," *Dallas Morning News*, November 8, 2003.

Schneider, Russ. " 'My Finest Game' Says Tiant After 19-Whiff Effort," *The Sporting News*, July 20, 1968.

———. "Lucky Luis? Modest Hurler Tiant Thinks So," *The Sporting News*, August 3, 1968.

Serby, Steve. "Expo Martinez savors escape from alcohol," *New York Post*, August 5, 1987.

———. "Serby's Q & A with Carlos Beltran," *New York Post*, January 16, 2005.

———. "Serby's Sunday Q & A with Bernie Williams," *New York Post*, June 26, 2005.

———. "Serby's Sunday Q & A with Jose Reyes," *New York Post*, May 20, 2007.

———. "Serby's Sunday Q & A with Julio Franco," *New York Post*, June 25, 2006.

Shah, Diane K. and Contreras, Joe. "The Most Happy Rookie," *Newsweek*, May 11, 1981.

Shaikin, Bill. "The Angels' $70 Million Homebody," *Los Angeles Times*, February 14, 2004.

Shatzkin, Mike (editor), *The Ballplayers: The Ultimate Baseball Biographical Reference*, excerpt sheet, 1990.

Shaughnessy, Dan. "Brotherly love, Martinez style, warms camp," *Boston Globe*, March 12, 1999.

———. "For end results, he's their man," *Boston Globe*, September 7, 2005.

Sherman, Ed. "The world discovers the other Ozzie Guillen," *Chicago Tribune*, July 8, 1990.

"Shortstop Finds Outlet in Paints and a Palette," Associated Press, July 17, 2005.

SI.com. "Longtime catcher ends career after getting sent down," March 22, 2008. Sports Illustrated, www.si.com.

Sipple, George. "Hernandez: All those games are unbelievable," *Detroit Free Press*, July 8, 2005.

Smith, Claire. "Baerga Turns New Leaf in His Life Style," *New York Times*, February 21, 1997.

Smith, James F., "Winter Wonder," *Los Angeles Times*, December 30, 2000.

Smith, Ken. Transcript of Interview with Manny Sanguillen, National Baseball Hall of Fame, March 23, 1974.

"Sosa becomes fifth player to blast 600 home runs," Associated Press, June 20, 2007.

Sosa, Sammy and Breton, Marcos. *Sosa: An Autobiography*. New York, Warner Books, 2000.

Souhan, Jim. "Baseball's Frontier: Venezuela fertile ground for Twins," *Minneapolis Star-Tribune*, January 14, 2003.

Spander, "Baseball Is Big In Mexico," *The Sporting News*, August 13, 1977.

Spander, Art. "The Mexican Cy Young," *San Francisco Chronicle*, May 29, 1983.

Spencer, Lyle. "Kelly's Heart Back in Panama," *New York Post*, May 19, 1989.

Stark, Jayson. "Having had four lives, Perez doesn't realize he's getting 'too old,' " *Philadelphia Inquirer*, May 9, 1983.

Stark, Jayson. "Jose Cruz: The Big Leagues' Most Unheralded Star," *Baseball Digest*, August, 1985.

Stevens, Bob. "Jesus Alou Could Be the Best in Family," *The Sporting News*, July 3, 1965.

———. "Why Does Marichal Run? He Remembers $1 Fines," *The Sporting News*, July 21, 1968.

Strauss, Joe. "Albert Pujols: Baseball's Best Player," *Baseball Digest*, August, 2009.

————. "Pujols' affection for Dominican is mutual," *St. Louis Post-Dispatch*, November 28, 2005.

Stump, Al. "Always They Want More, More, More," *The Saturday Evening Post*, July 29, 1967.

Sullivan, T.R. "Catchy situation," *Fort Worth Star-Telegram*, March 13, 1991.

"Tejada sentenced to a year's probation," Associated Press, March 26, 2009.

"They Said It," *Sports Illustrated*, March 24, 2008.

"Time for Fernando's Hideaway," *San Francisco Examiner*, May 19, 1981.

Topkin, Marc. "Dodgers' Ramon Martinez Chases Dream of Greatness," *Baseball Digest*, July, 1991.

Torre, Joe and Verducci, Tom. *The Yankee Years*. New York, Doubleday, 2009.

Turkin, Hy. "All About Olmo," *New York Daily News*, March 17, 1943.

Twombley, Wells. "Geronimo Jumps, Lands on A's," *San Francisco Examiner*, October 19, 1972.

Tye, Larry. *Satchel: The Life and Times of an American Legend*. New York, Random House, 2009.

Umich.edu, http://umich.edu/

Van Dyck, Dave. "Guillen grades himself an 'A'," *Chicago Tribune*, May 31, 2004.

————. "Guillen Shrugs Off Aparicio Label," *The Sporting News*, April 29, 1985.

————. "Obama makes nice pitch for marketing department," *Chicago Tribune*, July 19, 2009.

————. "Richard revival is vital," *Chicago Tribune*, July 19, 2009.

Vecsey, George. "Nicaragua's Best Pitcher," *New York Times*, 1981, National Baseball Hall of Fame Library archive (date missing).

————. "Now Cepeda Has His," *New York Times*, November 8, 1967.

————. "The Gift of Freedom," *New York Times*, December 24, 1982.

Verducci, Tom. "The Lone Ranger," *Sports Illustrated*, September 9, 2002.

————. "The Power of Pedro," *Sports Illustrated*, March 27, 2000.

"Vinny Castillo retires from baseball after 16 seasons and one final win with Mexico," Associated Press, February 7, 2007.

Viva Baseball! National Baseball Hall of Fame Exhibit, 2009.

Vizquel, Omar and Dryer, Bob. *Omar!* Cleveland, Gray & Company Publishers, 2000.

Walker, Ben. "Blue Jays' Delgado Protests War in Iraq," Associated Press, July 21, 2004.

Walter O'Malley.com, www.walteromalley.com.

Weir, Tom. "For some players, fudging age might be the key to success," *USA Today*, February 8, 2000.

Wendel, Tim and Villegas, Jose Luis. *Far From Home: Latino Baseball Players in America*. Washington, D.C., National Geographic Society, 2008.

White, Paul. "Before He Was A-Rod," *USA Today Sports Weekly*, February 16–22, 2005.

White, Russ, "Minnie's All For Laughs," National Baseball Hall of Fame Library archives, unattributed, April 4, 1963.

Whiteside, Larry. "Loss of Tiant 'Tears Out Heart' of Red Sox," *The Sporting News*, November 2, 1978.

Whitten, Leslie H. "Marichal's Political Magic," Hearst Headline Service, June 3, 1966.

Williams, Joe. "Minoso Is What Cuba Once Was," *New York World Telegram & Sun*, May 16, 1962.

Winston, Lisa. "There are few like Andruw," *USA Today Baseball Weekly*, September 25/October 1, 1996.

Wolf, Bob. "Alomar to Take Over at Shortstop for Braves," *Milwaukee Journal*, September 15, 1964.

———. "Puerto Rican Whiz on Way," *Milwaukee Journal*, November 8, 1963.

Yates, Ronald. "Fans, players beat path to Valenzuela," *Chicago Tribune*, May 3, 1981.

Ziff, Sid. "Dodgers on Marichal: 'Kick Him Out,' " *Los Angeles Times*, August 23, 1965.

Zimmer, Don. "Zim still pulling no punches," *New York Daily News*, June 27, 2004.

Zolecki, Todd. "Long arms of Chavez could hold Phils back," *Philadelphia Inquirer*, March 4, 2007.

Index

Aaron, Hank, 75, 97, 177, 251, 277
Abreu, Bobby, 30, 239
Abreu, Nelson, 239
Africa, xvii
Agence France Presse, 226
Aguada, Puerto Rico, 268
Aguadilla, Puerto Rico, 260
Aguilas Cibaenas, 16
Alabama, xvii
Alamo, 24
Alaska, 140
Albany, New York, 9
Alexander, Grover Cleveland, 278
Ali, Muhammad, 122
Allen, Martet, 81
Almada, Baldomero, 24
Almeida, Rafael, xviii
Alomar, Sandy, Jr., 59, 61, 62, 63, 64
Alomar, Roberto, 38, 59, 61, 62, 63,
    64, 65
Alomar, Sandy, 59, 60, 61, 62, 63,
    64, 313
Alou, Felipe, 19, 39, 43, 50, 66, 67,
    68, 69, 70, 71, 72, 88, 127, 129,
    290, 313
Alou, Jesus, 19, 43, 66, 67, 69, 70, 71
Alou, Matty, 19, 43, 66, 67, 69, 71, 313
Alou, Moises, 43, 66, 71, 72
Alou, Virginia, 68

Alston, Walter, 128
Amaro, Ruben, Jr., 239, 240
Amaro, Ruben, Sr., 239, 240
Amaro, Santos, 239
American League, xiv, 21, 28, 31, 60,
    62, 64, 68, 74, 75, 77, 78, 80, 83, 84,
    85, 90, 92, 109, 111, 112, 116, 137,
    139, 141, 149, 150, 155, 156, 157,
    166, 169, 172, 183, 185, 188, 192,
    193, 196, 197, 198, 200, 203, 218,
    220, 226, 233, 234, 235, 243, 245,
    249, 250, 252, 253, 259, 260, 262,
    263, 264, 265, 266, 267, 268, 269,
    270, 282, 283, 284, 287, 288, 289,
    292, 295, 297, 298, 300, 304, 307,
    315, 316
Amoros, Sandy, 6, 240, 241
Anderson, Sparky, 112, 161, 163,
    248, 268
Andorra, 11
Andujar, Joaquin, 19, 21, 210, 242
Angel Falls, Venezuela, 235
Aparicio III, Luis, 78
Aparicio, Luis, xiv, xxi, 30, 31, 38, 47,
    60, 73, 74, 75, 76, 77, 78, 79, 111,
    113, 230, 231, 257, 313, 320
Appalachian League, 182
Aragua, Venezuela, 256
Arecibo, Puerto Rico, 166, 266, 283

Argentino, 251
Arguello, Alexis, 131
Arias, Joaquin, 199
Arizona Diamondback, xiv, 28, 53
Arlington, Texas, 310
Armed Forces Radio, 82
Arroyo, Luis, 6, 242
Arroyo, Puerto Rico, 259
Aruba, xvii
Associated Press, 251
AstroTurf, 79
Atlanta Black Crackers, 301
Atlanta Braves, 52, 61, 68, 72, 92, 113, 133, 137, 249, 254, 264, 265, 272, 274, 276, 277, 280, 289
Atlanta, 43, 254
Atlantic Ocean, 5, 81, 101, 269
Austin, Texas, 47
Avila, Bobby, xiv, 90, 243, 244
Avila, Gabriel "Tito," 309
Azcue, Joe, 6, 218, 219

Baerga, Carlos, 233, 244
Baez, Danny, 8
Bailey, Ed, 126
Balaguer, Joaquin, 69, 128
Baltimore Orioles, 10, 64, 65, 75, 77, 78, 98, 113, 131, 132, 134, 135, 178, 195, 210, 227, 228, 260, 287, 300
Bando, Garcia, 9
Bankhead, Sam, 16, 157
Banks, Ernie, 96, 198
Barcelona, 11
Barceloneta, Puerto Rico, 286
Barranquilla, Colombia 293
Baseball Almanac, 219, 220, 221
Baseball America, 53
Baseball Digest, 178
Baseball Encyclopedia, 76, 154
Batista, Fulgencio, 5, 7, 10, 108

Battle Creek, Michigan, 21
Bauman, Clarence, 92
Bay of Pigs invasion, 6
Bay, Jason, 187
Baylor, Don, 322
Beisbol—The Latin Game, 36, 37, 38, 39, 40
Belen University, 7
Bell, Buddy, 233
Bell, Cool Papa, xviii, 16, 17, 103
Bell, George, 19, 21, 210, 245
Bellan, Esteban, xvii, 4, 5, 319
Beltran, Carlos, 245, 246, 279
Beltre, Adrian, 19, 54
Bench, Johnny, 161, 163, 205, 206, 208
Bender, Charles "Chief," xviii
Berger, Wally, 121
Bernazard, Tony, 279
Berra, Yogi, 76, 77, 205, 240, 241, 251
Berroa, Billy, 313
Big Bird, 232
Biggio, Craig, 323
Bithorn, Hiram, 247
Bjarkman, Peter C., 7, 8, 18, 104, 106, 123
Black Sox scandal, 77, 155
Black Spiders, 46
Black Sports magazine, 85
Blair, Chad, 178
Blass, Steve, 100
Bloomington, Minnesota, 305
Blowers, Mike, 141
Bonds, Barry, 196, 212, 247
Bonilla, Bobby, 38, 247, 248
Boone, Bob, 206
Boone, Bret, 142
Borbon, Pedro, Jr., 248, 249
Borbon, Pedro, Sr., 248
Boston Braves, xviii, 117, 118, 121, 283
Boston Globe, 150

Boston Red Sox, xvi, 13, 20, 24, 33, 39, 40, 41, 43, 48, 49, 55, 77, 92, 104, 148, 149, 150, 151, 152, 161, 163, 164, 182, 185, 186, 187, 190, 192, 199, 216, 220, 221, 222, 253, 265, 266, 277, 285, 286, 289, 293, 310, 316

Boston, xiii, 13, 220, 221, 285

Boudreau, Lou, 172

Bowden, Jim, 55

Boyer, Clete, 68

Boys and Girls Club, 179, 200

Bragan, Bobby, 60

Brazil, 232

Brennaman, Marty, 164

Brewer, Chet, 16, 18

Briggs Stadium, 305

Bristol, Dave, 160

Brito, Mike, 225, 228

Brock, Lou, 322

Bronx, New York, 247, 305

Brooke, Edward, 221

Brooklyn Dodgers, xv, 5, 15, 27, 44, 48, 68, 120, 240, 241, 243, 253, 275, 283

Brooklyn Royal Giants, 44

Brosnan, Timothy J., 26

Brown, Joe L., 22, 70, 101

"Buddy Walk in the Park Day," 179

Buenos Aires, Argentina, 251

Buffalo, 275

Bugs Bunny, 150, 266

Buhner, Jay, 140, 141

Busch Stadium, 173

Bush, George W., 267

Butte, Montana, 232

Bytner, Vince, 9

Cabrera, Asdrubal, 315

Cabrera, Miguel, 30, 249, 250

Cabrera, Orlando, 43, 293

Caguas, Puerto Rico, 168

California, 13, 219, 225, 265

Camaguey, Cuba, 160

Cambria, Joe, xx, xxi, 7

Campanella, Roy, xiv, 205

Campaneris, Bert, 6, 108, 250, 251, 302, 313

Canada, 26, 64, 134, 148, 169

Canadian Provincial League, 169

Canal Zone, Panama, 80, 81, 82

Canavati, Anuar, 25

Candlestick Park, 71, 89

Canel, Eloy "Buck," 251, 252, 272, 313

Cano, Robinson, 19, 21, 315

Canseco, Jose, 252, 253

Canseco, Ozzie, 252

Caracas, 30, 32, 34, 113, 230, 265, 284, 294, 302

Cardenal, Jose, 6

Cardenas, Cuba, 261, 278

Cardenas, Leo, 6

Cardenas, Rene, 253, 254, 313

Carew, Eric, 80

Carew, Marilyn Levy, 86

Carew, Michelle, 86

Carew, Olga, 80

Carew, Rod, xv, xxii, 38, 39, 40, 80, 81, 82, 83, 84, 85, 86, 96, 295, 303, 320, 322

Carew, Rodney Kline, 80

Caribbean Sea, 21

Caribbean Series, 255

Caribbean, 32, 41, 46, 47

Carlton, Steve, 70

Carmona, Fausto, 54, 315

Carolina League, 83

Carolina, Puerto Rico, 95

Carrasco, Carlos, 32

Carrasquel, Alex, 33

Carrasquel, Chico, xiv, xx, xxi, 30, 31, 32, 33, 73, 74, 76, 79, 109, 111, 113, 230, 231, 257

Carter, Gary, 322

Carty, Rico, xiv, xv, 20, 21, 210, 254, 255

Castilla, Vinny, 255

Castillo, Bobby, 225

Castillo, Luis, 21

Castro, Fidel, xi, xiii, xxiii, 3, 4, 5, 6, 7, 8, 9, 11, 13, 32, 50, 108, 158, 159, 217, 252, 257, 260, 269

Castro, Raul, 4, 11, 12, 13

Catano, Puerto Rico, 280

Cedeno, Cesar, 19, 256

Central Alara, Cuba, 299

Cepeda, Orlando, xiv, xvi, xxi, xxii, 16, 38, 40, 41, 47, 50, 87, 88, 89, 90, 91, 92, 93, 127, 286, 290, 291, 293, 309, 310, 313, 320

Cepeda, Pedro "Perucho," xvi, 16, 87, 88

Chamorro, Violetta, 137

Chandler, A.B. "Happy," 25, 262

Chapman, Aroldis, 11, 12, 13

Charleston, Oscar, 105

Charleston, West Virginia, 305

Chavez Ravine, 136, 224

Chavez, Hugo, xx, 31, 32, 115, 284

Chicago American Giants, 301

Chicago Cubs, 9, 30, 42, 176, 207, 210, 212, 214, 225, 245, 247, 266, 268, 280, 287, 291, 299, 303, 317

Chicago White Sox, xx, xxii, 9, 12, 30, 30, 31, 33, 36, 37, 44, 46, 48, 49, 55, 59, 61, 73, 74, 75, 76, 77, 78, 79, 109, 110, 111, 112, 113, 114, 115, 153, 155, 156, 157, 158, 187, 188, 210, 211, 212, 222, 230, 236, 245, 247, 258, 259, 269, 273, 274, 284, 289, 290, 310, 319

Chicago, x, xiii, 13, 30, 33, 37, 48, 75, 79, 103, 107, 111, 158, 213, 214

China, 9

Christopher, Joe, xv, 97

Chunichi Dragons, 11

Ciales, Puerto Rico, 263

Ciego de Avila, Cuba, 10, 159

Cienfuego, 154

Cienfuegos, Cuba, 103, 108, 301

Cincinnati Reds Hall of Fame, 122

Cincinnati Reds, xviii, 5, 10, 13, 44, 48, 55, 111, 117, 118, 122, 149, 159, 161, 163, 164, 191, 248, 257, 274, 275, 294, 295, 315

Cincinnati, 164, 221, 243, 248

Civil War, xvi, xvii

Claire, Fred, 147

Clariond, Fernando Canales, 27

Clark, Ron, 112

Clemente, Roberto, Jr., 38

Clemente, Luis, 38

Clemente, Luisa Walker de, 96

Clemente, Roberto, x, xi, xiv, xv, xxi, xxii, 22, 38, 39, 40, 61, 68, 93, 94, 95, 96, 97, 98, 99, 100, 101, 175, 256, 297, 306, 313, 319, 321

Clemente, Vera, 101

Cleveland Indians, xvi, xx, 31, 41, 43, 44, 48, 49, 54, 55, 62, 64, 74, 90, 133, 137, 150, 155, 157, 169, 172, 182, 183, 185, 216, 217, 218, 230, 233, 234, 235, 243, 244, 262, 264, 288, 303, 315

Cleveland, 37, 63, 182, 218, 219, 220

Cobb, Ty, xix, 80, 84, 106, 164, 283

Cocoa Beach, 83

Collins, Eddie, 311

Colombia, xvii, 3, 43, 59, 226, 291, 292, 293
Colon, Bartolo, 38
Colon, Panama, 275, 297
Colorado Rockies, 12, 26, 255, 258, 265
Colorado, 255
Comiskey Park, 48, 74, 79, 155, 158
Concepcion, Davey, 30, 76, 111, 113, 230, 231, 256, 256
Coney Island, 82
Congress, 52, 215, 286, 288, 300
Consuegra, Sandy, 6
Contras, 132, 133
Contreras, Jose, 8, 12, 257, 258
Cooper, Cecil, 322
Cora, Joey, 31
Cordova, Cuiqui, 19
Cramer, Emilio, 32
Crosby, Sidney, 198
Crosley Field, 120
Crutchfield, Jimmie, 17
Cruz, Jose, Jr., 259
Cruz, Jose, Sr., 259, 313
Cruz, Hector, 259
Cruz, Julio, 259
Cruz, Tommy, 259
Cuba, ix, x, xi. xii. xvi, xvii, xviii, xix, xx, xxiii, 3, 5, 6, 10, 11, 12, 13, 21, 24, 32, 44, 47, 49, 50, 51, 54, 59, 95, 103, 105, 107, 108, 109, 117, 118, 120, 121, 122, 132, 153, 154, 155, 158, 159, 161, 162, 163, 164, 165, 217, 221, 222, 239, 240, 241, 250, 252, 257, 259, 260, 261, 269, 283, 288, 291, 305, 310, 316, 320
Cuban Stars, 44, 47, 103, 105, 278
CubaTours, 10
Cuellar, Mike, 6, 259, 260
Cueto, Johnny, 21, 315, 316

Cunningham, Bill, 119
Cy Young Award, 111, 149, 150, 226, 260, 268, 297, 298

Dallas Cowboys, 27
Damon, Johnny, 190
Dark, Alvin, xii, 90, 91, 125, 127
Davenport, Iowa, xv
Davenport, Jim, 88
Davies, Kyle, 200
DaVinci, Leonardo, 127
Davis, Eric, 322
Dawson, Mark, 198
de la Rosa, Nelson, 151
Dean, Daffy, 150
Dean, Dizzy, 150
Debayle, Anastasio Somoza, 132
DeLeon, Jose, xv
Delgado, Carlos, 40, 260, 261, 279, 323
Delmonte, Wenceslao y, 5
Dennis Martinez National Stadium, 131
Denny's, 232
Deportibo, Walter Ferretti, 131
DeShields, Delino, 148
Detroit Free Press, 305
Detroit Tigers, xi, xxiii, 19, 30, 48, 72, 78, 112, 116, 191, 192, 203, 208, 219, 249, 250, 268, 284, 305
Detroit, 21, 34
Diamond, Neil, 186
Dihigo, Martin, Jr., 108
Dihigo, Gilbert, 38
Dihigo, Martin, xix, 16, 38, 44, 47, 102, 103, 104, 105, 106, 107, 108, 109, 290, 302, 313, 320
DiMaggio, Joe, xix, 25, 246
Dobson, Pat, 260
Doby, Larry, xiv
Dodgers Stadium, 148

Dominican Republic, ix, xi, xii, xiv,
xv, xvii, xix, xxii, xxiii, 3, 4, 15, 16,
17, 19, 20, 21, 22, 23, 36, 39, 40, 41,
42, 43, 44, 48, 50, 51, 52, 53, 54, 55,
59, 66, 67, 69, 72, 90, 95, 105, 110,
123, 124, 126, 127, 129, 130, 132,
145, 147, 148, 151, 152, 165, 175,
179, 180, 182, 183, 185, 194, 201,
208, 209, 210, 211, 214, 215, 242,
245, 248, 254, 256, 262, 263, 264,
267, 272, 279, 282, 285, 289, 290,
291, 294, 300, 305, 306, 312, 315,
316, 317, 319, 320
Don Gregorio, Dominican Republic,
267, 268
Donovan, Dick, 77
Dorado, Puerto Rico, 138
Doubleday, Abner, xvi
Downs Syndrome Awareness Day, 179
Drummondville, Ontario, 169
Drysdale, Don, 79
Duckett, Mahlon, 108
Dumbrowski, Dave, 249
Duncan, Mariano, 21
DuPuy, Bob, 55
Durango, 46
Durocher, Leo, 256
Dykes, Jimmy, 171

Easler, Mike, 176
Easter Bunny, xvi, 231
Eastern League, 125
East-West Classic, 104
Ecuador, 226, 271
Ed Sullivan Show, 70
El Caracas Base Ball Club, 32
El Paso, Texas, 310
Ellis Island, 166
Ellis, Doc, 99
Empire State Building, xv

Enter the Sandman, 193
Escalera, Nino, 48
Esculea Basica San Miguel School, 152
Espino, Hector, 26
ESPN, 40
Estalella, Bobby (grandfather), xx, 261
Estalella, Bobby (grandson), 262
Estrellas Orintales, 16, 17, 18
Etchohuaquila, Mexico, 224, 225
Europe, xx

Fairly, Ron, 128
Fan Fest, All Star Game, 310
Federal Bureau of Investigation
(FBI), 86
Fenway Park, 41, 185, 186, 221, 248,
266, 285
Fernandez, Alex, 313
Fernandez, Leonel, 214
Fernandez, Tony, 19, 21, 262, 263
Figueredo, Jorge, 8
Figueroa, Ed, 263, 264
Fisk, Carlton, 203, 204
Florida Marlins, 10, 13, 34, 114, 148,
165, 203, 206, 207, 208, 234, 249,
269, 293, 296, 299, 316
Florida State League, xv, 83
Florida, 5, 8, 86, 93, 95, 140, 170, 195,
206, 260, 299
Fomento, Cuba, 316
Forbes Field, 97
Ford Frick Award, 251, 271
Fordham University, 4, 5
Fort Knox, 18
Fort Myers, Florida, 95
Fox, Nellie, 74, 75, 77, 79
Foxx, Jimmy, 184, 197
Franco, Julio, 19, 264
Franks, Herman, 91, 92
Frick, Ford, 6

Frisch, Frankie, xix
Fryman, Travis, 185
Fuentes, Tito, 6, 310, 313
Furcal, Rafael, 19, 52, 53

Galarraga, Andres, 265, 284
Gamboa, Panama, 81
Garcia, Freddy, 19, 30
Garciaparra, Nomar, 235, 265, 266
Gardner, Paul, 122
Garvey, Steve, 322
Gatun, Panama, 80
Gehrig, Lou, 107, 227
Geneva, New York, 160
George Washington High School, 182
Georgia Tech, 265
Geronimo, Cesar, 19
Gettysburg Address, 191
Gibson, Bob, 125
Gibson, Josh, xviii, 16, 17, 45,
    103, 154
Gilbert, Andy, 125
Gillette, 252
Gomez, Elia, 9
Gomez, Lefty, 313
Gomez, Pedro, 9
Gomez, Preston, 6, 8, 9, 165, 313
Gonzalez, Adrian, 316
Gonzalez, Juan, 266, 267
Gonzalez, Mike, xix, 165
Gonzalez, Pedro, 21
Gonzalez, Tony, 6
Goodwin, Curtis, 255
Gordon, Joe, 243
Gottlieb, Eddie, 104
Graham, Frank, 123
Granada, Nicaragua, 131, 132
Granger, Wayne, 161
Granma, 8
Great American Ball Park, 257

Green, Pumpsie, 48
Greenlee, Gus, 16, 45
Greenwood, Lee, 186
Gregg, Tommy, 148
Griffey, Ken, Jr., 140, 142, 196
Griffin, Alfredo, 19, 96, 214, 313
Griffin, Rick, 143
Griffith, Calvin, 7, 83
Griffith, Clark, xx
Grim, Bob, 156
Grissom, Marquis, 136
Alexander, Manny, 21
Guerra, Mike, xx
Guerrero, Pedro, 19, 210
Guerrero, Vladimir, 19, 28, 249,
    267, 268
Guerrero, Wilton, 267
Guidry, Ron, 322
Guillen, Ibis, 115
Guillen, Oney, 115
Guillen, Ozzie, xxii, 30, 36, 37, 76,
    109, 110, 111, 112, 113, 114, 115,
    116, 230
Guillot, Nemesio, xvii, 5
Guinness Book of World Records, 151
Gullett, Don, 294
Gumbel, Bryant, 116
Gwynn, Chris, 136
Gwynn, Tony, 177, 322

Haak, Howie, xv, xvi, xxi, 7, 22, 95
Haddix, Harvey, 277
Hagler, Marvin, 211
Haina, Dominican Republic, 66, 68
Haiti, 17, 124
Hamm, Mia, 266
Haney, Fred, 252
Hansen, Ron, 78
Harrelson, Ken "Hawk," 189
Harris, Bucky, xxi, xxii

Hart, John, 182

Hato Mayor, Dominican Republic, 264

Havana Sugar Kings, 5, 6, 8, 217, 295

Havana, 3, 5, 33, 117, 123, 154, 162, 217, 239, 240, 252, 278, 287, 295, 310

Hearns, Thomas, 211

Hebner, Richie, 99

Hemond, Roland, 111

Hernandez, Guillermo "Willie," 268, 269

Hernandez, Jackie, 6

Hernandez, Keith, 195

Hernandez, Livan, 8, 269

Hernandez, Orlando, 8, 54, 114, 269, 270

Herrera, Antonio Jose, 31

Herrera, Pancho, 6

Hertz, 28

Hiatt, Jack, 126

Hicks, Tom, 197, 199

Hidalgo, Richard, 34

Higuera, Ted, 227, 270, 271

Hiram Bithorn Stadium, 247

Hirchback, John, 65

Hispanic Heritage Baseball Museum Hall of Fame, ix, xi, 44, 222, 243, 254, 259, 300, 309, 310, 311, 312

Hoak, Don, 7

Hodges, Gil, 240

Hoffman, Trevor, 189, 193

Hofman, Rich, 200

Homestead Grays, 46, 103, 108

House, Tom, 205

Houston Astros, 9, 31, 34, 37, 51, 52, 71, 203, 208, 239, 242, 246, 254, 259, 300, 311

Houston, 38, 310

Howard, Elston, 168

Hoyt, LaMarr, 111

Hriniak, Walt, 112

Hubbell, Carl, 224, 227

Hudson, Kate, 199

Hurricane Georges, 214

Idelson, Jeff, 319, 320

Independence, Missouri, 175

Indianapolis, 135, 248

International League, 5, 8, 275, 278

International Olympic Committee, 26

Irvin, Monte, xiv, 105, 290

Isaacs, Stan, 169

Jackie Robinson Lifetime Achievement Award, 158

Jacobs Field, 63, 183

Jamail, Milton H., xx, 32

James, LeBron, 198

Japan, 11, 214, 215, 262, 264

Jarrin, Jaime, 42, 271, 272, 313

Javier, Julian, 19, 272

Javier, Stan, 272

Jersey City, 6

Jeter, Derek, 190, 199, 235, 323

Johnson, Darrell, 221

Johnson, Josh, 108

Johnson, Randy, 140, 142, 196

Johnson, Walter, 10, 157, 278

Jones, Andruw, 273, 274

Jones, Chipper, 265

Jordan, Michael, 122

Junior World Series, 8

Jupiter, 126

Kaline, Al, 321

Kansas City Athletics, 49, 93, 170, 250, 251, 275

Kansas City Monarchs, 46, 278, 301

Kansas City Royals, 150, 176, 190, 200, 245, 246, 289, 295, 319

Kansas City, 168, 176
Kelly, Roberto, 274, 275
Key West, Florida, 290
Killebrew, Harmon, 79
Kirkland, Willie, 88
Kiss, 232
Klein, Alan M., 23
Klein, Joe, 191, 192
Klem, Bill, 119
Koufax, Sandy, 125, 128, 132, 147
Kralick, Jack, 171
Kress, Red, 74
Krich, John, 21, 22, 42
Kuhel, Joe, 122
Kuhn, Bowie, 100, 101

La Guaira Sharks, 31
La Guna Verde, Dominican
    Republic, 124
La Mesa, California, 25
La Prensa, 253, 254
La Russa, Tony, 177, 179, 313
Lake Michigan, 126
Landis, Kenesaw Mountain, xviii, 77
Lane, Frank, 155
Larkin, Barry, 322
Larsen, Don, 136
Las Martinas, Cuba, 257
Las Vegas, 26, 112
Lasorda, Tommy, 10, 225, 247, 282
Latino Legends, 38
Led Zeppelin, 232
Leesburg Florida, xv
Leiter, Al, 322
Leonard, Buck, xix, 45, 46, 47,
    103, 107
Leonard, Sugar Ray, 122, 211
Leyland, Jim, 203, 284
Linares, Omar, 11
Lincoln, Howard, 142

Linebrink, Scott, 110
Liriano, Francisco, 316
Little League World Series, 25
Lloyd, John Henry "Pop," 105
Logan Airport, 221
Lollar, Sherman, 77
Lone Ranger, 292
Long Branch, New Jersey, 117
Lopez, Al, 75, 290, 313
Lopez, Felix, 312
Lopez, Hector, 275, 276, 313
Lopez, Javy, 276, 277
Lopez, Marcelino, 6
Los Angeles (Anaheim, California)
    Angels, xxii, 9, 28, 30, 34, 35, 59,
    61, 80, 86, 151, 172, 197, 200, 227,
    239, 248, 263, 265, 267, 280, 295,
    296, 311, 316
Los Angeles Dodgers, xiv, 10, 27, 28,
    42, 50, 54, 77, 96, 125, 129, 132,
    136, 147, 148, 181, 187, 222, 223,
    224, 225, 226, 227, 228, 229, 247,
    254, 266, 268, 271, 272, 274
Los Angeles, 89, 140, 148, 228, 240,
    254, 271, 282
Los Dragones, 16, 18
Los Mochis, Mexico, 270
Louisville Slugger, 150
Lowell, Bertica, 13
Lowell, Mike, 13
Lown, Turk, 77
Lucchino, Larry, 40
Luque, Adolfo, x, xviii, xix, 5, 44, 106,
    107, 117, 118, 119, 120, 121, 122,
    123, 288
Luzinski, Greg, 322

Macias, Angel, 25
Macon, Georgia, 160
Maddox, Gary, 322

Maddux, Greg, 274
Madonna, 199
Maglie, Sal, 25
Maiz, Jose, 27, 29
Major League Baseball, ix, x, xi, xii,
    xiv, xvi, xvii, xviii, xix, xx, xxi, xxii,
    xxiii, 3, 6, 7, 8, 9, 11, 15, 19, 20, 22,
    23, 24, 25, 26, 27, 33, 34, 36, 37, 38,
    39, 41, 42, 43, 44, 47, 51, 52, 53, 54,
    55, 59, 62, 63, 66, 68, 72, 74, 78, 79,
    80, 82, 84, 86, 87, 88, 89, 90, 95, 99,
    103, 105, 106, 107, 108, 109, 114,
    115, 118, 119, 120, 126, 128, 130,
    131, 133, 135, 139, 143, 144, 146,
    149, 153, 154, 155, 158, 159, 168,
    169, 171, 172, 173, 175, 180, 181,
    182, 183, 187, 190, 191, 194, 203,
    204, 205, 207, 209, 210, 211, 214,
    215, 217, 221, 222, 226, 228, 231,
    232, 239, 243, 247, 248, 249, 250,
    252, 254, 255, 256, 257, 258, 259,
    260, 261, 262, 264, 265, 267, 272,
    279, 282, 283, 287, 289, 291, 295,
    297, 299, 300, 302, 307, 309, 311,
    315, 316, 321
Managua, 101, 131, 253
Manati, Puerto Rico, 204, 245
Mandel, Steve, 184, 185
Manning, Max, 107, 121
Manoguayabo, Dominican Republic,
    145, 152
Mantilla, Felix, 277
Mantle, Mickey, 75, 97, 213, 246, 275
Manuel, Charlie, 184
Manuel, Jose, 162
Mao, Dominican Republic, 248
Maplewoods Community College, 176
Maracaibo, 73, 74, 79
Maracay, Venezuela, 249
Marianao, 217

Mariano Tigers, 154
Marichal, Juan, xiv, xxi, xxii, 19, 36,
    38, 39, 40, 52, 67, 123, 124, 125,
    126, 127, 128, 129, 130, 131, 137,
    294, 313, 320
Marion, Marty, 157
Maris, Roger, 42, 209, 212, 213,
    214, 275
Mark Light Field at Alex Rodriguez
    Park, 198
Marsans, Armando, xviii
Martin, Billy, 83
Martinez, Dennis, 130, 131, 132, 133,
    134, 135, 136, 137
Martinez, Edgar, 38, 137, 139, 140,
    141, 142, 143, 144, 145, 313, 322
Martinez, Paolino, 146
Martinez, Pedro, 19, 20, 38, 145,
    146, 147, 148, 149, 150, 151, 152,
    279, 316
Martinez, Ramon, 19, 145, 146, 147,
    149, 150
Martinez, Victor, 43
Marx, Groucho, 220
Massachusetts, 221, 222
Mata, Victor, 20
Matanzas, Cuba, 5, 103
Mathewson, Christy, 5, 106, 118
Matlock, Leroy, 16
Mattingly, Don, 227
Mauch, Gene, 163, 296
Mayaguez, Puerto Rico, 168, 306
Mays, Willie, 75, 88, 89, 90, 97, 108,
    246, 251, 256, 274, 290, 321
Mazeroski, Bill, 243
McCarver, Tim, 39, 43, 91, 92
McCourt, Frank, 187
McCovey, Willie, 89, 92, 290
McDougald, Gil, 240
McGraw, John, 120, 278, 302

McGwire, Mark, 42, 209, 212, 213, 214, 215, 252

McKeon, Jack, 206, 207

McLain, Denny, 219, 220, 260

McNally, Dave, 260

McNamara, John, 257

Medellin cartel, 293

Mejias, Roman, 6

Mele, Sam, 83, 84, 170

Mendez, Jose, 10, 38, 44, 278, 313, 320

Mercado, Fabian Perez, 214

Mercado, Orlando, 313

Mesa, Jose, 19

Metallica, 193

Mexicali Aguilas, 228

Mexican Baseball Hall of Fame, 25, 26, 27

Mexican League, 24, 25, 27, 28, 33, 46, 59, 104, 217, 225, 227, 240, 244, 261, 262, 270, 283

Mexico City Reds, 27

Mexico City, 24, 27, 46, 125

Mexico, ix, xii, xvii, xix, xxii, 3, 4, 24, 25, 26, 27, 29, 36, 41, 44, 45, 46, 47, 59, 104, 105, 107, 109, 214, 222, 223, 224, 228, 239, 240, 243, 244, 247, 255, 258, 262, 264, 270, 310, 311, 316, 319

Miami, 10, 55, 110, 133, 135, 165, 186, 195, 208, 258, 290, 310

Michael, Gene, 191

Michigan City, Indiana, 126

Miller, Ray, 134

Milwaukee Braves, 20, 59, 61, 86, 125, 254, 277, 289, 290

Milwaukee, 252

Milwaukee, Brewers, 189, 213, 270

Minaya, Omar, xxii, 37, 211, 240, 279

Minneapolis, 83

Minnesota Twins Hall of Fame, 305

Minnesota Twins, xv, 6, 33, 34, 43, 49, 80, 82, 83, 169, 170, 171, 218, 220, 282, 285, 288, 292, 297, 302, 305, 316

Minnesota, 220, 283, 304, 305

Minoso, Minnie, x, xiv, xx, 5, 6, 44, 48, 49, 90, 105, 152, 153, 154, 155, 156, 157, 158, 159, 165, 169, 290, 310, 313

Mize, Johnny, 103

Molina, Bengie, 279, 280

Molina, Benjamin, 280

Molina, Jose, 279, 280

Molina, Yadier, 279, 280

Mondesi, Raul, 175

Montanez, Willie 280, 281

Monte Cristo, Dominican Republic, 289, 305

Monterrey Sultanes, 25

Monterrey, 25, 26, 27, 29

Montreal Expos, xxii, 26, 27, 37, 68, 72, 114, 133, 148, 149, 163, 211, 247, 265, 267, 279, 282

Moorad, Jeff, 185

Moore, Randy, 121

Morales, Kendry, 316

Moreno, Arturo, xxii, 28

Moreno, Omar, xv

Morgan, Joe, 161, 163, 257

Morgan, Mike, 136

Mota, Manny, 19, 50, 282, 313

The Mouse That Roared, 70

Moyer, Jamie, 322

Municipal Stadium, 218

Murphy, Dale, 322

Murray, Eddie, 136

Murtaugh, Danny, 99

Muser, Tony, 271

Musial, Stan, 75, 272

Narron, Jerry, 197

Nashville Elite Giants, 107

National Association of Professional Base Ball Players, 4

National Baseball Hall of Fame Veterans Committee, 93

National Baseball Hall of Fame, x, xix, 10, 20, 33, 36, 44, 45, 47, 48, 52, 65, 74, 76, 78, 79, 82, 86, 89, 102, 103, 105, 111, 112, 118, 119, 125, 129, 138, 144, 154, 161, 165, 172, 174, 177, 180, 182, 192, 194, 196, 199, 203, 215, 222, 224, 227, 232, 235, 247, 251, 257, 271, 272, 274, 278, 283, 286, 288, 290, 301, 319, 320, 321

National League, xiv, xix, 20, 26, 34, 39, 64, 67, 68, 69, 88, 89, 92, 96, 98, 104, 112, 118, 125, 132, 135, 136, 139, 140, 141, 149, 157, 161, 173, 178, 206, 207, 209, 212, 214, 224, 234, 242, 247, 254, 255, 257, 259, 262, 265, 269, 273, 276, 277, 280, 293, 298, 299, 303, 306, 311, 316, 317

National Series, 10, 11

Nava, Vincent, xvii

Navarro, Emilio, 312, 313

Navoja, Mexico, 223

Negro Leagues Baseball Museum, 158

Negro Leagues, xviii, xix, xx, 5, 15, 16, 17, 18, 27, 38, 44, 46, 104, 107, 121, 154, 155, 176, 177, 217, 246, 290, 301, 302, 312

Negron, Ray, 185

Netherlands, 11, 12, 273

New Jersey, 117, 183, 217

New Jersey-New York State League, 117

New Orleans, 16

New York City Fire Department, 191

New York City, 81, 182, 183, 194

New York Cubans, 5, 44, 48, 154, 217, 290, 312

New York Daily News, 199

New York Giants, 6, 7, 19, 48, 69, 88, 108, 119, 120, 246, 278, 302, 305

New York Mets, 27, 30, 34, 37, 71, 97, 108, 152, 189, 195, 208, 210, 240, 246, 248, 251, 260, 268, 277, 279, 295, 298, 316, 317

New York Post, 199

New York Yankees, xiv, 10, 12, 13, 20, 33, 37, 41, 49, 53, 55, 61, 82, 90, 134, 136, 150, 151, 156, 161, 166, 167, 168, 169, 170, 172, 185, 187, 188, 189, 190, 191, 192, 194, 195, 199, 200, 201, 203, 207, 211, 221, 222, 225, 235, 239, 240, 243, 244, 246, 258, 263, 269, 270, 274, 275, 279, 280, 292, 306, 307, 312, 315

New York, xvi, xvii, 37, 69, 103, 140, 155, 156, 160, 169, 183, 184, 184, 185, 195, 246, 247, 251, 269

Newark Eagles, 107

Newsweek, 85

Nicaragua, xvii, 3, 59, 61, 101, 130, 131, 132, 133, 134, 135, 136, 253, 320, 321

Nicaraguan Baseball Hall of Fame, 254

Nicholson, Dave, 78

Nickels, Greg, 144

Niehaus, Dave, 199

Niekro, Phil, 322

Nikaitani, Dr. Douglas, 143

Nixon, Richard, 166

Nixon, Russ, 147

Nizao, Dominican Republic, 267

Nobel Prize, 136

Nolte, Nick, 132
Noriega, Manuel, 274
North Dakota, 45
Northern League, 153
Notre Dame, 311
Nuevo Leon, 24
Nunez, Pablo, 226

Oakland Athletics, 52, 213, 252, 253, 254, 272, 279, 297, 302, 303, 309
Oaxaca, Mexico, 255
Obama, Barack, 173
Obregon, 46, 224
Oculaire Del Tuy, Venezuela, 111
Offerman, Jose, 19, 21
Ohio, 182
Oliva, Tony, 6, 38, 282
Oliver, Al, 99, 100
Olivo, Diomedes, 22
Olmo, Luis, 283, 284, 289
Olympic Games, 4, 8, 11, 133, 257, 269, 271
O'Malley, Walter, 272
O'Neil, Buck, 46, 176, 246
Ontario, 64
Ordonez, Magglio, 30, 110, 284
Orozco, Pascual, 310
Orta, Charolito, 46
Orta, Jorge, 29, 46
Ortiz, David, 19, 20, 39, 40, 185, 186, 200, 285, 286
Ortiz, Jorge, 37
Ortiz, Magdelena Rosales, 26
Oscar the Grouch, 232
Osvaldo Virgil National Airport, 306
Ott, Mel, 120

Pablo Sanchez High School, 191
Pacific Coast League, 175
Pacific, xx

Pagan, Jose, 99, 281, 286
Pagliaroni, Jim, 70
Paige, Satchel, xviii, xix, 16, 17, 18, 45, 46, 103, 121, 154, 164
Palmeiro, Rafael, 287, 288
Palmer, Jim, 260
Pan American Games, 4, 8, 12, 124, 129, 240, 255, 257
Panama City, Panama, 189
Panama, xv, xvii, 3, 39, 59, 80, 83, 86, 191, 192, 274, 275, 291, 320
Papelbon, Jonathan, 20
Parker, Dave, 176
Partagas Cigar Factory, 154
Pascual, Camilo, xxi, 6, 170, 171, 288
Pascual, Carlos, 288
Pasquel, Jorge, 24, 25, 27, 33
Paula, Carlos, 48
Pele, 232
Pembroke Pines, Florida, 183
Pena, Carlos, 19
Pena, Tony Francisco, 289
Pena, Tony, xv, 19, 38, 183, 289
Pentagon, 52
Pentland, Jeff, 212
Penuelas, Puerto Rico, 242
People magazine, 85
Perez, Eddie, 113
Perez, Teodora, 162
Perez, Tony, 10, 159, 160, 161, 163, 164, 165, 175, 251, 313, 320
Perez, Victor, 161
Perkins, Bill, 16
Perry, Alonso, 168
Peru, 226
Philadelphia Athletics, 168, 169, 262
Philadelphia Phillies, 32, 100, 104, 127, 151, 163, 164, 184, 225, 239, 240, 258, 262, 264, 281, 295, 298, 299, 303, 306, 311

Philadelphia Stars, 108
Philadelphia, 103, 104, 180, 228, 239
Phoenix, 309
Piazza, Mike, 148
Picasso, 234
Piedmont League, 283
Pierce, Billy, 74, 77
Pi-Gonzalez, Amaury, 309, 313
Pinar del Rio, Cuba, 11, 282, 292
Piniella, Lou, 140, 164, 200
Pittsburgh Crawfords, 16, 45
Pittsburgh Pirates, xv, 6, 7, 22, 37, 39,
    51, 67, 69, 70, 90, 95, 97, 98, 99,
    129, 150, 179, 187, 225, 243, 247,
    248, 272, 281, 286,
    289, 291, 297
Pittsburgh, 243, 248
Pizarro, Juan, 289, 290
Polo Grounds, 108
Pompez, Alex, 154, 290, 291, 313
Ponce Lions, 312
Ponce, Puerto Rico, 88, 276, 298, 312
Portland, Oregon, 26
Posada, Jorge, 194
Posnanski, Joe, 177
Power, Vic (Victor Pellot), 21, 49, 166,
    167, 168, 169, 170, 171, 172, 173
Progressive Field, 315
Providence Grays, xvii
Puckett, Kirby, 322
Pueblo Nuevo, Cuba, 250
Puerta La Cruz, Venezuela, 315
Puerto Cabello, Venezuela, 317
Puerto Caimito, Panama, 192
Puerto Rican Senate, 312
Puerto Rican Sports Hall of Fame, 312
Puerto Rico, ix, xvi, xvii, xxi, 3, 4, 13,
    16, 36, 37, 39, 40, 41, 44, 45, 47, 49,
    51, 50, 61, 87, 90, 93, 94, 95, 99,
    100, 101, 134, 138, 165, 168, 169,

172, 208, 242, 244, 245, 246, 247,
    259, 260, 261, 263, 266, 268, 279,
    283, 286, 289, 290, 291, 306, 309,
    311, 312, 319, 320
Pujols Family Foundation, 179
Pujols, Albert, x, xiv, 19, 38, 173,
    174, 175, 176, 177, 178, 179, 180,
    249, 323
Pujols, Bienvenido, 175
Pujols, Deidre, 176, 177, 179
Pujols, Isabella, 176, 179
Pulido, Carlos, 34

Quito, Ecuador, 271

Radatz, Dick, 190
Radio Nicaragua, 136
Ramirez, Aramis, 19, 291
Ramirez, Aristedes, 183, 184
Ramirez, Hanley, 19, 316
Ramirez, Manny, 19, 38, 40, 151, 180,
    181, 182, 183, 184, 185, 186, 249
Ramirez, Onelcida, 183, 184
Ramirez, Rafael, 313
Ramirez, Ruddy, 151
Ramos, Bombo, 126
Ramos, Pedro, xxi, 6, 292
Randolph, Willie, 279
Reese, Pee Wee, 240
Regalado, Samuel O., xxiii
Reinsdorf, Jerry, 114, 158
Renteria, Edgar, 292, 293
Rettenmund, Merv, 149
Reyes, Jose, 19, 316, 317
Reyna, Leonel Fernando, 39
Reynolds, Harold, 322
Rice University, 259
Richards, Paul, 75, 76
Rickey, Branch, 7, 155
Rigney, Bill, 88

Rijo, Jose, 19, 55, 294
Rincon, Juan, 34
Ripken, Cal, Jr., 195, 197, 227, 300, 322
Rivas, Luis, 34
Rivera, Clara, 192
Rivera, Mariano, 38, 187, 188, 189, 190, 191, 192, 193, 194
Riverfront Stadium, 164
Rizzuto, Phil, 275
Roberto Clemente Award, ix, 144, 176, 179, 239, 321
Roberto Clemente League, 272
Robinson, Brooks, 321
Robinson, Frank, 97
Robinson, Jackie, x, xv, 15, 27, 37, 44, 48, 68, 106, 120, 155, 159, 191, 275, 314, 315
Robinson, Wilbert, 120
Rocky Mountains, 232
Rodgers, Buck, 135
Rodriguez Jr., Jose, 204
Rodriguez, Alex, x, xiv, 38, 110, 142, 174, 194, 195, 196, 197, 198, 199, 200, 201, 235, 312
Rodriguez, Aurelio, 29
Rodriguez, Cynthia, 199
Rodriguez, Derick, 207
Rodriguez, Eddie, 200
Rodriguez, Eva Torres, 204
Rodriguez, Frankie, 30, 34, 35, 294, 295
Rodriguez, Ivan, 38, 202, 203, 204, 205, 206, 207, 208
Rodriguez, Jose, 204
Rodriguez, Lourdes, 195
Rodriguez, Maribel, 207
Rodriguez, Victor, 194, 195
Rodriguez, Wandy, 52
Rojas, Jose, 68

Rojas, Mel, 68
Rojas, Octavio "Cookie," xxiii, 165, 295, 296, 314
Rolaids Relief Man of the Year, 191
Rollins, Rich, 171
Roma, Enrique, 29
Ronald McDonald House, 179
Rose Hill College, xvii
Rose, Pete, 161, 163, 164, 303, 322
Roseboro, Johnny, 128, 129
Rotterdam, 11
Ruth, Babe, xix, 9, 20, 45, 103, 106, 179, 197, 212, 213, 227
Ryan, Nolan, 85

Saberhagen, Bret, 150
Sadecki, Ray, 91
Safeco Field, 144
Sain, Johnny, 243
Salina, Puerto Rico, 62, 63
Sally League, 160
Salt Lake City Trappers, 28
Samana, Dominican Republic, 316
Samuel, Juan, 19, 21
San Cristobal, Dominican Republic, 294, 316
San Diego Padres, 9, 26, 62, 63, 64, 228, 298
San Diego, 98, 214, 310, 311, 316
San Francisco Giants, xiv, xvi, xxii, 37, 39, 51, 66, 67, 68, 69, 70, 71, 72, 73, 87, 88, 89, 90, 91, 93, 124, 125, 126, 127, 128, 129, 130, 137, 207, 230, 235, 272, 275, 279, 280, 286, 290, 291, 293, 299, 309, 310, 317
San Francisco, 28
San Juan International Airport, 93, 99
San Juan, 13, 26, 27, 61, 306, 317
San Pedro de Macoris, 17, 20, 21, 210, 214, 242, 245, 254, 262, 272, 315

Sanchez, Alex, 244
Sandberg, Ryne, 65
Sandinista National Liberation Front, 132
Sandinistas, 132, 133
Sandoval, Pablo, 317
Sanguillen, Manny, xv, 99, 297
Santa Barbara, 311
Santa Clara, Cuba, 259
Santa Claus, xv, 231
Santana, Johan, xiv, 30, 34, 38, 297, 298
Santiago, Benito, Jr., 298, 299
Santo Domingo, 12, 53, 145, 174, 179, 182, 256, 282, 285, 291, 315
Santo Violetta, Cuba, 162
Santurce Crabbers, 88, 162
Santurce, Puerto Rico, 244, 247, 289
Sauer, Hank, 71
Savannah College of Art and Design, 222
Scheurholz, John, 273
Schilling, Curt, 322
Schmidt, Mike, 176
Schott, Marge, 165
Schultz, Dutch, 290
Scioscia, Mike, 197
Scully, Vince, 271
Seattle Mariners, 133, 137, 139, 140, 142, 195, 196, 197, 199, 225, 232, 233, 234
Seattle, 199, 233
Segui, Diego, 6, 314
Selig, Bud, 26, 72
Sesame Street, 232
Shakespeare, 191
Shaughnessy, Dan, 150
Shaw, Bob, 77
Sheffield, Gary, 212
Shibe Park, 104

Simmons, Al, 174
Simpson, O.J., 28
Singleton, Ken, 322
Smith, Ozzie, 112, 232, 322
Smith, Ron, 78
Smoltz, John, 322
Sockalexis, Louis, xviii
Soriano, Alfonso, 19, 199
Sosa, Jose, 211
Sosa, Lucrecia, 211
Sosa, Luis, 211
Sosa, Sammy, 19, 21, 38, 42, 175, 209, 210, 211, 212, 213, 214, 215, 322
Soto, Geovany, 317
South America, 31
South Bend, Indiana, 311
South Korea, 264
Spahn, Warren, 125, 289
Spander, Art, 28
Spanish American War, 118
The Sporting News, 28, 121, 177
Sport magazine, 85
Sports Illustrated, 85, 112, 150, 177, 201
Springfield, Massachusetts, 127
St. Louis Browns, 48, 78
St. Louis Cardinals, 91, 92, 112, 125, 150, 151, 157, 173, 175, 177, 178, 179, 208, 212, 213, 215, 227, 228, 239, 242, 272, 279, 280, 289, 293, 310
St. Louis, xiii, 103, 176, 243
St. Paul Saints, 153
St. Paul, Minnesota, 83
Staley, Gerry, 77
Stallings, George, 117
Stanford University, 240
Stargell, Willie, 99, 101, 176, 286, 321
Staten Island Advance, 251
Stengel, Casey, 75, 119, 172, 243

Stennett, Rennie, xv
Stewart, Dave, 322
Stoneham, Horace, 91
Strawberry, Darryl, 136
Stuart, Dick, 22
Suarez, Luis, 226
Sukeforth, Clyde, 120
Sutcliffe, Rick, 322

Tacoma, Washington, 127
"Take Me Out To The Ballgame," 307
Tampa Bay Devil Rays, 113, 114, 260
Tanner, Chuck, 297
Tarot cards, 78
Taylor, C.I., 302
Taylor, Tony, 6, 299, 314
Tejada, Miguel, 19, 52, 300
Terry, Bill, 122
Terry, Ralph, 243
Texas Rangers, 196, 197, 198, 201,
    203, 204, 205, 206, 210, 211, 253,
    264, 266, 267, 268, 272, 274, 275,
    279, 287
Texas, 27, 140, 199, 240
Thomas, Frank, 115
Thome, Jim, 322
Thompson, Hank, xiv
Thon, Dickie, 311, 314
Thon, Frankie, 311
Thon, Freddie, 311
Thorn, John, 39
Thornton, Andre, 322
Thorpe, Jim, xviii
Tiant, Luis, Sr., xvi, 16, 216, 217, 221
Tiant, Isabel, 217, 221
Tiant, Luis, xvi, 6, 38, 49, 54, 165,
    216, 217, 218, 219, 220, 221, 222,
    270, 314
Tijuana, Mexico, 214
Time magazine, 85

Toronto Blue Jays, 51, 64, 65, 211,
    245, 254, 260, 261, 262, 315
Toronto Sky Dome, 64
Torre, Joe, 192
Torreon Peas, 46
Torrez, Mike, 311
Torriente, Cristobal, 9, 10, 107, 154,
    301, 302, 314, 320
Tovar, Cesar, 33, 108, 302, 303
Tovar, Venezuela, 297
Trembley, Dave, 178
Trevino, Alex, 314
Trillo, Manny, 303
Trinidad, Felix, 244
Troy Haymakers, xvii, 4
Trujillo, Rafael, xi, 16, 17, 18, 19, 128
Trujillo, Ramis, 124
Tucson, Arizona, 28
Turmero, Venezuela, 239
Tye, Larry, 18

U.S. Cellular Field, 77, 79, 158
U.S. Consulate, 53
U.S. State Department, 10
Uncal, Luis, 226
Under Fire, 132
Underwood, John 310
United States, ix, xiii, xvi, xvii, xxi,
    xxii, xxiii, 3, 4, 5, 7, 10, 19, 20, 24,
    25, 26, 28, 30, 32, 37, 39, 42, 44, 46,
    47, 48, 50, 52, 59, 64, 82, 90, 102,
    103, 105, 106, 109, 117, 119, 126,
    127, 128, 129, 132, 133, 134, 145,
    151, 154, 158, 159, 160, 161, 175,
    182, 192, 208, 215, 217, 221, 222,
    223, 228, 231, 232, 233, 239, 244,
    253, 254, 257, 260, 269, 271, 286,
    290, 291, 305, 319
University of Havana, 7
University of Miami, 195, 198

Urbina, Ugueth, 34
USA Today, 37, 54

Valentine, Bobby, 205
Valenzuela, Fernando, Jr., 228
Valenzuela, Avelino, 223, 224
Valenzuela, Fernando, 29, 38, 222, 223, 224, 225, 226, 227, 228, 229, 244, 270, 271, 314
Valenzuela, Hermenegilda, 223
Van Gogh, Vincent, 127
Van Halen, 232
Vance, Dazzy, 219
Veeck, Bill, 9, 48, 153
Veeck, Mike, 153
Vega Baja, Puerto Rico, 204
Velelado, Cuba 304
Venezuela, xiv, xvii, xix, xx, xxi, xxiii, 4, 30, 31, 32, 33, 34, 35, 36, 37, 40, 41, 42, 43, 44, 47, 51, 59, 73, 74, 76, 79, 95, 105, 109, 111, 112, 113, 115, 132, 165, 226, 231, 232, 235, 239, 249, 250, 256, 265, 291, 295, 302, 303, 312, 315, 317
Ventura, Robin, 113
Vera Cruz, xix, 24, 45, 47, 104, 239, 240, 243
Vero Beach, 254
Versalles, Zoilo, 6, 283, 304, 305
Vieques, Puerto Rico, 261
Vietnam, 264
Villa Clara, Cuba, 269
Villa Gonzalez, Dominican Republic, 316
Violetta Central High School, 160
Virgil, Ozzie, Jr., 305, 306
Virgil, Ozzie, Sr., xi, 19, 48, 305, 306
Virgin Islands, xv
Viva Baseball, 319
Vizquel, Nico, 235

Vizquel, Nicole, 235
Vizquel, Omar, 33, 41, 229, 230, 231, 232, 233, 234, 235, 236, 314
Voice of America, 226

Waddell, Rube, 219
Wagner, Billy, 279
Wagner, Leon, 88
Walker, Harry, 70
The Walt Disney Company, 28
Ward, Pete, 78
Washington Nationals, 27, 48, 55, 72, 247, 256, 269
Washington Post, 227
Washington Senators, xx, xxi, 6, 7, 8, 33, 37, 85, 120, 157, 262, 288, 292, 304, 305
Washington, D.C., 26, 27, 170
Weaver, Earl, 134
Weiss, George, 168
Wells, David, 191
Wells, Willie, xix, 47
Western Europe, xvii
Westminster Christian High School, 195
White House, 267
Whittier, California, 265
Wilhelm, Hoyt, 78
Willemstad, Netherlands Antilles, 273
Williams, Bernie, 37, 38, 306, 307
Williams, Danny, 310
Williams, Kenny, 109, 114
Williams, Matt, 233
Williams, May Venzor, 310
Williams, Samuel, 310
Williams, Ted, 25, 70, 75, 80, 85, 104, 288, 310, 314
Williamsport, Pennsylvania, 25
Wills, Maury, 128

Wilson, Bill, 100
Wilson, Boojum, 121
Wilson, Hack, 197, 212
Winfield, Dave, 176, 322
World Amateur Baseball
    Championship, 33
World Baseball Classic, 4, 8, 12, 36,
    43, 110, 194, 201, 255, 271, 272,
    316, 317
World Cup, 8
World Port Tournament, 11
World Series MVP, 13, 165
World Series, 30, 35, 36, 37, 38, 63,
    77, 78, 79, 82, 90, 92, 98, 99, 115,
    122, 136, 150, 151, 152, 164, 167,
    182, 186, 189, 190, 199, 201, 203,
    206, 207, 208, 221, 234, 235, 240,
    241, 243, 248, 249, 251, 252, 257,
    258, 262, 268, 269, 270, 274, 275,
277, 280, 282, 286, 289, 293, 294,
    295, 297, 303, 305, 313, 321
World Trade Center, 52, 191
World War II, xviii, xx, 13, 33, 37, 89,
    107, 247
Wright, Burnis "Wild Bill," 107, 108
Wrigley Field, 209, 212, 213
Wynn, Early, 77

Xalapa Hot Peppers, 46, 312

Yankee Stadium, 41, 183, 207, 286,
    307, 310
Yastrzemski, Carl, 222, 303

Zambrano, Carlos, 30, 317
Zimmer, Don, 150
Zorilla, Pedro, 88
Zorro, 231

About the Author

LEW H. FREEDMAN is a veteran sports writer who is the author of 45 books, including ABC-CLIO and Greenwood Press titles on basketball star LeBron James, football star Peyton Manning, and African-American pioneers of baseball.

A former writer for the *Chicago Tribune*, *Anchorage Daily News*, and *Philadelphia Inquirer*, Freedman owns a B.S. degree from Boston University and a master's degree from Alaska Pacific University. He and his wife Debra live in Columbus, IN, where he is a sports editor of *The Republic*.